British Socialists

BRITISH SOCIALISTS

The Journey from
Fantasy to Politics

STANLEY PIERSON

Harvard University Press
Cambridge, Massachusetts
and London, England
1979

Library of Congress Cataloging in Publication Data

Pierson, Stanley, 1925-
  British socialists.

  Bibliography: p.
  Includes index.
  1. Socialism in Great Britain—History.   I. Title.
HX243.P49   335'.00941   78-25820
ISBN 0-674-08282-6

For Joan

Acknowledgments

I have been aided in this study by numerous British and American libraries. For help in locating and, in some cases, reproducing materials I thank the staffs of the British Library of Political and Economic Science; British Museum Reading Room and British Museum Newspaper Library at Colindale; Birmingham Central Reference Library; Brotherton Library, University of Leeds; Corpus Christi College Library, Oxford; Library of Congress, Washington, D.C.; Manchester Central Reference Library; National Library of Ireland, Dublin; National Library of Scotland, Edinburgh; Nuffield College Library, Oxford; Sheffield City Library; State Historical Society of Wisconsin; Public Record Office, London; University of Illinois Library; University of Victoria Library.

For permission to use or quote from unpublished materials I express my appreciation to the Manchester Public Libraries for the Robert Blatchford-A. M. Thompson correspondence; Sheffield City Library for the Edward Carpenter papers; Yale University and Elliott Chubb for the Chubb correspondence in the Thomas Davidson papers; International Institute for Social History for the Karl Katusky correspondence; Malcolm Glasier for the John Bruce Glasier correspondence and diaries; the Passfield Trustees and Derek A. Clarke for the Passfield papers and the Graham Wallas papers; Dan Laurence and the Society of Authors for the correspondence of George Bernard Shaw; Corpus Christi College, Oxford, for the R. C. K. Ensor correspondence; the Fabian Society for the Fabian papers and correspondence; the State Historical Society of Wisconsin for the correspondence of Morris Hillquit, Henry Demarest Lloyd, and Algernon Simons; Nan Milton for the John Maclean correspondence; Irene Wagner for the Labour Party papers and correspondence; Roddy Connolly for the James Connolly correspondence.

Permission to quote from Edwin Muir's novel *Poor Tom* has been gratefully received from Curtis Brown Ltd. The Hogarth Press and Gavin Muir have granted permission to quote from Edwin Muir, *An Autobiography*.

Support for travel and research was provided by the American Philosophical Society, the American Council of Learned Societies, and the Office of Scientific and Scholarly Research of the Graduate School of the University of Oregon.

Colleagues at the University of Oregon have contributed, through conversations and critical readings of sections of the manuscript. They include Steve Conway, Robert Worthington Smith, Robert Berdahl, Roger Chickering, Thomas Brady, and most of all, Val Lorwin and Thomas P. Govan. Among the British friends who have helped me at various stages I am especially grateful to Norman Mackenzie.

For her patience and efficiency in typing the manuscript I thank Erma Robbins. Additional help was provided by the staff in the History Department—Dana Bruns, Beverly Jordan, Vicki Tunnell, and Enid Scofield. My wife, Joan, has continued to be my most demanding critic; she must, therefore, share responsibility for the final form of the study.

Contents

BRITISH SOCIALISTS

INTRODUCTION

EVERYTHING BEGINS in "mystique" and ends in "politique," wrote Charles Peguy.[1] Thus he expressed his dismay at the outcome of the radical movements to which he had devoted his earlier years. This book examines the kind of transformation that angered Peguy; it deals with the loss of the qualities of vision and commitment which attended the passage of the British Socialist movement into the political process.

The capacity for a movement to attract and engage presupposes a certain state of readiness on the part of the convert. In Great Britain the early recruits to the Socialist movement were usually seeking to overcome a painful social and psychological condition: traditional institutions and value systems had ceased to provide any satisfactory orientation to life. In their initial efforts to overcome this state of estrangement they often resorted to flights of fantasy. Tracing the beginnings of the Socialist movement to exercises in fantasy is not intended to demean the movement. Rather the interpretation recognizes the intensely private nature of the first attempts of individuals to cope with a condition of social homelessness. Indeed, it acknowledges the potential value of a "detour through fantasy." Although "fantasy always implies an initial turning away from a real situation, it can also be a preparation for reality and lead to a better mastery of it."[2] For those who became Socialists, however, the path toward a better mastery of reality led beyond

1

fantasy into ideology. The Socialist ideology absorbed or displaced the fantasies of scattered individuals; it gave rise to a new outlook that made common action possible.

The term ideology has been used in such a variety of ways in modern thought as to raise doubts about its usefulness. But no term is better suited for conveying the combination of social vision and social energy evident in the British Socialist movement. Like a number of other ideologies, socialism mapped out the social landscape anew; it identified the sources of injustice and discord; it indicated the means of removing them, and charted the way to a new and better society. The Socialist ideology also generated new energies; it summoned men and women to create a movement and to seek power in the realm where authority is exercised and laws are made.

The study approaches the origins of modern British socialism through an examination of three cases of social homelessness, or the "divided consciousness," and a discussion of the historical background for that condition. The "divided consciousness" was not a necessary precondition for conversion to socialism, and the Socialist ideology was not the only remedy for this state of mind. But the Socialist movement drew much of its initial vitality as well as its continuing force from individuals who were suffering from an acute sense of self-division. They came for the most part from the lower middle class, and they entered the movement with aspirations quite different from those dominant in the movement's working class supporters. Many of the tensions within the Socialist movement can be traced to the different social backgrounds of its adherents.

Socialism gained significant support in Great Britain only after its initial Marxist form underwent a series of reinterpretations and mediations. Through the adaptation of Marxism to indigenous modes of thought and experience, three more or less distinct versions of the Socialist ideology emerged—Social Democracy, Fabianism, and a less coherent form I have called Ethical Socialism. These different versions of socialism gave rise to different organizations, styles of propaganda, and political strategies. But they constituted a common movement.

Three main organizations—the Social Democratic Federation, the Fabian Society, and the chief vehicle for Ethical Socialism, the Independent Labour Party—set out to translate Socialist principles into practical political terms. Their efforts engendered bitter disputes; the history of each of the organizations was marked by defections and schisms. A close examination of these internal disagreements will clarify the dilemmas arising from the struggle to relate the Socialist ideology to political realities. Except at a few points the study does not cross the threshold of parliamentary activity, for the failure of the movement was determined not by the policies of its parliamentary representatives but by the inability of the Socialists to convert a substantial part of the working classes.

The British Socialist movement can be studied from various perspectives. No treatment of the movement can ignore the influence of social and economic structures. And these influences are dealt with at certain points. But the movement can best be understood by following its development from within. The main concern here is with the individuals and groups calling themselves Socialist and, particularly, with those who served as organizers and propagandists. Their aspirations, dilemmas, and responses mirror most clearly the movement's growth and disintegration.

PART ONE

THE ORIGINS
AND EARLY YEARS OF
THE MOVEMENT

1

THE "DIVIDED CONSCIOUSNESS" AND THE EMERGENCE OF BRITISH SOCIALISM

"WHAT A SPLENDID thing it would be," a young man in London wrote in the spring of 1882, "not to have to undertake the laborious and unsatisfactory adjustment to the existing social order, involving so many painful compromises."[1] The writer was a clerk in the Civil Service, Percival Chubb, and he was addressing a recently discovered spiritual guide, the peripatetic philosopher—Thomas Davidson. Over the next few years, in a series of intensely personal letters, Chubb laid bare his discontents, his anxieties, and his hopes of finding a more satisfying way of life.

Chubb's letters to Davidson give access to a state of mind crucial to the development of socialism in Britain. An acute sense of division between personal ideals and the workings of social institutions characterized many of the young men and women who assumed the important roles in the Socialist movement during the three decades before World War I. This division provides a key to the early growth of socialism and to continuing dilemmas within the movement.

Chubb came to London in 1881 from the northeast, where his father, a successful tradesman in earlier years, had suffered a series of economic reverses which left the family in penury. At the age of seventeen Chubb had become a clerk in a merchant's office in Newcastle and, after moving to London, continued to send back to his family more than a quarter of his yearly earnings of ninety-five pounds. The move to London and a position in the postal service did not bring a sense of personal satisfaction or new opportunities in life. "I despise my present calling," he wrote Davidson. The fact that "thousands of young men" should be driven into a "sedentary pen pushing occupation" was "neither wholesome or natural." The "money making" ethos of London, moreover, seemed to him "sordid" and whenever possible he withdrew into the countryside for consolation.[2]

Before coming to London Chubb had been strongly influenced by the Romantic poets and, with a friend, had roamed through the "land of Wordsworth and Coleridge." Together they "conceived the hope" of entering the literary world and, after earning enough to support themselves, they planned to "retire into seclusion for culture" and the "creation of a general regenerative movement." Regeneration, Chubb believed, must begin within. And while he continued to suffer the "spirit of worldliness" he encountered in his daily life as a clerk in London, he concentrated on developing his "higher tastes and aspirations."[3]

To Davidson, Chubb confessed his "passion for perfection" and his dream of changing the "entire atmosphere of his life"— of destroying "old habits of mind" and "social ties." "I really do not know myself yet. I live too much in the world and too often adjust myself to others . . . It seems to me that mentally I must go into the wilderness. What I need to do is, so to speak, gather up myself to myself, centralize my energies. The sense of living from oneself, of the power to walk in life firm footed and self reliant, is to me of all things the most precious. I must have absolute loneliness."[4]

Chubb's desire to escape from society in order to achieve personal integrity did not prevent him from seeking new human relationships. And he found congenial spirits in groups which were growing up in London at this time to discuss philosophical, literary, and social questions. Through these activities and particularly his friendship with Davidson, his circle of acquaintances widened to include many of those who came to play prominent roles in the development of British socialism.

One of his new friends was William Clark, a free-lance journalist. Clarke's failure to earn more than enough for a bare subsistence had cast a "blight on life" and left him with a deep sense of futility and resentment. In the spring of 1882 he too was expressing his inner torment to Davidson. "I am as utterly at sea as any human being ever was . . . This is a miserable condition of mind—like a complete sceptic to have no belief, and to feel that there is no place for you in the world and that you have nothing to live for. Yet it really describes my case . . . If I once get an object to work for, I can work for it. Only it must be absorbing, dominant, really great. As it is I find nothing of the kind either inside or outside myself."[5]

Clarke was not as skeptical as his confession indicated. He believed firmly in the possibility of "an unselfish noble humane life" and shared Wordsworth's reverence for those "who regulate their lives by their few strong instincts and few plain rules." Yet his own sense that the "working I do" was not an expression of personal convictions but "mere wish or even prejudice" had plunged him into deep despair. His divided condition led him to suggest at one point that it might be better to be a "workman," producing "something of value and therefore useful to my fellow man." In the meantime he felt "powerless" and adrift in a "hazy dreamland," seeking knowledge of "what to believe and what to do." Life, he observed, was a "succession of illusions which are always breaking up." Clarke had, in fact, reached a state where he did not "in the least mind dieing" and even welcomed death.[6]

Chubb and Clarke were suffering from the crisis of identity widespread in modern society.[7] Their letters exhibit the loss of a stable sense of a self related satisfactorily to social institutions. They expressed feelings of emptiness and unworth, of powerlessness and lack of purpose, of the absence of meaningful social roles. "We are both heartily at one," Chubb wrote, "in our disquiet with the unreality and meanness of life as it is lived around us."[8]

Still the two men retained strong moral sentiments against which they could measure their feelings of inadequacy. They had found "greater faith and insight" in the Romantic poets, the writings of Carlyle and Ruskin, and especially in the American transcendentalists, Emerson and Whitman. From these sources they derived, at least intermittently, assurances that the universe was informed by spiritual purpose. But the influence of the Romantic writers also intensified the feelings of opposition between personal values and public mores and strengthened their tendencies to take refuge in fantasies of moral self perfection and absolute integrity. A true selfhood could only be envisioned in terms of a total withdrawal from the existing social order or through its complete transformation. At times both Chubb and Clarke considered emigration as one way of cutting "the thread to so much that now hampers . . . and retards."[9]

Association with Davidson encouraged their hopes of breaking sharply with the world of "mere money getting" and opened the "possibility of a great moral change." Davidson was developing the idea of a new and nobler mode of life by means of a kind of secularized monastic community, inspired mainly by the teachings of the Catholic philosopher Antonio Rosmini-Serbati. It requires "little inducement," Chubb told Davidson, "to follow your call . . . to the Utopian state." And by the fall of 1883, through Chubb's initiative, a "gathering of utopians" was discussing the possibility of building a "new life in the center of Babylon."[10]

It was a diverse group. And it included several young men—H. H. Champion, R. P. Frost, J. L. Joynes, and Hubert Bland—who were already involved in efforts to propagate Marxism in Britain. They were skeptical of Davidson's plan to cut "connections with the old world." So too were others in the group—Edward Pease, Frank Podmore, and Frank Keddell—who favored the reform of existing institutions. But Chubb and Clarke had little sympathy for the belief in institutional change. People like Champion, Pease, and Podmore, according to Chubb, were "too timid and reluctant to make themselves the living embodiment of a new spiritual gospel." Socialist agitation seemed to Chubb to entail a loss of "inwardness" and a submergence of "ends in means." It confirmed the truth of Emerson's criticism of the mere reformer.

The Reformers affirm the inner life but they do not trust it, but use outward and vulgar measures. They do not rely on precisely that strength which wins one to their cause: not on love, not on principle, but on men, on multitude, on circumstances, on money, on party, that is, on fear, on wrath, on pride . . . The Reformers have their high origins in an ideal justice but they do not retain the purity of an idea, they are quickly organized in some low inadequate form and present no more poetic image to the mind than the evil tradition which they reprobated.[11]

The disagreements between those who wished to concentrate on moral self-improvement, and those who favored institutional reform could not be resolved, and in December 1883 the group divided. Champion, Frost, Joynes, and others decided to work mainly with the new Marxist organization, the Social Democratic Federation, while Bland, Podmore, and Pease formed a new Socialist body, the Fabian Society. The "utopians," led by Chubb, reorganized as the Fellowship of the New Life, and set out through study and discussions to cultivate "a perfect character in each and all."[12]

The split between the two groups was not as sharp as it appeared. Members of the Fabian Society acknowledged the need for a higher personal morality while some members of the Fellowship, including Chubb and Clarke, were also attracted to the Socialist cause. For a time both men held back from socialism "because so much bad is mixed up with the good," but the new ideology offered a way of relating personal ideals to social action. Chubb, in fact, had begun to worry about his own tendency to fall into the "slough of subjectivism" and suffer a "rupture with common sense." And in the course of 1884 he joined the Fabian Society. Over the next few years, in the face of Davidson's disapproval, Chubb vigorously defended his ties with the Socialists.

I do not deny that [the Socialist] wants "inwardness" but the material problem is such a fiercely urgent one that the ordinary socialist may be forgiven if he devotes himself rather too exclusively to the task of the materialistic salvation. The truth is that the material conditions of life for hundreds of thousands of our people are so bad that there is no chance of human development of their victims until the material conditions are altered. It is the profound sympathy with these dehumanized folks that is the leading motive of the majority of Socialists here and the way in which many of them are working is simply heroic . . . We appear to you to be immersed in a struggle with wretchedness and squalor, too external . . . You appear to us in the pursuit of a spiritual religion to be . . . in danger of an unattractive quietism.[13]

Even within the Fabian Society Chubb was primarily concerned with enhancing the ethical element in socialism. And he continued to give himself mainly to the work of the Fellowship, where the members were committed to finding "a more natural and simpler life." Through the late eighties Chubb remained one of its leaders as the group discussed works of ethical and spiritual edification and developed plans for starting a "colony." He also participated in a new effort to raise the level of ethical sensitivity in Britain—the Ethical Societies—started by the American, Stanton Coit in 1887. It was through this movement and the help of Davidson that Chubb escaped "a life chained to a desk" and emigrated to America in the early nineties.[14]

Initially Clarke had been more hostile to the Socialists than Chubb. The Marxists, he felt, were seeking a "revolution quite as much for the sake of overthrowing ethics and the spiritual side of things as for the sake of improving the material condition of the people." Late in 1884, after "giving deep study to Socialism," he again concluded that it was "wrong on fundamental points." Because it ignored ethics it lacked "regenerative power" and was, indeed, "fatal to progress to freedom and love." It was simply the "old Proteus of greed and hate under a new form" and its collectivizing of property would only "transform society into a mechanism."[15]

Clarke's work as a journalist and his study of American capitalism, however, led him to "take stock of my whole category of political beliefs" and revise the individualistic form of political radicalism with which he had identified himself. Through his growing friendship with Henry Demarest Lloyd, the American crusader against monopoly capitalism, he also became convinced of the crucial role of economic factors in society. In 1885 he joined some of the Fabians in the study of Marx's *Capital* and before long began to apply a Marxist type of analysis to contemporary social developments. His lectures for the Fabian Society, which he joined in 1886, "provided the major economic argument for the Fabian policies of nationalization and municipalization."[16]

Although Clarke became convinced that "moral and spiritual progress" required radical changes in the material conditions of life, he did not give up his preoccupation with the problem of personal ethical transformation. He was reluctant, in fact, to join the Fabians in the "somewhat dirty political arena" for fear of "being defiled." He did not remain for long in the Fellowship of the New Life, but he played an active part with Chubb in the early development of the Ethical Societies. Despite his Marxist ideas and his role in the Fabian Society, Clarke continued to judge "the real world of men and institutions" in terms of progress to a higher ideal of unselfishness.[17] True political activity, he believed, was the direct expression of one's ethical or religious conviction. The Socialist cause remained for Clarke a means of ethical regeneration.

Still Clarke was forced to recognize that the Fabian Socialists were separating the two realms he was seeking to integrate. The political work of the Fabians, he observed in 1890, was only possible if the members kept to a "common ground" which excluded "vital differences . . . on ultimate questions of ethics and philosophy." And he complained of his "isolation among men who knew no ultimate aims." Meanwhile, his own hope for a unified conception of life increased. In a small study of Whitman, published in 1892, Clarke declared that the American poet answered the yearning of "our times . . . to reach the very foundation of being" and establish new links "between religion and democracy." He saw in Whitman's poetry a vision of mankind transforming "the world into . . . an ordered whole" in which the individual could identify with "a larger self" and find a new "spiritual solidarity."[18]

Clarke gradually withdrew from the Socialist movement during the nineties. Frustrated in his own efforts to promote a new form of radical politics, he also became convinced that the Fabian Society was "played out as a political force" because it rejected "large and far reaching ideas" in favor of "piddling points of factory legislation and municipal socialism." Before long he concluded, too, that the working classes were sunk in greed, ignorance, and apathy, and that England was becoming "more and more rotten every day." In his last years, before his death in 1901, he disassociated himself from socialism and all causes, and lamented the fact that he had given "so many of the best years of his life to barren questions."[19]

The Socialist movement did not in the end enable Chubb and Clarke to resolve their acute sense of division between personal values and social institutions. Chubb emigrated and pursued his ethical and religious quest in America, while Clarke, increasingly subject to a debilitating illness and fits of melancholy, withdrew to the countryside and found his main interest in art. A number of other young men and women in these years, however, were moving by means of the Socialist ideology out of a sphere of purely private ideals and imaginings onto the ground of common political action. No one provided such a clear record of this passage as George Bernard Shaw.

Shaw had come to London from Dublin in 1876 at the age of twenty. He was, in his own words, a social "downstart." His family had lost, through various misfortunes, its earlier economic security and social respectability and had reached a rather precarious position on the lower edges of the middle class. When he was fifteen Shaw took a job as a clerk in an estate office, but four and a half years in this position left him with a hatred for the routines of commercial life and an acute sense of self-division. "I was at home," he recalled, "only in the realm of my imagination, and . . . therefore I had to become an actor, and create for myself a fantastic personality fit and apt for dealing with men." Soon after arriving in London he wrote his closest friend back in Dublin: "You are the only person in the world to whom I am a person with an identity and a soul."[20]

Initially Shaw planned to enter the Civil Service but, lacking the necessary language qualifications, he abandoned this course. Over the next few years he worked from time to time as a journalist, a clerk, and a salesman. But for the most part he avoided full-time employment and, supported by a modest inheritance, fixed on a literary career. He was at the same time engaged in a program of self-discovery and social exploration. The five novels he wrote between 1879 and 1884 present an "autobiography of the artist's mind."[21]

These novels illuminate Shaw's London, where lonely young men of talent and ambition were seeking places in the various professions and attempting as well to develop a new and satisfying sense of selfhood.[22] The nature of the search and something of the range of possibilities Shaw discovered along the way was disclosed in his series of heroes. The series also charted his own movement away from the mode of extreme idealization which held Chubb and Clarke.

Robert Smith, the hero of Shaw's first novel, *Immaturity*, was, according to R. F. Dietrich, as "direct a view of his essential undisguised self" as the author ever gave; he served at the same time as a means of "spiritual clarification."[23] Shaw reenacted, in the figure of the young clerk, his experiences in the Dublin estate office as well as his first years in London. Smith was lonely and introverted, painfully shy in social relationships, and filled with loathing for the drudgery and servility of his clerical work. "Is there any profession in the world," he asked, "so contemptible as that of a clerk?"[24] Smith's response to this situation was much like that of Chubb and Clarke; he was, as Shaw described him, "all ethics." An uncompromising atheist and free thinker, he also was a person of absolute moral integrity. Indeed, his moral superiority was such that in the context of conventional social relations it often appeared monstrous. Between his private virtues and the practical world, in fact, no genuine ties were possible. It became a matter of personal honor to break with the crass commercial order in which he was employed.

Having cast off his conventional social role, however, Smith discovered that his emancipated self was precarious; he found that he was "virtually without identity," and as the normal directives and restraints of common sense fell away he became prey to fantasies which brought him to the edge of self-annihilation. But he returned, at least part way, to the real world, taking a position as a secretary to a member of Parliament while finding the main support for his ideal self in bohemian circles and the realm of art. At the end of the novel the division of Smith (or Shaw) was unresolved; he remained, as Shaw observed later, "resentfully insubordinate and seditious in a social order which he not only accepted but in which he actually claimed a privileged part."[25]

Immaturity did not solve the hero's quest for a reintegration of existence, but it mirrored Shaw's growing awareness of

the options available to the sensitive young man in London. For
Shaw the split between the self and his social roles proved to be
a liberating process; it enabled him to explore new possibilities
in life. His next three novels have been described as an attempt
to "experimentally piece together an identity." Shaw explored
such personality types or vocations as the engineer, the artist,
and the athlete. He was gradually composing a model, based
mainly on aristocratic or classical views of self-fulfillment,
which departed from the ascetic and self-sacrificing ideals of
Chubb and Clarke. At the same time Shaw was engaged in a
"long and arduous . . . struggle to extrovert himself" and find a
meaningful relationship to society.[26] By the time he wrote the
fifth novel, *An Unsocial Socialist*, he had discovered, in the
theory of Karl Marx, a convincing interpretation of the social
and economic order.

Shaw encountered Marxist ideas late in 1882 after a lecture
by Henry George had opened his eyes to the economic sources
of many social evils. And so he was drawn, in his words, "into
the Socialist revival" along with other young men "burning
with indignation at the very real and fundamental evils that af-
fected all the world." Marxism, he recalled, appealed "to an
unnamed unrecognized passion: the hatred in the more generous souls among the respectable and educated sections for the
middle class institutions that had starved, thwarted, misled,
and corrupted them spiritually."[27] But the Socialist ideology
also helped Shaw to look beyond his personal frustrations; the
fantasies projected in his novels gave way to a conscious
struggle for a different form of society. He stopped writing fiction and passed from the realm of imagination into the sphere of
reforming or revolutionary activity disclosed by Marxism.

Marxism did not, however, connect Shaw's personal
values with a clear program of political action. While he was
fascinated by the drama of history presented by the new social
theory, he was at the same time dedicated to ideals which
clashed with Marxism. Shaw remained committed to a radical
form of individualism, inspired by Shelley and others, that led
him towards anarchism.[28] Only after joining the Fabian Society
in 1884 did he begin to reconcile his personal ideals with the
Socialist call to action. In the process Shaw's Marxist faith was

largely dissolved and his anarchist bent checked. His "other self," as he called it, the impractical idealist and "impossibilist," was being excluded from his activity as a Fabian Socialist. But not, as Martin Meisel has recognized, from the movement of his imagination.[29] In committing himself as a Fabian to the task of altering British institutions Shaw had partitioned off aspirations for a radically different way of life which would in time reappear in his dramatic work.

The divisions and oppositions with which Chubb, Clarke, and Shaw struggled were not new. The "divided consciousness" was a common experience in British and European development throughout the century. A radical severance between private and public spheres of life has been characteristic of all industrializing societies. And it was among persons who were especially susceptible to the social and psychological stresses arising from this severance that the Socialist ideology found many of its early supporters. The origins of the Socialist movement in Britain may be clarified further through a brief discussion of the changing social structure.

THE VICTORIAN SOCIAL STRUCTURE

During the course of the century the British had developed what a recent historian has called "a viable class society." The highly integrated preindustrial social order had been transformed into a system of institutions through which new social classes and groups could "express themselves, safeguard or ameliorate their standards and conditions of life and channel their conflicts out of the path of violence into those of negotiation and compromise."[30]

In the new society the capitalistic middle classes assumed the dominant position. Although they had not been able to create political forms completely supportive of their interests, they had secured, through compromises with the traditional political leaders from the landed classes, a commanding influence on national policies. Their central demand—for free and open competition between economic producers—was reinforced by a powerful network of religious, educational, and cultural institutions. Their "entrepreneurial ideal" might find a sanction in religious conceptions of character or in the newer notions of the rational economic man, but it reflected a fairly well integrated scheme of life; middle class values and disciplines suited the practical tasks and opportunities presented by the social system.

Working class institutions lacked the strength and comprehensiveness of the middle class structures. To a large extent the workers had built their distinctive institutions as defenses against the steady conquest of British society by middle class energies, interests, and ideas. "Friendly societies" provided large numbers of workers with some insurance against the erratic workings of the market economy, or against the natural adversities of life; consumer cooperatives eliminated or reduced the profit of middle men in some sectors of commerce; the trade unions gave the more skilled sections of the working class the bargaining power necessary to protect their conditions of work and their living standards against the pressures, sanctioned by orthodox economic thinking, to drive wages down to bare minimum. Implicit in these working class institutions was a less individualistic view of society than that prevailing in the middle class and a greater recognition of the cooperative nature of economic life; it was expressed in the traditional ethical claim to a "fair day's wage for a fair day's work."[31]

The better-off sections of the working classes were, to be sure, highly susceptible to the values and ideas of the middle classes. In the Nonconformist chapels they often shared with the middle classes, they affirmed the ascetic virtues—hard work, prudence, thrift, and abstinence—which helped sustain the capitalistic order. Even when the skilled workers left the chapels and adopted "secularist" views, as they did in increasing numbers in the course of the century, they usually retained the middle class values. Earlier hopes that the competitive industrial order might be superseded by a "new moral world" had largely faded out during the mid-Victorian decades and given way to a "labourist" outlook which bound the workers to the "dominant ideas of the bourgeoisie."[32] The extension of the franchise to a substantial number of workers through the acts of 1867 and 1884, reinforced their willingness to accept the intellectual and political leadership of the Liberal and Conservative parties.

Still, the workers had developed in the course of the century a fuller awareness of their distinct interests as a class. A "robust working class sub culture, cradled in the traditions of early Victorian radicalism" persisted "in a state of tension" within the dominant middle class social and cultural system. Working class radicalism shared the dominant Victorian commitment to moral and material improvement, but it also affirmed democratic values and the right of all to "full participation in the heritage of the community."[33] This sense of working class identity was sharpened during the closing decades of the century by the rapid transformation of the economic system from small units of production, in which craftsmen and artisans played the dominant role, to a factory system. The change of scale tended to depersonalize and delocalize industrial relations, while the growing impact of international market forces encouraged new conceptions of class solidarity. Trade union practice, the give and take of industrial bargaining, moreover, made economic conflict explicit and endemic and at times generated a militant spirit of opposition to the employers. Although the trade union movement was stalled during the recession of the 1880s it developed rapidly in the decades ahead. By 1914 nearly four million workers had joined unions.

For the most part the trade unions and the other working class associations helped integrate the workers into the developing capitalistic system and strengthen the spirit of "labourism" and class collaboration. The narrow range of trade union concerns and their relative effectiveness in protecting the interests of the workers served, in fact, to inoculate broad sections of the British working classes against the appeal of socialism. During the early years of the movement the Socialists were more likely to reach the workers where trade unions were weak or where unemployment, widespread during the eighties, made them more receptive to basic challenges to the capitalistic order.

Most often the early Socialists came not from the working classes but, as the cases of Chubb, Clarke, and Shaw suggest, from the lower levels of the middle class. They came from the "salariat" or the "professional proletariat" which, as Eric Hobsbawm observed, was "rising through the interstices of the traditional social and economic structures of Victorian Britain."[34] Some were seeking careers in the civil service, journalism, teaching, or the literary world. Others were taking positions in the burgeoning world of business as commercial travelers, clerks, or shop assistants. They were young, usually single, and mostly of provincial background. They were particularly vulnerable to the anxieties attendant on the passage from comparatively well integrated family or social backgrounds to the strange highly impersonal and competitive world of London. Each of the major Socialist organizations—the Social Democratic Federation, the Fabian Society, and the Independent Labour Party—drew their propagandists and organizers largely from this sector of society.[35]

The early recruits to the Socialist movement had often been defeated or at least thwarted in their social ambitions. Lack of "suitable employment," Clarke observed, was "forcing young men of education and good breeding into the Socialist ranks." The sense of socially inflicted injury was felt most strongly perhaps by the young middle class women converts, for they had usually been stung to rebellion by the obstacles which Victorian conventions placed in their paths toward self-fulfillment. Frustrations encountered along normal avenues of social and political advance were especially evident among the leaders of the Independent Labour Party. Its most prominent figures, Keir Hardie, Ramsay MacDonald, and Philip Snowden, had grown up in the working classes and suffered reversals in their efforts to achieve a higher social status.[36]

The recruits to the Socialist cause might come from any section of society. In a few cases the movement attracted persons from the landed class who had been stranded by the industrial order. Thus, John Lister, the "squire of Halifax" and the first treasurer of the Independent Labour Party, hosted his Socialist colleagues in the great hall at Shibden Park in a setting reminiscent of an "older and merrier England." What distinguished many of the early converts was simply the absence of any well-defined class or social interests. And the Socialist ideology provided, like other ideologies, a new orientation to society. It served to "render otherwise incomprehensible social situations meaningful" and to "make it possible to act purposefully within them."[37]

The development of the Socialist ideology in Victorian Britain was not, however, a direct outcome of social and psychological stress. It emerged only through the adaptation of Marxism, a foreign system of thought, to indigenous habits of mind. The Socialists also drew on a century long cultural struggle to come to terms with the divisions of modern society.

THE CULTURAL BACKGROUND

When William Blake lamented the "fall into division" and "the war among our members," he voiced the feeling of a generation of European poets and writers who were confronting in a new and urgent way man's alienated condition. A sense of alienation—of a lost relationship with God, with nature, with a true community or an essential self—has been a central feature of human history. For the Romantics, however, the religious systems or "public philosophies" which had traditionally functioned to reconcile the individual to the alienated state, and provided a more or less meaningful sense of membership and participation in a higher order, had broken down. The Romantics inaugurated an era which, as Philip Rieff expressed it, had ceased to be "culturally positive." Not only did many individuals experience a new sense of opposition between the self and society, but they had lost the sense of a coherent self—of a more or less satisfactory relationship between will, intellect, and imagination. Hence the many sided struggle for new forms of integration. The Romantic movement, Rene Wellek observed, was a "great endeavor to overcome the split between subject and object, the self and the world, the consciousness and the unconscious."[38]

The promise of reintegration, or a restored wholeness, was deeply embedded in the Christian tradition. The millennial hope had emerged with a special force at those times in the development of Western civilization when the symbolic and institutional orders had lost their hold. Amid the social and cultural changes of the late eighteenth and early nineteenth centuries the millennial design surfaced once more and became a central element in the Romantic outlook. In appropriating the design, however, the Romantic artists and thinkers attempted to bring it into harmony with the assumptions of a more rationalistic age. The central place of the transcendent God in the Christian scheme was absorbed in the simple duality of the individual and the world, or mind and nature. Human redemption, the recovery of wholeness and harmony, would be achieved through the strivings of mankind without providential aid. It was a reconstruction which also eliminated, or sharply reduced, the older religious insistence on human sin and the power of evil in the world.[39]

The French Revolution seemed to provide objective historical support for the millennial design; it promised a "new man in a new world." The social upheaval inspired the British Romantic poets in particular with the hope of recovering a vital relationship between the artistic imagination and public affairs. Developments in France soon destroyed these hopes and most Romantic writers ceased to believe in human redemption through political action. While they retained their millennial aspirations, they transferred them from the processes of history to the inner life; the hope of transfiguring the individual consciousness by the creative imagination displaced the dream of a new social order. Art became the "reconciling and justifying agency in a disintegrated mental and social world of alien and warring fragments." In Great Britain the leading Romantics tended to abandon the "social dimension of human experience" or, as the development of Wordsworth and Coleridge indicated, to make their peace with traditional institutions.[40]

For most Victorians the divisions with which the Romantics had struggled were viewed in traditional religious terms. Christian renewal, particularly in its dominant evangelical form, revitalized the older interpretation of human alienation. With its strong emphasis on sin and evil and its promise of a perfect life beyond the grave, evangelicalism gave new intensity to the Christian drama of the divided soul. Evangelical Christianity probably increased the divorce between private sensibilities and institutional developments because its emphasis on personal regeneration encouraged the tendency for economic forces to unfold in ways little checked by older notions of community responsibility. Victorian religious development witnessed, in fact, a series of efforts to counter the individualistic bias of evangelicalism and bring Christian teachings to bear on the social disorders of the age. In their different ways, the

Tractarians, the "Broad Churchmen," the Christian Socialists, and the "immanentist" theologians of late nineteenth century Nonconformity, were seeking to recover the older ideal of an organic "Christian Commonwealth," in which public and private values were conceived as fully harmonious. The commonwealth ideal strongly influenced the British Socialists.

For nineteenth century intellectuals who had ceased to believe in Christianity and were not unduly troubled by metaphysical and religious questions, the philosophy of utilitarianism offered a new approach to the problem of the divided self. The Utilitarians, inspired by Jeremy Bentham, set out to bring human consciousness into closer conformity with the rational and contractual relationships characteristic of the emerging industrial society. Perhaps as Sheldon Wolin observed, Bentham "factored out the soul" and "reduced man to mere externality."[41] Bentham was mainly concerned, however, with the problem of reforming the public sphere of law and administration and was indifferent to the inner life of the psyche. Indeed, his attempt to formulate an ethic of consequences represented an acceptance of the growing separation between public and private realms. His leading disciple, James Mill, did attempt to integrate the two realms but he did this by expunging all sentiments and motives which did not make for a purely rational conception of self and society. This complete liquidation of inherited moral, aesthetic, and religious sentiments might, as John Stuart Mill discovered, threaten the very foundations of existence. And the younger Mill preserved his Utilitarian creed only by recovering ideas and values derived from the opposing Christian and Romantic currents of thought. Later Utilitarians did not entirely give up the dream of an integral rational world but they tended to accept Bentham's more limited mission and concern themselves with the public sphere of legal and administrative reform.

Evangelicalism and utilitarianism owed much of their force in "Victorian life" to their single-mindedness. And though the relationship between the two systems of thought was complex, marked by affinities as well as antagonisms, they functioned in complementary ways. The Utilitarian confidence in stable human characters, with well-defined interests, rested in part at least on the moral values and the modes of self discipline nurtured by evangelicalism.

The declining appeal of the Evangelical and Utilitarian systems of thought in the last third of the century prepared the way for the Socialist movement. Not only were the several forms of the new ideology built up in large part out of the ruins of the major Victorian belief systems, but socialism found its early adherents among those who had lost the security the two systems had provided. Many of the early converts were experiencing anew, as the cases of Chubb, Clarke, and Shaw suggest, the personal crisis which had found early and extreme expression in the Romantic writers.

Although mid-Victorian social and religious thinkers had temporarily resolved the dilemma of the "divided self," it had continued as a major problem in Victorian literature. A "knowledge of the Romantic failure in self-discovery," according to one literary historian, was a starting point for the major Victorian writers. Social and economic developments during the middle decades of the century increased the sense of social estrangement experienced by many artists and writers. To E. D. H. Johnson, in fact, the "whole hearted hostility to the progress of industrial civilization" was the main source of the "divided consciousness," which lay at the "core of Victorian literary" activity. The place of the artist in the emerging industrial and urban society was, at best, ambiguous; the economic and utilitarian preoccupations of the middle classes seemed to deny any valid function to the aesthetic impulses. Hence the deepening conflict evident in the major Victorian poets—Tennyson, Browning and Arnold—and in many of the novelists as well, between the norms of public life or popular expectations on the one hand, and their innermost feelings and perceptions on the other. The poets might, like Tennyson, explore the "mystery of man's inner being" and realms beyond ordinary consciousness through the experience of dreams, madness and visionary moments, or follow Browning in a search into man's instinctual and passional nature. Or they might, like Arnold, seek a "model for the integral self" in earlier historical periods.[42]

Insofar as the Victorian writers found a "middle ground on

which to arbitrate (their) dual allegiances," they discovered it in moral commitment.[43] Their reliance on the seemingly secure foundation of conscience was, like so many of the Victorian appeals to fact or experience amid the doubts of the age, an interim solution, dependent on intuitions which fastened onto deeply embedded but historically deposited sentiments. The strongly moralistic impulse in Victorian culture carried over not only the older Christian ethic of love and self-sacrifice but many of the ascetic and work oriented values of the later Puritan tradition as well.

Nowhere was the Victorian confidence in moral sentiments, disengaged from the traditional matrix of religious ritual and doctrine, more apparent than in the thought of Thomas Carlyle. His early work expressed the trauma of the sensitive young man who had left a comparatively well integrated pre-industrial society to enter the strange and estranging world of the metropolis. His reaction to the collision between the two ways of life and his attempt to reorder the world on moral foundations gave his writings a special appeal to young men and women of succeeding generations who experienced Carlyle's ordeal. But his moralistic approach to the social changes under way disqualified Carlyle for any realistic grasp of economic and political forces. Like Ruskin, whose response was so familiar in many ways, Carlyle turned to the past in search of institutions to repair a broken world.

During the closing decades of the century many Victorian writers and artists abandoned the effort to bridge the realm of private sensibilities and public affairs and sought in the exercise of the imagination its own justification. But the "hunger for wholeness" continued in the work of a new generation of writers, coming for the most part out of the lower middle classes of the provinces. They were, as Malcolm Bradbury observed, "culturally uncertain" yet "assertive" and filled with a sense that the "moral world and the world of things" had lost any satisfactory relationship. The anxieties and aspirations which fed the Socialist movement were mirrored in the fiction of such writers as Shaw, H. G. Wells, George Gissing, Arnold Bennett, and, somewhat later, Dorothy Richardson and D. H. Lawrence. It is not surprising that each of these writers turned for a time to the Socialist movement. For their creative work and the Socialist ideology may be seen as parallel strategies for dealing with the problem of the divided consciousness.[44]

There were other strategies. The eighties and the nineties witnessed a proliferation of cults and movements which promised to reorder a fragmented existence. Positivists and Socialists, theosophists and Spiritualists, Whitmanites and Swedenborgians, the Fellowship of the New Life and the Ethical Societies, even the more extreme adherents of vegetarianism and anti-vivisectionism, were participating in a common quest for a new unity amid the bewildering changes of modern life. Many of the early Socialist recruits had tested one or more of these faiths before joining the movement; many retained their earlier commitments and viewed socialism as the proper economic and social expression for their personal beliefs. Others transferred to the new cause their aspirations for a total integration.

The early development of socialism bore the marks of this chaotic cultural milieu. But the new ideology found points of growth in British life only after being adapted to the dominant Romantic, Christian, and Utilitarian modes of thought. In their efforts to apply the new ideas to British traditions, however, the Socialists soon diverged. And out of this process three more or less distinctive forms of the Socialist ideology emerged. The process began with the introduction of Marxist ideas in the early eighties.

The Differentiation of the Socialist Ideology

In 1881, when H. M. Hyndman began his Marxist propaganda in Britain, he was thirty-nine, older by some years than those who soon gathered around him. Raised in a well-to-do family, he had gained, through his experiences as a speculator in stocks, a company promoter, and journalist, a knowledge of the world of capitalism rare among the early Socialists. And over the next forty years he continued his financial speculations even as he invested his life in the work of overthrowing the capitalistic system.[45]

Hyndman's Marxism centered on the labor theory of value and the correlary doctrines of exploitation and the class struggle. He was committed to the goal of the public ownership of the means of production, distribution, and exchange, and he believed that it could be achieved through the political organization of the workers. To these basic Marxist ideas Hyndman added notions drawn from various sources. He accepted Ferdinand Lassalle's emphasis on the role of the traditional state in transforming society, as well as his version of the "iron law of wages," according to which the workers were inexorably driven down to a bare subsistence level by the operations of the capitalistic system.

Hyndman assimilated the ideas of Marx and Lassalle to traditions of British radicalism which, by the eighties, were less suspicious of state action. And he shared the utilitarian outlook underlying much of traditional radicalism; he believed that human beings were governed primarily by considerations of pain and pleasure and were capable of pursuing their interests in a rational manner. Fixed within a way of thinking which Marx himself regarded as a "sophistical rationalization of existing society," Hyndman made no place in his socialism for the dialectical view of social process on which the Marxian expectation of a qualitatively different way of life was based. Hyndman's Marxism was, in Willard Wolfe's words, heterodox and vulgarized. He "reduced Marxism so completely to the bare bones of economic theory and economic history" as to "obliterate all traces of Marx's philosophy and sociology."[46]

In 1881 Hyndman formed the Democratic Federation and set out to build a new political force. His attacks on prominent Radical political leaders and their policies soon cost him his initial support among the London working classes and by 1883, when he formed the Social Democratic Federation with an explicit Socialist program, its membership was mainly middle class. Unable to exploit the growing rift within the Liberal Party between its individualistic and collectivist wings, Hyndman and his associates adopted an increasingly militant posture. They did not abandon conventional political activity and practical proposals for reform but they emphasized the Marxist doctrines of exploitation and the class struggle.

The Social Democrats had little confidence in the economic associations through which the workers had attempted to advance their interests. From the beginning Hyndman rejected proposals for close cooperation with the trade unions. His belief in a fixed wage fund under capitalism made him doubt the effectiveness of industrial action, such as strikes, in improving the condition of the workers. Moreover, he believed that the unions were hopelessly implicated in the capitalistic order. With considerable justification, he argued that they served a working class elite, fragmented the proletariat, and impeded the growth of a broader awareness of class interests. Hyndman's antagonism toward the unions and his blindness to their potential role in a dialectical interplay between theory and practice, has been judged disastrous to the Marxist cause in Britain.[47] But his belief that the "labourist" outlook of the trade unions constituted a major barrier to Socialist advance was justified.

Convinced that Socialist advance would take place mainly through political action, the Social Democrats attempted from platform and press to give the workers a Marxist understanding of their exploited condition and create an awareness of class interests. The Federation's propaganda, derived chiefly from Hyndman's reading of Marx, remained narrowly economic, intellectualistic, and undialectical; like most contemporary versions of Marxism, it portrayed capitalism as inescapably doomed by its inner contradictions. But the practical, even opportunistic, bent among the Social Democrats was checked by a zeal for doctrinal rectitude, nurtured in their classes in Marxist economics. Their dogmatic outlook—their fierce attacks on rival creeds, especially orthodox religious beliefs—indicated that Hyndman's utilitarian form of Marxism was attaching itself to a much wider range of sentiments and aspirations. The early development of the new ideology in Britain witnessed a recovery, in fact, of the millennial drive for an undivided existence which Marx himself had carried over from the Romantics and the pioneer Socialist thinkers of the first half of the century. Although Marx, and particularly Engels, had tended in later years to emphasize objective economic forces in the movement of the dialectic, their system of thought still held a "vision of man returning to a perfect unity, expressing his personal life as a social force."[48]

Marxism appealed to a number of young middle class men who, like Chubb, Clarke and Shaw, were seeking an integral system of belief. Thus Clarke described Herbert Burrows, a civil servant and an early associate of Hyndman, as one who had "broken away from his old Unitarian moorings" and could "find no fresh ones . . . He takes up Socialism in a kind of despair. He inwardly revolts against its materialism but sees nothing else to work for." Burrows resolved his quest for a personal faith by accepting theosophy while adopting the Marxist view of social development. But other Social Democrats expanded their Marxism into a complete interpretation of life. Ernest Belfort Bax was the most energetic and influential of these. Having discovered Marxism while studying philosophy in Germany, he attempted in a series of books and articles to elaborate an ethic and a metaphysic by means of ideas drawn from Kant, Schopenhauer, and the late nineteenth century philosopher, Eduard von Hartmann. Bax's Marxist philosophy, or what he called the religion of socialism, culminated in a version of total human integration. The opposition between personal desires and social demands, as well as the disharmonies between cognitive and emotional faculties within the individual, would be overcome.[49]

Bax had introduced into British Social Democracy concerns which were ignored in Hyndman's Marxism. Those concerns were enlarged by the most famous of the British converts to Marxism, William Morris. As one who considered artistic activity "the crown of a full and noble life," he found in the "religion of socialism" an alternative to the commercialized civilization he despised. But not long after joining the Federation Morris concluded that Hyndman's form of socialism would lead only to "mechanical" changes and not to the "real revolution." Early in 1885 Morris, Bax, and others broke with Hyndman and set out to develop a new conception of socialism by means of the Socialist League.[50]

The new form of the Socialist ideology, expressed in the writings of Morris, and most fully in his utopian novel, *News from Nowhere*, drew on older and simpler modes of social life; it stressed the joys of the artisan in his work and in human fellowship, and it promised a natural, spontaneous, and harmonious existence. But in their recoil from the utilitarian and opportunist outlook of Hyndman, Morris and the other members of the

League scorned the political process and drifted into a anarchist outlook that proved suicidal. Morris, like Carlyle and Ruskin before him, tended to retreat into historical fantasies. Before its dissolution in the early nineties, however, the Socialist League planted its ethical and aesthetic approach to socialism in small but dedicated groups in several provincial centers.[51]

Although the defection of Morris and his followers confirmed the hold of Hyndman's Marxism on the SDF, its subsequent development exhibited the continuing play of attitudes and feelings of which Hyndman took little account. He had succeeded in excluding fundamental philosophical or religious issues from the ground of legitimate Socialist concern. But the rhetoric of the Social Democrats indicated the force of what Henri de Man called the eschatological sentiment.[52] And the periodic schisms which marked the subsequent life of the SDF can be traced to the desire for a more radical break with existing values and institutions than that envisioned in Hyndman's Marxism.

During the eighties and nineties, however, the Federation gained a modest following among the working classes in London and some sections of the industrial north. Its appeal to the workers was limited in many areas by its inflammatory and secularist rhetoric, and its hostility to the trade unions. But the Social Democrats remained a significant force within the movement.

The Fabian version of Socialism lacked the doctrinaire and systematic quality of Social Democracy. It grew more slowly out of a complex interplay of ideas and personalities.[53] Many of the early Fabians had experienced, as in the cases of Chubb, Clarke, and Shaw, a deep rift between private values and public mores. Nearly all the early Fabians had discarded Christianity and were seeking a new philosophy of life. But the development of Fabianism witnessed the gradual divorce of that search from the Socialist ideology; the Fabians developed a framework within which men and women of differing philosophical or religious beliefs could work together for political reforms.

A crucial stage in this process took place during 1885 and 1886 when members of the Society undertook a close study of Marx's *Capital*. The Marxist doctrines of surplus value and exploitation were soon called into question by Sidney Webb, who denied, on the basis of Ricardo's theory of rent, that labor was the only source of economic value. Already the lectures of Henry George had familiarized many of the Fabians with the radical social implications of the concept of rent. And following Webb's lead the Fabians expanded the concept of rent to include not only the variable fertility of land to which Ricardo had called attention but the "surplus values" of capital and special abilities as well. Since all three of the surplus rents could be seen as social creations, they were subject, according to the Fabians, to appropriation through taxation for the benefit of society as a whole. Capitalism, so the Fabians argued, meant the exploitation not only of the workers but of the entire community; the Marxist concept of a victimized proletariat driven toward revolution by the inexorable working of economic forces, gave way to a belief that socialism would be achieved through the general enlightenment of all classes.

The new form of the Socialist ideology was mainly the work of Webb. A lonely, introverted, and brooding young man, he was struggling in these years to overcome a condition of personal despair into which he had been plunged by the loss of religious belief and a disappointment in love. His rapid rise in the civil service probably helped reconcile him to the existing institutions. But he had also drawn from the writings of Mill and from the Positivist creed of Auguste Comte a confidence in the steady growth of rational understanding and a belief in the special role of the professional in public life. Convinced that prevailing institutions provided the means of achieving socialism, Webb dismissed the moralistic appeal, the call for a new spirit of altruism, still stressed by some of his Fabian colleagues. By 1888 he was making the case for socialism in terms of conventional notions of self interest. "It seems inevitable . . . that an at best instructed and unconscious egoism should predominate in the individual. It is the business of the community . . . so to develop social institutions that individual egoism is necessarily directed to promote the wellbeing of all."[54]

Shaw recognized more quickly than most Fabians that Webb's approach to socialism demanded the suppression of purely personal aspirations. The circle of Fabian concern was being drawn in such a way as to exclude what Shaw referred to as the impractical idealist. In 1888 he apologized, in fictional guise, for killing the idealist within himself—"my other self and the best fellow in the world." And Shaw chided Hyndman and Morris for being "so maddeningly, incorrigibly, hopelessly . . . unreasonable and impossible in every day work of the movement" that the Fabians were forced to rescue it. "Here are the pair of you, brilliant imaginative men of imposing posture and capable of stirring the imagination of young enthusiasts; and yet you have between you let the movement go to pieces . . . In the meantime the Fabians . . . are the only people who have been sufficiently in earnest to overcome very strong personal incompatibilities and teach themselves to sit at the same council table and work together."[55]

The Fabians were still, as Shaw conceded, "a head without a tail." But Webb's conception of a socialism achieved through the enlightenment of all classes and by means of existing political and administrative agencies brought the Fabians close to the developing outlook of the Radical wing of the Liberal party. And during the late eighties the Fabians, led by Annie Besant, began to work with Radical politicians in London and to apply their ideas to pressing social problems. Shaw, in fact, helped initiate a new Fabian strategy of infiltrating other parties by joining a Liberal caucus. He had become convinced, with Webb, that "Socialism, if it is to be realized at all, will be achieved unawares."[56] Before long the Fabians were cooperating with Radical leaders in London in a progressive alliance and, by means of their publications and lecture tours, were reaching a new generation of middle class reformers and working class leaders outside London.

The publication of the *Fabian Essays* in 1889 virtually completed the process of ideological clarification. Socialism was now defined by one of the essayists, Sydney Olivier, simply as "an industrial system for the material requisites of human existence." The central Socialist idea of public ownership remained. But the Fabian form of socialism had been limited to practical efforts to modify the existing industrial order. And it had come to rest on a form of utilitarianism which, as Clarke observed, simply served as "a useful provisional hypothesis for the rough and superficial work of the ordinary reformer."[57]

The Fabian contraction of socialism did not take place without resistance and defections. Clarke's disillusionment has been noted. Annie Besant also broke away in these years after finding a more satisfying belief system in theosophy. Moreover, members of the Society continued to quarrel over questions of political strategy and the proper scope of Socialist concern. But in 1896, when Shaw attempted to lay out in Tract 70, "the whole Fabian policy" as it had been built up over the years, he explicitly excluded from the Society's "special business" any "distinct opinions" on basic philosophical issues or even fixed views on economic and historical development. The object of the Society, he declared, was "to persuade the English people to make their institutions thoroughly democratic and to socialize their industries sufficiently to make the livelihood of the people completely independent of private Capitalism."[58]

The Fabians had carried further the process, initiated by Hyndman, of adapting the Socialist ideology to British traditions. Through Webb's leadership the Marxist notions of exploitation and common ownership had been grafted onto indigenous forms of economic and social thought. The historical determinism found in contemporary Marxism had been identified with the natural workings of British political institutions. Moreover, the Fabians had substituted for the militant rhetoric of the Social Democrats a style of propaganda marked by restraint and moderation. Though the Fabians also attempted to win over the working classes, their following remained predominantly middle class, and they looked mainly to existing political parties and administrative agencies to advance their Socialist goals.

Still, the Social Democratic and Fabian forms of socialism had much in common. Hyndman's Marxism was designed to draw the working classes into the political process and his utilitarian outlook entailed, despite his dogmatism, a conception of national integration rather similar to that developing among the Fabians. Both the Social Democratic and Fabian leaders were seeking a more equitable distribution of wealth, greater economic and social security for the lower classes, a more representative political system, increased educational opportunities, and greater efficiency in government. They paid little attention to those aspects of Marx's writings which dealt with the plight of the worker in the capitalistic mode of production.

Ethical Socialism, the third form of British socialism, lacked the systematic character of Hyndman's Marxism and owed little to the kind of clarification through rational discussion which issued in Fabianism. This version of socialism was not the creation of a specific person or group; it arose more or less spontaneously out of the interaction between various Socialist propagandists—Social Democrats, Fabians, and the followers of Morris—and the lower classes in the industrial centers of the north. But this new form of socialism gave scope to the ethical, aesthetic, and religious aspirations which the Marxists and the Fabians had, with varying degrees of success, excluded.[59] During the early nineties Ethical Socialism gained a following much greater than that obtained by the pioneering organizations.

Much of the inspiration for Ethical Socialism came from Morris and his vision of a world in which social institutions would fully express the human capacity for fellowship and pleasure in creative work. Through the propaganda activity of his disciples, for the most part young men from the lower middle classes, the socialism of Morris was translated into popular terms. Two figures were particularly important in this work of translation—Edward Carpenter and Robert Blatchford.

Carpenter was a Cambridge graduate, a former clergyman, and occasional visitor at the London meetings of the Social Democrats, the Fabians, and the Fellowship of the New Life. In his long prose poem, *Towards Democracy*, published in installments during the eighties and the nineties, he blended ideas from diverse sources—Carlyle, Ruskin, Whitman, Marx, Morris, and the religious mysticism of the east—into a new and extravagant version of the millennium.[60] He also relied greatly on Christian categories, symbols, and imagery in presenting a vision of a future in which mankind would recover an Adamite harmony with nature. Through his lectures and writings, as well as through his direct influence on the prominent Socialist propagandists who visited him at his rural retreat near Sheffield, he helped impart a strongly utopian impulse to the new movement. Carpenter's strong primitivist bent reinforced the social nostalgia evident in Morris. A regressive strain, a desire to escape from industrial society into a simpler and more natural community, entered into Ethical Socialism.

Blatchford was even more important in the development and dissemination of Ethical Socialism.[61] His weekly paper, the *Clarion*, begun in 1891, did much to popularize Socialist ideas in the industrial areas of Lancashire and Yorkshire. And his extraordinarily successful exposition of socialism, *Merrie England*, won thousands of converts. *Merrie England* gained a deceptive appearance of practicality and common sense from proposals and statistics borrowed from Fabian materials. But the force of the book derived from its picture of the Socialist future, inspired in large part by the ideas of Morris. Although agnostic and hostile to organized religion, Blatchford appealed directly to the moral sentiments nurtured in the churches and chapels. For Blatchford the new movement was essentially a religious crusade.

The new form of socialism took its distinctive cast from ethical, aesthetic, and religious ideas, but it also owed much to the work of the Marxists and the Fabians. During the late eighties a number of young Marxists, impatient with the reluctance of the SDF and the Socialist League to enter directly into the practical struggles of the workers, broke with these organizations and attempted to mobilize the workers for independent political action. They tended to surrender along the way much of their Marxism, but they paved the way for a new articulation of working class interests in Socialist terms.[62] Meanwhile, Fabian lecturers in the early nineties were providing a new generation of working class leaders in the northern industrial centers with a critique of capitalism and contributing, unintentionally, to the growing desire for a working class political party.

Ethical Socialism was highly eclectic. Around the central Socialist goal of public ownership were gathered many of the diverse and often contradictory ideas which had entered the movement during its first decade. Spokesmen for Ethical Socialism might employ Marxist ideas of exploitation and the class struggle, or Fabian notions of rent and general enlightenment. But they were distinguished by their appeals to moral and religious sentiment and they promised a fundamental change in the quality of life.

Ethical Socialism found its most enthusiastic response in the textile centers of Yorkshire, where a tradition of comparative class harmony, expressed in the common allegiance of working class leaders and employers to the Liberal Party and the Nonconformist chapels, was breaking down. Large-scale economic organization and technological changes, together with the impact of distant market forces, were generating new conflicts between the classes. Socialist propagandists were quick to recognize the way in which religious sentiments might be enlisted on behalf of working class grievances. Thus Keir Hardie, one of the most eloquent of the new labor leaders, claimed that socialism simply expressed the Christian gospel in new terms. The old "religious form may still exist," he declared, "but once again the spirit has passed away and found its embodiment elsewhere . . . But instead of calling it Christianity we call it Socialism."[63] In those areas of Great Britain where comparable economic and religious conditions prevailed, Ethical Socialism exercised a strong appeal.

Ethical Socialism had come to serve two more or less distinct functions. It reaffirmed the hope of Morris and his followers for a fundamental transformation of life; by tapping the reservoir of traditional moral and religious sentiments, the new propagandists gave new force to the earlier hope for a society in which a spirit of fellowship and creative labor would prevail. But the Ethical Socialists were also helping the workers awaken to a new conception of their interests as a class. Particularly in those areas of the north where the trade unions had not been able to protect the workers against the pressure to reduce wages, the Socialists gained support. Many of the younger working class leaders responded to the Socialist call to create, in the form of an independent political party, a new instrument for their interests.[64]

Both the expressive and the instrumental functions of Ethical Socialism were evident in the early growth of the ILP.[65] The leaders of the new party dropped the name Socialist from its title in order to appeal to the workers in general. For they hoped to draw much of their membership and financial support from the trade unions. And the party's program included proposals which had already been accepted by many labor leaders—an eight hour day, public provision of work for the unemployed, greatly increased educational opportunities, and the abolition of indirect taxation. Indeed, the failure of the Liberal Party to give sufficient support for these proposals supplied much of the impetus for the new party. Thus Ramsay MacDonald, still a member of the Liberal Party, believed that the ILP was not so much the outcome of socialism as an expression of "a desire for Labor representation among the Liberals."[66]

But the ILP was a Socialist party; its speakers and publications insisted on the public ownership of the means of production, distribution, and exchange as the key to social regeneration. And while the party's spokesmen might draw their ideas from the Marxists, the Fabians, or the Ethical Socialists, the latter registered most strongly on the ILP's propaganda. Its speakers appealed directly to the moral and religious sentiments and, in terms familiar to those who had been reared in the Nonconformist chapels, called for a "change of heart."

The ILP's blend of pragmatism and utopianism was a source of strength. Its propaganda could be attuned to the peculiarities of different localities. Moreover, the ILP bridged the gap between working class and middle class sensibilities more effectively than the older Socialist organizations. The new party drew a significant number of recruits, including most of its speakers and organizers, from the lower middle class or the "professional proletariat."

But the influence of the middle class recruits within the ILP was also one source of a continuing tension. For they saw in socialism the promise of a radically new way of life. And they were worried lest that goal be lost in the effort to advance the economic interests of the workers. Even before the founding of the new party a number of the middle class adherents of Ethical Socialism had developed, in the "Labour Churches," an institution designed to preserve the higher Socialist mission against the materialism, the compromises, and the moral hazards of political action. And a small section of the ILP, made up mostly of young men and women from the commercial middle classes, soon broke away from the party's political course in order to seek, in the form of small communities, a purer expression of their Socialist faith. "In the atmosphere of politics," their leader wrote, "the upright reformer cannot live and work; he loses honesty, purpose, and sight of his own ends. It is impossible to fight the system with its own weapons, one cannot touch pitch without being defiled." Blatchford soon soured of the new party and denounced the "tricks and intrigues of the lousy political crew" while restating his belief that Socialists were engaged primarily in a moral and a religious crusade.[67]

Within a year after its founding the ILP had become the largest of the Socialist organizations in Britain. Although it failed to gain support from the trade unions, it showed promise of becoming a mass party; by 1895 it had formed several hundred branches with perhaps twenty thousand members. In the general election of that year the ILP ran twenty-eight candidates for Parliament. All these, including the party's president, Keir Hardie, who had earlier won a seat in a London constituency, were defeated. While the party continued to grow for a time, the late nineties proved to be a difficult period for the ILP and the Socialist movement generally.

Relative economic prosperity after 1895, a Conservative government, and a strong surge of imperialist sentiment created a political climate less congenial for Socialist propaganda. The membership of the ILP fell off sharply and a number of its most effective speakers became discouraged and withdrew from propaganda work. Although the ILP played an increasingly active role in local politics, its leaders were forced to reassess their political strategy. They were now more convinced than ever that an effective working class party required the support of the trade unions and they began to revise their electoral tactics. This was largely the work of Ramsay MacDonald, a relative newcomer to the party's leadership.

Ten years earlier MacDonald had left his native village in Scotland to take a position as a clerk in Bristol.[68] There he joined the local branch of the SDF and, after moving to London in 1886, continued to take part in the Socialist movement. In an unpublished novel, written during these years, MacDonald dealt with the young professional people and artists, as well as the middle class reformers, who dominated the Socialist circles. And he expressed too his inability to find in socialism a solution to a crisis in his emotional life. Like many of his contemporaries MacDonald was simultaneously struggling to establish himself in one of the professions and to find a new belief system. In the years ahead, as he sought a career in journalism and in politics, his personal quest drew him to the Fellowship of the New Life, the Swedenborgians, and the Ethical Culture movement. He also joined the Fabian Society and shared for a time the Fabian belief that the Socialist cause could be advanced by infiltrating the Liberal Party. But in 1894, his hope of becoming a Liberal candidate for Parliament having been frustrated, he joined the ILP. He carried into his work for the new party, however, an approach to Socialism that remained much closer to Fabianism than to the utopian spirit of Ethical Socialism. In this new context he confessed to a close friend his sense of being "planted on the borders of socialism."[69]

MacDonald, with the support of Hardie, developed a new electoral policy for the ILP. It was designed to minimize conflicts with the Liberal Party, which still held the allegiance of most of the trade unionists, by emphasizing the practical goals they shared with the Socialists. Several major industrial defeats and signs that the legal position of the trade unions was in jeopardy made their leaders more receptive to proposals for independent political action. And in February 1900, the ILP leaders were able to form a political alliance with a number of the trade unions. By means of the Labour Representation Committee they set out to form a "definite Labour group in Parliament."[70]

The Social Democrats and the Fabians also participated in the founding of the Labour Representation Committee. Both of the older Socialist bodies had viewed the development of the ILP with misgivings. Hyndman and his colleagues believed that no working class party could be effective unless its members acquired a genuine Marxist understanding of the economic and social process; they were convinced that the new party's "sentimental socialism" guaranteed its political sterility. The Fabians, in contrast, believed that the ILP threatened the class collaboration on which they relied to advance socialism. But as the new party spread, the Fabians accepted it as a force for socialism and sought to educate it through their speakers, the dissemination of their literature, and the holding of conferences to deal with the pressing problems of local government.

Both the Social Democrats and the Fabians had suffered a decline in members and vigor during the late nineties. And despite their reservations they accepted the political alliance with the trade unions as a new means of advancing the Socialist cause. It was time, as Hyndman put it, to set first principles aside.[71]

But even as the various sections of the Socialist movement found a ground for cooperation, the outbreak of the Boer War challenged each of the organizations to reconsider its relationship to national development. In fact, the war, as Shaw said, dragged into prominence the fact that "the political solidarity of the Socialists was an illusion."[72] The war brought out some of the pre-Socialist attitudes and loyalties in which the new ideology had taken root.

For most members of the ILP and the SDF the issues posed by the war were fairly simple. Spokesmen for both groups blamed the war on the capitalists and employed Marxist theory to explain imperialism. But their opposition to the war was more directly a reflection of older radical hostility to imperialistic ventures. Even Hyndman, whose own attitude toward the British empire was somewhat ambivalent, held that Social Democratic opposition to the war was "a matter of general ethics rather than of Socialism." Both the SDF and the ILP set aside their Socialist commitments to support pro-Boer members of the Liberal Party in by-elections. Indeed, Hardie at one point called on John Morley, the chief spokesman for this section of the Liberals, to lead the "disordered and almost despairing hosts of those who are literally sheep without a shepherd." No wonder one Socialist defender of the war charged that the ILP had been swept "into the most reactionary wing of the broken forces of Liberalism" while the SDF was but a "trifle less enslaved."[73]

Socialists who did not share these older radical attitudes tended to support the war. Thus Blatchford and most of his colleagues on the *Clarion*, whose Socialist outlook carried over many of the attitudes of an older, even Tory Britain, took a strongly patriotic position. So too did several of the Fabians, like Hubert Bland, who had little sympathy for the tradition of liberal radicalism.

Only the Fabians experienced a serious internal conflict over the war. And the dispute indicated the precariousness of the framework of concern into which Webb had guided the Society. Webb and Shaw contended that the issues raised by the war "lay outside the special province of the Society." And Bland warned the members against throwing themselves "athwart the Imperialist or any strong stream of national life." But Sam Hobson, a vigorous newcomer on the executive, called on the Society to "extend the scope of its criticism and propaganda" beyond the "details of industry and municipal politics" to which it had become "increasingly restricted." It was time, he argued, for the Fabians to recover their position as a "leading force in the Socialist movement" by influencing a democratic public opinion on larger issues. Olivier agreed; he claimed that the surge of imperialistic feeling in Britain demonstrated the bankruptcy of official Fabianism. "Imperialism is in fact a living power because it represents a sort of primitive avatar of real elemental force . . . You can't get ahead of a real elementary force except by going better in elemental force yourself." In the end the society's executive defeated the challenge to the "perfect single-mindedness" of the Fabians. But the refusal to take a collective stand against the war led to several resignations, including that of Ramsay MacDonald.[74]

Socialist responses to the war, like the earlier process of ideological differentiation, indicated the diversity of impulses within the movement. But Socialists retained a strong sense of participating in a common cause. Thus in the midst of the Boer War, the Marxist Hyndman could reach across the spectrum of Socialist ideas and share his dismay over the corruption of British life with the prophet of Ethical Socialism, Edward Carpenter. And a year later, when Webb began to develop close ties with the "imperialist" wing of the Liberal Party, Shaw warned him against "going back on our Socialism." "We are committed for life," he told Beatrice Webb, and "any appearance of backing out of it would leave us less influence than Hyndman or Keir Hardie."[75]

The Socialist ideology had drawn a number of men and women out of their private worlds of frustration and fantasy; it had freed others, especially in the working classes, from older political loyalties. Socialism had enabled the alienated and the discontented to "size up the situation," map out the social landscape anew, and come together for political action. After the turn of the century the Socialists would enter more fully into the political process. They would also find themselves increasingly torn between their Socialist commitments and the exigencies of parliamentary politics.

PART TWO

POLITICAL INVOLVEMENT AND DEEPENING DILEMMAS

2

ETHICAL SOCIALISM 1900-1905: THE PARTING OF THE WAYS

T HE GENERAL ELECTION of 1900, so the ILP secretary observed, "lifted the movement from the abyss into which it had fallen, and awakened new zeal and enthusiasm."[1] During the next few years, as the war ended and interest in domestic problems revived, the Socialists gradually regained the ground they had lost in the late nineties and extended their propaganda into new areas. For the ILP, in particular, the change was dramatic, because the alliance with the trade unions decisively altered its relationship to the political process. Party leaders could now concentrate on the task of drawing the members and resources of the unions into the cause of working class political independence and, at the same time, pursue their new strategy for converting the workers to socialism.

The strategy had become apparent at the founding conference of the Labour Representation Committee. MacDonald and Hardie had set aside their Socialist principles in deference to the "labourist" outlook of most of the trade union leaders. During the next few years the ILP leaders allowed their Socialist ideology to recede further into the background as they became convinced that a strong espousal of socialism would impede the cause of working class political independence. Not all members of the ILP were willing to accept this policy; the party's course, charted mainly by MacDonald, met a growing criticism. The ILP policy also evoked a counter strategy among those Ethical

Socialists gathered around the *Clarion*. Convinced that the Socialist vision was being sacrificed to political expediency, Blatchford attempted to revitalize the cause by giving it a new philosophical basis. He launched a campaign to de-Christianize the British people and propagate his own creed of "Determinism."

THE ILP AND THE ALLIANCE WITH THE TRADE UNIONS

As the ILP renewed its growth after 1900 it again found its main support in the industrial areas of Yorkshire and Lancashire-Cheshire. Nearly 60 percent of the party's three hundred or more branches were located in this region. There were additional pockets of support in Scotland and the Midlands while new branches in the mining areas of Wales and the northeast promised a wider reach. Yet, the ILP had failed to make much headway in London and exercised virtually no appeal to the mass of the rural workers. At its 1905 conference the delegates voted to elect nine of the fourteen places on the party's administrative council on the basis of geographical divisions in the hope of developing a more truly national basis. But in these years the ILP was still, as Henry Pelling observed, "a sectional rather than a national party."[2] The ILP and the other Socialist groups continued to draw an important part of their memberships from the lower middle class. Thus the description by Montague Blatchford, brother of the *Clarion* editor, of the typical recruits into the movement at the turn of the century. "My experience is that our raw material consists mostly of young men who have a little above the average intelligence; of young clerks, shop assistants, school teachers, and even young professional men who have education but little money. These young men have usually been active members of Sunday Schools, debating societies, or political clubs, or at least have held some sort of intellectual positions among their mates in mills or workshops. They join at personal sacrifice in the esteem of their mates." Only a strong belief in the justice of the Socialist cause, Blatchford added, could compensate for the "obvious fact that socially (the converts) have lost rather than gained." But the middle class element was viewed with some suspicion within the Socialist-trade union alliance. From time to time the trade unionists attacked the "professional men, journalists, and adventurers" who were trying to "creep into the movement."[3]

ILP propaganda continued to swing between pragmatic and utopian poles. After 1900 the party's spokesmen addressed themselves more effectively than they had earlier to national issues; pamphlets dealing with trade policy and unemployment gained wide circulation. But ILP propaganda was still distinguished by its strong appeal to moral and religious sentiments. No figure exhibited this appeal more clearly than Philip Snowden, who performed at this time "a missionary work unsurpassed among his contemporaries . . . in arousing the masses to self awareness."[4] Snowden's early life, situated in the most fertile soil for Ethical Socialism, the West Riding of Yorkshire, exemplified many of the aspirations which entered the popular Socialist movement.

Snowden was born of working class parents in the small textile town of Cowling in the northern part of the West Riding. His family was firmly rooted in a local tradition of political radicalism reaching back to the time of Chartism. "I imbibed," Snowden recalled late in life, "the political and social principles which I have had fundamentally ever since." Closely attached to a local Wesleyan Methodist chapel, Snowden accepted as a young man the liberal religious views of the American Unitarian, William Ellery Channing. He also advanced beyond the educational level of most of his social peers and served as a student teacher for several years before taking a job in an insurance company's office. Then, disenchanted with the life of a clerk, he took the civil service examinations and entered the excise service. A series of positions introduced him to a wider social and cultural world, and he became fascinated with the theater. He studied closely the styles of the leading actors of the day and participated in an amateur dramatic society. A critic of one of these performances commended Snowden for his "perfect aplomb," his "dexterous manipulation of voice," and his "easy grace of style."[5]

In 1891 a spinal disorder, which crippled Snowden permanently, forced him to leave the civil service. He returned home to recuperate and prepare for work in journalism or law. An invitation to the local Liberal club to speak against socialism led Snowden to Socialist writings. He read Hyndman, Morris, Carpenter, Lawrence Gronlund, and the *Fabian Essays*, discovering in the process, "ideas and aims" he had already held in "vague and indefinite form."[6] Soon his cottage in Cowling became a center for the discussion of Socialist ideas. After visits by several prominent ILP speakers—James Sexton, Enid Stacy, Sam Hobson, and Edward Hartley—Snowden organized a branch of the new party. He also began to speak for the new cause throughout the West Riding, and during the late nineties became one of the ILP's most popular figures. Like many of the party's prominent speakers he often claimed that socialism had come to revitalize religious truths which had been betrayed by the churches. Thus he contrasted the "tramping Socialist of Nazareth with the modern bishops who draw big salaries while thousands of their countrymen starved."[7]

Sam Hobson, looking back out of his later disillusionment with the movement, declared that Snowden's "real claim to fame" lay in his great skill, among a "considerable group of political hot gospellers," in evolving a new platform technique.[8] The judgment was too cynical. Snowden's Socialist rhetoric developed naturally out of the social and religious setting in which he had grown up. But he worked exceedingly hard perfecting his platform style; as he moved out from the West Riding he even studied the idiosyncracies of language in various parts of the country in order to touch his audiences more effectively. But his addresses in the early years of the century gave new and extraordinary force to the mixture of ideas and sentiments making up Ethical Socialism. This mixture was displayed most fully in his popular talk, "The Christ That Is to Be."[9]

In this talk Snowden denounced organized religion in terms characteristic of much of Socialist propaganda. "Never did the Church cling more tenaciously to its pagan creeds," he declared, for the clergy recognized that "the final struggle between reason and superstition is close at hand." Yet, Snowden went on to appropriate the Christian teachings of love and service for the Socialist cause. "A new conception of the meaning and purpose of the sacrifice of the cross" was dawning; Christ's sacrifice was not a "substitution for the sacrifice of others" but an "example that only by such sacrifice can others be saved." Snowden also struck out against the suspicion of the secular world encouraged by so much of Victorian Christianity and declared that the religion of the future would be a "political religion." It would apply the "moral truths of religion . . . to our industrial and social affairs." Snowden condemned individualism and, in words reminiscent of Edward Carpenter, predicted that "individual consciousness" would pass into a "social consciousness" and bring "the complete organic unity of the whole human race." A Marxist element also entered the address. The coming moral and religious era would be aided by "great social forces . . . ever moving on in their might and majesty" and not "for a moment" impeded or disturbed by the "tumult of our debates." Snowden normally concluded his Socialist addresses on a millennialist note; he might refer to the hope for beauty and joy in common things inspired by Ruskin and Morris. But he relied mainly on Christian imagery. In the Socialist society the "spirit of love and sacrifice . . . which shone with the glory of full perfection in the life of Jesus of Nazareth" would "animate all men." "The new humanity" could only be attained, however, along the "old hard road of Calvary—through persecution, through poverty, through temptation, by the agony and bloody sweat, by the crown of thorns, by the agonizing death. And then the resurrection to the new humanity—purified by suffering, triumphant through sacrifice."

There was another side to Snowden's propaganda work. Increasingly, after the turn of the century he used the "come to Jesus" appeal in those places where he was "breaking new ground for socialism." Where the Socialist cause had gained support he concentrated on current social and political issues. Indeed, he concluded before long that Socialists were "overflowing with sentiments and ideals" and "sadly deficient in practical knowledge of economics." He decided, therefore, to concentrate on "driving economic common sense" into the movement. Snowden's economic common sense, however, came from the political radicalism of his background. He tended, in fact, to "take whole areas of Liberal principles into his Socialist theory." Alongside his advocacy of nationalization and the progressive tax measures designed to bring a cooperative commonwealth, were orthodox liberal views of such matters as free trade, the empire, the drink traffic, and budgeting policies. Until the end of his life the contradiction between Philip Snowden, Socialist, and Philip Snowden, the economist "still under the influence of Mill, Ricardo, and Henry George," seemed to some observers to "defy explanation."[10]

The contradiction within Snowden was built into the ILP. Its ethically charged Socialist ideology still rested in large part on an earlier set of social and political attitudes derived from nineteenth century radicalism. Though this legacy tended to check efforts to develop distinctly Socialist positions on a number of political issues it facilitated the party's cooperation with most of the trade union leaders.

After a slow start the alliance had grown rapidly and by 1903 it contained all the major trade unions except those of the miners. In that year, at the LRC conference in Newcastle, the delegates adopted resolutions which ensured a much greater degree of political independence, solidarity, and discipline and created a fund to support the Committee's members in Parliament. The chief impetus for this growth came from a judicial decision. In 1901 the Law Lords had placed the entire trade union movement in jeopardy. The Lords had upheld a lower court verdict in favor of a claim by the Taff Vale Railway Company against the Amalgamated Society of Railway Servants for losses resulting from a strike. The decision meant that a union's financial resources were no longer secure against claims for damages arising out of the acts of individual members. In the face of this threat many trade union leaders now accepted the Socialist call for working class political independence. But they turned to politics mainly to defend or restore the legal position which their unions had gained in the eighteen seventies; they were still little disposed to adopt the Socialist view of capitalist exploitation and the Socialist argument for collective ownership.[11]

The ILP leaders continued to test the attitudes of their trade union allies by introducing Socialist resolutions at the annual conferences of the Committee. And in 1905 they were able to pass a vaguely worded resolution in favor of nationalization. But they addressed themselves mainly to the work of strengthening the alliance and giving it practical political meaning. It was soon apparent that a practical political tactic might be at odds with the advance of Socialist propaganda. The five by-election contests in which the alliance participated during 1902 and 1903 indicated a clear tendency for the ILP leaders to sacrifice Socialist propaganda in the interest of electoral success.

In March 1902, Philip Snowden stood for a seat at Wakefield against a Conservative in a contest still dominated by the war issue. He campaigned hard and effectively, and his poll of nearly 40 percent of the vote indicated his strong appeal to anti-war Liberals. But late in the campaign the *Clarion* criticized Snowden's tendency to "shrink from using the word Socialist at all," in order to gain a few votes. Hyndman also concluded, on the basis of his electoral addresses, that Snowden was not a genuine Socialist.[12]

Several months later a seat fell vacant at Clitheroe in northeastern Lancashire, a constituency ideally suited to Snowden's candidacy.[13] The chances were good that the ILP would return its second Socialist to Parliament. Tactical considerations dictated otherwise. Snowden withdrew in favor of David Shackleton, a trade union leader and a Liberal who agreed to run under the auspices of the LRC. Not only was Shackleton less likely to draw a Liberal opponent but his candidacy was regarded by the Committee leaders as an opportunity for luring one of the most powerful trade union federations, embracing the Lancashire textile operatives, into the new political alliance. Both these aims were realized. Shackleton was returned unopposed as the Conservatives, who had a strong working class following in the area, also stood aside. In January 1903, the cotton unions, 103,000 strong, joined the Committee. It was the largest single addition up to this time. But the setback to ILP propaganda was clear. Glasier wrote Hardie that they "must not seem to act as though they were disappointed." Hardie, meanwhile, assured his readers that Shackleton's declaration of independence from the two older parties was precisely what the ILP was striving for. "There can be no fear," he wrote, that Shackleton would not be a "Socialist in practice."[14]

The addition of the cotton textile workers was important because it brought a sizable bloc of conservative working men into an electoral alliance which had hitherto depended mainly on the support of working class Liberals. Since the 1880s the conservatives had been attracting a growing working class vote in the larger urban centers to add to the substantial working class support they had gained earlier in the Lancashire towns. To pry these workers loose the leaders of the alliance had to convince them of their independence from both traditional parties. Will Crooks, a popular figure in London progressive politics and the Committee's candidate at Woolwich early in 1903, demonstrated the potentiality of such an appeal by converting what had been a Conservative margin of 2800 votes to a Labor margin of over 3200. But Crooks, like Shackleton, had only recently accepted the need for labor's political independence. Socialism played little part in his campaign.[15]

The other contests in 1903 revealed a positive reluctance on the part of the Committee's candidates to accept the help of Socialists or ILP speakers. At Preston, another Tory stronghold, John Hodge, general secretary of the steel smelters' union, lost a straight fight with a Conservative. Hardie had polled over four thousand votes there during the general election but Hodge was informed by his managers that Hardie's appearance would offend working class Conservatives. No wonder Glasier commented ruefully that "those who teach the faith" are "held to be a bit disqualified these days."[16]

At Barnard Castle, Durham, in August, where the Committee won its first three-cornered fight, the ILP men were again warned off. The candidate was Arthur Henderson, until shortly before the contest a Liberal party agent. He accepted the Committee's platform, but his campaign was more in the nature of an intra-party fight among the Liberals. His program differed little from that of his Liberal opponent and he secured most of the official Liberal support. The local labor leaders informed Hardie and Glasier that "it would not be prudent for any of the prominent men of the ILP to share in the fun." Only after MacDonald protested to Henderson was Snowden invited to represent the ILP in the campaign. The episode so disturbed Hardie and Glasier that they determined to publicize the dispute. With Henderson's narrow victory, however, their indignation cooled and the article Glasier planned to write was put off until it would lose "all personal point."[17]

Shackleton, Crooks, and Henderson, the three LRC candidates returned to Parliament between 1900 and 1906, were not Socialists in any strict sense of the term. They exemplified the older "labourist" outlook which did not question the legitimacy of the capitalistic order.[18] The outlook was already expressed in the House of Commons in the small "Lib Lab" section of the Liberal Party. These working class representatives came mainly from the mining areas of the northeast and Wales where the numbers and solidarity of the workers gave them considerable political leverage.

The "Lib Lab" group remained aloof from the LRC and opposed its efforts to develop a new party, convinced that working class interests could be pursued more effectively within the Liberal Party.[19] Moreover, the "labourist" outlook characteristic of this older form of working class politics, presented a special obstacle to the growth of socialism. For it was usually connected closely with Nonconformist religious commitments which resisted the special appeal of Ethical Socialism. Thus Henderson, deeply rooted in the Methodism of the north, felt it necessary at times to defend himself against ILP members who criticized him for spending time as a lay preacher. "It is not independence they want (but) automatic machines . . . It is a misfortune for some of us that we have not seen our way to join you Saints of the Movement" and travel the "narrow way" to salvation.[20]

While Henderson, Crooks, and Shackleton had abandoned the "Lib Lab" political strategy in favor of the idea of working class independence, they remained strangers to the ethically charged ideology of their Socialist colleagues. Godfrey Elton's summary description of Henderson's "labourist" and pragmatic approach to the advance of working class interests might be applied to all three. "Though he had shared and felt for the hardships of his class it is difficult to resist the conclusion that spiritually he belonged always to the bourgeoisie. He had all the strength and something of the weakness of that largely fictitious class, respectable, God fearing, kind, industrious, magnanimous, destitute of aesthetic and intellectual tastes and—astute."[21]

The difference between the Socialist and the "labourist" outlook was largely ignored, however, in a common drive to increase the political power of the working classes. Meanwhile, the ILP leaders were losing their earlier confidence about the rapid spread of Socialist ideas through their political alliance with the trade unionists. Russell Smart, editor of the *ILP News*, observed in 1902 that Socialist propaganda had reached a saturation point in many working class areas. There was a point, "varying with the circumstances, beyond which the polls of mere propagandist candidates refused to go." Where these "quite futile contests" were undertaken the vote tended to "fall unmistakeably back." And Smart concluded that the ILP had to decide, in view of the "sudden uprising of Trade Union demands for parliamentary candidates," whether the trade unionist vote would be "for or against our candidates at the polls."[22]

The task of linking the Socialists to the trade union vote was mainly the responsibility of MacDonald, as secretary of the LRC. In that role he soon assumed powers of initiative scarcely anticipated by those who had elected him. Committed to the goal of transforming the political alliance into a new party, he concentrated on the immediate possibilities of the political situation and set out to develop a policy which corresponded to the varied interests and strengths of the Socialists, the trade unionists, and the Liberals. Having tied the interests of the trade unionists and the hopes of the Socialists together in the idea of working class political independence, he used the potential electoral power which this alliance provided in many constituencies to seek concessions from the Liberals. And the Liberal leaders were quick to recognize the advantages which working class candidates in marginal constituencies might give them in their efforts to defeat the Conservatives.

MacDonald reduced the offense of this policy to the Socialists of the ILP and to the former Conservatives among the LRC's working class supporters by avoiding any public acknowledgment of formal cooperation with the Liberals. But he denied the contention of some ILP members that they should seek to identify the LRC more closely with socialism. "I think such a view disastrous. What our Socialists will have to do more and more is to carry on a Socialist propaganda and for political purposes to cooperate loyally with local unions and other similar organizations that are [inclined] to advance legislation in our direction. I think there must be a division of labour in this matter . . . At the present moment [the Socialist movement] is in great danger of becoming confused between two distinct objects." Socialists, he argued, should practice self-restraint. "We have failed over and over again in definite work because we . . . felt impelled to drag in general questions upon which we are fighting as members of Socialist organizations."[23] And MacDonald steadfastly resisted the efforts of Social Democratic candidates to secure LRC endorsement for their contests.

In the fall of 1903 MacDonald's negotiations with the Liberals led to a secret arrangement which virtually assured the return of a substantial bloc of independent labor representatives to the House of Commons.[24] With the knowledge and support of Hardie he concluded an agreement with Herbert Gladstone, the Liberal leader, to divide up constituencies in such a way as to give thirty or more candidates of the LRC a straight run at the Conservatives in the next general election. The agreement was not accompanied by any party debate or discussion. Party policy was, in fact, being determined by a few men working behind the scenes. The rank and file of the ILP, like their counterparts in the older political parties, were placing their fortunes more and more in the hands of their leaders. By virtue of the confidence and loyalty they inspired in their followers, the ILP leaders now possessed considerable room for maneuver in their pursuit of political power.

Still, the tension between the ILP's Socialist commitment and its political strategy was increasingly apparent. And party leaders were being forced to adapt their Socialist beliefs to the changing political situation. The modes of adaptation varied. Hardie, MacDonald, and John Bruce Glasier, who became chairman of the ILP in 1900, responded in quite different ways to the growing divergence between politics and ideology.

THREE MODES OF POLITICAL ACCOMMODATION:
Hardie, Glasier, and MacDonald

Hardie played a dual role in the life of the ILP.[25] As a spokesman for Ethical Socialism he called men and women to look beyond their immediate interests and seek, both within themselves and in society, a new moral order. As working class politician he pursued power, shrewdly gauging the possibilities for action and accepting the need for compromises which characterizes the political vocation. It was easier to combine the two roles as long as the ILP occupied a position outside the mainstream of political life. Moreover, Hardie's Socialist faith, like that of many of his ILP colleagues, was at times no more than a thin cover for older radical and liberal attitudes. But as the ILP became, through its electoral alliance with the trade unionists, more and more deeply involved in the political process, the tension between the Socialist prophet and the Socialist politician increased.

After the turn of the century Hardie continued, on the platform and in the press, to describe the Socialist as one who viewed "life from a different standpoint than that of the non-Socialist" and accepted the ethical as the "all important standard of conduct." The primary requirement for reform was the "formation and development of character." Character was inevitably "weakened by compromise and arrangements." At times Hardie's words recalled the purism of William Morris.

> We will not and can not and dare not smirch our ideal by associating it with the shifting measures of party politics. The faith of Socialists must be kept pure, that it may be clearly comprehended by the people. Thus and thus only will they be inspired to noble effort for the attainment of that higher life which Socialism offers. And this is why we cannot have any working agreement or even joint committee with those whose aim is to uphold a degrading, though fortunately decaying and worn out creed.

He continued to share something of Morris's hatred of modern industry and urban life and visualized the Socialist future as a return to a decentralized and less artificial community. A year after he and MacDonald had concluded the electoral pact with the Liberals, Hardie reaffirmed his determination to guard the purity of the Socialist ideal. "I cannot conceive of any set of circumstances as likely to arise in my life time which would lead me to agree to any alliance with any party now existing. Working arrangements with Liberals or Conservatives would spell ruin."[26]

Meanwhile, in his practical political work, as he sought to enhance the power of the ILP and advance the interests of the workers, Hardie was little inhibited by fears for the integrity of the Socialist cause. Convinced that the traditional party structure in Britain was breaking up, he saw possibilities for political alliances both with the Irish and with the Radical section of the Liberal party. His extreme opportunism led one *Labour Leader* correspondent in 1902 to ask why Hardie was "abandoning the ILP." Later, when Hardie suggested that they might cooperate with the Liberals in order to "save the country from reaction," his remarks created consternation in the ILP rank and file. Glasier told Hardie that he had not acted with his usual discretion.[27]

Hardie's statements in these years displayed the inconsistency which convention has usually allowed the politician in his efforts to connect human aspirations with practical possibilities. But Hardie's Socialist faith and his political activity were losing any plausible connection. An article he contributed to the *Nineteenth Century* in 1904 exhibited the contradictory impulses of the Socialist prophet and the politician. Here Hardie suggested that the Socialists might take the lead in "creating a new combination of progressive forces." But, he added, it would have to "be done so as in no way to impair the freedom of action of the Socialist party or to blur the vision of the Socialist ideal."[28]

Hardie recognized the contradiction. He conceded that the political alliance with the trade unionists, and the "more pressing needs of the hour" were taking the "keen edge" off the ILP's Socialist propaganda. And he confessed that the condition of the proletariat was a "sad bar to close adherence to logical principle." But only those who were not "feeling the pinch" could "afford to be logical and consistent." Indeed, for Hardie consistency in this new situation would jeopardize the work with which he had identified himself. He noted on one occasion that he had "no personality, no separate identity" apart from the interests of the ILP. His life's work was closely bound up with the fate of that party. When the choice between the two aims of the party was unavoidable, as the trade union alliance demanded at times, he usually sacrificed the remote goal of a Socialist society to the immediate advantages of labor. The Socialist inspiration remained, however, and in the years ahead it would rob his political work of some of its effectiveness and, in time perhaps, its conviction.[29]

The dilemmas with which Hardie struggled were less painful for Glasier and MacDonald. But for very different reasons. Glasier was not so deeply involved in the ILP's political work; MacDonald was little burdened by its utopian form of the Socialist ideology. Glasier and MacDonald proceeded in quite distinct ways to adapt their Socialist ideas to the changing political situation.

Glasier had joined the ILP late in 1893 following a decade of work in the Socialist movement. After helping start the Glasgow branch of the SDF he followed Morris into the Socialist League, became one of his most ardent disciples, and adopted his ethical and aesthetic form of socialism. Along the way he also gave up his goal of becoming an architect and decided to devote himself full time to the new cause. "Free and unconventional in dress and manner," he carried into his propaganda work something of the style of the vagabond poet. During the early nineties he moved into the growing stream of Ethical Socialism and became one of its most popular speakers.[30]

Initially Glasier, like Morris, was hostile to political action and he regarded the ILP with suspicion. But his strongly aesthetic and ethical bent, together with his marriage to one of the new party's leading speakers, Katharine St. John Conway, drew him into its work. Soon he had aligned himself closely behind Hardie's leadership. In 1895 he confessed that many of his "life's hopes" were in Hardie's keeping and in the years ahead he tended to efface his own personality before that of the ILP leader. Glasier invested Hardie with qualities which reflected his mystical view of the movement. When Hardie proposed that his colleague write his biography Glasier replied: "I feel that there is a great artistic and moral advantage in a leader's position being not too clearly defined, and indeed in there being a veil of reserve, if not mystery between him and the eyes of all the world . . . I think you have more spiritual significance in our midst with only the few essential features of your life outlined to us." In 1900, Glasier succeeded Hardie as chairman of the ILP and dutifully submitted his conference address for the latter's approval.[31]

As chairman Glasier did not exercise a strong and independent influence on the development of the party. He viewed his role mainly as inspirational and to this end he employed the rhetorical style which he had developed in his popular propaganda work. "How quite undisturbed are the rock beds of society," he observed after the general election, for in politics as in geology the "important movements of social reconstruction" were "accomplished by processes hardly discernible to the eye." This tendency to rely on hidden processes behind appearances characterized much of Ethical Socialism. In Glasier it was accentuated by a strongly poetic temperament. His style did not make for a clear or realistic confrontation of the problems facing the ILP. Glasier often evaded intellectual or strategical difficulties by falling back on personal feelings. Thus when two ILP leaders in Bradford came under attack for collaborating with the Liberals, Glasier dismissed the charges. "However mistaken their tactics may be, they are incomparably better and truer Socialists than many of those who bitterly attack them." Defending Hardie in a letter to Blatchford, he insisted that the "heart" was "the decisive thing."[32]

Lacking any real basis in theory, Glasier's Socialist creed began to function in a new way after 1900. It lost much of its inspirational quality and became apologetic. It ceased to call men out from conventional society to take a heroic stand on new principles. More and more it served to justify the ILP's policies and reconcile its members to the "blurring of lines" between the party and the trade unions, between Socialists and non-Socialists. Glasier's new role separated him from old comrades. His friendship with Blatchford continued into 1902 but it did not survive a bitter dispute among Socialists over a by-election in Dewsbury. Soon Glasier was criticizing the *Clarion* men for their "impertinent interference from outside." "We have created," he added, "a Labour Representative movement far bigger than the Socialist movement. We must now turn Labour Representation into Socialist sentiment."[33]

Glasier recognized that his conception of socialism was

changing. He justified himself in a letter to Edward Carpenter in the spring of 1903.

It [the ILP] has been the means of restoring the English tradition into our Socialist agitation—a tradition which was lost by the usurpation of the Marxist and Communards. For myself, I feel as one set free now that I am able to speak and work for Socialism without feeling that I belong to a different cast of beings from that of the ordinary Liberal or Tory. I feel much joy, too, now that I realize that Socialism is not a thing that a few refugees and philosophers brought into the world from twenty to forty years ago, but that it is a power that began with the beginning of the world and permeates infinitude.[34]

Glasier also attempted to explain the change to the ILP rank and file. Reviewing its twenty-year history in 1904, he recalled the "early days of faith," when Socialists possessed an "inquisitorial and catechismic air" and were regarded as "men who had been initiated into some inner mysteries of brotherhood." But the original "predictions and dogmas" had been "to a great extent falsified or ignored by events."

In a word Socialism in Britain . . . has chosen its own path for itself; which is another way of saying that the people have determined for themselves what Socialism is and what their method of realising it shall be. The history of the ILP is the history of this development. It is in a measure the revolt of democracy against dogma, the overleaping of a living form from the artificial mold . . . The ILP has achieved this position to some extent in spite of itself [and] . . . saved the British Socialist movement from political nullity.[35]

Glasier continued to insist that the "ILP tone is grander, more tender, and more idealistic than years ago," but the party had, in fact, now entered onto a path which increasingly demanded the skills of the negotiator rather than those of the prophet.[36] Glasier was not totally lacking in the former. As chairman he played a mediating role in intraparty disputes and undertook delicate missions to discourage candidacies in unpromising constituencies. And not long after Snowden succeeded him as party chairman in 1903 he assumed the editorship of the ILP organ, *Labour Leader.* His new responsibility, however, would bring an ever widening gap between his idealistic rhetoric and the practical problems facing the party.

MacDonald was not indifferent to the moralistic spirit within the ILP and could at times employ the party's rhetoric with great effect. But his own development within the Socialist movement had witnessed the gradual displacement of its utopian bent by a more traditional conception of politics. His association with the Fabians during the nineties strengthened this outlook but he did not share Webb's hostility to the growth of a working class party. Socialist progress, he wrote in 1899, would not "spring from the generosity of the enlightened, but from the common intelligence."[37] And his active role in the Ethical Culture movement in the late nineties reflected his deep commitment to the task of developing a new concept of citizenship. Still, MacDonald's socialism remained essentially Fabian; he envisioned the gradual modification of existing institutional arrangements through an extension of collectivist principles already accepted by progressive elements in the traditional parties.

It was a concept well suited to the strategical course he charted, first within the ILP, and then as the secretary of the LRC. It permitted him virtually to ignore the differences between the ILP and the left wing of the Liberal Party. Such a course was made easier by the survival of Liberal sentiments within the ILP. On major questions of policy Hardie readily followed MacDonald's lead and by 1902 was praising him as the best all around man the movement had produced.[38] But socialism, in any strict sense of the term, had little to do with MacDonald's work in consolidating the alliance with the trade unionists. He worked mainly behind the scenes, shrewdly assessing the interests and the tolerances of both the trade union leaders and the ILP members, as he attempted to promote independent labor candidacies.[39]

MacDonald stated his view of Socialist strategy most fully perhaps during 1904 in a report of the Amsterdam Congress of the Socialist International. There the militant position of the German Social Democrats had prevailed over the moderate views expressed by the French leader, Jean Jaures. In identifying himself with the moderates, MacDonald conceded the "ineradicable opposition between profits and wages, capital and labour, bourgeois and proletariat." But this did not necessitate class war. Democracy was "intellectual and moral" as well as economic. There was broad ground for cooperation between Socialists and non-Socialists on behalf of intermediate reforms which might lead toward "revolutionary" or "fundamental" change. He concluded that a "labour party would be justified in giving general support" to a Liberal government on such issues as imperialism and trade union legislation and "protecting it from defeat" if necessary. His remarks brought sharp protests from ILP members. Glasier deplored MacDonald's statement as "hardly an act of statesmanship" and raised the issue in a "half jesting, half serious way" in the party's administrative council.[40]

Still, MacDonald recognized that the ILP was endangering its identity as a Socialist party. A *Labour Leader* editorial in 1904, apparently written by MacDonald, announced that the ILP leaders had triumphantly accomplished the work of consolidation; it was time for the party to renew its "distinctive principles" and return to the "more direct work of Socialist propaganda." The ILP must demonstrate that its principles and motives went beyond mere radicalism and distinguished it from the other parties on such pressing issues as free trade, education, and "Chinese slavery." Neither MacDonald nor any other ILP leader succeeded in extending the Socialist critique effectively into new economic and political areas. His own insights into the possibility of a more distinctive program were, as David Marquand observed, left "hanging in mid air" as hints rather than policy. But MacDonald did attempt to reformulate the Socialist ideology and, at the same time, raise the level of theoretical understanding within the rank and file.[41]

Early in 1905 he launched a Socialist library designed to overcome the "deplorable lack of a Socialist literature more exhaustive and systematic than pamphlets and newspaper articles." The library would include translations of important continental works on socialism as well as contributions from British writers. Glasier, now editor of the *Labour Leader*, warmly welcomed the venture.

A common Socialist faith, simple as the gospels, has hitherto afforded motive and enthusiasm enough for the work of agitation. And of itself that faith, if sincere and powerful enough to surmount all obstacles of personal self interest and political opposition, is the one thing essential. But everywhere, Socialists, as they come to grapple at close quarters with the problems presented in the innumerable issues of our industrial, political, and domestic life, begin to realize their defects in knowledge, and their need of guidance from history and experience outside of themselves and their own country.[42]

MacDonald selected *Socialism and Positive Science*, a work by an Italian Marxist, Enrico Ferri, as the first volume in the series. The second, *Socialism and Society*, he wrote himself during stray hours taken from a busy round of political activity.

MacDonald gave his book a measure of coherence by adopting a form of Social Darwinism. Darwin, he declared, had provided socialism with a "definitely scientific foundation" superseding that of Marx. Like Peter Kropotkin, whose book *Mutual Aid* had been published three years earlier, MacDonald rejected the competitive struggle for existence as the chief characteristic of social evolution in favor of an increasing tendency toward cooperation. Viewed biologically, social development represented a series of adaptations, or the emergence of groups and institutions to perform functions required by the changing needs of society. The overall process, according to MacDonald, brought increasing social integration. Socialism was simply the late phase in a "steady subordination of all functional and sectional interests to the living needs of the whole community." Since this process of adaptation was necessarily gradual, both the revolutionary and the utopian leaps into the future were ruled out.[43]

MacDonald emphasized the role of economic factors when he described the past. New ideas and moral motives, he wrote, could operate only within the narrow limits set by changing economic functions. In his discussion of the contemporary situation, however, this determinism faded, and human initiatives found greater scope. Economic development was "the mainspring of history," but man's reason gave shape and direction to the demands for change. Socialism was inevitable, not

because "men were exploited, or because capitalism was col-
lapsing," but because "men are rational." Socialists must, therefore, place the "intellectual motive . . . above the economic."
A narrow appeal to class interests, as in Marxism or the old
trade unionism, was ultimately an appeal to the selfish interests
of the individual. The consciousness which Socialists sought
to quicken was that of "social unity and growth toward organic
wholeness."[44]

In discussing the future MacDonald reinstated the moral
idealism, and something of the utopianism, which informed
Ethical Socialism. He referred to an underlying development
through which "humanity evolved to higher and more humane
stages." History had already passed from a political into an
economic stage and would next enter a moral or Socialist stage;
society would become "more and more capable of expressing
the moral consciousness of man."[45]

Socialism and Society was not a serious contribution to
Socialist theory. It was an intellectual patchwork in which the
varied strands in the Socialist ideology were cleverly combined.
Both the economic determinism of the Marxists and the moral
idealism of the Ethical Socialists were given a place in his scheme
but he had reaffirmed the Fabian belief that the central Socialist
goal of public ownership could be achieved through the gradual
modification of existing institutions. MacDonald's book, like
so much of Fabian writing, did not, in fact, serve to clarify
socialism so much as to blur its outlines and stress its continuity
with tendencies already under way in British development.

MacDonald had become convinced that the British political
process resisted ideological systems. Parliamentary activity, he
observed, "cripples intellectual movements in politics." British
Socialists could not emulate their counterparts on the continent
by creating a "party founded on dogma" and professing its
creed "as the church fathers profess that of Athanasius." Although a new party in Britain had to prove that it possessed
a "foundation in principle separate from existing parties," it
had to demonstrate the practicality of its ideas in minor fields
before it could be entrusted with the responsibilities of national
power. And for this work a "special phraseology and method"
were necessary.[46]

MacDonald's book, with its eclectic blend of ideas, was a contribution to this special phraseology and method. It was the intellectual counterpart of the Socialist-trade union alliance. The book justified what MacDonald described as a new "political organism . . . capable of embodying all the tendencies, gropings, thoughts, ideas," which, he maintained, were "urging the society forward to greater perfection." The new political organism was designed, moreover, to digest a substantial portion of the Liberal party, since, MacDonald believed, that party was "about to divide."[47]

Hardie, Glasier, and MacDonald expressed, through their varied forms of adaptation, the retreat from socialism which followed the ILP's alliance with the trade unionists. The party was losing its sense of bringing a qualitative transformation of society. "Socialist human nature," Hardie observed, was "after all but a slice from the common stock, and is not cast in any ultra heroic mold."[48]

Most of the ILP's rank and file accepted the change in the party and the assurance by their leaders that the growth of a labor group in Parliament was the most effective way of converting the working classes to socialism. A few, however, did not. They concluded that the ILP was paying too high a price for its political gains and they demanded that it reassert its Socialist principles.

CRITICS WITHIN THE ILP: *Hartley and Hobson*

The ILP had never been fully united on questions of strategy. During the late nineties the policies of the leaders—their resistance to plans for unity with the Social Democrats, their alteration of the party's electoral tactics, and their formation of the political alliance with the trade unionists—had evoked sporadic criticism. Now, as the gap between the ILP's Socialist aspirations and its political practice widened, the opposition mounted. It was voiced most strongly by two of the party's prominent members, both of whom had been victims of the ILP's political maneuvering.

Edward Hartley, of working class background, had been active in a Methodist chapel and had performed before groups as an elocutionist before joining the Socialist movement. During the nineties he was one of the most active figures in the Bradford ILP; he was elected twice to the city council, presided over the local Labour Church, and stood for Parliament at nearby Dewsbury. At the turn of the century he was traveling extensively with the *Clarion* van, a gypsy-like mode of extending Socialist propaganda into remote areas. He had begun to question the party's electoral policy shortly before the general election of 1900, deploring the new "eagerness to get men in" rather than seek a "strong, reliable, thoughtful electorate" distinct from the Liberals and the Conservatives.[49] Late in 1901, when a vacancy became imminent at Dewsbury, Hartley prepared to contest the seat again.

The Dewsbury constituency had once contained four thriving ILP branches but only one remained in 1901. The ILP leaders were eager, however, to test their alliance with the trade unionists and began discussions with local labor leaders. It was soon clear that the Liberals might leave the LRC a straight fight with the Conservatives if a candidate congenial to their working class supporters was presented. The ILP leaders then attempted to persuade Hartley to withdraw. While negotiations were still under way the Social Democrats moved in with their own candidate, Harry Quelch, and charged that the ILP had abandoned Hartley. Hartley decided, in fact, to support Quelch and again attacked the ILP leadership for trying to "intrigue some half dozen persons into parliament" rather than "push Socialism."[50] Angered by the Federation's move, and embarrassed by Hartley's action, the ILP Council recommended that the local Socialists and labor men abstain from voting. Local working class feeling for independence was strong, however, and Quelch drew considerable support. Though he fell far short of victory, his poll was three times that anticipated by the ILP leaders. They were further embarrassed by declarations supporting Quelch by a number of ILP branches.

For Hartley, Dewsbury was "merely an incident in a trend." He charged that prominent members of the ILP were "coming to understandings with the Liberals . . . without consulting the party." The best way for the Liberal Party to end the ILP, he warned, was to "get twenty or thirty members of the ILP returned to Parliament with Liberal support." He continued to urge the prior necessity of making men Socialists. "Nothing can be done of value," he argued, until the working classes were united "into one solid body voting against all forms of rent, interest, and profit."[51]

The Dewsbury episode enabled the Social Democrats to exploit the rift opening within the ILP as a result of the trade union alliance. It also encouraged the *Clarion* men to renew their earlier efforts to bring about Socialist unity. Relations between the ILP leaders and the *Clarion* had not been good and in the heat of this controversy they deteriorated further. A *Clarion* proposal for a unity conference, from which the leaders would be excluded, was scornfully dismissed by the ILP men as an attempt to wreck the party.

Despite the furor over Dewsbury, the ILP annual conference in April 1902 demonstrated the firm hold of the party's leadership. For the first time in the party's history the entire administrative council was returned on the first ballot and Hartley drew only fifteen votes in challenging Glasier for the chairmanship. The delegates also rejected by a large majority a resolution to get all ILP candidates to stand as avowed Socialists, as well as several attempts to check the power of the leaders. The conference seemed to Glasier a "splendid reply to the SDF and the *Clarion*."[52]

Early in 1903, as the ILP's deference to trade union interests became more and more apparent, Sam Hobson launched a new attack. Hobson was also a veteran party worker, and well equipped intellectually to analyze ILP policies in terms of its Socialist objectives.[53] He had entered the movement from Cardiff in the early nineties after the *Fabian Essays* had generated great excitement in a small discussion group there. A commercial traveler by occupation, Hobson served as Hardie's secretary for a time and worked on the *Labor Leader*. He also took an active part in the Labour Church movement and in the Fabian Society, where he challenged from time to time the policies of Webb. Initially Hobson was a strong supporter of the Socialist-trade union alliance and, at the time of its formation, proposed an ambitious scheme for financing parliamentary candidates. At the ILP conference in 1900 he moved a resolution commending the administrative council for its work. Late in 1902, however, Hobson became a bitter critic of the alliance.

Hobson's opposition arose in circumstances which illustrate

the dilemmas of those within the ILP who gave priority to its Socialist ideology. He had been adopted as a parliamentary candidate by the Rochdale ILP but party leaders did not want to contest the seat. Rochdale, where the Liberal Party had lost by a narrow margin in the previous general election, had become a pawn in the political maneuvers between the ILP and the Liberals. Hobson, however, refused to withdraw. He had the support of both the ILP and the Social Democrats locally. But unity between the Socialist groups had made it more difficult to find a common political ground with the trade unions in the area. Socialism, a veteran ILP member in Rochdale wrote MacDonald, had become "completely divorced from . . . the principle of independent labour . . . The pity of it is that we have so many avowed Socialists here and an even greater number of others so dissatisfied with Liberal and Tory who would vote for an avowed Labour candidate but will not work with some of Hobson's leading supporters."[54]

The episode convinced Hobson that the ILP had reached a critical point in its development. In two letters to the *Labour Leader* in February 1903 he noted the growing "doubts and misgivings" among the friends of the ILP. Did anyone possess a "tolerably accurate working theory of what the ILP was driving at?" The Clitheroe by-election, he argued, had demonstrated the need of recognizing frankly the differences between Socialism and trade unionism; it was not a "cause for rejoicing" but a "serious warning." Hobson placed most of the blame on the "curiously narrow and restricted views of its functions" taken by the party's administrative council. At the same time he accused party leaders of making a fetish out of working class political independence and failing to see that this was a means of achieving socialism and not an end in itself. Hobson also criticized the party for its lack of intellectual effort and noted a growing "habit of impatience towards those who criticize the party from a frankly Socialist point of view." The ILP, he concluded, faced a "parting of the ways." He proposed that it now add the term Socialist to its title.[55]

Other critics joined Hobson, including Hartley, Leonard Hall, a Manchester leader, and H. C. Rowe. When, in March of 1903, Hardie proposed to a group of trade unionists and

Socialists in York that the labor men in Parliament cooperate with the Liberals to "throw out the party in power," Hartley attacked Hardie for compromising the ILP without giving it a chance to discuss and decide the question. The York branch of the ILP also repudiated the proposal, and even Glasier criticized Hardie. But the party conference, held soon afterwards, did not discuss the episode and the opposition to official policies mustered less support than the year before. There was little evidence, as Glasier wrote Hardie, that Hobson had "much weight behind him."[56]

Sporadic criticism continued. It flared up in the summer of 1904, after Henderson, Shackleton, and Crooks appeared in support of a Liberal candidate in Devonport. The *Labour Leader*, now the party's official organ, quickly condemned the action of the three MP's as "plainly contrary to the LRC constitution." For one member of the party the event signaled the "passing of the ILP."

The position of the ILP would not be so hard had we of the rank and file had an opportunity of expressing ourselves pro and con during the initiatory stages of the LRC movement. But the democracy and independence of the old days has apparently broken down under a continuous obedience to political exigency, and the rank and file are as much under the stigma of having their thinking done for them as the adherents of orthodox political parties . . . The ILP has lost its political and Socialist identity in a frantic effort to gloat over superficial successes.[57]

The ILP leaders were also becoming vulnerable to attacks from the opportunistic wing of the party. When the *Labour Leader* criticized James Sexton, the dockers' leader, for his support of the Liberals at Devonport, he charged that ILP officials had already reached an understanding with the Liberals at Halifax and Leicester. In the face of their denials he branded them a "despicable cabal."[58]

MacDonald's report to the party on the international Socialist congress at Amsterdam in August of 1904, in which he attacked the militant position of the German Socialists, and his intimation of an understanding with the Liberals at the next general election also drew a stinging rebuke from Hobson. He

called MacDonald's report a caricature, insisted that most Socialists retained the idea of the class struggle, and repudiated
the idea of cooperating with the Liberals. "The Socialist section"
of the alliance, he declared, "would not touch such a proposition with a pitchfork."[59]

In the closing months of 1905, as the ILP approached a
new general election, there were further signs that its political
strategy had made the ILP more and more wary of offending
the mores of the working classes. The caution was reflected in
the campaign at Bordesley, a constituency in Birmingham,
where Glasier had accepted the prospect of "imprisonment in
the House of Commons." His wife Katharine, who for years
had graced the Socialist platform in colorful but unconventional
dress, now "yielded to the necessity of the campaign" and ordered a "tailor made rig." As Glasier explained to his sister,
"any special unconventionalness in a political campaign is a
source of comment . . . and she will be able to speak with
greater freedom."[60]

The main critics, Hartley and Hobson, had not left the ILP
but they stood for Parliament under other auspices. Hartley
was put up by the Social Democrats in East Bradford, and Hobson, having been denied official ILP support, ran as an independent Socialist at Rochdale. He adopted the position that it
was "just as bad tactics for Socialists to combine with labor
as with Liberals."[61]

The critics had failed to gain much support for their challenge to the policies of the ILP leaders. Nor had they grappled
seriously with the theoretical and strategical problems of the
party. But they expressed the deepening concern of many Socialists over the fate of their ideals amid the maneuvers and
compromises of practical politics.

Meanwhile, outside the ILP other Socialists were reflecting
anew on the position of the movement. One was Blatchford,
who a decade earlier had provided much of the inspiration for
Ethical Socialism. At the end of 1901 he was discouraged and
disgusted with the "wrangle, vulgarity, and blind jealousy of
politics."[62] A year later he led his associates on the *Clarion* into
a bold new campaign to transform the intellectual foundations
of popular socialism.

BLATCHFORD'S WAR ON CHRISTIANITY

Blatchford's weekly paper, the *Clarion*, continued to provide guidance for a substantial section of the Socialist movement. Its circulation in 1900, between 35,000 and 45,000, was three times that of Hardie's *Labour Leader*. Most *Clarion* readers probably supported the ILP, but Blatchford and his close associate, A. M. Thompson, viewed the paper and the local groups inspired by it as expressions of the Socialist movement as a whole. Indeed, Thompson, who directed the *Clarion's* editorial policies during the late nineties, devoted much of his energy to the promotion of Socialist unity.

The unity campaign failed but it revealed that a large percentage of the *Clarion* readers were not attached to any Socialist organization. And the ensuing discussion of this problem led to the formation of the *Clarion* Fellowship. It supplemented the other *Clarion* organizations which had sprung up in the nineties, the Scouts, the Cinderella children's groups, and the choirs, with a new kind of club, more "social and intellectual" than the ordinary labor or Socialist club. An Anglican clergyman, Cartmel Robinson, was one of the chief promoters of the idea; he described it in religious terms.

> The Clarion Fellowship does not . . . limit itself . . . or exist for any special purpose . . . Of all that Socialism is or ever can be, this fellowship must ever be nearest the heart of it, this pleasant intercourse one with another, bound together in a common faith of the goodness of man and the final victory of right and the consummation of every pure wish for every man in the presence of the All Father . . . Fellowship of communion—that sums up everything, it will remove mountains.

Few of the *Clarion* men would have accepted his Christian interpretation. But during 1900, despite the low ebb of the movement generally, the fellowship grew rapidly, stimulated by a series of dinners in the major towns of the north. Perhaps, as Glasier felt, it developed at the expense of other Socialist organizations.[63]

The fellowship also drew Blatchford out of his semi-retirement from the movement; it seemed "a new duty and a new hope." But he had come to feel that the *Clarion* group had been right in its original idea that the "chief duty of a Socialist press-man must be of an educational kind." The energies the *Clarion* groups had expended on national politics were, Blatchford concluded, largely wasted, for "parliament was a worn-out force." He continued to view *News from Nowhere* as the chief source of his socialism, though he was now less sanguine about its early realization. Most of the working men were simply not ready.[64]

For a year or more following the election of 1900, the *Clarion*'s policy vacillated. Thompson supported the trade union alliance against the "sea green incorruptibles" who with their "utterly meaningless formulae" had "greatly delayed the Socialist advance." Montague Blatchford, who had begun to take an active part on his brother's paper, declared that the movement had now grown up. It was time to put aside "erratic enthusiasms" and "impress people with [its] sense of responsi-bility." Robert Blatchford was more cautious. He sought closer relations with the ILP and favored informal conferences with the radical Liberals, but he remained hostile to alliances and worried, in letters to Glasier, lest Hardie "break the Socialist line."[65]

Late in 1901 Blatchford decided to write a new popular exposition of socialism. The book, *Britain for the British*, pub-lished in the spring of 1902, indicated that Blatchford shared something of the ILP disposition to accommodate Socialist ideals to present realities. The book was more utilitarian in tone than *Merrie England*, for Blatchford now conceded that self-interest was the "strongest motive of human nature." He sought a "more direct appeal to the class consciousness of the masses."[66]

Even before the publication of *Britain for the British* the *Clarion* leaders had begun to veer away from the ILP's course. The Dewsbury episode, where *Clarion* men at the local and the national level supported Quelch, provoked a series of sharp exchanges between the *Clarion* and the *Labour Leader*. Thompson's effort to organize a new unity conference, which would be held without the leaders, further embittered relations. The *Clarion* equivocated a while longer, but in the course of 1902 even Thompson's views hardened. The greatest danger, he wrote, was that socialism might become "modified out of all meaning and purpose by the characteristic British spirit of 'practical' political compromise." Socialism was a "religion or a moral system rather than a party program."[67] Early in 1903 Blatchford led the *Clarion* off in a radically new direction. He opened a campaign to destroy traditional religious beliefs and provide a new philosophical foundation for the Socialist movement.

Ethical Socialism had contained almost from the beginning two rather different orientations toward life. The dominant set of attitudes in popular socialism was strongly puritanical; this outlook pervaded the ILP, whose speakers often employed the rhetoric of the Nonconformist chapels or the temperance platforms. But the *Clarion* propaganda of the early nineties had also helped popularize the humanistic and naturalistic values found in the socialism of Morris. While the ILP, from Hardie down, retained the moral tone of the Nonconformist chapels, the *Clarion* groups often exuded a bohemian spirit of liberation from conventional values and restraints. The ILP speakers might attack the churches for betraying the moral values they identified with true Christianity; a number of the *Clarion* writers, however, questioned the ascetic ethic associated with the traditional faith.

Thompson recalled that a strong antagonism toward Christianity had been implicit in much of the work of the *Clarion* writers but they "had feared to retard the advance of Socialism by mixing the acrimonies of religious controversy with our propaganda." By the late nineties this caution was being dropped. Against "sickly asceticism" Thompson wrote in 1898, "I am supporting the cheerful modern revolt back toward Paganism, back toward the old Greek faith that nothing in the world is more beautiful than the human body, nothing more moral than nature's laws." One spokesman for the *Clarion* Fellowship saw it as the vehicle for a "new hedonism" which would stress self-development over self-sacrifice and "throw contempt upon the base results of the unhealthy idea of asceticism." These *Clarion* writers shared the militant atheism of the Social Democratic philosopher, Belfort Bax, who was convinced that Socialists would have to destroy the "poisonous infection of super-stition amongst the masses."[68]

Blatchford's campaign against organized religion was not premeditated. It developed out of a "small sermon," shortly before Christmas, 1902, in which he disparaged Christianity. "The religious standard of charity," he wrote, was "easier to attain . . . than the Socialist standard of complete justice." "Christianity," he added, "has always feared truth."[69] The comment brought a deluge of correspondence, most of it critical of Blatchford.

The resulting controversy led Blatchford to state his opposition to Christianity more fully and to offer an alternative faith based on science. "Science has destroyed the foundations of all the religions of the world. I oppose supernaturalism and dogmatic religion for many cogent reasons. Socialism is part of a religion. It is part of a religion more reasonable and more merciful than Christianity is at its best. I want to speak for that religion and I cannot speak without saying what I think about the religion now accepted, but not believed by the great mass of the British people." Thompson and others on the staff warned him that he might ruin all they had built up, but Blatchford was adamant. "I have been much alone these last two years," he confided to Thompson, "and have brooded and read a good deal. I feel as if I am now upon the threshold of the work which I was evolved to do." Over the next four years, despite an occasional pause to attack the "clique running the ILP," or express his suspicions about secret deals with the Liberals, Blatchford concentrated on the campaign.[70]

Early in the campaign he decided it would require two phases. First, preliminary skirmishing would draw out the spokesmen for Christianity and clear the air so that Blatchford could destroy "block by block" the old beliefs of the religious rank and file. But since the "parsons don't seem to have much of the old religion left," a second phase would be necessary in order to demolish the new, more liberal forms of religion. A year and a half later, in October 1904, Blatchford announced that he had "split the enemy into the new and the old." Discussion up to this point had been dominated by attacks on the Bible, inspired by higher criticism and evolutionary theory. He could now focus on the doctrine which underlay all forms of contemporary morality—the doctrine of free will.[71]

The problem of free will had been central to the discussion from the beginning. Along with his attacks on Christianity, Blatchford had attempted to demonstrate that there was a new religion, whose central doctrine was determinism. He had held this belief as far back as the late eighties, and preached it periodically through the nineties. But his determinism did not find a place in a coherent system of thought until he read Ernest Haeckel's *Riddle of the Universe*, published in an English translation by the Rationalist Press Association in 1901. Haeckel himself was hostile to socialism, but his mechanistic and evolutionary cosmology attracted Blatchford, who used it to fortify his Socialist faith. The *Clarion* articles in which he worked out his new creed were gathered together in *Not Guilty: A Defense of the Bottom Dog*, published in 1904.

The term "bottom dog" referred mainly to the great mass of individuals living in the slums of the large cities, with seemingly little control over their lives. Their condition had been fixed, according to Blatchford, by their physical or social environment, or by heredity. It was a "self-evident and undeniable fact that man has no part in the creation of his own nature." Since every "member of the body, every faculty, every impulse is fixed for him by heredity," and "every kind of encouragement or discouragement comes of environment," it followed that "everything a man does, is, at the instant when he does it, the only thing he can do" at that moment.[72]

Traditional religious, moral, and legal categories, such as good, sinful, innocent, guilty, and criminal, were false and pernicious in their effect on society. Men should be "classified as . . . fortunate and unfortunate." Criminals should be "pitied, and not blamed, helped instead of punished." The murderer usually sprang from "a selfish and cowardly society." He should not be punished but simply confined like a "smallpox patient or a lunatic." True morality, Blatchford argued, sprang from "the social feelings . . . inherited by man from his animal ancestors" or "imitated from observation of the animals he knew so well in his old life." Human existence was completely explained, determined, and bounded by the stream of evolution.

Those whom "civilized persons" chose to regard as criminals were simply cases of arrested development, victims of heredity or of the "ancestral struggle within." "Unhappy unblest atavistic man, that in lieu of love has only lust, in lieu of wisdom only cunning, in lieu of power, violence; and with the whole world to walk in, as in a garden fair, lies wallowing hideously in the foul dungeons of his own unlighted soul." Although he denied personal responsibility Blatchford did not believe that his creed was fatalistic. On the contrary he attacked the "delusion" of the "religious folks" that "God will see us right." This was the main barrier to efforts by people to "right themselves."[73]

Blatchford had defined his two crucial determinants, heredity and environment, so broadly as to include nearly all of man's self-improving activities. Not only was there a biological basis for altruism, but men could overcome their atavisms through education and the reform of laws and institutions. Determinism sanctioned the moral feelings on which most Ethical Socialists relied. Moreover, despite Blatchford's mechanistic view of reality he made room for beneficent natural or supernatural forces. "But because I believe 'men must love the highest when they see it,' because I believe that the universal heart is sweet and sound, because I believe that there are many who honour truth and seek happiness and peace for all I do not fear to plead for the Bottom Dog, nor to ask a patient hearing."[74]

In the midst of his campaign, Blatchford invited his religious opponents to reply in the columns of the *Clarion*. The Christian counterattack was led by G. K. Chesterton. A few years earlier Chesterton had become both a Socialist and a follower of Whitman, but amid the political and spiritual ferment generated by the Boer War he had rejected "modernism," and returned to "theological ethics." His reconversion, he wrote later, was induced in part by the "unbelievers," who "began by disbelieving even in normal things" and proceeded to destroy "any sane and rational possibility of secular ethics."[75]

Chesterton's reply to Blatchford did not involve a serious defense of Christian doctrine; he simply focused on the denial of human freedom and accountability. The failure of men to 'live up to ideals," Chesterton wrote, had never "been met by a more astounding cure" than the idea that no one "should be responsible for anything." To associate violence and vice so closely with poverty and slums was an insult to the poor. It suggested that "wickedness and folly raged only among the unfortunate." Blatchford's denial of freedom was, Chesterton argued, closely tied to his failure to understand the Christian doctrine of sin. He associated the idea of a sinner with a "drunkard or a thieving tramp," who were often, Chesterton conceded, victims of a "gravely unjust social system." But Blatchford "was so anxious to forgive that he denied the need of forgiveness."[76]

Chesterton was supported by a number of clergymen and by several Socialists who had returned to orthodox religion. One was George Lansbury. His reply to Blatchford was simply autobiographical. He had become a Social Democrat and agnostic in the nineties and sat "at the feet of Stanton Coit," the leader of the Ethical Culture movement. But "disappointment with the cause" and "twelve months of reading and prayer" had led him to put his "trust not in men but in God." Percy Redfern, who also answered Blatchford, had moved from secularism to Tolstoyism and then to the Anglican church after the "trust in nature and ego and the secular world," on which he had rested his socialism, collapsed.[77]

Blatchford's campaign reached beyond his readers and entered into the work of some of the popular Socialist propagandists. A summary of Fred Bramley's lecture, the "Religion of Socialism," before an ILP branch in Birmingham showed both the characteristic appeal to orthodox religious sentiments and the influence of the new determinist creed. "He stated that the purpose of all religions was to do good, and that in condemning the orthodox churches, which were commercial in character, he was not condemning Christianity itself . . . He pointed out that the orthodox moralist failed to realize that the individual must be looked upon but as a manifestation of the conditions over which he has as a unit, little or no control."[78]

It is difficult to assess the impact of Blatchford's campaign. Prominent Socialists disagreed about his influence. Joe Burgess, one of the founders of the ILP, declared that it had not "made a single convert" to socialism and had created a "stumbling block for many." Religious belief, Burgess added, was "general in the rank and file of the movement" and among the propagandists.

George Haw claimed that Blatchford had "scattered the old army" and "irretrievably injured the cause." But Hartley challenged these views. He maintained that the great majority of Socialist speakers were not believers and insisted that the "great body" of the movement agreed with Blatchford. Henry Snell, a Socialist and leader in the Ethical Culture movement, welcomed the *Clarion's* discovery that "one of the chief hindrances" to socialism was Christianity, and praised Blatchford for opposing the "capitalist-Priesthood alliance which every sensible man knows to exist."[79]

The Social Democrats cautiously approved of Blatchford's new work, while the Fabians ignored it. The ILP leaders were alarmed about the damage it might do to their political prospects. Glasier repeatedly disassociated the ILP from Blatchford's views on religion and even began a small campaign of his own to get clergymen into the ILP. As he explained to his sister, "I am trying to draw the English Clergy because I wish to undo the impression of the *Clarion* that our movement is entirely anti-Church."[80]

Blatchford claimed that his anti-Christian books, *God and My Neighbor* and *Not Guilty*, had done much more good than *Merrie England* by making "thousands of humanists." There was some support for his claim. In 1908, Graham Wallas, after lecturing in the West Riding, asked his hosts what the "best of the young men read," and was told that "the one man who has really got hold of them is Blatchford."[81] There were scattered reports of conversions and the *Clarion's* circulation jumped markedly during the campaign. Yet, the sale of the books did not approach that attained by the earlier books on socialism. Moreover, Blatchford and his colleagues made no effort to institutionalize their creed or use the fellowship to advance it. The campaign was simply educational.

Blatchford's attempt to reestablish Ethical Socialism on the foundation of Haeckel's determinist creed was naive philosophically. He claimed the sanction of science not only for metaphysical propositions but for his personal values. His crude materialistic and mechanistic conception of the teachings of science had already been superseded by the advanced thinkers in the positivist tradition.

From the standpoint of the Socialist movement Blatchford's campaign was quixotic. He ignored the urgent theoretical and strategical issues which were now emerging within the wider world of European socialism and displayed no appreciation for the political dilemmas facing the ILP leaders. But the remoteness of his campaign from the realities of the movement was most apparent at the level of those moral and religious sentiments where Blatchford had, in earlier years, exerted his greatest influence; his deterministic creed tended, in fact, to cut him off from the attitudes and feelings of the Socialist rank and file. Three years after he began his campaign Blatchford conceded that the Socialist movement was still "out of touch with Determinism" and "therefore out of touch and out of tune with me."[82]

In their diverse ways, Blatchford, Hobson, Hartley, MacDonald, Glasier, and Hardie were responding to the altered relationship between the Socialist movement and the political process. Meanwhile, the issues which were dividing the Ethical Socialists in the early years of the century were also troubling the Marxists and the Fabians.

3

SOCIAL DEMOCRATS
AND FABIANS:
QUESTIONS OF SCOPE
AND STRATEGY

THE PIONEERING SOCIALIST organizations—the Social Democratic Federation and the Fabian Society—had joined the ILP in forming the Labour Representation Committee. But both of the older Socialist bodies soon drew back from any active role in its development. They drew back for different reasons. Social Democrats worried lest the political alliance with the trade unions endanger the integrity of their Marxism while the Fabians opposed the goal of an independent working class party.

Social Democrats were not, however, of one mind. Almost from the beginning the Federation's Marxism had inspired different interpretations by its followers. Some Social Democrats gave priority to doctrine and sought to nurture a pure Socialist consciousness; others stressed the necessity of adapting their Marxist ideas to the immediate interests and aspirations of the workers. After the turn of the century the development of the Socialist-trade union alliance forced these ambivalent tendencies within British Social Democracy to the surface. The renewal of the dispute was evident in 1901 when the Federation decided to break with the LRC.

The Fabians did not leave the LRC. Edward Pease continued to represent the Society on its executive. But his presence simply indicated the Fabian attempt to infiltrate all promising political agencies and to appeal to the enlightened members of all classes. He resisted the efforts of MacDonald and the ILP leaders to guide the LRC toward full political independence. Webb, meanwhile, continued to urge Fabians to limit the scope of socialism to those questions of public policy which held a promise of broad nonpartisan support. Conceived in this way, however, the Society's role was too narrow to accommodate the social aspirations of some of its members. Indeed the Fabian strategy might, as Graham Wallas concluded, threaten one's basic commitments. For the Fabians generally, as for the other sections of the movement, deepening involvement in the political process raised new questions regarding the scope of socialism and the means of implementing it.

DIVISIONS AMONG THE SOCIAL DEMOCRATS, 1900-1905

At the end of the century Hyndman's interpretation of Marxism still dominated the SDF. Over the years he had struggled, more or less successfully, against the polar tendencies among Social Democrats. He had resisted those members, like William Morris, who sought to create a party of pure principle and escape from the contagion of bourgeois institutions; he had opposed as well those who were willing to sacrifice doctrinal rectitude in order to employ the established methods by which the workers had advanced their material well-being.

Hyndman was attempting to reconcile his Marxist theory and political practice. He was critical of the German Social Democrats for being too doctrinaire and "putting Marx on a pedestal of infallibility." While he believed in the validity of Marx's economic analysis, the importance of the class struggle, and the inevitable breakdown of capitalism, his socialism was set firmly within a nationalistic framework. The "extension of the sphere of collective action" was desirable in order to provide the "higher standard of citizenship which alone can develop the individual and strengthen the nation." Hyndman exalted the state in a manner which clashed directly with Marxist theory. "Above the combatants [stands] the State, which . . . has been compelled, as the organized form of the community, to intervene in order to protect, for the national benefit, the lives and health of the workers . . . [and] to mitigate the class war." At times Hyndman viewed British development in the evolutionary and reformist terms characteristic of the Fabians. The "gropings" toward socialism by public authorities, both at the national and the municipal levels, were "reducing the distance we have to traverse before we attain the full stage of a co-operative commonwealth." The Federation had developed a program of practical reform, including the eight hour day, sub-sidized housing for the lower classes, increased educational op-portunities, and public maintenance of children.[1]

In the late nineties Hyndman was still, despite the small following of the SDF, hopeful about the prospects for socialism. "There never was a period," he wrote in 1898, "when Socialists regarded the immediate future with more confidence than they do today." "The great capitalist period . . . is coming to an end; not by reason of the disgust of mankind at large with its ethical wrong-doing, or class injustices, but because like all the old systems of production which have preceded it, and have passed away, it blocks the path of further progress, and is, there-fore, now engaged in digging its own grave." The chief task of Social Democrats was the education of the workers. Only those who had "grasped the Marxist evolutionary-revolutionary theory" could be "relied upon when affairs became difficult." Hyndman was even concerned lest the capitalistic system be destroyed by irresistible economic forces "before the people at large have been educated sufficiently to appreciate what is taking place around them or to organize their methods of pro-duction and distribution on a new basis."[2]

In 1900 Hyndman and his colleagues on the executive had set aside their Marxist scruples and joined the ILP in the con-ference which drew Socialists and trade unionists together in order to promote greater working class representation in Parliament.[3] Although delegates of the Federation failed in their efforts to commit the Labour Representation Committee to the principle of the class war, they had, for the moment, accepted the ILP lead and entered into a new relationship with the British labor movement. In the general election of 1900 three SDF can-didates ran for Parliament with the endorsement of the LRC.

The willingness of the Social Democrats to attach them-selves to the new working class political force was soon reduced by Hyndman's decision to give up his position of leadership. He was troubled during 1900 by personal financial difficulties. Moreover, the disunity of the Socialists in the face of the Boer War led him to doubt the future of the movement. The British people, he told Edward Carpenter, were "played out—decayed and done for morally, mentally, and physically." The workers especially were sunk in "ignorance and cowardice" or addicted to drink and gambling.[4] He was dismayed too at the lack of political aptitude within the Social Democratic branches and their failure to attract educated members from the middle classes. In August 1901 he resigned as chairman of the Federation and gave up his place on the executive.

Hyndman had no intention of leaving the movement. He had simply retired to the sidelines in order to "criticize our proceedings from a more independent standpoint." Two months after his resignation he reaffirmed his faith in the soundness of the Federation's principles and their relevance to the "conditions of the times." Indeed, something of his earlier optimism soon returned. He foresaw a coming "consolidation of Socialist forces" in Britain which would witness the disappearance of Fabianism, for Hyndman the only serious rival to Marxist theory within the working class movement.[5]

Hyndman's withdrawal, though temporary, was quickly followed by a change in the SDF's policy. Led by Harry Quelch, editor of *Justice* and one of the most militant spirits on the executive, the delegates at the Federation's annual conference in September 1901 voted to pull out of the LRC. Its unwillingness to acknowledge the class struggle and develop a political program "clearly antagonistic" to the programs of the Liberals and the Conservatives meant, according to Quelch, that the Socialist-trade union alliance was bound to "deceive the expectations of the workers." In a different context, he conceded that the spread of Socialist ideas among the unions would modify "their exclusive character," but for the time being they remained, in a way Marx had not anticipated, "a reactionary mass, opposing the progress of the mere proletarian outside their ranks." Quelch urged Social Democrats to concentrate on building a united Socialist party. The ILP had now "proved itself to be Socialist" and would be forced in time to choose between its Socialist commitment and its political alliance with the unions.

"Either the ILP will break away and help to form a Socialist party, or it will allow itself to be led further and further away from Socialism and then the Socialists in the organization will leave it and combine with other Socialists."[6] It was a fairly accurate forecast. But the decision of the Social Democrats to reject the alliance with the trade unionists in favor of the goal of Socialist unity inaugurated a period of friction within the Federation, as contending individuals and groups attempted to work out anew the implications of Marxism. The SDF's Marxism was challenged both on philosophical and strategical grounds.

From its beginnings in the eighties the SDF had enrolled persons who wished to augment Hyndman's narrow economic conception of socialism with distinctive ethical and metaphysical meanings. Such an aspiration, encouraged by the later writings of Engels, was expressed in the British movement most clearly by Belfort Bax. Having refused to accept Marx's claim that his theory superseded formal philosophy, Bax had attempted to develop in a series of books and articles the ethical and metaphysical implications of socialism. And over the years he continued to insist, against Social Democrats who wished to avoid the political liabilities of religious disputes, that socialism entailed specific ethical and metaphysical views.

When the Social Democratic Party in Germany, the main center of European Marxism, was disturbed by the "revisionist" controversy in the late nineties, Bax rushed into the fray. He had no sympathy for Eduard Bernstein's challenge to the orthodox Marxist position of Karl Kautsky and urged the German party to expel its heretic. But Bax also rejected the positivistic and deterministic interpretation of Marxism which Kautsky was carrying forward from Engels. In an essay published in Kautsky's journal, *Neue Zeit*, Bax insisted on the "relatively substantial and independent role of consciousness" in history; social development involved the "reciprocal determination of outward material circumstances and inward ideological spontaneity." To Kautsky such a position seemed mere "utopianism concealed behind Marxist phraseology."[7]

It was not simply an academic dispute. Unlike Hyndman, who was occupied mainly with what can be called utilitarian levels of consciousness, Bax was convinced that Socialists must destroy and replace deep-seated attitudes and sentiments. He recognized the resistance which inherited habits of mind offered to the growth of Marxism among the lower classes; he had seen the emergence, at the expense of Marxism, of a popular social-ism which drew much of its vitality from traditional religious and moral feelings. The surge of popular patriotism during the Boer War had reinforced his sense of the encounter of differing belief systems. But the war had also demonstrated the "hopeless impotence of the old Christian ethic of personal character . . . to guide man's political thoughts and actions" and sub-stituted "the moral shoddy . . . of Patriotism." The coming "ethic of Socialism" would make public duty rather than private life the "central spring of morality."[8]

Bax believed that the subtlest enemy of the Socialist move-ment consisted of the "antipathies and aspirations" and the "moral catchwords" of the "small bourgeoisie." Unless the "embryonic proletariat" could free itself from their infection and the "poisonous superstition" of religion, it could not develop the new "moral consciousness," centered on the ideal of social solidarity, which Bax saw as an essential feature of a Socialist society. Marxism alone, he argued, overcame the two major fallacies of modern thought. It corrected the tendency for Christians and idealists to build a "spurious abstract spiritual world" in which the moral sentiments were divorced from man's social life and his material needs. Marxism also corrected the main tendency in the utilitarian outlook—to hypostasize the "individual animal consciousness" and rest in a shallow materialism.[9]

Bax's renewed attempt to nurture a deeper and wider Marxist faith among the British Social Democrats was chal-lenged within the Federation by Theodore Rothstein. An im-migrant from Russia, Rothstein had joined the Federation in 1895, espousing a form of Marxism much like that of his friend Kautsky. He rapidly became influential in the affairs of the SDF. His election to its executive in 1900 dismayed Hyndman, for he saw in Rothstein's internationalist outlook an indif-ference to the peculiarities of national traditions. Rothstein in turn was, as he told Kautsky, "thoroughly ashamed" of the

Federation's policies and the absence of any clear "theoretical exposition of our principles." He assured the German leader that he was attempting to transform his British colleagues into "decent Social Democrats."[10]

Rothstein vigorously attacked Bax's version of Marxism. Bax, he declared, had failed to grasp the "real, unadulterated monism" for which Marx laid the foundations; he had reintroduced a dualism which expressed the "worst features of modern bourgeois belief." Rothstein argued too that the Federation was mistaken in concentrating on the task of educating the workers in theoretical truths. Through its preoccupation with abstract principles the Federation had "become a stranger . . . to life," passively watching the "passing show of events." In order to move from sect to party the Social Democrats needed to enter more actively into "the course of events." Action was the "greatest educator." Strikes, for example, were not primarily occasions to preach socialism but "incidents in the great class war which claims all our sympathy and support." Above all, Rothstein argued, the Social Democrats should develop the "anticipative faculty," a form of intelligence capable of accelerating "the natural course of the evolution of things." He was seeking, in fact, a dialectical relationship between theory and practice like that envisioned by Marx and Engels.[11]

In their efforts to overcome the limitations of Hyndman's Marxism, Bax and Rothstein were pushing the Social Democrats in different directions—the former toward a more comprehensive Socialist faith, the latter toward a fuller engagement with objective social forces. Neither figure, however, questioned the Federation's break with the LRC. Despite Rothstein's demand for a "deep and precise insight into the correlation of things and the psychology of men," he rejected proposals for closer relations with the trade unionists because their political programs contained "nothing indistinguishable from any average Liberal." The SDF's isolation, he conceded to Kautsky, was a paradox, but it was the paradox of a "thorough-going Socialist group" amidst the "wilderness of stupidity and trimming dishonesty" presented by British political life.[12]

Bax too was firmly opposed to the political alliance with

the trade unionists. The unions represented the "greatest obstacle to the formation of a solid Socialist party." Even Quelch's plan for Socialist unity was unacceptable if it threatened the Federation's ideals. Apart from their ideals the Social Democrats had no "object of significance." "By the sacrifice of the integrity of principle . . . the SDF might possibly succeed . . . in realizing, say payment of members, or such an undoubted social reform as the eight hours day in various industries. But the SDF would see greater things than these . . . It is for something else that a whole generation of Socialists in Great Britain have learned to labor and to wait."[13]

But if Bax and Rothstein, from their differing philosophical perspectives, gave support to the Federation's renewed determination to guard its ideological integrity, some members wished to free it completely from compromising political tactics. They had become dissatisfied with Hyndman's leadership, which seemed, as one of them recalled, to oscillate between opportunistic and revolutionary positions, "each dogmatically to the exclusion of the other as the fit took him."[14] His withdrawal from the executive and the decision of the Federation to leave the LRC encouraged them to demand a genuinely revolutionary strategy.

The new spirit centered in Scotland, where educational and religious traditions nurtured an especially rigorous cast of mind. A number of the Scottish Social Democrats had been inspired to seek a more consistent Marxist policy by the publications of the Socialist Labour Party in America, and the writings of its leader, Daniel De Leon. At the International Socialist Congress in Paris in 1900 several of the Scottish Marxists joined De Leon in opposing a resolution proposed by Kautsky and supported by Hyndman, which permitted Socialists to enter bourgeois governments under "exceptional circumstances." During 1902 lecture tours by De Leon's chief British disciple, James Connolly, generated growing support in the north for a militant policy.[15]

De Leon was convinced, on the basis of American experience, that the typical trade union was simply a "limb of capitalism." He held that the Socialist movement required industrial unions, which would include the entire working class within their ranks, utilize the general strike to help the workers gain power, and function as constituent organs in the future Socialist republic. In his struggle to reorient American Marxists De Leon developed a party marked by intense commitment, strict discipline, and a rigid adherence to principle. The ideas and methods of De Leon seemed to offer the Scottish Marxists a way of escaping from the "bourgeois corruptions" of Hyndman. Indeed, they were motivated in part by a desire to rid the movement of "middle class men who had never divested themselves from Bourgeois habits of thought" and by a sense of the "snobbishness and pretentiousness" of the London leaders.[16]

During 1902 and 1903, at the annual conferences of the SDF, and by means of a new monthly paper, the *Socialist*, these Marxists challenged the compromising political activities which characterized a number of the local branches. They were attacked sharply by Quelch and other Social Democratic leaders as "impossibilists" and, at the 1903 conference, the leader of the Scottish group, George Yates, was expelled. Within a short time the bulk of the Federation's Scottish branches broke away to form a new Socialist Labour Party. It was necessary, a spokesman for the rebels declared, to "vindicate the theory of scientific and revolutionary socialism from the degraded position which the SDF had dragged it into." Subsequently a group of London Social Democrats, also influenced by De Leon, organized the Socialist Party of Great Britain. Both bodies had decided that the SDF, along with the ILP and the Fabian Society, were "consciously or unconsciously the tools of capitalism."[17]

The "impossibilists" were developing, with the aid of De Leon, an ideological posture which radically separated them from conventional society. They were realizing something of Bax's hope for a total reordering of consciousness. Marxism, as one of the rebels recalled, "gave me in a flash of blazing revelation, a completely interrelated Universe, in which mankind and human society and their history were details in an endlessly developing whole." *The Communist Manifesto* and Engels' *Socialism, Scientific and Utopian*, in particular, provided a "vital core around which" he could integrate his scattered readings. To pursue a "completely logical line of action," as the SLP leaders demanded, however, was not sufficient. The new spirit also required a special vigilance against the "frauds" who continually appeared in "revolutionary movements, . . . ready to adopt its external symbols and phrases and some of its teachings to cover their reactionary designs."[18]

Although the Socialist Labour Party, the chief agency for this new and militant form of socialism, rapidly assumed the character of a narrow dogmatic sect, its leaders were gaining a fresh understanding of Marxism. They discovered in De Leon's emphasis on the role of the worker in the productive process, and the reduction of labor to "animated pieces of merchandise," aspects of Marx's analysis of capitalism which had been largely ignored in the distributive concerns of Hyndman. Indeed, the new party soon followed De Leon in placing major emphasis on the need for an industrial strategy. Their efforts to form Socialist unions made little headway, but the SLP leaders were moving away from political action. During the general election of 1906 they urged their members to abstain from voting, not simply because their party had been unable to put up any candidates, but because all the electoral issues were "phony."[19]

The shift in strategy reflected the rapid decline of electoral appeal, both in America and Britain, which followed the adoption of an uncompromising policy. Connolly, who had gone to America to work with the Socialist Labor Party there, observed that no one "spoke of political organization as being but the 'shadow' of the economic until the vote began to dwindle." He had, in fact, quickly become disillusioned with De Leon after questioning the American leader's views on religion and the family. The episode convinced Connolly that most working class Socialists in America were, like those in Britain, only "half-emancipated slaves" and reluctant to doubt "a trusted leader from a class above them." And before long he concluded that De Leon's view of the party reduced his followers to "automatons whose duty is to repeat in varying accents the words of our director general."[20]

Perhaps, as one Marxist observed, the influence of De Leon contributed to the "disintegration of Hyndmanism" within the British movement. The American leader's "lack of dialectic" and his "virtually idealistic" emphasis on understanding prevented any serious engagement with social institutions or objective developments.[21] But "Hyndmanism," and indeed Marxism generally, were periodically breaking apart; it is difficult to find in any of the European Socialist movements the kind of reciprocating, mutually informing relationship between theory and practice envisioned in Marx's dialectic.

The SDF leaders continued to seek a course which was both politically practical and theoretically sound. By 1903 the Federation, along with the Socialist movement generally, was growing again. Over the next two years it regained the strength, in numbers and branches, it had attained at its peak in the nineties. During 1904 the Social Democrats took the initiative in agitation on behalf of the unemployed. And despite its separation from the LRC, the secretary's report at the SDF's annual conference of that year urged the branches to join local LRC's in order to "influence such in a Socialist direction."[22] Social Democrats had discovered, in fact, that their candidates rarely attracted much electoral support unless they appealed to the immediate concerns of the working classes.

Branches of the Federation in Lancashire provided the strongest backing for a reformist strategy. Unlike London, where Social Democrats were usually employed in small workshops or in occupations which did not support strong unions, most of the Lancashire members belonged to the powerful cotton union. During the nineties the SDF's strength in the area had come to exceed that in London; it was the only area in the industrial north where the Federation had held its own against the ILP. It owed its success in large part to the religious and political peculiarities of the region, but an effective electoral campaign still presupposed an appeal to the non-Socialist working classes. Local leaders, like Dan Irving, secretary of the large Burnley branch, had adopted a much more pragmatic policy than that characteristic of the Federation elsewhere.[23]

At the annual conferences of 1904 and 1905 the Lancashire Social Democrats introduced resolutions in favor of reaffiliation with the LRC. "Others are getting credit for our spade work," John Moore of Rochdale observed. They were leaving the "molding of the working class to the leaders of the ILP." Irving confessed that he was an opportunist and insisted that there was "little difference between the ILP and ourselves." The motion was defeated at both conferences, however, by a wide margin.[24]

Hyndman gave some support to this move within the SDF. He had resumed a dominant role in the life of the Federation in 1903 and during the following year stumped the country with a series of speeches opposing Joseph Chamberlain's proposal for a preferential tariff system. He also began to cultivate the Burnley constituency, where the strength of the Social Democrats gave him hope of entering Parliament. But Hyndman's opportunistic tendencies were still checked by his concern for the integrity of his Marxist doctrines. Although he had supported the Lancashire effort to take the Federation back into the LRC in 1904, he reversed his position a year later, arguing that reaffiliation could only take place at the expense of socialism. And even as he cultivated the Burnley constituency he contended in private that socialism would not "be brought about by the vote" but only through a "bloody and desperate struggle." In 1905 he abandoned for a time his strong hostility to industrial action and welcomed the prospect of "a general strike . . . as the first step towards national and international Socialist revolution."[25]

The dual impulses in Hyndman's Marxism, and the struggle to maintain a meaningful connection between theory and practical action, had virtually reduced the Social Democrats to a state of immobility in the early years of the century. Indeed, the vitality of the SDF seemed to lie mainly in its capacity for negation and denunciation. By virtue of its commitment to principle it did serve as a kind of conscience within the wider Socialist movement, challenging the ILP and the *Clarion* groups in particular to seek greater rigor in their propaganda work. But the scholastic character of the exchanges between Bax and Rothstein, the most significant theoretical debate among Social Democrats in these years, suggested the extent to which they had sealed themselves off from the main currents of British thought and culture.

The Fabians, in contrast, had come to view socialism as the natural outcome of native traditions of social thought. And Webb had succeeded in limiting the scope of the Society's work to that of developing practical legislative and administrative proposals. Individual Fabians continued, however, to nourish hopes for a fundamental transformation of British institutions and values. The problem which exercised the Social Democrats—that of finding the proper relationship between theory and practice—was paralleled in the efforts of Fabians to deal with the tension between the Society's official policies and their personal aspirations.

THE SCOPE OF FABIANISM: *Webb versus Wallas*

The Fabian Society lost something of its vitality in the early years of the century. Between 1899 and 1904 its membership declined from 860 to 730, and the sale of its tracts and pamphlets fell off by nearly a third. The Society's failure to take a stand against the Boer War had increased its distance from other sections of the Socialist movement. And despite the Society's participation in the LRC, Fabian leaders saw little promise in political alliance with the trade unionists. Webb was convinced by 1901 that the ILP was "hopelessly out of the running" and, as late as 1904, believed that the "Labour Party" would never amount to anything. Most Fabians favored the Society's older strategy of working through existing parties or administrative agencies. In practice this policy of "permeation" had normally meant close cooperation with the Radical wing of the Liberal Party.[26]

Fabianism remained highly eclectic; it was woven out of diverse strands in late Victorian thought. To the rationalistic outlook and the ethic of service found in the utilitarian tradition the Fabians had added ideas drawn from Marx, Comte, the Neo-Hegelians, and Spencer. Insofar as these elements had been fashioned into a coherent approach to social reform this was largely the achievement of Webb. "We have lived," as Pease put it, "for years on Webb's new ideas of politics."[27] And it is to the outlook of Webb that one must turn, not only to understand the Fabian policies in these years, but to grasp as well the growing disagreements within the Society.

Webb's marriage to Beatrice Potter in 1892 had given him financial independence and enabled him to devote full time to public service. He hoped, through "serious study," to work out the "detailed application of collective principles to the actual problems of modern life."[28] During the nineties the Webbs had begun a close historical study of English institutions which seemed to them the necessary foundation for the work of the modern social reformer. Their inquiry into the growth of trade unions, culminating in the publication of *Industrial Democracy* in 1897, acquainted them with one of the crucial ways in which the working classes had responded to the challenges of industrialization. The growth of the unions not only disclosed a process of "functional differentiation," central to the Webbs' picture of social evolution, but it exhibited the "issues and controversies" increasingly characteristic of the "larger world of politics."[29] The book presents, in fact, an interpretation of British development which informed the work of Webb as a Fabian leader.

The crucial problem of modern society, according to the Webbs, was that of combining "administrative efficiency and popular control." They saw in the development of the most successful trade unions, especially those of the cotton operatives and the miners, a solution to the problem. For these unions had put their initial "primitive democracy" behind them and developed the specialization of function demanded by the complexities of the modern economic system. They had clearly distinguished between the electoral role of their members, the policy making and deliberative work of their representative bodies, and the administrative task of their "permanent civil service." They had created a "fully equipped democratic state of the modern type."[30]

Study of trade union development also helped the Webbs define the major task of modern society—the fuller integration of the lower classes through an enlargement of the concept of citizenship. By pressing working class claims for social and economic justice, the trade unions had helped enlarge the meaning of the rights and duties of the individual citizen. The trade union drive for a fair day's pay or a "living wage" was translated by the Webbs into the idea that all members of society were entitled to a "national minimum" standard of living.[31]

The Webbs viewed the trade unions as vital forces in the regrowth of "social tissue," necessitated first by the breakdown of the traditional social and political order, and then by the "administrative nihilism" of nineteenth century liberalism. The functions of the unions, however, were limited to such issues as the working conditions and wages of their workers. They were not competent to decide what should be produced or how wealth should be distributed in society at large. These were political matters. To the "elected representatives and trained civil servants is entrusted the duty of perpetually considering the permanent interests of the state as a whole."[32]

Convinced that the functions of the trade unions disqualified them for a direct role in politics, the Webbs opposed the efforts of Socialists who were seeking to enlist the unions in a political alliance. They scolded trade union leaders for "meddling with wider issues of general politics" and they criticized Socialists for their "deficiency of technical knowledge" and their facile use of "revolutionary shibboleths like nationalization." The trade unions, as such, had "no logical connection with any particular form of ownership." The workers would have to "decide between rival forms of social organization" in their capacity "as citizens, not as trade unionists." Politics, like religion, was a sphere where men chose their associations on grounds different than those of immediate economic interest.[33]

The Webbs predicted that working men would enter the House of Commons in growing numbers. They would do so, however, not as trade union representatives but as part of a wider emergence of a new type of professional politician. Parliamentary work presented the trade union official with tasks as different from his union duties as those were from the work of the ordinary mechanic. Not only did parliamentary activity require a high level of intelligence and training on the part of the representative but it demanded a capacity to learn from parliamentary experience and to help educate his constituency. Modern democracy, according to the Webbs, would tend to "exalt the real power of the representative" while differentiating his functions from "those of the ordinary citizens on the one hand and the expert administrator on the other." The clearer separation of roles foreshadowed major changes in political life.

How far such a development of the representative will fit in with the party system as we now know it—how far it will promote collective action and tend to increasing bureaucracy—how far on the other hand it will bring the ordinary man into effective political citizenship and rehabilitate the House of Commons in popular estimation—how far, therefore, it will increase the real authority of the people over the representative assembly and of the representative assembly over the permanent civil services—how far, in short, it will give us that combination of administrative efficiency with popular control which is the requisite and the ideal of all democracy—all these are questions that make the future interesting.[34]

The questions were largely rhetorical; they outlined, in fact, the Webbs' expectations about the political future. For they envisioned a collectivist order, defined as the "conscious and deliberate organization of society based . . . on the scientifically ascertained needs of each section of citizens." Collectivism would not come through "the chances of the [political] fight" or through class conflict; it would come from a general growth of enlightment and particularly through the acquisition of scientific knowledge. Such knowledge, however, must act "on and through the minds . . . of the 'average sensual man'." Even the wisest of men could not be "trusted with supreme authority in the absence of a means of securing popular consent." Democracy, according to the Webbs, was the "irresistible tendency" of the age.[35]

The Webbs did not attempt to connect the analysis in *Industrial Democracy* directly to socialism; they were seeking to instruct all political parties and reformers. But their attempt to establish a dispassionate and rational vantage point beyond the clash of interest groups was closely related to Webb's conception of Fabian socialism. For he saw the Fabians as part of a new class of experts capable of providing the scientific knowledge necessary to cope with the complex problems of modern government. His collectivism tended, in fact, to reduce socialism to a science of public administration.

The Webbs attempted to protect the sphere of the expert from the contagion of interests or personal values by limiting the area to which scientific knowledge was applicable. Science dealt with the realm of means; it possessed no authority to define social ends. For the Webbs these were matters of personal taste. Hence the necessity for a democratic process to determine the goals of society. Experts should instruct the politicians and administrators, but decisions about basic values should be referred to the people.

The analysis presented in *Industrial Democracy* was not disinterested; it contained, as Hobsbawm observed, a "theory of democracy, the state, and the transition to Socialism."[36] In their account of the growth of trade unionism the Webbs had reaffirmed the Fabian policy of permeation. They had also separated themselves once more from Socialists who were attempting to create a new party. After 1900 Webb continued to disparage Socialists who were still committed to the "primitive policy of the conversion of England." Confident that a Socialist outcome was implicit in existing political and administrative tendencies, he claimed that the actual "increase of socialism" was "much faster than that of professed and organized socialism." A labor or Socialist party constituted, in fact, a threat to Webb's conception of national development. Most Socialist leaders, he observed, failed to recognize the way in which the "political horizons" had been widened by "imperial questions" and global rivalries. Outside the sphere of labor interests and local government, Webb charged, most Socialists were "mere administrative nihilists."[37]

The Fabian conception of Socialist development left the Society's members free to decide their own relationship to the political process. Convinced of his own disinterestedness, Webb was willing to work with whatever political group seemed most receptive to his ideas at the moment. To Shaw he appeared to be "the freest man in England." Webb expressed this freedom at the turn of the century by abandoning the Liberal radicals, with whom he had worked closely in earlier years, in favor of the "imperialist" wing of the Liberal Party. The interest of Lord Rosebery, Herbert Asquith, and others in the notion of "national efficiency" seemed to open a way for Fabian influence. The Webbs, Beatrice observed, were being "carried there by the currents of our work." Since "England is governed by cliques of friends and acquaintances," she noted, "you help to rule" only "if you are inside the clique."[38]

To some of their Socialist colleagues the Webbs' decision to work with the Liberal imperialists seemed in retrospect a clear case of "putting money on the wrong horses," since it estranged the Webbs from the increasingly influential radical leaders of the party. But politics, so Beatrice claimed at this time, was a "mere by product of our life," secondary to the work of investigating society. She had few illusions about the consequences of their new association for any personal political ambitions. "If we came to throw our main stream of energy into political life," she observed in 1901, "we should have to choose our comrades more carefully." From that standpoint their new political ties were "suicidal."[39]

Webb's "freedom" and "disinterestedness" in political matters expressed an extraordinary single-mindedness. He had long since left behind those existential dilemmas he had shared with many of the early Socialists. Speculations about metaphysics or ultimate questions of belief now seemed futile to him; they were not susceptible to "valid discussion" and led "nowhere." He was finding, so far as one can see, complete self-fulfillment in the tasks presented by public affairs. For Beatrice, who continued to struggle with religious issues, Sidney's one-dimensionality was inhibiting. In the privacy of her diary she confessed that her husband's presence sent her most intimate self into hiding.

When Sidney is with me I cannot talk to the "other self" with whom I commune when I am alone. "It" ceases to be present and only reappears when he becomes absent. Then the old self, who knew me and whom I have known, for that long period before Sidney entered into my life, who seems to be that which is *permanent* in me, sits again in the judgement seat and listens to the tale of the hour's and day's acts, thoughts and feelings, which the earthly one has experienced.[40]

The self-denial required by Webb's approach to socialism had enabled the Fabians to draw together men and women of diverse outlooks. In its pluralism and its capacity to circumscribe the area of political discussion, the meeting of the Fabian Society bore some resemblance to the parliamentary process itself. To carry a proposal through the Society, with its varied perspectives, meant that it had a reasonable chance for passage through Parliament. But a number of the Fabians continued to chafe under the restraints imposed by the Society's policy, for it demanded the suppression of aspirations that interfered with the development of practical political proposals; it ruled out fundamental challenges to prevailing institutional structures and values. Fabians who retained such hopes were likely to become frustrated. So it was with Graham Wallas. His opposition to Fabianism emerged during the campaign to reform secondary education.

Education had been a central concern for Fabians almost from the beginning. In the nineties Wallas and Stewart Headlam, as members of the London School Board, had helped shape its policies in the areas of elementary education. Webb was chairman of the Technical Education Board of the London County Council where he attempted to expand both technical and secondary educational opportunities. He and his wife had also played the leading role in founding the London School of Economics and continued to influence its development. By the end of the century Webb was a recognized expert in the field of education and in close contact with governmental officials who were seeking to reform secondary education.

Reform in this area was long overdue. The Education Act of 1870 had accomplished its main goal, the conquest of illiteracy. But efforts to expand the public educational system beyond the elementary level had been delayed by intense religious rivalries and by a division of responsibility between school boards and county or borough councils. In 1899, however, the creation of a national Board of Education centralized educational administration and encouraged a new effort at comprehensive reform. In May of that year Webb presented a plan for educational reform to the Fabian Society. He proposed that the school boards be abolished and educational authority be vested in the councils. After eighteen months of discussion, and modification of the proposal to preserve school boards in the larger cities, the plan was accepted and presented in a Fabian tract, "The Education Muddle and the Way Out," published in the spring of 1901. Webb's relations with the government officials working on the problem were now so close that they requested proofs of the tract before its publication. And over the next two years, as the Conservatives carried their education proposals through Parliament, the Webbs and other Fabians provided technical assistance and campaigned vigorously for the legislation by means of lectures and newspaper articles.[41]

The government passed two education bills, the second of which dealt with the problem of London separately. They abolished all school boards and provided public subsidies for voluntary or denominational schools, most of which were run by the Church of England. And while the influence of the Fabians on this legislation has been questioned, it seems clear that Webb's influence, at least on the bill dealing with London, was important. "You have toiled in the background," Robert Morant, the framer of the bill, wrote Webb, and "you have achieved the unification and true coordination of Education in London."[42]

The Fabian decision to support legislation to subsidize traditional religious teachings had important consequences for the Society. It identified the Society with the Conservatives on an emotionally charged political issue and deepened the estrangement between the Fabians and the radical sectors of the Liberal Party. Nonconformists were outraged by the plan to put Church of England schools "on the rates." As Beatrice Webb conceded, the acts forced many a rate payer to "maintain the teaching of a religion in which he did not believe and which he often regarded as damnably injurious to both his children and the community."[43]

This sense of injury was felt by many Socialists. Some held the extremely anti-Christian views of Blatchford and Bax; others were secularists, or simply shared the general Nonconformist hostility to the established church. The education bills, according to these Socialists, strengthened teachings which were outmoded and pernicious. Within the Fabian Society such a view was held most strongly by Wallas.

Wallas had been Webb's closest friend and strongest ally in the development of the Society. He had also been deeply concerned with the problem of education. The son of an Anglican parson, he had become an agnostic while attending Oxford. His dismissal from a teaching position at Highgate School in London in 1885 because he refused to take part in religious exercises had made him particularly sensitive to the need for safeguarding the intellectual freedom of the teacher. In the early years of the movement he regarded an improved educational system as an alternative to a Socialist revolution; his first public lecture, at the home of William Morris in 1886, had dealt with this subject.[44]

Educational reform possessed a religious significance for Wallas. He expected that the schoolroom would take the place of the church and nurture the new social faith of the future. Wallas' own humanistic faith owed much to Aristotle and the Greek ideal of the polis. Utilitarianism and Darwinian science had strengthened his rationalistic bent. But Wallas was also influenced by Ruskin's insistence that the lower classes could only be rescued from the "immoral principles" of the commercial system by new ethical or social motives. Convinced that the Christian church was disintegrating, he foresaw a time of profound religious transition.

When [the collapse] does come the last fragment of the old social organism will have disappeared and material and spiritual anarchy will be alike complete. The social idea alone will be able to reintroduce order and happiness. And just because the social ideal is a new religion, because it acts in a field of thought left hitherto untouched and unrealized, we shall be able to preach it without compromise alike to believers and disbelievers in any theological system . . . Our religion will find its noblest sphere not in churches or on death beds but in the workshop or corn field, the assembly and wherever associated human life is most strong and most delightful.[45]

It was not easy to reconcile such an aspiration with Webb's approach to educational reform.

Yet, Wallas and Webb had much in common. They were both committed to the growth of a new kind of political leadership, devoted to the "painful process of conscious inference from consciously coordinated premises." Wallas' stress on the role of experts had made him especially vulnerable to charges of elitism which dogged the Fabians. Beatrice noted his "growing distaste . . . for Democracy" and his "distrust for the devices and expedients that Sidney is ready to adapt for making the democratic *form* practical and efficient." But Wallas probably envisioned for future citizens a more active role than the "consciousness of consent," to which the Webbs seemed to reduce ordinary individuals.[46]

Wallas had begun to question, moreover, the intellectualistic assumptions of Webb and most contemporary reformers. The nineteenth century rationalist tradition, he observed in 1901, had been shaken by a growing recognition of the "irrational, the subconscious, and the passionate, as the really significant quality of mankind."[47] And while he remained committed to the goal of achieving an organic community life in accordance with "pure reason," Wallas hoped to deepen the rationalistic tradition by means of a close study of the psychological dimension of political activity. Unlike Webb, who was preoccupied with institutional change and skeptical of the ability of the reformer to influence motives in any direct way, Wallas wished to alter fundamental beliefs and values.

During the Fabian discussions about educational reform the disagreement between Wallas and Webb approached the breaking point. Wallas was especially upset by Webb's proposal to subsidize the church schools. He was little moved by Webb's argument that such a measure was necessary to place education "on a much higher plane of efficiency." At issue was the character of the education being provided. For Webb the continuation, even strengthening, of church teachings was a small price to pay for a general improvement in the kind of education necessary for a more productive citizenship. Wallas, however, felt that Webb was promoting an "insidious ecclesiasticism." He was appalled by Webb's acceptance of the principle that "every child should be educated in schools supported by the religion of their parents." If consistently applied, Wallas told Webb, the principle would have "kept England in the condition of A.D. 500 and if adopted now would soon reduce it to the condition of Spain."[48]

Wallas was committed, as his brother-in-law, J. H. Muirhead, put it, to the task of nurturing new motives in the common man and creating in "the minds of the coming generation a desire for a higher level of life." Hence he regarded the Fabian handling of the education issue as a lost opportunity to work for the abolition of traditional religious teachings. Although Wallas did not press the issue strongly within the Society, he left no doubt about the strength of his convictions in conversations with Beatrice Webb. Indeed, his objections to Fabian policy soon led to his resignation. His departure from the Society in 1904 was actually occasioned by a disagreement over a Fabian tract on fiscal and trade policy. But it reflected his growing sense of the narrowness of the Society's frame of reference. Other things than the Fabians' "own special business," he wrote later, "were always breaking in." And in the years ahead, as he pursued his pioneering study into the psychology of politics, his rationalist and secularist convictions deepened. He became more and more convinced that the "special task" of his generation was to develop "a world outlook deeper and wider and more helpful than modern Christendom."[49]

Fabians who sought social changes more fundamental than those encompassed by the Society's policies did not, however, have to break away. They might seek them through other channels. This was the solution of Shaw, whose theatrical work in these years may be seen as a series of inquiries into issues which could not be treated within the boundaries of Fabianism.

The Two Worlds of George Bernard Shaw

Shaw once observed that had it not been for Webb he "might have become a mere literary wise cracker like Carlyle and Ruskin." His scornful dismissal of the two Victorian sages was unfair; it concealed his intellectual debts to their writings. But the remark expressed Shaw's confidence that he had escaped from the "chains of Socialist idealism" and discovered in the "disillusioned Socialism" of the Fabians the only secure basis for the practical work of the social reformer. By the late eighties he had rejected the revolutionary catastrophic view of social change encouraged by his early Marxism, and he had also moved beyond the moralistic and quasi-anarchistic alternative expressed most fully by William Morris. To Blatchford, the chief spokesman for this current of socialism during the early nineties, Shaw observed: "You will never be worth your salt" as a serious reviewer of literature "until you learn to face the world without imposing your trumpery little moral system upon it."[50]

The appearance of the *Fabian Essays* in 1889 had demonstrated Shaw's crucial position in the life of the Society. Not only did he edit the volume but he wrote two of the essays and, with Webb, assumed the major responsibility in defining the Fabian position. Over the next twenty years Shaw remained the Society's chief publicist, drafting its most important statements of policy and often playing a critical role as mediator in its controversies. Yet, while Shaw was "in the center" of the Fabian stage, he acknowledged that "Webb has been prompting me, invisible from the side." He was convinced that Webb was "one of the most extraordinary and capable men alive," who, in placing his abilities at Shaw's disposal, had enormously increased the latter's effectiveness.[51]

By the end of the century Shaw had emerged as a leading dramatist and gained a place in British cultural life which overshadowed his Fabian activity. His work as a dramatist and his work as a Fabian reformer, however, were increasingly separated. "My accursed talent for pure literature," he told Webb, meant "the division of my energies and the destruction of my singleness of purpose."[52] By means of pure literature, however, the ideals and hopes which he had dissociated from his Fabianism earlier were becoming vital once more.

Shaw's commitment to Fabianism had not mitigated his hatred of middle class values and conventions. Strongly influenced by Morris, he shared the latter's desire for a far-reaching transformation of the ethical and aesthetic quality of life. Such an aspiration informed Shaw's writings as a drama critic during the nineties as he set out to demonstrate the claim of Morris and the earlier romantics that the artist had a special role in the civilizing process. The artist was charged with the task of nurturing man's moral sensibility, heightening his social understanding, and leading men toward a better society. Where Morris, however, had tended in his art to retreat from contemporary life into the past or into fantasy, Shaw regarded present social reality as the true material of art. Ibsen and others had demonstrated that the theater, properly employed, could replace the church and the school as the chief instrument of enlightenment and social progress.[53]

Shaw attempted to carry out the program in his early drama. Initially his plays undertook a limited utilitarian task. The "momentous social problems" which had diverted Carlyle, Ruskin, and Morris from their artistic interests to become "revolutionary pamphleteers" imposed on the dramatist the need to "turn the theatre into a platform for propaganda." Until the "ordinary bread and butter questions" were solved the artist must neglect the loftiest human concerns.[54]

Shaw's "unpleasant plays," Widowers' Houses, The Philanderer, and Mrs. Warren's Profession, were "dramatic pictures of middle class society from the point of view of the Socialist, who regards the basis of that society as thoroughly rotten economically and morally." They were criticisms of the capitalist phase of modern social organization; they sought to "make people thoroughly uncomfortable while entertaining them artistically."[55] Thus Shaw's early dramatic work and his Fabianism were complementary efforts to permeate important sectors of national life.

Shaw soon concluded that this effort to integrate his Fabianism and his art had failed, both aesthetically and as social propaganda. A drama tightly controlled by Socialist preoccupations was too limited. He did not reject social questions as material for the dramatist, but in the plays which followed, Shaw attempted to emulate the great dramatists of the past and rise above ideological commitments in order to explore "life at large," or "human nature as it presents itself through all economic and social phases." The "pleasant plays," Arms and the Man, Candida, and The Man of Destiny, written after 1894, had "no purpose except the purpose of all poets and dramatists." Shaw's Fabianism ceased to be integrally related to his drama. Socialist concerns were still evident in the "pleasant plays" and the "plays for puritans" which followed, but the plays were no longer controlled by Shaw's socialism. Shaw the artist could now create his characters and "let them rip." Faithful to the possibilities of the concrete human situation, Shaw's imagination displayed "an awkward inclination to get out of hand." His characters escaped from the lead strings of his social and ethical aims.[56]

The tradition of comic drama on which Shaw drew was well suited to his talent for social exposure, for tearing aside the masks of conventional attitudes in order to reveal the play of vital passions and interests underneath. Comic drama was also compatible with Shaw's continuing ethical concern. For comedy, like tragedy, had traditionally presupposed moral judgments by the dramatist. In the hands of Shakespeare and Molière, comedy had often functioned to explore the contradictions between human ideals or pretensions, and behavior. But while these dramatists could accept conventional social wisdom and moral standards, Shaw was living in a society where such conventions had become problematical. Indeed, he employed comic drama to attack prevailing norms. "The function of comedy," he wrote in 1896, was "nothing less than the destruction of established morals." Only after this work of demolition, could art, "as the sole possible method of revelation for the forecasts of the spirit," bring man into a "purifying consciousness of the deepest struggles of the human soul with itself."[57]

During the nineties, moreover, Shaw was rethinking the problem of the meaning of life. Like a number of modern artists for whom traditional interpretations had collapsed, he began to construct a personal religion or mythology. He had become convinced that the Secularists and other popularizers of nineteenth century science had failed to explain the "mystery of consciousness." He also rejected the Darwinian conception of natural selection in favor of Samuel Butler's argument that man's mind disclosed the presence of a cosmic force working through biological evolution. Schopenhauer, Nietzsche, and others helped Shaw identify that force with the will. But Shaw avoided the irrationalism and the strong pessimism of the German thinkers by incorporating into his doctrine of the will man's drive for intellectual enlightenment and, indeed, for such civilized virtues as kindness and a sense of justice. Man's rational bent, Shaw maintained, was "essentially a passion." Not only did Shaw's myth of the "life force" provide a legitimizing framework for his art but it also supported his continuing hope for a revolutionary transformation of life, encouraged earlier by Marx and Morris, and then excluded from his Fabianism.[58]

Several studies of Shaw have argued that his plays after the turn of the century exhibit his disillusionment with Fabian socialism.[59] To identify his dramatic creations with Shaw's general attitude toward social and economic developments, however, is mistaken. Shaw tried, as he put it, to separate his activities into "water-tight compartments." During the early years of the century he continued to play his customary role in the Fabian Society, taking the lead in developing its position on such critical issues as the Empire and trade, and striving to reconcile the strongly opposed views on these issues within the Society. Shaw was also an active politician in these years, serving as a borough councillor in London and dealing with the practical matters such a position demanded. To Beatrice Webb he seemed "hopelessly intractable" on the political platform; both his lack of respect for "other people's prejudices" and his "quixotic chivalry to his opponents" seemed to her "magnificent but not war." Still, Shaw prided himself on his "contact with life and experience by public work" and dismissed the urgings of friends to "use your imagination whilst it is still in its prime."[60] His experience in the movement, however, had led Shaw to reassess the prospects for socialism. It was clear, he observed in 1903, that the working classes, despite the efforts of Fabians and others, remained firmly "anti-socialistic."[61]

Shaw's concern with the state of the movement was evident in the three major plays in the early years of the century—*Man and Superman*, *John Bull's Other Island*, and *Major Barbara*. These plays demonstrated Shaw's growing power as an artist and his comparative freedom from ideological commitments in his drama, but they also reflected his political frustrations. *Man and Superman*, he told John Burns, has "relieved me of a great deal that has been on my chest for a long time." He was employing his artistic imagination, in fact, to explore the emerging dilemmas of the British Socialists. He was, as James Hulse has argued, putting the "various types of Socialism . . . and the ideals he had studied between 1882 and 1900 . . . into dramatic form for three dimensional investigation." Within the conventions of drama Shaw could experiment freely with the alternative strategies toward social reconstruction.[62]

Socialism was not a central concern of *Man and Superman*. The play derived its dramatic force from Shaw's skillful interweaving of sexual and romantic themes with speculations about the nature of biological evolution. Socialist ideas were, however, held up for artistic scrutiny in the figure of Tanner, a political revolutionary modeled on the personality of Hyndman. And Tanner did mirror certain features of the Social Democratic leader; he was strongly rationalistic, consistent in his theory, and politically impotent. For all his penetrating intelligence Tanner was captured by nonrational but vital forces of which he took little account, and by the social conventions which he consciously despised. Shaw extended the criticism of dogmatic Marxism in the "Revolutionary Handbook," a collection of essays and maxims, appended to the play. "We have yet to see the man," Shaw concluded, "who, having any practical experience of proletarian democracy, has any belief in its capacity for solving the great political problems." But the "Handbook" also dismissed the permeative tactic of the Fabians as "fundamentally futile." Man's political capacity was "clearly beaten by the vastness and complexity of the problems forced on him." No serious revolutionary movement could rescue man from his "idols and cupidities" until "human nature was changed." The only solution, Shaw declared, lay in the development of superior human beings through the new science of eugenics or selective breeding.[63] Shaw's bold attempt to transcend existing social and human realities pleased at least one Fabian. Beatrice Webb wrote in her diary: "I am delighted with his choice of subject. We can't touch the subject of human breeding—it is not ripe for the mere industry of induction, and yet I realize that it is the most important of all questions, this breeding of the right sort of man. [Shaw's] audacious genius can reach out to it." It was not a reach that pleased her husband. "I have just read Shaw's Don Juan play," Sidney wrote to Pease, "and I do not admire it at all."[64]

The political pessimism of the "Handbook" was fully integrated into the dramatic texture of the next play, *John Bull's Other Island*. It imparted an underlying tone of melancholy and bitterness to what was on the surface a light-hearted comedy. This was a play about politics, and specifically about the relationship between England and Ireland. But in Shaw's treat-

ment of the political issues the dominant features were demagoguery and opportunism at one end, a hopeless gullibility at
the other. Socialism again was a peripheral concern of the play
and treated in a way which indicated its radical divorce from
reality. In the unfrocked priest, Keegan, regarded as mad by
his fellow men, Shaw presented a figure whose vision epito-
mized the utopianism of Morris, Carpenter, and the Ethical
Socialists. Keegan envisioned a perfect community where work
would be transformed into aesthetic pleasure through the spontaneous workings of a common faith and morality.

> In my dreams [the new social order] is a country where the State
> is the Church and the Church the people; three in one and one in
> three. It is a Commonwealth in which work is play and play is life;
> three in one and one in three. It is a temple in which the priest is
> the worshipper and the worshipper the worshipped; three in one
> and one in three. It is a godhead in which all life is human and all
> humanity divine; three in one and one in three.[65]

For Shaw the Fabian, however, the lyrical affirmation of the
mad priest could only be a lament for a lost Socialist innocence.

    Major Barbara is the most complex and puzzling of the
plays of this period and the work by Shaw which has elicited
the most critical commentary. Recent interpretations have
tended to stress those qualities of wit, satire, and symbolic in-
ventiveness, together with the comic affirmation of life, which
dominate Shaw's aesthetic.[66] And yet the play can also be seen
as the "most powerful dramatization of Shaw's conflicting ideas
and feelings in these years." It exhibited the two more or less
autonomous sides of the author's development. The opposition
between Shaw the Fabian Socialist and Shaw the artist-prophet,
was evident both in the structure of the play and in the central
figure of Undershaft. No wonder one critic has seen Undershaft
as a projection of "the two selves of Shaw."[67]

    The Fabian theme in *Major Barbara* was expressed in the
claim that "poverty is the greatest of our evils and the worst
of our crimes." The play unfolded the logic of this assertion.
It demonstrated that the absence of material security destroyed
human dignity and prevented the growth of self-respect and

civilized values. It also demonstrated that the power of the capitalist was too strong for the religious idealist. The Salvation Army which Barbara had joined to save souls proved to be an unwitting tool of the propertied interests; the Christian virtues it inculcated simply rendered the lower classes more docile.[68]

The conversion of Barbara and her fiancé, Cusins, to the harshly realistic outlook of her father, Undershaft, opened the way for a strategy of permeation. The social system might be captured from within by the Socialist reformer. Indeed, to some extent Undershaft, the enlightened capitalist, had anticipated the Fabian design. His model village incorporated many of the features of the Collectivist order envisioned by Webb. Life was arranged in such a way as to promote a maximum efficiency in the productive process while ensuring the workers at least a "national minimum" in terms of wages, housing, and the amenities of civilization.

From a Fabian point of view Undershaft's model village was still inadequate. In solving the problem of poverty Undershaft had deprived the workers of much of their freedom as well as any significant role in shaping their social and political environment. "When you organize civilization," Undershaft observed, "you have to make up your own mind whether trouble and anxiety are good things." If not, "you may as well go through with it." Life in the village suggested, in fact, how a Fabianism preoccupied with economic security and divorced from liberal values and democratic methods might enter into the service of an authoritarian capitalist order. But the play went on to reaffirm the Fabian demand for democratic control. As Cusins prepared to enter into the Undershaft inheritance he declared: "I want a democratic power strong enough to force the intellectual oligarchy to use its genius for the common good."[69]

Barbara, however, wanted much more than the democratic welfare state of the Fabians. At the end of the play she spoke of "human souls to be saved" and of the task of "raising hell to heaven" and "man to God."[70] And the play was concerned in large part with the problem of moving beyond the Fabian conception of social reform. Shaw's desire for a more radical transformation of society was evident in his treatment of two phenomena which the Fabians tended to ignore—power and religion.

Undershaft's understanding of the role of force and violence in human affairs introduced a Marxist-like realism into the play. The capitalist scoffed at the efforts of moralistic reformers, dismissed conventional political activity as make-believe, and proclaimed the primacy of economic power. The "government of your country" he asserted, was run from the "counting house." The only "lever strong enough to overturn the social system was the machine gun." Yet, this was not the realism of Marx. Although Undershaft symbolized the massive strength of the capitalistic order, the social analysis in the play veered away from collective social forces and the possibility of revolutionary violence, to the inner lives of individuals. Society as portrayed in *Major Barbara* was not the complex system of institutions illuminated by Marxist theory, but a field where individual wills contested for supremacy. Power was not, in fact, the key to social change. Power was essentially spiritual; its exercise presupposed a will rooted in a religious faith. And for the author, as he observed in the Preface of the play, "the most stupendous fact in the whole world situation" was the complete disappearance of any "credible established religion." Undershaft not only exemplified the realities of power and violence in human affairs; he embodied, as did Barbara, Shaw's faith in the "life force."[71]

The notion of a cosmic force working out its purposes through the lives of outstanding individuals, particularly artists, had been a major theme in *Man and Superman*. Undershaft now gave clearer meaning to the doctrine. He was inspired by a "constant sense" that he was "only an instrument of a Will or Life Force which uses him for purposes wider than his own." This, Shaw explained, was the "consciousness of all genuinely religious people."[72] In the course of the play Barbara and Cusins embraced the creed of Undershaft and thus became members of a vanguard who by virtue of their superior wills and creative participation in the cosmic process would lead mankind beyond capitalism, and beyond Fabianism as well.

In search of a force capable of raising mankind to a new level of existence Shaw had turned to potential energies lying beneath the threshold of consciousness. He had long been fascinated by the mixture of martial ardor and joy expressed in the Salvation Army, and his sense that religion provided a source for socially redeeming energies had been strengthened by Gilbert Murray's recent translations of Euripides. Shaw's treatment of Undershaft, as the "new Dionysius," lacked the enigmatic blend of terror, cruelty, and ecstatic transport which lends such power to the *Bacchae*.[73] But it presents a sharp contradiction to the conventional motives and rational outlook on which the Fabians relied. Indeed, "Dionysian energies" could only be purchased through a repudiation of Fabian attitudes and methods.

The contradiction was not overcome in *Major Barbara*. The play was, as Margery Morgan observed, "a paradox in which antitheses retained their full values and cannot be resolved away." The work did offer, however, in the notion of religious conversion, a possible bridge between Shaw's Fabian ideology and his utopian vision. "A new Socialism" and a "great change," he had told an audience late in 1904, "could only come about through a religious motive." And in the period after the writing of *Major Barbara* the religious problem would increasingly occupy Shaw.[74]

The intense intellectual and imaginative effort which went into *Man and Superman, John Bull's Other Island,* and *Major Barbara* did not shake Shaw's loyalty to the Fabian Society. It continued to be a place where he found meaningful work for socialism and a satisfying contact with the real world. He was, to be sure, periodically skeptical of the Fabian strategy. Shortly after finishing *Major Barbara*, he expressed his fear that the Society was getting stale and needed a "stock taking." But he disclaimed any "far reaching design" or any intention beyond "a genuine desire to reflect on our past life."[75] Within a few months, in fact, Shaw again assumed the lead in defending the official policies of the Society against the strongest challenge they had faced thus far.

The challenge was led by H. G. Wells. For Wells, like Wallas and Shaw, was developing a picture of the social future which could not be fitted within the frame of Fabianism. Wallas had left the Society in order to follow his deepest bent while

Shaw generally succeeded in separating his work as an artist-prophet from that of the political reformer. Wells, in contrast, was determined to reshape Fabian policy to serve his own bold social design.

THE UTOPIAN AS FABIAN: *H. G. Wells*

Wells described himself, along with Shaw and MacDonald, as the type of "adventuresome outsider" who was "inevitable in a period of obsolete educational ideas and decaying social traditions."[76] He represents another case of the gifted young man of the lower middle classes, undergoing a process of inner division and social estrangement and setting off in search of an integral scheme of life, first through fantasies and then by means of the Socialist ideology. Wells affords an especially revealing account of the development of the divided sensibility in late Victorian and Edwardian society. Not only did he express many of its characteristic hopes, fears, and anxieties, but he indicated, through his refusal to accept the successive claims of the scientific, political, and artistic vocations, something of its compelling nature. Wells' stormy relations with the Fabians also exhibited the suppressed aspirations ever threatening their form of socialism.

Wells came from a family which had been left, because of the failures of the father, clinging precariously to middle class conventions. Like Shaw and so many others he escaped from a cramping existence into a wider world opened by books. The imaginative enlargement he underwent helped disqualify him for the "despised identities" he experienced, first as an assistant in a drapery shop and then as a student teacher. Before long he was traveling the road on which "at various paces a large section of the intelligentsia of my generation was moving—towards religious skepticism, socialism, and sexual rationalism."[77]

The road was charted for Wells by romantic writers—Blake, Carlyle, and Ruskin—and given a new social turn by the ideas of Henry George. During a "resentful phase" in the mid-eighties Wells discovered the Socialists; he attended Fabian meetings and for a time hung silently on the outer edges of the circle around Morris. But he did not, like many of his contemporaries, find in socialism a reorientation to life. Science, which he had begun to study by means of a scholarship, was providing a "New Word," and the Socialists, so he concluded, lacked the "scientific habit of mind."[78]

Norman and Jeanne MacKenzie, in their biography of Wells, have described the way in which the "new science slipped into the space left by the rout of the old religion," without, however, completing the rout.[79] For the millennial and apocalyptic cast of mind, derived from his discarded Calvinistic and evangelical beliefs, remained to shape his attitudes toward science. His refusal to grant ultimate intellectual sovereignty to science was encouraged by one of his teachers, Thomas Huxley, who had insisted that man must create his own order of values and meaning in the face of an amoral physical universe. By the early nineties Wells had concluded, in fact, that scientific modes of explanation could not reach man's most intimate sense of self and the sphere of values. He had also abandoned the vocational avenues opened by science in order to become a writer.

Having been schooled in science without submitting to its special discipline, Wells could put the new ideas of the biologists and the physicists in the service of a powerful imagination. It was an imagination energized by the wishes and the anxieties of an individual who, as he confessed to a friend, was struggling "to shake off the last vestiges of convention." Lonely, impoverished, desperately ill at times, Wells gained that "easy communication with unconscious materials" which frequently comes to those for whom customary securities, and inhibitions as well, have fallen away. Wells' method in writing his early science fiction has been likened to a "process of dreaming," in which "powerful and primitive emotions were translated into visual images." His extraordinary gift for constructing strange new worlds out of the ideas provided by science won him rapid success as a writer.[80]

Wells' science fantasies in the nineties reveal a bent of mind in which many of the assumptions of Victorian life—the stability of human nature, an orderly social process, the absolute nature of time and space—are dissolving and all things are becoming possible. Civilizations collapse, planets wage war, men become invisible, race back through time and emerge from or revert into animalism.[81] Yet, the enduring force of Wells' Calvinistic inheritance was apparent too in the pessimistic and apocalyptic vision which informed many of these stories. In that vision, however, the hope of man's redemption had faded out and the universe described by science, together with the scientific intelligence itself, assumed menacing and, indeed, diabolical qualities. While something of the older religious structure of meaning remained, the stories laid bare a state of mind which was nihilistic and despairing.

Literary success, financial security, and marriage probably helped Wells develop a more sanguine view of man and society. By the late nineties his writings exhibited a renewed search for redeeming truths; the free flow of fantasy began to give way to social diagnosis and prophecy. Where Shaw in these years was freeing his artistic imagination from explicit didactic or ideological aims, Wells moved in the opposite direction. His imagination, as Bernard Bergonzi observed, was "increasingly coerced by intellectual conviction."[82]

The shift from fantasy toward ideology, from a purely imaginative ordering of life to a scheme devised by the rational intellect, was expressed in a series of articles published in 1901, "Anticipations of the Reaction of Mechanical and Scientific Progress upon Human Life and Thought," and printed in book form later in the year. Ostensibly the book dealt with the social ramifications of scientific and technological progress, as Wells employed the techniques used so successfully in his fiction, of selecting out and exaggerating certain tendencies in contemporary life in such a way as to create new and strange perspectives. In *Anticipations*, according to one admirer, Henry James, the author's "disencumbered intelligence" had enabled him to run ahead of his time and enter the world of the future.[83] The intelligence displayed in the volume was more encumbered than James realized. *Anticipations* represents, in fact, a series of shrewd observations and projections, bad guesses, and rational arguments, held together by an imaginative structure which expressed the wishes, fears, and anxieties of an alienated and divided self.

Wells argued that the process of mechanization had irreparably broken down the old social classifications in Britain.

A vast "social liquefaction" was under way, reflected in the development of an irresponsible and functionless rich on the one hand, and a mass of the socially submerged, "drifting aimlessly towards the abyss" on the other. In between lay the "really living portion of the social organism," an emerging section of the old middle class which was drawing into itself all functioning groups. The development of this "large fairly homogenous body" of disciplined specialists and scientifically minded men represented a "new force in history." Indeed, they would "confessedly ignore most of the existing apparatus of political control," for the parliamentary system had "long ceased to bear any real relationship to current social processes." It functioned simply to guard the interests of the wealthy as society broke down into antagonistic classes. Political democracy provided a mere stopgap between a ruling class which was declining and a "new collective intelligence or purpose."[84]

Anticipations contained little serious social analysis. Its readers were carried quickly from recognizable social facts or tendencies into a realm of fantasy where vivid images and metaphors predominated. At times Wells portrayed social processes in terms of colors. The "grey confusion" of democracy, or existing political leadership, would gradually be segregated into tints and shades with new social significance. Hydraulic metaphors were also prominent. Present society was a molten mass in which various groups were swimming or sinking or floating or drowning.[85] This play of the imagination was controlled in large part, however, by three powerful desires or anxieties; *Anticipations* exhibited the author's almost obsessive concern with the social menace of the lower classes, his own urge toward freedom in sexual conduct, and his strong personal drive toward power.

The lower classes constituted a serious menace to the development of a society dedicated to the procreation of "the fine, and the efficient, and the beautiful." Darwinian science had demonstrated that the "whole mass of the human population are inferior." Therefore, the rulers of the coming New Republic could not afford to be squeamish. They would have "little pity and less benevolence" for the "vile" and "wretched multitudes . . . of contemptible and useless creatures" who endangered social progress through "sheer incontinence" and "un-restricted lust."[86]

The demand that procreation by the lower classes be subject to social control did not involve any defense of existing conventions regarding marriage or sexual relations. The present system of "wild permissions and insane prohibitions" in sexual matters was absolute lunacy. Apart from society's legitimate concern with the birth of children, sexual relations were of no more public interest than "one's deportment at chess."[87]

Wells' attitude toward political power also suggested the play of strong personal desires. For power in the new society would go, as Beatrice Webb observed, to a type of person who represented an idealization of Wells himself. "Altogether outside of the official state system of today," Wells wrote, the new men would win their way through sheer intelligence and scientific training. They would not be encumbered by the now exploded values of political liberalism.[88]

While *Anticipations* was shaped by the personal desires of the author, it also carried over many of the inhibitions of the Victorian world he was seeking to displace. Despite his claim that the coming life would be "wonderfully arbitrary and experimental," Wells reinstated many of the old moral and religious sentiments. The "new republicans" would be "religious men," convinced of the "final rightness of all being" and determined to pattern their lives accordingly. They would acknowledge the notion of a God or "greater will" working independently of any conscious human will toward a "greater synthesis." Yet, their future ethical and religious system would be constructed in the light of modern science. Wells had, at least for the moment, left behind his earlier skepticism and placed science, or the "critical thinking" he identified with science, at the center of his hopes. Science, he argued, would gradually reveal "the common reason of things" and make "scientific people . . . more and more homogenous in their fundamental culture." Wells had returned, in fact, with the aid of science, to the religious vision of a millennium; he predicted that men would "become consciously integral" and gain "a harmony with the universal will."[89]

It is not difficult to explain the appeal of *Anticipations* to the Fabians. Wells had amplified and dramatized the historical importance of the force on which the Fabians had placed such emphasis—the scientifically trained experts. Shortly after the publication of the volume, Edward Pease wrote to Wells to find out if he was aware of the work of the Webbs, the "pioneers of your New Republic." But Sidney Webb had already written Wells, expressing his admiration for the book, and particularly for its stress on the "coming predominance of the man of science." He criticized *Anticipations* on two grounds. By viewing the "trained professional expert . . . too exclusively as an engineer, a chemist or an electrician," Wells had failed to recognize the need for trained administrators "equipped with an Economics or a Sociology which would be scientific." He had also underestimated, according to Webb, "the capacity of the wage earning class to differentiate itself," take on "bourgeois characteristics," and contribute to "a new governing class."[90] To acquaint Wells with his own view of British social development, Webb sent him a copy of *Industrial Democracy*.

The disagreement between Wells and Webb was more fundamental than the latter recognized. Wells had scant respect for the social, economic, and political institutions on which the Fabian leader was attempting to build a collectivist order. Indeed, his whole bent was hostile to the pragmatic and accommodating reform methods of the Fabians. Wells' "anticipatory habit of mind" and "other wordly bent," as he himself described it, disqualified him for the close attention to immediate details on which the Fabians insisted. The differences in outlook were evident in Wells' first talk before the Society, after joining in 1903. His lecture, "Locomotion and Administration," called into question the Fabian reliance on existing bodies of local government. They had been rendered obsolete, Wells argued, by the change of scale and the altered patterns of population resulting from "a revolution in the methods of locomotion." Speaking on behalf of the growing "delocalized class," he called on the Fabians to discover the "larger community of a new type . . . which your working theory of local government ignores."[91]

To Beatrice Webb it was clear that Wells lacked much understanding of the actual operations of administrative agencies. But she welcomed him as a useful ally in the work of the Society; his loose generalizations would be useful as instruments of research. Wells was also invited to join a small dinner club the Webbs had organized outside the Fabian Society to discuss "the aims, policy, and methods of imperial efficiency at home and abroad."[92]

Wells found congenial spirits among the Fabians. He was drawn to Wallas especially and came to rely on him for critical appraisals of the manuscripts in which he developed further the ideas advanced in *Anticipations*. Both Wells and Wallas had been strongly influenced by Moisoi Ostrogorski's criticism of modern democracy and his challenge to conventional approaches to the study of politics.[93] Wells shared the doubts of Wallas about the Fabian educational policy as well as his opposition to the Society's tract on trade policy. Upon the publication of the tract, Wells, like Wallas, resigned, changing his mind only after Pease and Shaw had urged him to consider the merits of the Fabian method of collective thinking.[94] Meanwhile, Wells was developing his picture of the good society more fully; in 1905 he published *A Modern Utopia*.

The new book, unlike *Anticipations*, was a deliberate fantasy. It also displayed more clearly the author's inner discords; the three main figures in *A Modern Utopia* can be seen as projections of a fragmented consciousness. The narrator-hero embodied Wells' searching intelligence and imagination. His traveling companion, described at one point as an "introspective carcass" suggested the drag of the author's lower self, because his banal and sentimental remarks about a thwarted love affair back on earth continually distracted the hero from his utopian quest. The higher possibilities of the hero were embodied in a double he encountered at the climax of his passage through utopia. In this figure, "at once so strangely alien and so totally me," the hero discovered the self he "might have been." This ideal self had overcome the petty vanities and erotic impulses which held earthbound men back from noble and steadfast lives.[95]

The private concerns and anxieties evident in *Anticipations* were again apparent in *A Modern Utopia*. The "labouring and servile classes" had been virtually eliminated through acts of "social surgery" and the feeble-minded and criminal types had been safely confined on islands. Men of will and ability enjoyed to the full the "human power of self-escape" from traditional restraints, including those of monogamy, at least insofar as their wives tolerated extramarital affairs. Gone too was the cumbersome and inefficient political system prevailing on earth, together with the "accidental" classifications of social and economic interest groups on which it had rested.[96]

In the Wellsian utopia individuals were classified according to temperaments or "differences in the range, and quality and character of the individual imagination." Those blessed with a high degree of imagination were called poetic types; they "ranged beyond the known and the accepted," and created the basic forms of civilization. To this obvious celebration of his own bent Wells added kinetic types—individuals whose "truthful, moral and trustworthy" qualities made them ideal administrators. This type, as Wells explained later, was an expression of his "marriage" with the Webbs and an effort to make room for individuals of their outlook and abilities. Poetic and kinetic types were clearly marked off, in turn, from the dull, who lacked imagination, and the base, who were without moral sense. Out of the kinetic and poetic types, moreover, came the samurai, the ruling elite in utopia. By virtue of their force of will, their moral strength and their powers of intellect, the samurai alone possessed political power.[97]

Wells claimed that a concern for individual uniqueness was the central principle of his modern utopia. But the claim was largely canceled by an elaborate scheme of social controls. The new order required a "will to override all these incurably egotistical dissentients" and, indeed, demanded a state that "effectually chipped away just all those spendthrift liberties that waste liberty." To some extent the harmony between individual desires and community needs would come through science, or mechanical design. "The plain message physical science has for the world at large is this, that were our political and social and moral devices only as well contrived to their ends as a linotype machine . . . or an electric tram, there need now at the present moment be no appreciable toil in the world and only the smallest fraction of the pain, the fear, and the anxiety, that now make human life so doubtful of its value."[98] Yet, science no longer held the primacy of place and the integrating power assigned to it in *Anticipations*.

In a lecture delivered in 1903, "The Skepticism of the Instrument," Wells had reinstated his earlier view that science, or reasoning powers, could not deal with the "finer and subtler" issues of religion, ethics, and art. These issues belonged to the "province of poetry"; they were essentially modes of self-expression. His insistence on a private realm of initiatives, beyond the reach of science, did not prevent Wells from developing a new religion and ethical system for his samurai. This system provided the linchpin which held his utopia together; it also suggested Wells' continuing captivity to the Victorian moral world.[99]

Although the basic premise of the samurai's religion was a "denial of original sin," Wells elaborated a scheme of rules and prohibitions which matched the asceticism of the more rigorous of the Victorian sects. Members of this ruling elite were required to "renounce the richness and elaborations of the sensuous life, to master emotions and control impulses." The samurai were bound to a common rule which forbade the use of alcohol and tobacco, access to "painted women" and dramatic entertainments, as well as participation in games in public. And while the new religion had been purged of all "magic and emotion," "organ music and incense," and "creeds and . . . catechisms," its members spent ten minutes daily reading from its "Book," and undertook a seven day vigil each into the wilderness.[100]

A Modern Utopia, like *Anticipations*, was a blend of fantasy, rationalism, and Victorian moralism. But while the anarchic bent of Wells' imagination was still constrained by the older ascetic code, the conflict-ridden self he displayed in these writings lacked any positive relationship to society. Wells' continuing state of acute social alienation was evident both in his scornful dismissal of the existing political system and in his indifference to economic institutions. It was reflected too in his desire to replace the prevailing society with an order built out of temperamental or imaginative types. This absence of institutional ties encouraged what the MacKenzies called the latent messianism in Wells. During 1905 he conceived the mission of transforming the Fabian Society into the "beginnings of an order akin to the Samurai."[101]

The writings of Wells helped release aspirations among Fabians which had been excluded from the framework of concern developed by Webb. Members who had challenged the Society's policies at the time of the Boer War, particularly Olivier and Hobson, now saw a new opportunity to enlarge the scope of Fabianism. Olivier was convinced that the Society had "ossified," and he was toying, in the notion of a "League of Sane Men," with a way of developing a new kind of social leadership. Even Shaw had concluded that it was necessary to "make Fabianism interesting again," though he remained committed to the old policy and attempted to tutor Wells in the Society's practice of mutual criticism.[102]

During 1905 Wells published an article, "The Misery of Boots," which made his challenge to the policies of the Society explicit. Socialism, he declared, meant "revolution . . . a complete change, a break with history." He scoffed at Fabian attempts to achieve socialism by "odd little jobbing about municipal gas and water" or by "backstairs intervention among the Conservatives and Liberals." He called on those in the movement to give their "best energies to making other people Socialists." "For us, as for the early Christians," he wrote, "preaching our gospel is the supreme duty." Not only was Wells seeking to enlarge the scope of Fabian socialism but he was advocating a strategy of conversion which Webb believed the movement had outgrown.[103]

Wells won considerable support for a change of policy from some of the older members, and from new recruits who were entering the Society. By the end of 1905 Hobson could claim that the reformers possessed a clear majority on the Fabian executive.[104] But their efforts were interrupted by the general election in January 1906. The landslide victory of the Liberals, together with the return of twenty-nine candidates of the Labour Representation Committee, dramatically altered the political context for all sections of the Socialist movement.

PART THREE

Ethical Socialists and the Political Process

4

ETHICAL SOCIALISM 1906-1908: THE CLIMAX

THE ELECTION OF twenty-nine candidates of the Labour Representation Committee to Parliament early in 1906, including seven sponsored by the ILP, raised the hopes of British Socialists to new heights. "We walked with a new confidence," a Scottish veteran recalled, "conscious of an unfamiliar prestige."[1] Over the next two and a half years all sections of the movement shared in a Socialist revival.

The chief center of growth was again the textile manufacturing region of Yorkshire. And in a by-election in the summer of 1907 the Socialists mobilized sufficient support behind their candidate, Victor Grayson, to defeat both the Conservatives and the Liberals. His campaign demonstrated once more the way in which the popular form of the Socialist ideology had engaged sentiments of a declining Nonconformist religion. Indeed, a number of clergymen, confronted with a movement drawing so much of its moral outlook and rhetoric from the chapels and the churches, began to support the Socialist cause. Several of the clergymen set out to demonstrate the close relationship, even identity, between Ethical Socialism and Christianity.

With the emergence of a distinct Labour Party in Parliament, however, the dilemmas of the Socialists increased. Direct involvement in the parliamentary process brought out more fully the dualism within the ILP as well as the divergent aims within the Socialist-trade union alliance. Although Socialists who had questioned the worth of the alliance had been silenced for a time by the electoral successes, little more than a year after the general election they were again challenging the ILP policies.

THE SOCIALIST REVIVAL

The magnitude if not the quality of the revival can be shown by the rise in the number of Socialist groups. The Social Democrats added nearly a hundred branches and affiliated societies during 1906, 1907, and 1908, bringing their total to 232. In the same period the Federation increased its membership to 12,000. The ILP, with 375 branches in March 1906, listed 765 branches two years later and over 900 by the spring of 1909. Its dues paying members rose to over 30,000 with perhaps double that number connected with the local branches. The circulation of the *Clarion* soared from 56,000 at the beginning of 1906 to 74,000 two and a half months later and 81,000 in May 1908. *Clarion* organizations were again playing an important role in recruiting Socialists. The Fellowship revived although the Scouts and the cycling clubs were probably more popular. The *Clarion* van campaigns, started a decade earlier, quickly expanded and by 1908 six vans were working in various parts of Great Britain. They were joined in these years by a "red" van of the Social Democrats. Fabianism again flourished in the provinces. The new local Fabian groups, largely independent of the parent London society, also tended to draw closer to the other sections of the movement. By 1911 they numbered more than fifty and contained over 2000 members.[2]

The Socialist movement continued to embrace a wide range of ideas and aspirations. With some justification a *Times* reporter described socialism as "a theme so large, so facile, so elastic" as to be "adjustable to every mood."[3] But Socialists agreed in repudiating the capitalist order and in seeking some form of common ownership of the means of production, distribution, and exchange. Most Socialists, including the Marxists, also sought such "palliatives" as the eight hour day, right to work legislation, old age pensions, and a minimum wage. Beyond the common commitment to public ownership, however, the major sections of the movement were characterized by distinct political strategies and styles of propaganda.

Social Democrats were still dedicated to the task of building a working class political party informed by Marxist doctrines. As if to emphasize the fact they replaced the term "federation" in their title by the term "party" in 1907. At elections they appealed, much like the ILP, to the immediate interests of the workers. But the Social Democrats steadfastly refused to rejoin the political alliance with the trade unionists, fearful lest their advocacy of Marxism be weakened. Their continuing attempt to find a middle road between "opportunism" and "impossibilism" soon evoked new attacks from both wings of the party. Still the greater militance and theoretical seriousness of the Social Democrats enabled them to compete with the ILP. The ILP, one of the Social Democratic recruits observed, was "too much like the Sunday school which we were trying to get away from."[4]

For the Fabians these were troubled years. They continued to produce tracts on a wide range of public issues, particularly at the level of local government. But the substantial influx of new and young members introduced into the Society aspirations which clashed with the policy developed earlier. Moreover, the emergence of the Labour Party led some of the older members to question the Society's political strategy. The executive led by Webb and Shaw faced a series of challenges as Wells and others attempted to revise the Fabian Basis and redefine the Society's mission.

Ethical Socialism remained the most popular form of the Socialist ideology. Indeed, the revival called back into action several of those who in earlier years had been most influential in transforming socialism into ethical and religious terms. Edward Carpenter was once more a familiar figure on Socialist platforms, preaching a gospel which had lost none of its apocalyptic and messianic tone with the passage of time. His notion of a "super consciousness," beyond the fragmented, anxiety-ridden, individualistic existence of contemporary life, had been developed further in *The Art of Creation* published in 1904. In an article on "The New Morality" in 1907 Carpenter predicted the total disappearance of the ethic of responsibility and duty in an integral, spontaneous, instinctive life. The vision of mankind achieving a state of perfect integration and escaping from the repressions of civilization also appeared in a pamphlet,

"The One Life," published by the founder of the Labour Churches, John Trevor. Now retired to a chicken farm in southern England, Trevor attacked the restraints which civilization imposed on sexual drives. He proposed the formation of a new community, modeled on the American Oneida experiment, in which youth would have the "right to love."[5]

Blatchford remained engrossed in his religious campaign during 1906. "I am only out of the firing line," he wrote, "because I have gone far ahead of it." He did bring out a new edition of *Merrie England* and wrote a charming utopian novel, *The Sorcerer's Shop*, in which he portrayed Manchester in the aftermath of a Morris-inspired revolution. Before long, stirred by the Socialist revival, Blatchford would take a more active part in the movement. Meanwhile, Tom Groom ran the *Clarion* Scouts, Fred Hagger the Fellowship, and R. B. Suthers assumed responsibility for maintaining the flow of cheap *Clarion* tracts on socialism. One of these, Fred Henderson's "The Case for Socialism," was a particularly lucid and forceful statement of the ideas of surplus value and exploitation. It became one of the most effective tracts in the whole body of popular Socialist literature.[6]

In the period after 1906 many of the Socialist converts were coming, as in the early years of the movement, from the lower ranks of the professional or salaried sections of society. A "middle class proletariat," Sam Hobson observed, was again "greedily absorbing Socialism, slaking that intellectual thirst which neither the old political ideas nor the churches can now satisfy." They might occupy positions as teachers, civil servants, journalists, clergymen, or, as students, be seeking to enter the professions. More often, they were clerks, shop assistants, or commercial travelers. These sections of society were particularly vulnerable to the impoverishment of human relations experienced in the large cities, to the sense of losing a meaningful orientation to life left by the breakdown of religious faith, and to the boredom of commercial routines. In the Socialist movement they found a new fellowship, new purpose in life, new scope for unrealized talents, and opportunities for service. They also discovered the vision of a new social world. Edwin Muir, a clerk and ardent member of the Glasgow *Clarion* Scouts and the ILP, recalled the emotional transformation wrought by the movement. "Having discovered a future in which everything, including myself, was transfigured, I flung myself into it, lived in it, though everyday I still worked in the office of a beer bottling factory . . . My sense of human potentialities was so strong that even the lorry men and the slum boys were transformed by it; I no longer saw them as they were, but as they would be when the society of which I dreamed was realized."[7]

The most effective propagandists for Ethical Socialism were appealing once more to the sentiments and symbolism nurtured in the popular religious tradition. New tracts were designed for this purpose and the movement continued to draw some of its ablest speakers from young men who had planned to become clergymen. The renewed vigor of the Labour Churches again demonstrated the tendency for Socialists to seek religious expression for their faith. A dozen Labour Churches had survived into the new century and these reported a quickening of interest. At Bradford hundreds were turned away at several services. More than a score of new churches started up in the next three years, most of them in connection with ILP branches. They rarely lasted more than a few months and the churches recovered little of their earlier sense of common spiritual enterprise. Several, in fact, formed ties with the Union of Ethical Societies in an effort to find fresh inspiration.[8]

The development of the Labour Churches suggested that the moral and religious sentiments which had helped to energize Ethical Socialism in the early nineties were, despite the Socialist revival, losing something of their force. The new leaders of the churches were inclined to play down their religious significance, in fact, and view them frankly as political recruiting agencies. Hence the comment by Henry Brockhouse, president of the Labour Church Union in 1907 and also a member of the ILP's National Administrative Council. "As a flank movement the Labour Church is more effective in destroying the opposition of the orthodox churches to Socialism than is a direct frontal attack on orthodoxy itself. Its services with hymns, readings and general orderliness and decorum are a concession without loss of principle to the susceptibilities of our one time orthodox brethren who are gradually weaned from narrower views."[9]

Many of the newer recruits to the movement, particularly those from the middle classes, were no longer seeking traditional religious sanctions for their Socialist faith. Blatchford's anti-Christian campaign was one sign of the change; so too was the growing influence of Wells and his form of rationalism.[10] The changing sensibility was also reflected in the impact of thinkers from outside Britain. In the early years many Socialists had sought inspiration in the American transcendentalists, Emerson and Whitman. Later Tolstoy had helped fortify an ethical outlook, rooted in Christianity and successively recast by Carlyle, Ruskin, and Morris. After the turn of the century the new generation of Socialists began to read Nietzsche. The initial appeal of the German philosopher probably lay in his social iconoclasm, but he encouraged Socialists to abandon the ascetic and altruistic values of Christianity in favor of a heroic and vitalistic outlook. The ideas of Nietzsche also helped articulate the distrust with which some of the middle class Socialists were beginning to view the political development of the working classes.

The distrust was directed mainly at the policies of the ILP. For the electoral successes of the alliance with the trade unionists accentuated the party's drive to advance the immediate interests of labor and thrust its Socialist aims further into the background. A number of the ILP leaders, including Hardie, MacDonald, and Snowden, were now sitting in the House of Commons, and they were under renewed pressure from their trade union associates who noted the great discrepancy between the voting power and the financial resources provided by the two sides of the alliance. MacDonald and the other ILP leaders conceded, in fact, that they had secured more than their share of parliamentary candidates and began to favor trade union nominees over their own men. At the same time they went out of their way to emphasize the working class character of the Labour Party.

Despite the ILP's preoccupation with what Glasier referred to as "the sordid side of the movement," both he and Hardie took time to restate at length their Socialist faith. "Socialism," Glasier wrote, in a series of *Labour Leader* articles, was "but the reincarnation of those noble and holy aspirations" rising from the "remote recesses of our being . . . upon which new systems of religious thought have been built." And in a popular exposition of his faith Hardie claimed that "state Socialism, with all its drawbacks," would prepare the way for the simplification of life and the "free Communism in which the rule, not merely the law, will be—from each according to his ability, to each according to his needs."[11]

Meanwhile, MacDonald was seeking to adapt the ILP's Socialist ideology to the party's new political role. He also continued his efforts to raise the level of theoretical awareness among Socialists. The Socialist Library added volumes by Eduard Bernstein, Emil Vandervelde, and Jean Jaurès, the three most influential reformist Socialist thinkers on the continent. MacDonald founded a new monthly journal in 1908, the *Socialist Review*, to present serious articles on a variety of practical political and social questions. He was seeking, as he told R. C. K. Ensor, to "get round the *Review* a group of original thinkers working out Socialism in new directions as far as the English movement is concerned, and restating our principles and our policy in view of modern experience and conditions." But while the *Review* proved of "educational value for the thoughtful members" of the movement, it proved "too heavy and dry for the average reader."[12]

Most members of the ILP were still wedded, in fact, to a form of socialism which was highly moralistic in its appeal. And during the summer of 1907, at a by-election in the West Riding, Ethical Socialism achieved a striking political success when a young former divinity student, Victor Grayson, defeated candidates from both the Conservative and Liberal parties. Grayson's victory, however, also dramatized the divergence between the ILP's Socialist commitment and its political practice.

Victor Grayson and the Colne Valley Campaign

In 1906 the West Riding, with over one hundred ILP branches, still provided the party with its densest popular support. Yet the ILP had not been able to convert this strength into parliamentary electoral successes. The Liberal party's dominance in the region made its leaders reluctant to accept the kind of arrangements which in Lancashire had given the Labour Party twelve seats at the general election. Only in Halifax, where John Parker won a seat in a double constituency, and in Leeds, where James O'Grady won a seat, did the ILP receive the tacit blessing of the Liberals. The ILP's electoral polls in the West Riding did indicate, however, its real following and the serious challenge the party now presented to the Liberals. Not only did Fred Jowett win a three-cornered fight in West Bradford but Stanton Coit at Wakefield and Russell Williams at Huddersfield each came within a few hundred votes of the Liberal victors.[13]

In the months following the general election the rising fortunes of the Socialist movement were most apparent in the Huddersfield area. Here Russell Williams, a librarian, remained the most active propagandist, preaching a socialism well suited to "the native penchant for religiosity." A veteran of the early days of the movement, Williams had turned to socialism after his hopes of pursuing a career in the civil service had been frustrated. In a series of talks before the Methodist Pleasant Sunday Afternoon audiences and ILP branches during 1906 he appealed both to the moral feelings and the material interests of his listeners. There was, he told one audience, "no height of moral obligation to which Socialism would not help them aspire, no altitude of comfort which it would not help them attain."[14] Meanwhile the local Socialists were gaining new leadership from a vigorous weekly paper, the *Huddersfield Worker*.

Williams stood for the Huddersfield seat again in November 1906 at a by-election against Liberal and Conservative candidates. Once more he fell short of victory though he narrowed the Liberal margin. Glasier, in reporting the campaign, noted the remarkable but inexplicable political transformation there as well as the "exasperating sense of self-sufficiency" among the local men. He noted, too, that Williams had centered his campaign on the principle that "all things socially needed should be socially owned." The Huddersfield campaign, he concluded, "has been the most distinctively socialist contest fought in this country."[15]

This development was not altogether welcome to the ILP leaders. Williams' candidacy in the General Election had been denounced by Asquith as "an act of aggression" and the ILP leaders were not eager to enter the contest lest it damage relations with the Liberals and the trade unionists. Had it not been for the strong local enthusiasm they probably would have refrained. In assessing the results Hardie acknowledged that the Liberals had made socialism the central issue and that Williams had "eagerly taken up the challenge." As a Socialist he did not regret this, but he noted that it had led to defeat. Hardie was particularly disturbed by the signs at Huddersfield of new efforts to force the Socialists and the trade unionists apart. He cautioned the party not to "wrangle over what their principles . . . should be ten or twenty years hence" but to concentrate on "the cry for food for the starving child, the demand for work from the workers."[16]

Two weeks after the Huddersfield by-election a twenty-five year old Socialist speaker from Manchester, Victor Grayson, arrived in the nearby Holne Valley to conduct a week's "mission" on behalf of the ILP. During the next two months he extended his work into the neighboring Colne Valley. Grayson did not ignore the industrial grievances and the material claims of the workers but he appealed most directly to ethical and religious feelings, relying strongly on the Biblical phrases familiar to the chapel goer. He injected a new fervor into the Socialist rhetoric already familiar in the area.

Born in the Liverpool working classes, Grayson was serving as an apprentice with an engineering firm when a Unitarian minister picked him out as a "lad of promise" and secured a scholarship for him at a Unitarian college in Manchester.[17] During the early years of the century Grayson prepared for the Unitarian ministry although he aspired, a close acquaintance recalled, to the role of a "meteoric missioner." Grayson had become a Socialist while working as an apprentice and continued to take an active part in the local movement. By 1904 he was editing a small Socialist paper and devoting more and more of his time to Socialist propaganda. The college authorities even called Snowden in to urge the young man to concentrate on his studies, but without success. During 1905 and 1906 Grayson gained a reputation as the "mob leader of the Manchester unemployed"; some called him the "young Bradlaugh" because of his rich and powerful voice. He decided to abandon plans for the ministry in order to devote himself to the cause of socialism.[18]

In the winter of 1906-07 Grayson spoke extensively for the ILP in the area with which he became most closely associated, the Colne Valley. Part of a sprawling parliamentary constituency, reaching from the outskirts of Huddersfield into Lancashire, the Colne Valley shared fully in the dominant characteristics of the West Riding. Most of its workers specialized in the production of medium tweeds carried on in family mills which had developed in the nineteenth century. But new manufacturing techniques and the increased scale of industrial organization had served to break down the older sense of social and political solidarity between workers and employers. A local "labour league" had been formed in the early nineties and became one of the first affiliates of the ILP. In 1895 the Colne Valley Labour League put Tom Mann up for the parliamentary seat and he polled twelve hundred votes. In subsequent elections the League did not nominate a candidate, owing to the popularity of the Liberal incumbent, Sir James Kitson, and to the paucity of party funds. But during 1906, when it appeared that Kitson might be advanced to the Lords, the leaders of the League determined to fight the seat, convinced that "we shall be able to make a good show." Meanwhile Socialist sentiment was growing. A history of the valley written in 1906 took special note of the "influence which the socialist leaven has had on the thoughts, the aspirations and the struggles" of its workers. Early in 1907 Williams summed up the state of the movement there.

There is no hamlet in it without its body of workers. The hills are literally aglow with the light of a reforming passion . . . Liberalism does not appeal to the young men. They want something to fight for; a living soul-moving ideal. They want to feel the pulse of a new time, to thrill with the hope of a brighter era . . . The inspiration of Socialism is filling their souls with a new sensation, gladdening them with a new joy and helping them to realize the inadequacy of their fathers' creed.[19]

Grayson pitched his appeal to the sensibility described by Williams. Socialism, he declared, "taught new ideas of life," it "is a religion of the present . . . a religion which teaches us to think and feel straight and be moved to a consciousness to alter the ghastly horrors perpetrated in our midst." And he contrasted socialism with the religion fashioned in the theological schools, subsidized by employers and "molded to keep the workers in their places." Later, in the course of an election campaign, Grayson said that he had not entered the church because "it was useless to expect true religion in a social system such as the present." The Socialist movement was the "only movement . . . fit for men and women of spirit and religion." He also maintained that the chapels were "emptying themselves into the Socialist halls." A local church worker conceded this. "Many young people were disturbed in their faith by Grayson's claims that capitalists owned and controlled the pulpit, and the churches suffered seriously."[20]

In the spring of 1906 the Colne Valley Labour League had contacted the ILP council about the possibility of adopting Grayson as its parliamentary candidate. MacDonald was cool to the proposal but urged the Colne Valley Socialists to form a local LRC along with trade unionists in the area. He also sent a list of the Labour Party's recommended candidates, which did not include Grayson. Efforts to organize a local LRC failed, apparently because of the apathy of the trade unionists. And when, early in 1907, the League chose Grayson as its candidate and forwarded his name to the ILP's council for endorsement it was rejected, ostensibly on the basis of the lack of official trade union support. However, the council was increasingly concerned about the complaints from its trade union allies that the ILP was seeking too many candidacies and making excessive demands on funds provided mainly by the unions. Moreover, as Glasier observed some time later, Grayson was viewed as "a young cheap orator, not at all the type we want to get into Parliament."[21]

Early in April the ILP sent Snowden and James Howard to the Colne Valley in an effort to resolve the issue. Convinced that the League was determined to run Grayson, they recommended to the ILP Council that it "try to meet the branch in its desires" for it was "extremely healthy." The council, however, did not act. And late in June after the Colne Valley seat was declared vacant and Grayson was formally adopted by the

League, a subcommittee was appointed by the Labour Party executive to consider the problem. It concluded that the candidacy was not in accord with its constitution and declared that Labour Party officials should not take part in the campaign.[22]

"I have never been in such an unpleasant fix in all my life," MacDonald wrote at the time. In a "personal and confidential" letter to Grayson he attempted to be conciliatory but suggested that the Colne Valley men had "insisted on forcing our hands" in a situation where "local desires run counter to national interests." While he assured Grayson that the ILP would help him "as much as it can off its own bat," the fight would "lie very much upon your own shoulders."[23]

In response Grayson accused the ILP Council of "evasive action" and the Labour Party of "pettiness." And he questioned the viability of the political alliance. "I think most sincerely this cleavage will have to come some time and nothing will be lost by precipitating it. As things stand therefore, I gather that in the event of my success at the polls, I shall be a free lance socialist member, independent of the Labour group. So be it. By diverse ways we shall arrive. Believe me."[24]

In the electoral campaign that followed, Grayson was more accommodating. He associated his candidacy with the work of the Labour Party and presented an electoral program much like that of the party's candidates. It included the right to work, old age pensions, free trade, and free meals for schoolchildren. Moreover, he exploited the widespread discontent among the workers in the area over the introduction of new high speed looms. But Grayson did not stress immediate benefits, preaching socialism instead as a "deliverance." Indeed, a writer in the *Yorkshire Factory Times* criticized his campaign for dealing so little with trade union issues. Grayson, however, recognized that the Colne Valley workers were comparatively well off; later he observed that his "one hope for socialism" lay with the "educated and materially contented portion of the working classes—those who had risen above the immediate carking care of making ends meet."[25]

Grayson's campaign evoked an extraordinary spirit of self-sacrifice. He received support from nearly all the ILP branches in the West Riding. Despite the Labour Party's boycott,

Snowden and Glasier took part and Hardie, about to embark on a voyage for reasons of health, sent his blessing. Some of Grayson's followers abandoned their regular employment for days in order to give full time to the campaign. Their enthusiasm was described by a Liberal leader, T. J. Macnamara.

> Night by night, week by week, month by month, a new and attractive appeal has been made to the people by enthusiasts filled with a burning faith. They stood at the street corners and preached the gospel of Socialism with all the fervor of the early Christian missionaries. They were not paid hacks . . . The night before the poll it so happened I found myself in the same hotel as Mr. Grayson and his right hand men and women. I sat amongst them for an hour or so filled with admiration for their enthusiasm, their grim purpose and their deep attachment to their cause. (If I dare say so I was also filled with an equal amazement at their lack of a real grip of economic hard facts and possibilities, but let that pass.) As I sat amongst them I said to myself, these people ought to beat us because their political creed is a religion.[26]

Grayson's margin of victory was small, some three hundred votes in a total poll of twelve thousand. But it was a sensational political upset. According to Charles Masterman it created an "excitement . . . unmatched by any political phenomenon in recent years." Coming shortly after a by-election victory of an ILP leader at Jarrow, Peter Curran, the Colne Valley result seemed to spokesmen for the propertied classes a "menacing portent." The conservative *Daily Express* immediately started a series of articles dealing with the "menace of socialism," and within a few weeks the first concerted anti-Socialist campaign in Great Britain was under way.[27]

The Colne Valley result stirred the movement deeply. Glasier attempted to moderate the enthusiasm; he attributed the victory to the close cooperation between the forces of socialism and labor. But Grayson immediately became the symbol of a "clean" socialism, untouched by the compromises into which the ILP leaders had been drawn. He did not sign the constitution of the Labour party and did not accept its discipline in Parliament. He also rejected peace overtures from the ILP leaders, refused to speak from a platform on which MacDonald presided, and expressed a desire for an alternative political policy. Hardie, he declared after his election, had done "great work . . . in disentangling Labour from Liberalism," but the ILP's "great task now" was "to keep Socialism from coming under the tutelage of Labour." A short time later he expressed his scorn for the Labour Party and its respect for parliamentary traditions. "Revolutionary and unconstitutional means were needed to break up the tremendous mountains of tradition that persist in Parliament . . . What he wanted to do in the House of Commons was not to talk and become an indifferent Parliamentary debater, but to convey the impression he had received of the life he had lived and to make those languid politicians see that they were not worth the snap of the finger when the country was behind a real cause." Small wonder that Grayson soon became the spokesman for a growing number of Socialists who were losing confidence in the ILP leaders in Parliament.[28]

Grayson's victory was the most dramatic expression of the resurgence of Ethical Socialism. But the Colne Valley campaign had also revealed a significant new factor within the movement. Eleven clergymen, six Anglicans and five Nonconformists, worked alongside Grayson to secure his return. "Without their aid," Joseph Burgess observed, "it is probable that the Socialist poll would have been a minority."[29] In the months ahead Socialist clergymen generated much of the movement's vitality in the West Riding and assumed a major role in disseminating Socialist ideas across Britain. At a time when a new generation of middle class Socialists was following Blatchford, Shaw, Wells, Nietzsche, and others in a search for a new philosophical basis for social and ethical reconstruction, these clergymen were seeking to make explicit the connection between the popular form of socialism and the traditional religious faith.

THE SOCIALIST CLERGYMEN

The great majority of the British clergy had been hostile or indifferent to the growth of socialism. Yet, from the beginning of the movement individual clergymen within the Anglican church and the Nonconformist denominations had played active roles. Even where a clergyman denied the need for a new political party, as in the case of the Baptist leader, John Clifford, he might accept the Socialist vision of the future. Clifford denounced those who claimed that Christianity does not have answers to "questions of land ownership" or "modes of industry," as guilty of "flat paganism." And he joined with other Nonconformist ministers in organizing a Christian Socialist League during the nineties to apply the "principles of Jesus Christ directly to all social and economic questions." By the turn of the century a few clergymen of liberal theological outlook were willing to go much further in seeking a common ground with the new movement and even submit orthodox religious claims to the test of socialism. Thus Bodell Smith, a Manchester Unitarian, predicted that the churches would "ultimately free themselves from every theological doctrine that is not in harmony with the spirit and the principles of Socialism."[30]

Following the general election of 1906 socialism appeared to many clergymen to represent a prophetic force. It appealed particularly to those clergymen who had rejected the evangelical preoccupation with individual salvation and the other world. Anglican Socialists were likely to be high churchmen, for the sacramental and corporative concerns of the high church tradition made them especially sympathetic to the Socialist stress on the redemption of secular life and the importance of human solidarity. The stronger a man's faith in the true church, one sacramentalist declared, the more likely it was that he favored "the common ownership of goods."[31] The Nonconformist clergymen who joined the movement tended, in contrast, to hold a rather free view of the church and to emphasize God's redemptive activity within history.

During 1906 and 1907 many clergymen developed close ties with the movement. A few months after the general election an Anglican order in the West Riding, "The Community of the House of Resurrection" at Mirfield, invited Socialists and labor leaders to a conference to discuss the social problem. Commenting on the "inspiring weekend," Hardie declared that socialism had demonstrated once more its capacity to attract "men of all classes and creeds to its standards." A short time later a *Labour Leader* reporter described the members of the community as "men who have heard even as we ourselves have [heard] the call of Socialism."[32] In the months ahead several of the Anglicans from Mirfield would speak frequently from ILP platforms.

The new Socialist enthusiasm among the Anglicans found organized expression in June of 1906 in the Church Socialist League. Its initial leaders were clergymen in the Newcastle area who had been influenced by the Guild of St. Matthew, started thirty years earlier by Stewart Headlam. But they had come to see the Guild's program, with its concentration on land nationalization, as too narrow. At the outset the League committed itself to the "establishment of a democratic commonwealth in which the community shall own the land and capital and use them cooperatively for the good of all." During its first year the League grew to include eighteen branches with over six hundred members.[33]

To these Anglicans the Socialist movement promised a remedy for the disintegrative social and economic changes of the nineteenth century. In the Socialist concept of fellowship they saw a new form of the older Anglican ideal of a church commonwealth.

> It is significant that this doctrine of the fellowship of the Church, obscured in Britain during the last two hundred years, during which our industrial system has been developed, has been revived during the period of the growth of Socialism in the latter half of the last century . . . Socialism will upraise the outward fabric which will correspond to the inner motives of the Kingdom of God throbbing in the hearts of his people . . . The Catholic Church . . . is sooner or later bound to find in Socialism its own political reflection.[34]

To clergymen who had struggled unsuccessfully to make their faith meaningful to the industrial and urban populations, the Socialist movement seemed to be the only force capable of saving the established church from social sterility. Socialism had demonstrated, according to Algernon West, the League's president, its capacity to transform "thoughtless and selfish and vicious lives" and to exercise the "ethical influence of religion on character." For another leader, James Adderley, socialism had "come to our rescue" and offered "a great moral lead."

It dares to attack the whole system and that not merely in a destructive way . . . Socialism gives new life to the Christian faith.
It is worthwhile being a Christian. The soldiers of Christ, pent up
for three hundred years in their barracks, meditating on a far off
heaven, are summoned to Socialism to take part in a Holy War . . .
If those who summon us are "atheists" or "heretics," the shame is
on us, not on them.

Lewis Donaldson welcomed the millennial strain in socialism.
He compared the Socialist agitator to the Christian apostles
who in the "first days . . . turned the world upside down."
Through the work of Blatchford and others the church could
recover its "attitude of expectancy." "We thank these atheists,"
Donaldson wrote, " and hold out to them hands of comradeship
in social service."[35]

The League made significant contributions to the Socialist
cause. Its members provided strong support for Pete Curran at
his successful by-election campaign at Jarrow in the summer of
1907 and they were even more prominent at Colne Valley where
W. B. Graham, the curate at Thongsbridge near Bradford,
was described as the "life and soul of the party" around Grayson.[36] At the ILP conference of 1907 W. E. Moll, a leader in
the League, was elected to the administrative council and served
for three years.

Yet, their religious ties usually limited the extent to which
the Anglican Socialists could identify themselves with the
movement. The decision of the Church Socialist League to
restrict its membership to Anglicans had drawn a sharp rebuke
from the Labour Leader. "What many people had hoped for,"
the writer observed, "was the Socialist clergy, few as they
are, boldly proclaiming themselves on the side of the political
movement against the flesh and devil of Capitalism and
Mammon worship."[37] The League's secretary, Conrad Noel,
denied that church ties prevented full fellowship in the cause,
but this and other exchanges expressed a tension between
religious and ideological commitments which became more and
more evident.

Nonconformist clergymen who joined the movement were
less susceptible to this tension. They came for the most part

from denominations marked by considerable congregational autonomy. And usually they were drawing on an "immanent-ist" theological outlook in which the sharp distinction between the secular and the sacred had broken down. For these clergy-men socialism could appear more readily as a vehicle for God's work in history. Indeed, the new social gospel might pull the clergymen away from organized religion. Such was the case of Frederick J. Swan of the Marsden Congregational chapel in the Colne Valley.

Swan had gained a reputation in the valley as a "gifted preacher and a man of wide culture." He was also a man of very free theological views and early in 1907 he published a book in which he declared that most of the traditional doctrines of Christianity were not essential to the faith. It was time to re-place "old and worn out symbols" with "new and living forms." They key to the new religious outlook, immanence, explained what evolution really was—"namely the Divine development of all creation into a preordained perfection." In Swan's discussion the Socialist movement received special attention. He warned against the tendency of religious people to "regard it with suspicion" and let it grow "beyond all control." "Unless the or-ganized Church gets in closer touch with the new social move-ment and gives a generous welcome to every good work for social reform and more clearly distinguishes between anti-Christian and anti-Ecclesiastical then there is a probability that the Church as an organized society will be left behind, as outgrown clothes are quietly discarded and as useless out of date weapons are put into the museum." "If God be in the world," Swan concluded, "he is behind this development."[38]

Swan's views antagonized the leaders of his congregation and in March 1907 he was forced to resign. Commenting on his "persecution," he observed that "any church which could not include such men as Carlyle, Ruskin and Tolstoy was not a true church." He now felt, as he confessed later, that he "was not making the best of [his] life in the limited sphere of a private enterprise church." Following his resignation Swan went to work for the local Socialist movement. He conducted a series of "missions" on its behalf and served as a contributor, then as editor, of the *Huddersfield Worker*. He played an important role in Grayson's campaign and after the election accepted a position with the Colne Valley Labour League. When Blatchford came to the valley to speak in September 1907 Swan introduced him to "his harvest." Blatchford, like Morris, he observed, possessed "that tremendous faith in human nature and its perfectibility without which all preaching of Socialism is in vain."[39]

Meanwhile, other Nonconformist clergymen were seeking to demonstrate the essential agreement between the Christian faith and socialism. A strong stimulus for this development came from the visit of an American Methodist, J. Stitt Wilson, who opened the first of a series of "social crusades" in the West Riding late in 1907. Employing techniques much like those of the traditional religious revival meeting, Wilson preached socialism. He assured his audiences that there was "nothing in the Universe . . . that human desire can want but cannot be realized" by means of "intellect and love." With local Socialist clergymen, Swan and others, helping him as "attorneys for humanity," Wilson's campaign "ran like fire among the stubble" during the next six months, making many converts for socialism. In Halifax alone more than three hundred names were added to the rolls of the ILP following his "crusade."[40]

In a series of pamphlets Wilson proceeded to translate Christian doctrines into the terms of Socialist ideology. "I do not discuss theological categories," he said in an interview, "I discuss questions of capital and labor and human life and mutual duty . . . The issue at the present time is not theologic but economic." Wilson argued that the "commonplace vocabulary of materialism" was the only medium through which Christian principles could "effect an entrance" into human affairs; the "lowly science of economics" held the key to "world deliverance." Thus he reinterpreted the Christian doctrine of the atonement in social and economic terms. "The individual who acknowledged his complicity with the social crime of capitalism" became part of the "messianic soul, taking upon himself the race sin and bearing it away in his efforts with his brother to establish social justice on earth." Indeed, the Socialist movement was a new expression of the age-old messianic impulse. Its "motive and spirit" alone could save the modern church from "her flirtation and harlotry with the money Gods." The conversion experience had ceased, for Wilson, to be a conquest of personal sin; it was a social struggle to free mankind from the bondage of capitalism. "The individual Socialist [is] in the transitional period—convinced against Capitalism from which personally he cannot extricate himself, and in which he still must live . . . This individual Socialist passes through a personal psychological experience, a social 'new birth,' in his mind and spirit towards all life. This social 'new birth' might not ineptly be called the Socialization of personality."[41]

The attempt to translate Christian doctrines into Socialist ideas found its most influential expression in the work of the popular London Congregationalist, R. J. Campbell. He also developed a new organization and a weekly paper to spread his form of Christian socialism.

Campbell had already established himself as extremely liberal in theological matters. An interview published in the *Daily Mail* late in 1906 had shocked many of his fellow Congregationalists. Here "in plain language, free from all technicalities, he threw over the doctrine of the Fall, the Pauline Plan of Salvation and roundabout a half dozen doctrines that had been the very citadel of the Evangelical faith."[42] This was the beginning of the New Theology controversy which, in early months of 1907, dominated not only the religious press in Britain but much of the secular press as well.

In the course of defending his religious views Campbell suggested that the churches should seek to rescue socialism from materialism. The remark brought a sharp reply from Hardie. "There is in the Socialist movement," he declared, "more of that asceticism, that simplicity of life and love of the natural which characterized the early Christian movement, than there is in the churches." Only if the churches "assimilated the beautiful ethic of Socialism" would they gain "a spiritual message to which man will gladly pay heed." Stung by Hardie's response, Campbell conceded that "if he were not a preacher with his life work already marked out" he would join "the pioneers of the Golden Age in the ranks of the Labour party." The New Theology, he added, was "simply Mr. Hardie's social gospel articulated from a definitely religious standpoint . . . It is the gospel of the humanity of God and the divinity of Man." Hardie then invited Campbell to join in the work of Socialist propaganda and subsequently the two men addressed large audiences in many of the major cities.[43]

To convinced Socialists Campbell's speeches were "thin politically" and made little impression, but their effect on the unconverted was extraordinary. "For a time," Fenner Brockway recalled, "R. J. Campbell, New Theologian and Socialist, was the most popular orator in the land." Impressed with the response to his addresses from the Socialist platform at a time when most of the Nonconformist pulpits were closed to him, Campbell began to view the Socialist movement as "the true Catholic Church although," he added, "it does not know itself by that name." He developed this idea in a book published in the summer of 1907, *Christianity and the Social Order*.[44]

The "decline of the churches" and "the rise of socialism," Campbell argued, were integrally related. "What appears to me to be going on," he wrote, is "simply the revival of Christianity in the form best suited to the modern mind." Indeed, the Socialist movement threatened the present forms of religious life.

> [Socialism] may work the overthrow of the churches as we now know them—that is religious organizations held together by dogmatic statements of belief rather than by the perception of a practical end to be attained . . . The practical end which alone could justify the existence of the Churches is the realization of the Kingdom of God, which only means the reconstruction of society on a basis of mutual helpfulness instead of strife and competition.

Socialism, according to Campbell, would rescue the churches from the "false emphasis on sin" and the belief in an "individualistic salvation in the next world." Socialism, properly understood, meant "the laying down of life in a noble self-forgetfulness to take it up again in a greater sense of solidarity and brightening of the common lot of the human kind."[45]

In the spring of 1908 Campbell founded the League of Progressive Religious and Social Thought in order to "provide spiritual fellowship for those who believe in Christianity without dogma" and "to help spiritualize the social movement of the age."[46] Swan gave up his post with the Colne Valley Labour League to serve as the secretary of the new organization, and it quickly attracted widespread support from Nonconformist clergymen of progressive religious and social views.

The newspaper of the League, the *Christian Commonwealth*, became a significant part of the Socialist press. There was an ILP subeditor and full coverage of the party's affairs. Snowden wrote regularly for the paper. But its columns were open to all who wished to contribute ideas to the movement for social regeneration. Carpenter presented several articles on sun worship. Annie Besant wrote on theosophy. One column carried news of the now declining Ethical Culture movement. Stanton Coit, the leader of the movement and an active member of the ILP, saw the God of the "new theology" as much the same as his own "moral ideal." The paper also courted Blatchford claiming that he was "a Christian at heart" and noting the strength he would bring to "our side." Blatchford held back, for the new theologians had not "mastered the problem of free will." Shaw, in contrast, employed the platform provided by the new theology movement to propagate his own conception of the God of the evolutionary process. During 1908 and 1909 the *Christian Commonwealth* displayed the diverse currents of thought and aspiration making up the broad stream of Ethical Socialism.[47]

To submerge the Christian faith in this stream, however, might mean a tacit surrender of the distinctive claims of the traditional religion. Ethical Socialists and Christian clergymen could find a common ground in the struggle for social justice and the effort to achieve a community characterized by cooperation rather than competition. But this essentially ethical ground left no room for the central Christian pronouncements about sin, grace, salvation, and judgment. Clergymen who reduced their gospel to the terms of Ethical Socialism were, in fact, losing any basis for their ministry. Hence the dilemma of a minister in 1908, identified simply as "one of the earliest members of the ILP," who had converted a number of those in his congregation to socialism through his preaching. As members of the local ILP they were now deserting his Sunday evening services for the meetings of the party. "I am compelled to ask," the minister wrote in the *Labour Leader*, "what is going to become of the church if my making of Socialists is a means of causing the church to be deserted?" "No doubt," he added, "many other Socialist parsons are in the same dilemma." He insisted that it would be a great misfortune if the church were to "disappear in the face of Socialist propaganda," but he had clearly surrendered religious authority. "I know that there is nothing in my church that need keep Socialists out of it . . . No question is asked about beliefs; no one is tied down to any creeds. Everyone is left free to think out his own beliefs and to form his own creed . . . If the majority happen to be Socialists they can socialize the church and all its institutions . . . They could surely if gradually make it a Socialist church." Glasier, commenting on the minister's dilemma, reminded him that socialism brought "no revelation concerning God, creation, death or judgment" and professed "no knowledge of the riddle of the universe or the mystery of life."[48] In their eagerness to demonstrate the close ties between the Christian tradition and the popular form of socialism the Nonconformist clergymen were undermining their religious authority. Those who went very far in identifying socialism and Christianity soon faced a choice of either leaving organized religion and devoting themselves fully to the movement, or retreating to a more orthodox form of Christianity.

Anglican and Nonconformist clergymen who took active roles in the movement also became vulnerable to the growing political dilemmas of the Socialists. The place of the Socialist ideology in the work of the parliamentary Labour Party was, by 1908, increasingly problematical.

SOCIALISM AND PARLIAMENTARY POLITICS, 1906-1908

The most prominent of the ILP leaders in Parliament, Hardie, MacDonald, and Snowden, played important roles in the Labour Party.[49] Hardie accepted the chairmanship of the parliamentary party, despite the misgivings of Glasier. MacDonald continued his work as secretary and also established himself as the party's most effective speaker in the House of Commons. Snowden, too, developed considerable skill in parliamentary debate and became the party's chief spokesman on fiscal or budgetary issues. All three of these leaders served on the Labour Party executive. They were thus well placed to pursue the ILP's goal of converting their trade union allies to Socialist principles. In this new phase of the alliance, however, that goal faded further from sight. The reasons were fairly clear.

The ILP leaders were still worried about the permanence of the alliance. Many of the trade union leaders distrusted the Socialists and argued that the ILP, by dominating the list of candidates and tapping the financial resources of the unions, gained far more from the alliance than it contributed. They attempted at Labour Party conferences to limit the influence of the Socialists, and on one occasion nearly succeeded in restricting the party's parliamentary members to "bona fide" trade unionists.[50] Fear of Liberal reactions also checked any inclination on the part of the ILP leaders to press more vigorously for Socialist objectives. The Liberals had accepted labor candidates in the general election partly to hurt the Conservatives but also because they assumed that they would support Liberal policies in the House of Commons. With their overwhelming majority the Liberals were still in a position to punish, perhaps destroy, the young party. Hence the caution of the ILP leaders. They were little disposed, as MacDonald put it, to return to the "wilderness."[51]

Yet, the ILP leaders were still satisfied with their first year in Parliament. The Liberal government passed a series of bills, giving the trade unions the legislation they needed to undo the consequences of the Taff Vale decision, improving compensation for injured workmen, and permitting local authorities to provide free lunches for schoolchildren. In the process the Liberals accepted the advice, the amendments, and in the case of the free lunches bill, the initiative of the labor and Socialist MP's.

During 1907 Liberal and Labour Party legislative priorities diverged. Through its preoccupation with the problems of education and liquor licensing, the ministry indicated how little real weight the Labour Party possessed in the House. Moreover, it was becoming evident to MacDonald at least that socialism did not provide any clear guidance in legislative matters. "Mere principles of Socialism," he told the ILP's annual conference in the spring, "do not carry very far because they are capable of application in so many different ways and their meaning in relation to existing things is so general."[52]

The difficulty of translating socialism into practical legislative terms was suggested by the fate of the proposal that had become the Labour Party's primary legislative goal—the Unemployed Workmen Bill. Introduced into the House by MacDonald in July 1907, the bill was hailed by some Socialists as bringing a "new day." MacDonald himself, in a pamphlet designed to publicize the bill, called it the "beginning of the Socialist state."[53] The treatment of the measure in Parliament invites examination because it illuminated the problem of translating the ILP's Socialist ideology into practical political terms.

Unemployment had been a critical issue for both the Socialists and the trade unionists. Socialists insisted that unemployment would only disappear with the abolition of capitalism, but the ILP had developed proposals designed to alleviate the plight of those without work under the existing economic system. And in 1905 ILP leaders and Social Democrats had cooperated in developing a nationwide agitation on behalf of the "right to work." Trade unionist approaches to the problem differed, placing the major stress on the need to limit hours in order to spread the work. But during 1905 the ILP Socialists and the trade union leaders had arrived at a common program which incorporated their different remedies. In the same year the Conservative government passed the Unemployed Workmen Act, which acknowledged greater public responsibility for the problem by providing funds for local distress committees to aid the unemployed. The Conservative legislation made no concessions to the proposals of the labor and Socialist leaders and was scheduled to terminate in 1908. Within this context the Labour Party leaders attempted to persuade the Liberals to deal more vigorously with the problem.[54]

By 1907, having failed to gain Liberal support for their efforts to amend the previous legislation, the Labour Party leaders developed their own bill. Presented by MacDonald, who had helped draft the bill, it included provisions for a central unemployment authority with a staff of experts to plan public works and coordinate the efforts of local authorities. Its crucial third clause required that local unemployment committees either find work for those seeking it or maintain them in the "necessaries of life." The pace of legislative activity precluded a second reading of the bill in the 1907 session and it did not receive extended debate until it was reintroduced in March 1908.

Socialism figured prominently in the debate. Fred Maddison, a "Lib Lab" opponent of the measure, called it the "first fruits of Socialist agitation" and warned that it would lead to a degree of state control over the "lives of the workers, to which no self-respecting people would submit." His fears, which centered on the right-to-work clause, were echoed by Herbert Asquith, now acting head of the government. The application of the clause, he argued, would involve "the complete ultimate control by the State of the full machinery of production." Victor Grayson, on the other hand, speaking in support of the bill, noted its limitations from a Socialist standpoint. The "organic social problem of the unemployed," he declared, would only be solved when the "means of production, distribution, and exchange . . . were in the hands of the people."[55]

Yet, the general tendency of the debate was to blur, indeed deny, these sharp ideological distinctions. Thus P. W. Wilson, a Liberal who introduced the bill for the Labour Party, did so as a "convinced Liberal" whose faith was "based on respect for the individual." He viewed the measure as "the only hint of a positive policy" on behalf of the unemployed. And William Brace, a trade unionist and member of the Labour Party, argued that the bill simply provided "a rallying ground of all reformers who wanted to deal with the unemployed problem in a way which would carry hope." He was "not a Socialist" but he believed in the principle of the right to work; it offered "new dignity and new hope to human life." Another Liberal, E. G. Hemmerde, opposed the bill, not because he rejected the right-to-work principle or, indeed, "any amount of Socialist measures," but because he did not think it provided any solution to the problem of the unemployed.[56]

Much of the discussion focused, in fact, on the ambiguities of what was admittedly a poorly drafted bill, and on its practical effects. Would it weaken the trade unions? Was it reasonable to assume that local authorities could develop meaningful public work projects? What level of wages was appropriate for those accepting such work? The discussion displayed the mixture of arguments—ideological, moral, and rational, interested and disinterested—characteristic of serious political debate.

MacDonald attempted to play down the Socialistic aspects of the bill and stress purely practical considerations. Two years earlier he had noted that parliamentary activity required a "special phraseology and method." His speech on behalf of the Labour Party measure illustrated his approach to legislative issues. Responding to those who saw the "nightmare of Socialism" in the right-to-work principle, he claimed that the principle was inherent in the Conservative act of 1905. This Fabian-like argument that the measure before the House was simply a logical extension of a legislative process already under way was vigorously rejected by the Conservative sponsor of the 1905 act, Walter Long. Not only was Long indignant over the attempt to "give to me . . . the credit" for aiding the Socialist movement but he warned MacDonald that his tactics would hinder efforts to develop progressive legislation.[57]

The power of the Liberals in the House of Commons ensured the overwhelming defeat of the Labour Party's bill. But for the Socialists the results of the parliamentary debate were not entirely negative. They had secured the support of their trade union allies for a principle, the right to work, which though admittedly a mere palliative from the Socialist standpoint, represented an important step toward fuller public responsibility for those victimized by economic fluctuations. Moreover, sixty-five Liberals broke away from their party leadership to vote for the bill. Increasingly restive over the failure of their party to confront the problem of the unemployed, these Liberals gave some credence to MacDonald's belief that there were no serious barriers to the growth of a broadly based progressive party moving toward socialism. At the same time the Labour Party initiative in the House, together with the mounting nationwide Socialist agitation over the plight of the unemployed during 1907 and 1908, helped push the Liberal leaders toward new remedies.

The right-to-work principle did not, however, go very far

to connect the "primary sentiments" and "fine phrases" of the Socialists, as MacDonald put it, to "the conditions of present day capitalism." It was, a writer in the *Socialist Review* conceded, more in the nature of a manifesto than a statement of practical policy. The episode pointed up once more the inability of the ILP Socialists up to this time to cultivate the middle ground of legislative politics effectively. Indeed, initiative in dealing with unemployment from a Socialist standpoint soon passed to the Fabians while the Liberals were already scouting different approaches to the problem.[58]

For a growing number of the ILP rank and file, the failure of the Socialists in Parliament to make headway on the unemployment issue was not to be attributed simply to their political impotence or their intellectual shortcomings, but rather to their timidity. During 1907 and 1908 a new wave of criticism rose within the party, directly mainly at MacDonald, who had now added the chairmanship of the ILP to his other responsibilities. The challenge to MacDonald's leadership had been initiated in the spring of 1907 by H. Russell Smart.

Smart, a commercial traveler by occupation, was one of the pioneer members of the ILP. He had served on the administrative council and he had edited the *ILP News*. An Ethical Socialist, he anticipated the "extension of the loving communism prevailing in the highest type of family life" into "the whole community." But from his pamphlet "Socialism and the Drink Question," published in 1890, to his "Socialism and the Middle Classes," twenty years later, Smart concentrated on proposals designed to advance the material welfare of the workers. As long as the party was faithful to such "living questions" as the right to work, the minimum wage, and pensions for the sick and aged, he would rather work for it than for a party of "sentimental idealists who turn deaf ears to the cry of poverty clamoring at the door." By May 1907, however, Smart had concluded that there was a "fatal rot" in the party which must be arrested before it was too late.[59]

To the task of criticizing the tactics of the ILP leaders Smart brought intelligence and vigor. Smart's political experience was limited and many of his views were naive. But he recognized the growing divergence between the activities of the Socialists in

Parliament and their Socialist principles. He attacked MacDonald especially for his reluctance to articulate these principles in the House. MacDonald, according to Smart, was essentially an administrator and lacked "imagination and audacity." He cited MacDonald's approach to the right-to-work bill as an example of his shortcomings; the bill was a "great moral cry for justice." It should be used to "raise in the clearest and most definite manner, and in practical form, a social issue which would separate the country into two political camps." The Labour Party, he charged, was drifting into "mere radicalism."[60]

MacDonald responded. He denied Smart's claim that the people were "too far off and indifferent to catch anything but broad effects," and that they would rally only to "a cry." "If it is true, I grant that my Parliamentary policy will not be accepted by the ILP, and in my pessimistic moments I sometimes think that it is true. But I think it underestimates the ILP intelligence. If the ILP active spirits understand and support us—as surely they must—the inert mass must follow. But Smart says no. The ILP needs the tipple of political alcoholism—phrases, demonstrations, and partisan fighting."[61] It was not a fair reply. But it indicated the contrast between MacDonald the politician, attuned to the practical possibilities of the parliamentary situation, and Smart, who viewed political activity in the light of the advance of Socialist principles.

The contrast was also increasingly evident at the level of electoral politics during 1907 and 1908. Advocates of a principled approach could take heart in the by-election victory of Grayson in the summer of 1907. But in the fall another by-election campaign demonstrated the political liabilities that might be attached to the Socialist commitment. The contest in the Kirkdale division of Liverpool suggested that the Labour Party could, at least in the special circumstances prevailing in this constituency, be greatly damaged by its association with socialism.

At Kirkdale, a working class district, the Liberals stepped aside as they had at the general election to allow labor a straight fight with the Conservatives. The Labour Party candidate, John Hill, was not a Socialist. But his campaign drew strong support from the movement, still excited by the successful contests at

Jarrow and the Colne Valley in the summer. Faced with a barrage of Socialist enthusiasm, the Conservatives seized on an issue which had long been a major factor in the voting habits of the Liverpool working classes—religion.

> The Socialists were receiving the support of the *Clarion* and out of that paper extracts from Robert Blatchford's atheistic writings were carefully selected and distributed wholesale in the form of handbills. From that moment the fate of the Socialist candidate was sealed. The Protestantism always latent in the Liverpool masses was aroused. Before the Socialist candidate quite knew what had happened he found himself regarded, not only as one who denied the Bible, but as an advocate of free love and the State ownership of children.

The Conservatives retained the seat by a slightly increased margin and MacDonald admitted to one of their leaders that the "election has been won by your atheistical pamphlet."[62]

The Kirkdale setback coincided with the emergence of a much more concerted public opposition to socialism than the movement had encountered thus far. Heretofore, popular anti-Socialist propaganda had been mainly the work of aroused individuals like W. H. Mallock or George Brooks, or of obscure religious writers. Following the general election the Harmsworth press began to criticize socialism and during the first half of 1907 the Socialist Sunday schools came under attack. But with the Grayson victory the Conservatives—and many Liberals—became alarmed. The *Daily Express* devoted a series of articles to the threat of socialism and other newspapers took up the cry. Over the next several years an Anti-Socialist Union published scores of tracts and pamphlets, many of which featured damaging quotations on religion or marriage from Blatchford, Bax, or prominent continental Socialists. The National Union of Conservative Associations emulated the *Clarion* organization with vans, street meetings, scouts, and posters to fight socialism. Catholic writers took an important part in this counter propaganda for they were sensitive to the appeal of socialism to the Irish workers. Joseph Rickaby, a Jesuit priest, summed up their fears. "Priests who work in the large towns of the North declare that our Christian young men are 'dying like flies' of Socialism. First they begin to tamper with Socialism and still come to Church . . . finally Socialism has become their religion and has supplanted the faith of their baptism as it is ultimately designed to do."[63]

The Kirkdale by-election and the anti-Socialist campaign which followed exposed once more the disagreements between the various Socialist groups. Social Democrats responded to the charges of atheism by taking refuge in a strictly economic definition of socialism. Questions of religion, like those dealing with sexual relationships, were strictly private matters. But the issue again provoked a spirited discussion in the correspondence columns of *Justice*, with Bax once more challenging the official position.[64]

Blatchford, like Bax, welcomed the confrontation. He conceded that "my infidelity has cost Labour the Kirkdale seat." But he was unrepentant and again defended his position. If Socialists hedged on the religious question they would "court defeat." He received support from a new Socialist weekly, the *New Age*, which was becoming an important forum for Socialist intellectuals. Referring to the attack on the Socialists at Kirkdale, an editorial urged them not to retreat, for "nothing is alien" to socialism.[65]

The ILP leaders in contrast deplored the intrusion of the religious issue, and Glasier attempted to launch a counteroffensive in the columns of the *Labour Leader*. He presented a series of articles on prominent Tories and Liberals, past and present, who held heterodox views on religion and sex. Yet, he also conceded that there were ILP branches whose bookstalls were "simply emporiums of Rationalist Press publications," and he urged the movement to "sweep completely from our propaganda all controversy about religious creeds."[66] Glasier did not, however, moderate his own claims about the religious significance of socialism or criticize those who claimed for it the sanction of Christianity.

For the Ethical Socialists in the ILP the tension between their political and their ideological commitments was becoming acute. Hardie was increasingly worried about the threat that the party's parliamentary activity posed to its socialist aims. His decision not to seek reelection to the position of chairman of the party was in part at least a reflection of this concern. "I shall be able to do better work for the Socialist side of the movement," he wrote, "as a free lance, unburdened by the responsibilities of office." Hardie said he would "oppose anything that savors of disloyalty to our trade union allies," but the ILP men must not allow themselves "to forget that the object we have in view is socialism." Frank Smith, Hardie's closest associate in these years, confided to Glasier that they might even have to "come out and be separate."[67]

When the ILP met at Huddersfield for its annual conference in April 1908, many observers expected a major assault on the party's policies. The handling of the Grayson candidacy the previous summer, the recent defeat of the right-to-work bill, and the impotence of the Labour Party in Parliament had generated considerable discontent in the rank and file. But the strong attack on the ILP policy did not materialize. It was forestalled to some extent by the conciliatory attitude of the leaders. The main debate centered on the Colne Valley episode and it ended in a compromise. Grayson was not required to sign the Labour Party constitution, but he was granted the regular salary paid to the ILP's parliamentary representatives in return for his agreement to cooperate with the Labour Party in the House.

In his address as chairman, MacDonald attempted to reconcile the divergent attitudes within the ILP. The party's role, he said, was twofold; it must "remain propagandist like John the Baptist" and "political like the Apostle Paul." It would be a "bad day for Socialism in this country," he added, "if ever the two missions became separated." While he attempted to give the visionary side of the ILP its due, he defended the work of the men in Parliament and restated his own form of Fabian gradualism. The "giddy and enticing prospects" raised by electoral successes should not divert the ILP from its main task of developing socialism as a "rational theory of social organization" and working "that theory into present day policy."[68]

The harmony of the Huddersfield conference proved temporary. Within a few weeks the criticism of the ILP leaders and their policies was renewed. It opened a period of conflict within the party which reached a climax a year later at the Edinburgh conference. But the ensuing controversy indicated that the ILP's ethically centered socialism was virtually exhausted.

5

THE EXHAUSTION
OF ETHICAL SOCIALISM

EARLY LEADERS of the Socialist movement had anticipated the crisis which overtook the ILP during 1908. Writing in 1888, William Morris had warned that the entrance of the Socialists into Parliament would bring the "almost inevitable danger" that they would become absorbed in the struggle for immediate gains and lose sight of their "ultimate aims." Shaw, writing from a different perspective a decade later, also had anticipated the crisis.

> For when the reality at last comes to men who have been nursed on the dramatization of it, they do not recognize it. Its prosaic aspect revolts them; and since it must necessarily come by penurious installments—each maimed by the inevitable compromise with powerful hostile interests—its advent has neither the splendid magnitude nor the absolute integrity of principle, dramatic and religious, necessary to impress them.[1]

During 1908 and 1909 the dual impulses within the ILP separated under the pressure of its political role. Its members began to choose between the party's Socialist vision and its drive, reinforced by the alliance with the trade unionists, to advance the immediate interests of the workers. For Hardie and Glasier, who struggled unsuccessfully to find a meaningful relationship between the party's socialism and its political activity the years ahead were especially painful. The deepening dilem-

mas of the movement were also reflected in the personal disintegration of its most effective younger spokesman—Victor
Grayson. Meanwhile, many of the clergymen who had been
drawn to the Socialist cause were forced to reexamine its re- ·
lationship to Christianity. But the exhaustion of Ethical Socialism prompted a few of its adherents to search for new religious or philosophical foundations for the movement.

The Crisis of the ILP, 1908-1909

"Who says organization," wrote Robert Michels in 1911,
"says oligarchy." In his classic study of European Socialist
parties in the early years of the century Michels found that the
psychological and administrative pressures inherent in modern
democratic political organization led invariably to domination
by a few leaders. The development of the ILP corresponded
closely to the pattern described by Michels. During the party's
short history the delegates to the annual conference, given sov-
ereign authority by the constitution, had seen initiative in making policy pass to the National Administrative Council. The
drift toward centralized control was not, as Michels recognized,
the outcome of conscious designs by the leaders; in the ILP it
proceeded in the face of a deterioration of their personal relationships. Moreover the shift of power to the center also reflected wider developments in British political life as national
issues were increasingly emphasized at the expense of local
problems and the influence of local personalities.[2]

The decline of democratic or conference control over the
ILP's policies was felt most acutely by some of the veteran members of the party— Smart, Hobson, Joseph Burgess, and others—
who had not risen to positions of official leadership. Less burdened by practical responsibilities and less solicitous of the interests of the trade unionists, they remained closer to the letter
and spirit of the party's propaganda. During the course of 1908
they set out to alter the organization of the ILP in such a way
as to make it a true vehicle for Socialist principles.

The effort was led by Smart. A few weeks after the Huddersfield conference in 1908 he renewed his attack on the ILP
leaders, charging that they had abandoned the idea of a "sover-
eign conference" for a "cabinet system." He maintained that

basic issues confronting the ILP, such as electoral policy and parliamentary strategy, were not discussed in the report of the Administrative Council or even at the council's meetings. The ILP, he concluded, had become a "mere machine for registering the decrees of three or four able men."[3]

Glasier responded with an attack on Smart's character. He accused him of resigning from the council "during the darkest days of the party's history" and attempting to return in the "floodtime of prosperity." But Margaret McMillan, a member of the council, commended Smart for his "great penetration" and his freedom from "personal animosity." She noted, however, the great difficulties of the council's work and its increasingly complex administrative tasks, as well as the anxieties and limitations produced by the political alliance. These factors explained why five men (she included T. D. Benson, the party treasurer) were "the leaders and umpires on every question."

> These decide who shall be elected for offices and what shall be done generally. Between them there is mutual understanding which is not, I think, based entirely on personal friendship. Their ascendancy was won doubtless by great and long service to the people, and it is maintained also, probably by their remarkable knowledge of all that takes place within the movement . . . The situation cannot have been created deliberately. It was created by circumstances over which neither party or leaders have any control. It is quite accurately described by Mr. Russell Smart.

Miss McMillan also observed that "the people, by their unbounded and indiscriminate admiration, had induced an intolerance of criticism" among the leaders.[4]

Smart developed several proposals designed to restore democratic control over the council as well as over the ILP men in Parliament. He recommended that salaried officials of the party, including the MP's be excluded from the council, that council members be limited to three year terms, and that they be elected on a regional basis rather than by the delegates at the annual conferences. Smart argued that a council reconstructed in this way would be effective in supervising the actions of the MP's. And during the fall of 1908 he set out to mobilize branch support for these proposals; they were subsequently embodied in a series of resolutions prepared for the 1909 conference at Edinburgh.[5]

In the meantime the struggle to extricate the ILP from its compromising political course centered on a series of unauthorized parliamentary candidates put up by local branches. Grayson's victory a year earlier encouraged Socialists in several areas to exaggerate their own chances for success, and they refused to accept the decisions of the ILP council or the Labour Party. The local initiatives also expressed a new determination to give priority to Socialist propaganda. Social Democrats and *Clarion* groups strongly supported this line of action. In April 1908, after the ILP had declined to contest a seat in Manchester, the local Socialists decided to support the Social Democrat, Dan Irving. Irving also received, despite the misgivings of the ILP leaders, "fraternal greetings" from the delegates at the Huddersfield conference then in session. His poll was humiliating to the Socialist cause. Irving drew only 276 votes out of the more than 11,000 cast, prompting MacDonald to scold the ILP for associating itself with the fight "simply because someone lisping the shibboleths of Socialism has sounded a trumpet."[6]

Other episodes followed. At Dundee in May the local Socialists and labor leaders defied the executive of the Labour Party and put up a candidate. At Pudsey in June the decision of the ILP's administrative council to stay out of an electoral fight was ignored by the local branches. And at Newcastle in September the local men again rejected a decision by the Labour Party. Here the unauthorized candidate was Hartley and he drew support from all sections of the movement—the ILP, the Social Democrats, the *Clarion* men, and an enthusiastic group of Socialist clergy. Socialist unity, *Justice* announced, "has arrived."[7]

The polls of these candidates were not large but they probably cost the Liberals both the Pudsey and the Newcastle seats. Many Socialists cheered the Liberal losses, convinced that a heightened sense of antagonism between the parties was necessary for Socialist independence. For the ILP leaders, however, these developments were embarrassing and, indeed, dangerous. They threatened, MacDonald told the members of the NAC, the existence of the ILP as a "national party with a national policy." Branches which ignored the decisions of the NAC and the Labour Party, to which they professed loyalty, were guilty, he claimed, of "political cynicism."[8]

Glasier launched a strong attack on the wildcat candidacies. The Pudsey campaign, he wrote, carried the "Socialist flag back eleven years" to the Barnsley by-election of 1897 where the ILP had attempted unsuccessfully to win the support of the Liberal trade unionists.[9] Glasier criticized the Newcastle Socialists for jeopardizing the position of the Labour Party MP who had already gained, through the abstention of the Liberals, the other seat in the constituency.

MacDonald was more willing to acknowledge the party's dilemma. He conceded that local Socialist morale was damaged by decisions not to contest seats. But he insisted that the "fighting appetites" had to be checked in favor of the "whole national policy of the party." The annual conferences, MacDonald argued, should settle the question of local autonomy. In the meantime the administrative council was simply "practicing the policy it was elected to guard." This policy opposed a "general fight."[10]

The critics, led now by Burgess, argued that the party conferences had not spoken on the specific question of by-elections. The ILP leaders, he charged, were "thoroughly out of touch . . . with local opinion." In their eagerness to please their trade union allies they were discouraging potential ILP candidates and losing their independence. Burgess was still convinced that the ILP could make the Labour Party "precisely what it desires" but only if it continued to stand clearly for Socialist principles. In the face of the "shameless calculations" of their leaders, he concluded, the true Socialists in the ILP might "have to go into the wilderness." Sam Hobson now recommended a break with the trade unions, convinced that the remnant would be "infinitely stronger as a fighting force."[11]

The Newcastle by-election contest was an important stage in the growing crisis within the ILP. Not only were the opponents of the party's electoral policy drawing together, but they were also developing an alternative view of the function of the Socialist in Parliament. If Hartley was elected, Grayson declared in the course of the campaign, the two of them would "make the workings of Parliament impossible while we are in it." "If they throw me out," he added, "I shall resign, and go back to the Colne Valley and be sent again and be thrown out again."[12] Three weeks after the Newcastle poll Grayson put this new obstructionist tactic into practice.

On October 15 the House of Commons was discussing a licensing bill designed by the Liberal ministry to check the evils of the drink traffic. Grayson had come in late, taken a seat on one of the Labour Party benches, and "with his green Tyrolese hat pulled low over his forehead, listened with a gloomy expression to the debate." Ten minutes later, "his face flushed with excitement," he leaped to his feet to demand that the House immediately turn its attention to the plight of the unemployed. Informed by the Speaker that the rules governing debate made his request impossible, Grayson declared that he would not "be bound by such rules." Then, amid cries of order from all parts of the House, he attempted to plead the case of those without work. When the Sergeant of Arms stepped forward to remove him Grayson offered no resistance, delaying his exit only to charge that the labor members were traitors to their class. The next day Grayson again defied parliamentary procedure to demand that the House do something for the people who were "starving wholesale." He was, therefore, "named" and suspended for the remainder of the 1908 session. On departing from the House, Grayson asserted that he had "gained in dignity by leaving" and then shouted that it was a "house of murderers."[13]

Grayson's scenes in Parliament sent a wave of excitement through the movement and he became more than ever a rallying point for opposition to the official policies of the ILP. Hundreds of telegrams and letters, as well as branch resolutions, poured into the Socialist newspapers. The great majority of these commended Grayson. Blatchford thanked him "from the bottom of my heart." Hyndman declared that he had "divided the sheep from the goats" and shown that the country was in "a never ending class war;" he praised Grayson for his pluck and common sense. Shaw declared that Grayson was "as completely justified as Plimsoll."[14]

The ILP leaders, on the other hand, were furious. Snowden called the scenes "theatrical and contemptible," Hardie described them as "part of a campaign designed to produce discord in the ranks," and MacDonald denounced the "silly tub thumping spirit of anarchy." Fred Jowett complained that Grayson had made no attempt to confide in or cooperate with his Socialist colleagues.[15]

Grayson's action hastened the realignment of groups already under way within the movement. The rebellious elements among the Ethical Socialists drew closer to the Social Democrats. During the closing months of 1908 Grayson, Blatchford and Hyndman appeared together frequently on Socialist platforms and were hailed as the new "Socialist triumvirate."

The ILP leaders were in a difficult position. Their policies were endangered not only by the rebels within the party but by the trade union section of the Labour Party. In the fall of 1908 the trade unionists were complaining again that they were "taking second place in the matter of candidates to the ILP." To Hardie, observing the working of the alliance, it seemed at times as though the fruits of the Socialists' struggle were "being garnered by men who were never of us."[16]

Still, the major threat to the ILP was coming from its own ranks. "It would seem," Glasier wrote in October, "as if we had been nourishing them too much in mere aggressiveness and we are reaping the harvest." He found it "deeply humiliating" that there should be "an appearance of doubt as to the choice between us" and, referring to Grayson, the "footlight heroics of a blatant windbag." But Glasier and the other leaders were contending with a form of Socialist enthusiasm much like that which had energized the ILP in its early years. It came in large part from new converts; Grayson claimed in fact that he spoke for "a younger generation of Socialists." After Katharine Glasier had been "hooted down" and prevented from speaking in Liverpool by a group shouting "Dare to be Grayson," she blamed the episode on the "rush of new recruits into our movement who know nothing about the ILP's rise." Snowden would maintain in the spring of 1909 that a third of the party's membership had come in within the past year.[17]

The influx of new young members accentuated an important element in the ILP's outlook. From the beginning the party had appealed mainly to men and women in their thirties or younger. A romantic belief in the trustworthiness of spontaneous youthful feeling had been a part of Ethical Socialism. "The first inspirations of youth," one Socialist writer declared, were "often the nearest to the truth. They are fresh from nature. The prison walls of custom have not yet closed around them." Even Hardie expressed his fear that the movement might be stalled by its "aged retainers." But the upsurge of youthful enthusiasm was now threatening the ILP's hard won political position.[18]

The rebellious spirit gathering around Grayson dismayed Smart and those who were supporting his effort to reform the party, for it endangered the labor alliance, on behalf of which, Smart observed, "some of us have devoted the efforts of half a lifetime." While he continued to concentrate on the task of winning broad support for a series of resolutions to overcome "oligarchic rule" in the party, Smart condemned Grayson's work as "essentially disruptive and reactionary." The threat to separate labor and socialism, he argued, played into the hands of the leaders by forcing the moderate critics to rally to their side. As the 1909 conference grew near, Smart disassociated his own campaign from the "noisy extremists" and "wreckers" and appealed to MacDonald to "treat us as comrades and carry us with you through argument." The ILP, he said, could not "be driven against the essential character of the men who made it." No one, Smart said to MacDonald, could "heal our sores as well as you." But MacDonald was no longer inclined toward conciliation. He even attempted to stop the circulation of Smart's resolutions to the branches, an action which drew a sharp rebuke from another veteran, S. D. Shallard. "In the early days," Shallard declared, such an "assumption of authority on the part of any chairman would have speedily ended his term in office."[19]

The ILP conference at Edinburgh early in April 1909 brought the disputes to a climax as the delegates were presented with a series of resolutions dealing with the makeup of the administrative council, electoral policy, and parliamentary tactics. The political alliance with the trade unionists was not seriously challenged; a resolution to end it secured only eight votes. But the other polls revealed a significant division of opinion. A resolution to exclude the party's MP's from the administrative council was defeated 265 to 158, and a motion to give ILP branches freedom to put up candidates without the council's authorization lost 244 to 136. An effort to commit the Labour Party to a tactic of obstructionism if the Liberals failed to enact a right-to-work bill was voted down 193 to 136.

The leaders were thus vindicated on all the major policy questions. But there was a consistent vote of a third or more of the delegates against the official policy. Toward the end of the conference, moreover, a majority voted to refer back a paragraph in the council's annual report which had censured Grayson and canceled his speaking engagements for the ILP because he had refused to share a platform with Hardie at a London meeting. MacDonald, Hardie, Snowden, and Glasier chose to interpret the referral as a censure of themselves and immediately resigned their party posts. They announced that they would enter the ranks and fight what MacDonald called the "movement of irresponsibility within the party."[20] Shocked, the delegates quickly reversed their vote and called on the leaders to reconsider. But the resignations stood.

The action of the "big four" was designed, as Snowden observed, to restore discipline.[21] In a measure it succeeded; the critics were routed while the leaders, at least MacDonald, Hardie, and Snowden, lost little of their influence in the party. But it was something of a pyrrhic victory. The resignations virtually destroyed the possibility of constructive debate on the issues the reformers had raised. The ILP still provided most of the propaganda and organizing activity within the alliance and its leaders had been able to resist any move to build local branches of the Labour Party. But unless the ILP could maintain a strong Socialist identity it would become superfluous. For the Labour Party was quite capable of taking over the drive to advance the immediate interests of the workers.

The resignations embittered critics within the ILP. Smart accused the leaders of an attempt to "dragoon the movement into passive obedience." "Never once have they tried conciliation . . . And so they have led us from one disaster to another.

They have weakened our influence over the country, wasted our money, nearly wrecked our paper . . . and now like unfaithful officers abandoned the ship because the crew complains of unskilful management." James Allan, one of the ILP's wealthy middle class supporters, agreed with Smart. And he warned the leaders that they were endangering, through their political policies, the support of the "unorganized Socialists, and the middle class." A party which could not carry these groups, he maintained, would be as little likely to bring "a permanent solution to the social problem as armed revolution itself."[22]

Smart believed that a truly democratic structure would prevent the ILP from reaching a condition, characteristic of the Liberals and the Conservatives, where there would be "no room in it for men of intellect and character." Unless the ILP could control its parliamentary representatives it would become "merely the ladder by which clever and . . . self-seeking politicians may climb to office." The reform of the party was crucial, not only for the "future of the movement," but for the reform of British political life as a whole.[23] But proposals for a party organization capable of transmitting Socialist principles clearly and directly into the political process did not go very far toward meeting the problems now confronting the ILP.

Ten years of political cooperation with the trade unionists had dispelled the initial hopes of the ILP leaders that they would rapidly convert their allies to socialism. The trade unionists had entered the alliance mainly to defend their economic position; they had refused to adopt a systematic political program, Socialist or other, in order to respond pragmatically to current issues in the light of working class interests. Despite some support for schemes of nationalization, most of the trade union leaders had not moved very far from the "labourist" outlook which accepted the legitimacy of the capitalistic order. Unable to alter in any fundamental way the beliefs of their allies, the ILP leaders had increasingly submitted to the trade union conception of working class advance; they had become captives of the alliance.[24]

One middle class member of the ILP's administrative council, R. C. K. Ensor, argued that the party would be rescued from its impasse and the "slavery of phrases" by the Fabian element it had absorbed.[25] But during 1909 the ILP leaders turned instead back to the simple version of Marxism which had helped to inspire the movement toward independent political action twenty years earlier. Marxism, with its strong emphasis on class interests, provided a sharper ideological identity and a clearer justification for the position in which the ILP now found itself.

Paradoxically it was MacDonald, the most Fabian of the ILP leaders, who prompted the retreat towards Marxism. In the spring of 1908 he published in the *Socialist Review* selections from the correspondence of Engels which condemned the policies of the British Social Democrats and urged a course of action much like that adopted by the ILP. Other attempts to attach the prestige of Marx and Engels to the ILP and the Labour Party followed. A manifesto issued by the ILP leaders after their resignations contended that the party had been formed "by Socialists who desired to follow the Marxian policy of uniting the working classes into an independent party for the conquest of political power." And a short time later, when Hardie wrote a defense of the labor alliance, he claimed that the ILP "and even more the Labour party are . . . in the direct line of apostolic succession from Marx and the other great master minds of Socialist theory and policy." The Labour Party, he insisted, was the "only expression of orthodox Marxian Socialist tactics in Great Britain." Even Glasier came down on the side of the Marxist theory of value while reasserting at the same time the ideal of brotherhood.[26]

Social Democrats viewed the ILP's patronage of Marx with a mixture of amusement and scorn. It was, a columnist for *Justice* observed, analogous to the discovery of the "bourgeois gentleman" that he had been speaking prose all his life.[27] Certainly the turn toward Marx did not indicate any serious search for theoretical insight or political guidance. It served, ironically, as a rationalization for the political impasse into which the alliance with the trade unionists had carried the ILP Socialists.

By the spring of 1909, moreover, the Socialist revival was over. Each succeeding ILP conference recorded a decline of members, branches, and financial reserves. Within a year there was a feeling generally in the movement that socialism was again in a slump. The phenomena of the post-1895 period reappeared. Socialist meetings in the West Riding had to be canceled because the Socialists were off to the football matches. Some ILP branches and clubs fell apart in this period through excessive interests in social activity, or in "beer and Billiards."[28]

Developments over the next few years further diminished the influence of the Socialists within the Labour Party. The decision of the Miners Federation of Great Britain, the largest single block of organized workers, to join the Labour Party greatly strengthened the pragmatic trade union orientation of the party. A new judicial decision, the Osborne Judgment of 1909, denied the legality of the financial support given to the Labour Party by the trade unions and made the party dependent on the Liberals for remedial legislation. The Labour Party also drew closer to the Liberals during their struggle against the obstructive role of the House of Lords in legislative affairs. And finally, the Liberal government's new program for social reform, expressed in the Lloyd George budget of 1909 and the National Insurance Act of 1911, damaged the claims of the Socialists that they held the key to social progress. "A big slice of the ILP's immediate program," Glasier conceded, had been given legislative form.[29]

The dilemmas of the ILP deepened in the years just ahead. The two general elections of 1910, in which the Labour Party was hard pressed to hold its seats, seemed to its critics to demonstrate the sterility of the ILP's policies. In the summer of 1911 four members of the NAC resigned, charging that the party was, through its "suicidal revisionist policy . . . bartering the soul of a great cause for the off chance of an occasional bare bone."[30] A short time later a section of the ILP, including Grayson, Smart, and Hall, broke away to join the Marxists of the SDP and the *Clarion* groups in forming a new Socialist party (a development which belongs to the history of British Social Democracy).

During the years just before the war the efforts of Hardie, Snowden, Jowett, and others enabled the ILP to reassert something of its Socialist mission within the Labour Party. But only the outbreak of the war, according to one historian of the ILP, saved the party from further decline and perhaps extinction.[31] The ILP's strong pacifist stand during the war helped solidify its ranks and attract new recruits. They came, however, mainly from the middle class while the party's opposition to the war cost it a substantial part of its working class following. Indeed, its influence within the Labour Party rapidly diminished. And while the ILP would undergo an ideological revitalization in the postwar years its renewed commitment to socialism served in the long run to widen its distance from the main course of the Labour Party.

The plight of the ILP in the years just before World War I presented particular dilemmas for Hardie, Glasier, and Mac-Donald. As in earlier years their responses were shaped both by their individual temperaments and by their special roles in the movement. But their attempts to cope with the growing divorce between the party's ideological and political commitments throw further light on the decline of Ethical Socialism.

THE DILEMMAS OF LEADERSHIP: *Hardie, Glasier, and MacDonald*

Hardie's later years were marked by deepening frustration. His leadership of the parliamentary Labour Party during 1906 and 1907 had been, by all accounts, a failure. Perhaps his career as an agitator, perhaps personal shortcomings, disqualified him for the political role into which he had been thrust. But his firm though sometimes quixotic determination to follow his own judgment rather than the needs of party unity or the demands of practical politics, can also be traced to his continuing commitment to a Socialist vision which could not be equated with the interests of the trade unionists. From time to time he contemplated a break with the Labour Party so that the Socialists who "believed in fighting" could "go together on their own." He was much more willing than the other ILP leaders to compromise with the rebels within the party; concessions might be necessary, he told Glasier, in order "to save *our* party."[32]

But Hardie followed an erratic course. At times, as at Edinburgh and its immediate aftermath, his socialism seemed to dissolve into mere "labourism."

We no longer come as missionaries to the trade unionist with the suspicion lurking in his mind that we are trying to divert him from the true political faith and convert him to some heterodox belief of our own; we come to him as part of his own movement, proclaiming his own gospel . . .

To defend such a position he even employed the rhetoric of Marxism. "I shall end my political career as I began it, by raising the old slogan—workers of the world unite; you have all to gain and nothing to lose but your chains." In the face of attacks on the party's leaders Hardie resorted to irrational forms of self-justification. The "same instinct which leads a herd of buffalo or a pack of wolves to follow the oldest and strongest of the herd or pack," he wrote, "operates in . . . a great democratic movement."[33]

Some of his critics like Smart, who had become targets of Hardie's abuse, were unwilling to respond in kind, "out of respect and reverence" for his service to the cause. A writer in the *New Age* was less restrained.

You have written the epitaph of your dead self as a Socialist prophet and proclaimed your new career as a third rate politician . . . The rank and file may still revere you; they may even yet a little longer follow you. But . . . the farce of combining platform Socialism with Parliamentary dignity and inaction is played out. Your attempt to straddle both has failed. You must choose the one or the other.[34]

Through the two general elections of 1910 Hardie continued to play the political game, pitching his electoral appeal in the terms necessary to hold his working class constituents in Wales. But he was returning, in Kenneth Morgan's words, to "his most natural role as the great agitator and propagandist of the secular faith in Socialism." To some extent he was resuming the work of those critics within the ILP who had been defeated at Edinburgh. Hence the deterioration of his relations with his colleagues on the National Administrative Council, which he rejoined in 1911, and with the Labour Party leaders. Glasier attributed Hardie's disaffection in these years to the wounded vanity of a leader who was losing his old place of honor and adulation. And Benson explained his idiosyncratic course as that of an individual who preferred "always to plough a lonely furrow and . . . do things off his own bat." But beneath the frequent churlishness of Hardie's manner and the inconsistencies of his political behavior was a struggle to reassert the Socialist mission.[35]

The reassertion of his socialism—eclectic, contradictory, and still essentially ethical—drew Hardie away from practical political concerns. In the course of 1911 he proposed, by means of a new national daily paper, a fresh Socialist appeal to the masses. But the scheme was soon captured by those committed to a "labourist" line and Hardie disassociated himself from the venture.[36] He found a more modest outlet for his Socialist propaganda in the columns of a new paper in his Welsh constituency, the *Merthyr Pioneer*. Wales had proven, in fact, increasingly receptive to the Socialist message and the political mission to which Hardie had devoted his life. But the growth of Ethical Socialism in Wales simply recapitulated in a shorter time span its development in England.

Wales presented, in the decade before World War I, a conjunction of economic, religious, and political conditions much like those characteristic of the areas in England where Ethical Socialism had taken root most readily. Although Welsh Nonconformity had experienced a great revival during 1904-1905, the industrial communities where it flourished were being disrupted by changes in economic organization and technology. Relative class harmony, based on traditional Liberal and nationalistic attitudes, was giving way to a new sense of distinctively working class interests. Here as in England a form of socialism in which the moral and religious sentiments of the chapels were attached to the cause of working class political independence exercised a powerful appeal without, however, completely displacing the earlier political outlook. Hardie's blend of traditional radicalism and Ethical Socialism gave him a special rapport with the workers. Indeed, in Wales as in England, the new cause attracted a number of young Nonconformist ministers and drew several completely away from organized religion. But the ILP was no more successful in Wales than in England in creating a truly independent and consciously Socialist political force. During the war years many of the ILP branches in Wales were rapidly absorbed by a Labour Party, which there, as elsewhere, had not broken decisively with the older tradition of working class radicalism.[37]

Hardie's last years before his death in 1915 present a picture of growing loneliness and sadness as physical infirmities, disappointments with the movement, and dismay over the collapse of working class solidarity in the face of war dimmed the hopes of earlier years. His comparison of his trials to the "blood and sweat of Gethsemane" might appear to some as extraordinary vanity, but given Hardie's humanized version of Christianity, the sufferings of Jesus were the obvious analogy of his own experiences. There were signs that he was reflecting anew on the religious sources of his Socialist faith. If he had his life to live over again, he told a religious gathering in 1913, he would devote himself to the task of spreading the Christian gospel.[38] Looking back on his life in terms of those ethical aims which were central to his socialism, Hardie may have been left in the end with a sense of defeat. But the diminishing appeal of his form of socialism was in part a result of that growing political consciousness among the working classes to which he was equally dedicated and to which he had contributed so much.

When, at the ILP's "coming of age" conference in 1914 Katharine Glasier confessed her "sense of heartbreak at the cruelty" of the party's later history, she was referring, in part no doubt, to her husband's fate. Bruce Glasier was a victim of a process in which he had, in his own words, "submerged my personal identity."[39]

As editor of the ILP's paper, Glasier had doggedly defended the party leadership during 1908 and 1909. He did not encourage any serious exchange of views on the issues facing the party. Contributions from critics were rejected because their tone seemed to him objectionable or because he questioned the motives of the writers. He saw his role as that of "holding the bridge against wreckers." His strongly moralistic outlook tended, in fact, to harden into self-righteousness.[40]

By the closing weeks of 1908 Glasier's editorship of the *Labour Leader* had become a major target for the dissenters within the ILP. Moreover, he was losing the support of his colleagues, both on the ILP council and the paper's board of directors. After criticism by Hardie, Glasier vowed, in the pages of his diary, to "throw up the paper" if those for whom he was fighting were "not going to stand up for him." And a short time later, when the London branches of the ILP voted sixty to two in favor of a resolution "disparaging my editorship," he asked for a full review by the council. Although the members "unanimously and gratefully approved" his handling of political issues, their criticism of other aspects of the *Leader* left him without the assurance he sought. He submitted his resignation, agreeing only to remain as editor through the spring conference. Following a bitter debate at the Edinburgh conference over his policies, he announced his liberation from the "chains of editorship."[41]

Glasier's popularity within the ILP, as measured by the voting for the council, had steadily declined. At Edinburgh he experienced the humiliation of trailing Smart on the first ballot. He had come to feel that all the accumulating spite within the party was being directed against himself. After his resignation he likened his fate to that of William Morris, who, in the late eighties, had seen a dissident anarchist faction capture his paper, the *Commonweal*. And since he viewed himself, like Morris, as a victim of a selfish group, Glasier set out in the month following Edinburgh to combat "demagoguery and the spirit of individualism" and "rebuild idealism in the movement."[42] Such a diagnosis exhibited little insight into the situation.

Glasier was reelected to the ILP council in 1910 and over the next few years he recovered something of his earlier popularity. But the image of the Socialist prophet and pioneer, to which he owed his renewed popularity, bore little relationship to his new role within the party, for he now claimed that "labourism" was the "only real socialism." In the affairs of the ILP he found himself more and more a part of the "MacDonald caucus" and opposed to Hardie and others who were seeking to reestablish the party's Socialist identity. Indeed, Glasier had little sympathy for those in the party who feared the Liberal embrace. When the ILP held a special conference on the eve of the first general election of 1910 to consider strategy, Glasier was distressed because no speaker "dared to say what I meant to say, i.e., that we should boldly support the Liberals." Those who urged a different course of action seemed to him to be guilty of "treachery" or moved by "selfishness."[43]

Glasier's Socialist faith had lost any plausible connection with political practice. The disjunction, together with the tendency for older radical attitudes to resurface, was apparent in a letter in which he attempted to console MacDonald over the death of his wife.

I am still, perhaps because my work lies chiefly in the propaganda field, almost crudely idealist in my inclination, but I am at the same time quite latitudinarian in my eagerness to see even the very least definite advance made in legislation. My feeling of dread lest the budget be defeated, or the Lords should triumph, or Tariff Reform be carried, has been such as even an unregenerate radical might be ashamed to confess. Yet, could I but see the way to accomplish it, I would disestablish landlordism or capitalism tomorrow at noon with a stroke of my pen or a sweep of my sword.

To overcome the widening gulf between his socialism and his political allegiances Glasier tended to take flight into metaphors. After all, he told MacDonald, "Our British movement is still in its infancy . . . It must have room to sprawl and kick and tumble . . . How preposterous it would be to demand of a child that . . . its rushings and tumblings should have a definite conscious or rational aim."[44]

Neither the catastrophe of war nor the onset of a fatal illness broke Glasier's fundamental optimism. To sustain his Socialist faith in his last years, however, he retreated more and more into his memories. In the two small books written on his deathbed during 1919 and 1920—*The Meaning of Socialism* and *William Morris and the Early Days of British Socialism*—he recaptured the hopes and the experiences of the earlier years of the movement. Socialism, he continued to insist, "goes beyond all existing political systems, and ranks in precepts with the higher religions. It belongs in ethical affirmation to the common stream from which the social idealism is nourished. It defines man's duty towards man in terms of fellowship and love as well as of citizen and justice."[45] At the end of his life Glasier still saw his socialism embodied most fully in the life and work of Morris and the spirit of fellowship which surrounded him.

To MacDonald fell the major responsibility for leading the ILP during its time of crisis. He was chairman of the party from 1906 into the spring of 1909 and, as secretary of the Labour Party, did much to shape the relationship between the Socialists and their trade union allies.[46] His role was a difficult one, for the unacknowledged electoral understanding with the Liberals precluded open discussion of a number of the problems facing the ILP. Still, the course which MacDonald followed was clear and consistent. It also rendered the ILP's Socialist ideology superfluous and indeed, called into question the need for a Socialist party.

Parliamentary experience had reinforced MacDonald's evolutionary and pragmatic political outlook. It was time, he repeatedly told the ILP membership, to "return from its Edens of perfection" and concentrate on the task of aiding the "Socialist tendencies" in existing political and economic institutions. He was confident, like the Fabians, that it was possible to identify and support legislative trends which were "truly progressive" and leading toward a "higher social organization." What MacDonald regarded as progressive, however, was scarcely distinguishable from advanced liberalism. Although he held fast to the concept of nationalization, he generally discouraged advocacy of distinctly Socialist measures for fear that this would damage relations with the trade unions and retard reformist legislation.[47]

As criticism of the Labour Party grew during 1908 and 1909, MacDonald abandoned his customary bent toward conciliation. He attacked the middle class critics in particular for their arrogance and their destructive spirit. And, in a rare public display of his exasperation, he declared that the "neurotic diseases" which seemed to afflict the "middle class mind . . . ought to be stamped out of our Socialist movement as the gardener destroys slugs." He was scarcely more patient with the ILP branches which supported Grayson after his declaration that the plight of the unemployed should take precedence over all other parliamentary business. Yet in the face of demands for an obstructionist tactic, MacDonald also attempted to instruct the branches in the meaning of the democratic process.

> You and I look forward to a time when laws will be passed which will be enforced and respected. Neither you nor I can consequently do anything at the moment which will make the enforcement of Socialist law impossible and deprive it beforehand of any chance of getting that respect. In addition to that you and I are Democrats . . . We are therefore bound to believe that the majority in the House of Commons must take upon itself the responsibility of its action. We must use every form that the House of Commons provides for the expression of our opinion . . . but there comes a point when the action of a minority becomes a tyranny and becomes the subversion of democratic justice. Today it may be very heroic to do violence to our democratic principles; tomorrow, however, I can assure you, you will discover that the penalty is much greater than the gain. The Socialist Movement, the Labour Movement, the Unemployed—every cause for which you and I stand and have fought for so many years, are to be advanced only by scrupulous regard for honest statement and for the democratic spirit.

To "indulge in expressions of our own feelings in intemperate ways," MacDonald added, would "smash up the whole movement." It was "sheer madness for us to assume" in the light of election results, "that we have got the masses of the people behind us." MacDonald also rejected the changes urged by Smart, through which the parliamentary members of the ILP would become faithful servants of the party or its council. Given its place in the Labour Party, the ILP could not "pursue its course with absolute indifference" to the desires of the latter without running "the risk of being expelled."[48]

Smart charged that MacDonald had "lost faith in the ILP . . . as an engine for reform." There was evidence for this. "Unless something can be done" to keep the ILP from "sinking back into its easy slackness of mind," he told Ensor shortly after the Edinburgh conference, "it will disappear altogether." What MacDonald viewed as slackness of mind included a large part of the party's moralistic and utopian appeal.[49]

It was becoming more and more difficult for MacDonald to connect the ILP and its Socialist vision with the political problems of the Labour Party. The ILP had not, except in a few geographical areas, been able to convert its Socialist enthusiasm into a strong electoral force. Although the ILP retained a virtual monopoly of propaganda activity within the Labour Party it had failed to develop an effective relationship with well-defined working class interests at the local level. Indeed, Henderson was beginning in these years to develop a network of local branches of the party.[50]

The two general elections of 1910 demonstrated both the political realism of MacDonald and Henderson and the growing dilemmas of the Socialists.

Although the electoral agreements with the Liberals enabled the Labour Party to hold nearly all its seats, the outcome also indicated the party's "humiliating dependence" on Liberal voters. Indeed, the success of the Liberal Party in "containing" the challenge of the Labour Party encouraged some Liberals to seek seats allocated to labor. MacDonald, as the party's chief strategist, was increasingly occupied in fighting off the Liberal encroachments, while simultaneously combatting "wild cat candidates" promoted by Socialist groups. He was engaged in a holding action, struggling to preserve a Labour Party clearly "separate from the Liberals in its members and aims." Extremely cautious in his approach to issues, content to rely on short term electoral arrangements with the Liberals to preserve the party's parliamentary seats, MacDonald's strategy has been described as a "coherent and predictable consequence of the political climate of the period."[51]

MacDonald kept one foot in the ILP, having returned to the NAC in 1911, but he was shifting his weight mainly to the Labour Party. He was encouraged to do so by several of his ILP colleagues. "If you can't pull the [Labour] party round," Benson told him, then "God help us." By 1911 MacDonald had clearly established himself as the labor movement's leading political figure. Not only was he, with the possible exception of Henderson, the Labour Party's most effective "broker," mediating between the various groups, but he had become to some extent the "manufacturer" of its ideas, developing through his writings

and speeches in Parliament the party's approach to major political questions. And while his rhetoric often blurred critical
issues, it also served the political function of avoiding potential
conflicts within the party. His ascendancy recorded in fact the
triumph of politics over ideology.[52]

MacDonald's style as a leader—charismatic at times and
yet essentially rational, even cold and forbidding—suggested
the constraints which the political role may place on ideologi-
cally motivated activity. He had long since reduced his Socialist
commitment to terms which enabled him to respond more or
less freely to the immediate possibilities of the political arena.
Perhaps the death of his wife in 1911 left him "more and more
an actor on the public stage" and made him vulnerable to the
growth of the mindless opportunism which is one of the hazards
of the political vocation. But others in these years might have
echoed the words of his younger ILP colleague, W. C. Anderson. "You have powerfully helped to bring sanity and common
sense and constructiveness into the British Socialist movement . . . All this means much to those of us who are anxious
to rescue Socialism entirely from the tyranny of phrases and
impossibilist policies."[53]

It may be questioned whether there was in MacDonald's
Socialist views much that was worthy of the term. But certainly
he had not completely surrendered to the immediate play of the
political game. His decision to oppose the war, however hesi-
tant and equivocal, expressed strong convictions. The decision
ended his chairmanship of the Labour Party, sent him into the
political wilderness and, ironically, bound him closely once
more to the Socialists of the ILP. Not until the postwar years,
when MacDonald again found himself straddling the divergent
paths of the Labour Party and the ILP, did he separate himself
from the latter's Socialist mission.

For Ethical Socialists who rejected the leads, however
varied, of Hardie, Glasier, and MacDonald, the activities of
Grayson seemed for a time to promise new direction. But the
pathos of Grayson's later career was further evidence of the
exhaustion of the popular form of socialism. His political and
personal decline record the dissolution of that blend of ethical
and material aspiration which had informed the ILP.

Grayson: A "Despiritualized Fury"

On one occasion Grayson told an audience that his freedom from ordinary social ties permitted him to "stand alone, self reliant, defiant, and reckless," as a champion of the disinherited. Certainly Grayson was not attracted to the work of the conventional politician. During the year following his election to the House of Commons he took little part in the debates and discussions and the detailed tasks of the committees which made up parliamentary routine. He appeared in the House infrequently, registering for only thirty-two out of a possible three hundred divisions for voting. Grayson remained primarily the Socialist propagandist caught up in an unceasing round of meetings and demonstrations up and down the country. His spectacular by-election victory had made him the most sought-after speaker in the movement during the closing months of 1907. When the *Leeds Mercury* conducted a poll early in 1908 to discover the most popular MP in the county Grayson won by a wide margin.[54]

Grayson brought many talents to his propaganda work—a flare for the dramatic, a gift for vivid imagery, a ready sense of humor, and skill in repartee. Like any successful agitator he could sense the mood of the crowd and find words capable of focusing its latent hopes, anxieties, and resentments. He played to a wide range of emotions and placed more stress than most Ethical Socialists on class feeling. At times, carried away in the excitement of the moment, Grayson would say things which he would later deny having said. On one occasion he urged violent action against the authorities. Yet, Grayson continued to emphasize those ethical and religious themes characteristic of the ILP tradition. They were prominent in one of his most popular talks, "The Destiny of the Mob."

It is against the prevailing materialism that modern Socialists are flinging the weight of their protests. What passes for atheism in our ranks is more often a natural reaction and a healthy rebellion against the sickly religiosity and hidebound Churchianity that has so long obscured the spiritual purpose of humanity. It is the task of the humanist to divert the eyes of a pessimistic society to the golden thread of beneficent purpose running all through history.

Grayson also struck the aesthetic note common to much of Ethical Socialism. He offered his working class audiences a vision of life as a "gorgeous feast," made up of poetry, fine art and literature, and natural beauty. "It is the strangling of the mind more than the starvation of the body," he insisted, "that the Socialist mostly deplores."[55]

Grayson, like a number of the most active Socialist propagandists before him, broke down under the strain of constant speaking and traveling. Early in 1908 he was forced to withdraw for a time and rest. The next two years witnessed a series of physical breakdowns and the steady deterioration of his health. Meanwhile, Grayson's standards of personal behaviour were changing. Having discarded his earlier religious beliefs he consciously attempted to fashion a new code of conduct, acknowledging, however, that the movement provided little guidance for this task. He was drawn to the styles of the gentleman and the hedonist. He caused "much heart searching among his friends" by appearing in evening dress to debate with the Conservative MP, William Joynson-Hicks, in Manchester. Replying to criticism, Grayson denounced the efforts of some Socialists to make the simple life a part of their faith and defended the ideal of the bon vivant. "I love good food. I love a beautiful dwelling. I love good wine, good cigars, soft beds. My attitude toward life is that of the Greek hedonist, with a dash of the ethics of Epicurus. Socialism has nothing to do with the "Simple life." It is a theory of social and industrial organization involving the social ownership of the means of life." Grayson's frank hedonism provided few defenses against the temptations which came with his rapid rise. There were, as his friend Hobson recalled, "dangerous hospitalities," and Grayson began to indulge freely. Blatchford had introduced him to drink and he began to rely on alcohol for quick stimulus amid the constant round of Socialist propaganda activity.[56]

During 1908, as discontent mounted within the ILP rank and file, many Socialists began to call on Grayson for a new lead. But as a member of Parliament Grayson's position was equivocal. While he continued on the propaganda platform to denounce parliamentary procedures as archaic and futile, and dismissed the Labour Party's unemployment bill as "insufficient," he still sat passively in the House. In the summer of 1908 as the nation experienced the most serious wave of unemployment in over a decade, there were increasing demands from within the movement for protests against the government's inaction. Where, a writer in the *New Age* asked, is the leader with "the courage to be rash," and he praised the "picturesque exaggeration of Grayson." The paper's dramatic critic, L. Haden-Guest, argued that the Socialist politician, like the Socialist dramatist, should expose the vital conflicts of the time. "What Socialists are trying to do in the social and political way is to clear the field of the unessential complexities that prevent conflict in order to get at the real conflict. Socialists desire the struggle of personality in the world to be a struggle in which all the gladiators are as well equipped as possible . . . Every advance toward Socialism is an advance toward real and vital conflict."[57]

Early in the fall, after a trip to America for rest and recuperation, Grayson returned to take part in the Newcastle by-election campaign and engage in a series of demonstrations on behalf of the unemployed. Within the movement there was growing anger over the failure of the Liberal government to take steps to relieve the plight of the unemployed. This was the setting for Grayson's two scenes in Parliament in mid-October.

Grayson expressed through his scenes some of the growing bitterness among the lower classes over the inaction of Parliament. Perhaps, too, he was attempting, as Hardie had attempted earlier, to shock the House into a fuller appreciation of the extent of social misery. But Grayson also projected into parliamentary life an attitude toward politics which was deeply rooted in Ethical Socialism and the thought of Morris, Carlyle, and Ruskin. These men had tended to view political activity as a form of heroic moral action. The attitude continued to run strongly through popular socialism. "It is the moral effect of the victory which we value," Blatchford had declared in the middle of the Newcastle by-election campaign. "It would mean the revolt of another great industrial center against the established order of things." "Great reforms," he added, "are born in the heart of the people, not in the brains of legislators." The writer of a popular life of Grayson made much the same point. "[The House of Commons] is a conspicuous site for scenes' in which some dramatic defiance of its rules by a Socialist member may furnish a striking tableau illustrative of the contrast between the irrepressible human indignation of that member against the horrible system of capitalism." To many within the Socialist movement Grayson's bold defiance of Parliament was heroic. During the weeks which followed, Social Democrats and *Clarion* groups, as well as a number of ILP branches, received him with great enthusiasm.[58]

In November, however, Grayson committed a blunder. He refused to share a platform with Hardie at a *Clarion* meeting in London. ILP branches which had praised him earlier now condemned him. The episode helped the ILP leaders to counter the challenge of the militants. But the challenge of Grayson and his followers was also weakened by their failure to develop a practical alternative to the existing strategy. At two critical moments—the Portsmouth conference of the Labour Party in February 1909 and the ILP conference at Edinburgh two months later—Grayson failed to offer constructive ideas.

For the opposition, inside and outside the ILP, the Portsmouth conference seemed an opportune time to state the case for a more militant policy by the labor and Socialist group in Parliament. At Portsmouth, Hyndman, Hobson, and others counted on Grayson, an ILP delegate, to speak out. He failed them completely. Grayson did not appear on the first day when discussion was directed to the problem of the unemployed. On the second day, when Hyndman pleaded with him to speak, Grayson "lounged elegantly against one of the pillars of the hall, and—carefully held his peace." Hobson and others then prepared a resolution for Grayson to move on the last day of the conference. But when the time came to make the motion Grayson was absent. Late that evening "he came into the hotel plainly the worse for wear. He told us a strange story of some nice and friendly fellows who had taken him for a ride."[59]

Smart warned Grayson. Referring to his "abduction" at Portsmouth, Smart wrote: "They are driving you on a beautiful, attractive road where at intervals you may call the ephemeral primroses of public applause: but they will carry you away from the pace of life and action."[60] Grayson did not alter his course. He continued, despite physical deterioration, to speak incessantly during 1909. And though he remained a member of the ILP he talked from time to time of a plan to form a new Socialist party. In private life he drifted into a series of difficulties involving drink, women, and money. For friendship he turned increasingly to the world of the theatre, particularly to that of the music halls.

At the general election early in 1910 Grayson again contested the Colne Valley seat. But he had now estranged a substantial section of his following by his public and private behavior. The chairman of the Colne Valley Socialist League opposed his renomination and resigned when 70 percent of its membership supported Grayson's refusal to sign the Labour Party constitution.[61] Divided within and lacking much outside Socialist support, most of which was engaged in other electoral contests, the local organization could not match the campaign of 1907. Meanwhile the Liberals, having overhauled their party organization, were primed for the fight. Their candidate, Charles Leach, was perfectly suited for the task of drawing votes away from Grayson. Formerly a Congregational minister, Leach had been a member of the ILP for a time in the mid-nineties and still described himself as an evolutionary socialist. Grayson ran a poor third in the contest, polling 3149 votes to Leach's 4741. Later in the year Grayson stood at Kensington in London but drew only 400 votes.

Grayson became "political editor" of the *Clarion* during 1909 and he continued in the position through 1910 and 1911. His contributions were infrequent and shallow; they consisted most often of parables or stories designed to illustrate the theft and destruction of the Socialist vision by the politician. He saw no merit at all in the major Liberal reform measures—the budget of 1909 and the Insurance Bill of 1911. Grayson's attacks on Parliament grew more and more extreme. He spoke of burning the many volumes of the parliamentary debates, blue books, and reports and giving Parliament "a chance to start afresh." "Indeed, I sometimes wonder as I look around, if it would not be a blessing to extend the conflagration and start life all over again with a clean piece of protoplasm. In politics we should get rid of the incubus of precedent, and morality would be rescued from the blight of tradition."[62]

Late in 1911, after several false starts, Grayson helped launch the British Socialist Party. The place of the party in the development of the Socialist movement will be discussed later. But Grayson's role was one of rapidly diminishing importance. Within a few months he had ceased to exercise any influence in its upper councils though he remained for a time one of its leading speakers.

The remainder of Grayson's life may be told briefly. In 1913 he married a London actress and they traveled to America on funds raised by Socialists. Later Hobson found them down and out in New York and helped them return to England. In hopes of making a fresh start Grayson and his wife went to Australia, then moved on to New Zealand. After some dubious monetary transactions in the Socialist movement there, Grayson went into the army. Wounded in France he returned to England to participate, with several other former Socialists, in prowar propaganda. He was now increasingly prey to drink. In 1920 he disappeared.

A later observer attributed the "tragedy of Victor Grayson" to the fact that he remained true to the Socialist vision at a time when the older leaders of the ILP had thrown it aside in favor of political expediency.[63] There was an element of truth in the judgment. But Grayson's fate was more intimately related to the fate of Ethical Socialism itself; his personal disintegration mirrored the breakup of those elements which had given vitality to this form of socialism.

Ethical Socialism had gained significant popular support only where it was connected with the material aspirations of the workers. Through his drift toward political nihilism Grayson was cutting himself off from any intelligible relationship to those aspirations. He could still voice the frustrations of the unemployed or resentments of a vaguer kind. And he did consider, in the development of a new Socialist party and in the industrial strategy of the Syndicalists, alternative modes of action. More and more, however, his Socialist vision lost any support in objective social or political forces and was reduced to its subjective basis. And yet this basis too was disappearing. Grayson's personal life after 1908 indicated the weakening of those moral and religious feelings which had informed his Socialist enthusiasm. When, shortly after his suspension from the House of Commons, he described himself as "an outcast following Jesus Christ," the earlier sentiments had clearly dissolved into mere sentimentality—into an affectation of feelings he no longer possessed. The rhetoric of Ethical Socialism remained; the vital substance was gone. The hysterical, pseudo-apocalyptic message of Grayson's later *Clarion* articles suggested that Ethical Socialism could, like other ideologies past and future, leave behind what Karl Mannheim described as a "despiritualized fury."[64]

The discords among the Ethical Socialists also presented difficulties for the clergymen who had been attracted to the movement. They had seen in the social cause a new way of applying Christian teachings to public affairs. But as the political dilemmas of the ILP and the Labour Party increased, clergymen were subject to much the same process of frustration and disagreement apparent among the Socialists generally. In the same period two of the most perceptive religious thinkers of the period, J. N. Figgis and P. T. Forsyth, attempted to clarify the relationships between socialism, Christianity, and politics.

The Disillusionment of the Clergy and Christian Reappraisals of Socialism

In their initial enthusiasm for the Socialist movement the clergymen had "swallowed," as one Anglican put it, "the formula of the nationalization of the land, the means of production and exchange," as the only way of "giving practical effect to our religion in our national life." They assumed that socialism provided them "with a ready-made Sociology." By the closing months of 1908, however, the issues which disturbed Socialists generally were dividing the Anglicans of the Church Socialist League and the Nonconformists of the Progressive League. They were discovering that Socialists too might fall into a "most pronounced pharisaism" and they began to examine more closely the meaning of their Socialist commitment.[65]

The Church Socialist League had rapidly succeeded in developing a new appreciation for Socialist ideas within the established church. In little more than two years it had formed twenty-five branches with a thousand active members. Representatives of the League presented statements on behalf of socialism at the important Anglican conferences and its members continued to be active in by-elections involving Socialist candidates. But they were also inevitably drawn into the debates within the movement concerning electoral policy and parliamentary tactics.

The League's annual meeting in the spring of 1909, like that of the ILP conference a short time earlier, brought a sharp clash of views. One section, led by the League's president, Algernon West, supported the ILP leaders and attempted to identify the League closely with the Labour Party. The other, more radical section, rejected this course in favor of greater political independence for the Socialists and a stronger assertion of Socialist principles. But it included a wide range of viewpoints. Thus, the religious "modernist," N. E. Egerton Swann, viewed socialism and Christianity as two sides of the "passing of the community" toward a new consciousness of itself as a "corporate and organic unity." P. E. T. Widdrington, a high churchman, hoped that the League might develop a distinctive theological and sociological basis for socialism. Cecil Chesterton, on the other hand, took a very militant position and defended the obstructionist political tactics of Grayson.[66]

Although the members of the League defeated a proposal by West that they affiliate with the Labour Party no clear-cut policy emerged. The new president, A. T. B. Pinchard, argued, in fact, that it would be undesirable for them to favor one of the various Socialist factions. Their primary task was simply to convert Anglicans to socialism.

On this vague basis the League continued to grow during the next three years. But the disagreements among the members became more and more evident. At one extreme Chesterton urged Anglican Socialists to maintain contact with the "really fertile revolutionary activity" and adopt a parliamentary tactic of defiance in the face of the "collapse of the [Labour] party." Meanwhile, others in the League were becoming convinced that the possibility of forming a Socialist party had "vanished forever." The "great capitalist parties" had stolen the "only essential Socialist principle"—the doctrine of the state as an "aid to the enlargement of human liberty." Socialists should, therefore, concentrate on converting the Liberals to socialism. Still another group within the League abandoned the hope of "saving the cause in Parliament." They turned to the new industrial strategy being developed after 1911 by the Guild Socialists. To a number of Anglicans Guild Socialism brought a "welcome emphasis on personality" and promised a way of recovering human initiative against the relentless march of the collectivist state. But the Guild Socialists were also attempting to rescue the Socialist vision from the erosive effects of the political process.[67]

One Anglican thinker in these years, J. N. Figgis, was examining more closely the modes of thought on which so much of the popular Socialist appeal rested. Figgis was not a Socialist but he was a member of the House of the Resurrection at Mirfield and especially sensitive to the moral and religious claims of the Socialists.[68] In the preface to a series of lectures published in 1907 he noted the declaration of Shaw's hero, Undershaft: "We have had enough of shams, and must at last demand a religion that fits the facts."[69] Figgis attempted, in his lectures and writings of these years, to answer the challenge of Shaw and others who were seeking to develop a new faith.

Figgis attacked the form of ethical idealism which had become increasingly prominent in late Victorian and Edwardian culture and had found popular expression in socialism. Whether expressed in terms of philosophical idealism, evolutionary optimism, or immanentist religion, it was, according to Figgis, an unhealthy deviation from the historical tendencies of the English mind. The British people, he argued, had resisted the temptation to give the ideal and the theoretical an independent status; they had favored the immediate and the concrete. In general the British had recognized that the "springs of life are deeper than all reasoning and are to be found in the power to act and love." To this traditional bent, Figgis maintained, Christianity, with its unflinching sense of sin and its acceptance of the "limitations of external fact" together with its realistic grappling with the actual "vulgarity of institutional life," corresponded most deeply.[70]

The form of ethical idealism which had superseded Christianity among many intellectuals was, according to Figgis, rapidly degenerating into "sentimental altruism." The advanced thinkers of the age were moving on to new positions. And as they did so the "great common ground of ethical values" assumed by Christian and non-Christian thinkers as well, was vanishing. Moreover, the two main trends of post-Christian or post-Idealist thought both menaced human dignity. One trend, expressed in the determinism of a popularized science, imprisoned man in an "iron law of physical sequences," in which there were no discontinuities, "no unique personalities, no really new events." The other trend, exemplified in such contemporary "makers of religion" as Shaw and Wells, and above all Nietzsche, led to a demonic form of life which "discards the notion of love, ridicules sacrifice and pity, and pours a virulence of scornful hatred on Christ Himself." The new apostles of the will to power, according to Figgis, were preparing the way for a "saturnalia of selfish pride."[71]

Against the intellectual and spiritual errors of the age, Figgis reaffirmed the distinctively religious feelings of awe, sin, and mystery as fundamental elements in human consciousness. And he insisted, in contrast to those clergymen who identified the workings of God with the struggle for social justice, on the transcendence of God, the fallen state of mankind, and the need for grace. He argued that Christianity alone provided the truly revolutionary power to penetrate to the foundations of the individual self and, by transforming the quality of human desires, to alter the "whole scale of . . . values."[72]

For Figgis Christian renewal provided the only basis for a reconstructed national community. He reaffirmed, in fact, something of the older Anglican vision of a Christian commonwealth in which there was a close relationship between personal beliefs and public institutions. But the vision was no longer, as in earlier times, integrally bound up with the political order. For the decline of religious observance and the growing power of the modern state meant that the Christian church needed protection against possible encroachments from the secular authority. Figgis went on to develop a fresh defense for the autonomy of the church and for all those basic associations in society which held "a principle of inherent life" and "inherent principles of development."[73] Through his emphasis on the crucial role of associations in nurturing personality, Figgis provided arguments for those Socialists who, amid growing political disenchantment, attempted to reformulate their goals.

Nonconformist clergymen were undergoing a parallel process of religious and ideological reappraisal. The process unfolded most clearly in the development of the Progressive League, founded by R. J. Campbell to give expression and direction to the growing sympathy between religious leaders and the Socialists.

From the beginning the Progressive League had contained two distinct orientations. Those members who followed the lead of Campbell, for the most part clergymen, were concerned mainly with the task of bringing out and enhancing the Christian meeting of the Socialist cause. They might, like Campbell, be closely associated with the ILP but they shared his view that the League itself should not be identified with any political party or even with specific economic doctrines. They simply sought to nurture what Campbell called the "zeitgeist for tomorrow."[74]

The other main section of the League, which included Hardie and a number of the Socialist leaders, was primarily concerned with the advance of the Socialist cause and its political fortunes. They regarded the League as a new instrument for that purpose. After all, Hardie observed, there could be no Christianity "apart from socialism."[75]

This ambivalent orientation no doubt helped the League grow rapidly. By the fall of 1909 it embraced a hundred and twenty-two branches and between four and five thousand members. But Campbell had already begun to regret the fact that they had made the League's basis so wide. For it had come to include persons who had "no real sympathy with . . . religious faith." He and his supporters were now struggling against the tendency of many of the League's members to view it simply as a political organization. At the same time they attempted to commit the League more fully to the "spiritual ideal . . . associated with the name of our Lord Jesus Christ." And in the spring of 1910 Campbell succeeded in changing the organization's name to the Liberal Christian League. A few months later the League's Christian character was strengthened when it was identified with such doctrines as the incarnation, the uniqueness of Christ, and immortality. This action was challenged by a number of clergymen and lay members, and amid deepening disagreements the League began to fall apart.[76]

The tension between religious and ideological commitments was apparent in Campbell's own development. For his work in the movement led him to include that it was necessary to choose between "the particular passion and idealism" of the ILP and his own "vocation as a preacher." He was losing his confidence in the immanentist theology and the ethically centered version of Christianity which had encouraged him, like many of the Nonconformist clergymen, to identify the divine will with the Socialist movement. As this common ethical ground dissolved a few of the Socialist clergymen left organized religion to devote themselves fully to the movement. But Campbell turned instead to a stronger form of religious authority; in time he left Congregationalism and entered the Anglican church.[77]

The moral and religious sentiments which drew the Socialists and the Nonconformist clergymen together in these years were also being subjected to a searching analysis by P. T. Forsyth, the leading theologian among the Congregationalists.[78] Forsyth challenged Socialists who claimed a religious status for their cause; he also attempted to distinguish between the essential doctrines of Christianity and ideological concerns.

In earlier years Forsyth had been a leader of the liberalizing theological and social tendencies within Congregationalism. He had studied with Albrecht Ritschl in Germany and subsequently blended the strongly ethical impulse of the German thinker with the concern for social redemption found in the Anglican, F. D. Maurice, and the nineteenth century Congregational leaders, Baldwin Brown and Robert Dale. He had also been drawn to socialism and accepted its stress on the organic nature of society and the need for mutuality in economic life. Forsyth was convinced that capitalism had "announced its own end in becoming de-ethicized in plutocracy."[79]

By the turn of the century Forsyth had concluded, however, that "conscience," or the ethical feelings, could not carry the weight which was being placed on them by many contemporary social and religious thinkers. Insofar as religious thinkers, in particular, simply concentrated on the workings of Christian love in the world, they tended to rob their faith of its power to confront the realities of human nature. Forsyth did not give up his own strong emphasis on the need for a new social ethic, but he attempted to balance it by restating what he felt to be the essential truths of the evangelical position.

The "old orthodoxies" were dead but they had possessed, according to Forsyth, "a true eye for what really mattered in Christianity." They saw deeply into the "abyss of moral experience" and grappled with the "final facts of human nature." The human spirit was inescapably divided; it was in a state of "collision—war and sin." Unless the ethical teacher had felt "the ground give way beneath [his own] moral nature," he remained a mere "dilettante of the moral soul." Christians who stressed the power of God's love at the expense of his holiness and the need for obedience drifted into "unreality" and "sentimentalism." "Only the cross" could "preserve the love of man for man from futile sentiment." For the acknowledgment of the "mighty saving act of God in Christ" was also a recognition of human limitation and of man's need for divine grace and power.[80]

Contemporary socialism, to which so many, according to Forsyth, were turning "in despair of personal faith," suffered from "an arrest of thought." The moral passion of the Socialists went deeper than "their consciousness." Shaw, in particular, seemed to Forsyth to be one who "feels things to be wrong without heart enough to find how wrong." But in fixing on moral ideals and attributing a self-sustaining power to them, popular socialism, like the more humanistic versions of Christianity from which it had largely derived, had "come to a point of strain." A deeper inspiration would be necessary to overcome the "disillusionments that await a democracy merely human and a socialism chiefly concerned with rights and comfort." Ethical ideals required religious faith "to force them into public life."[81]

Forsyth accepted some of the goals of the Socialists; they were, he acknowledged, the "fruits" of his own Christian faith. But he denounced the efforts of Socialists "to exploit for a certain economic program a Church whose fundamental principles of conversion it either ignored or scorns." Their fundamental error lay in the attempt to identify the Socialist order with the Christian Kingdom of God. The Christian Kingdom was not, according to Forsyth, a future "type of society . . . like other historic types" but an authority or "lordship" with its own special demands here and now. Forsyth was reaffirming a distinct and transcendental ground for Christian faith. And he insisted that such a perspective made possible a kind of disinterestedness denied to those who were wedded completely to socialism, for it corrected the inescapable tendency for human ideas and moral principles to harden into self-righteousness.[82]

The intellectual bases of popular socialism, which Figgis and Forsyth were criticizing from an orthodox religious perspective, were also undergoing reexamination by Socialists who had rejected Christianity. They were following the path of Carpenter, Bax, Blatchford, Shaw, and Wells, in a search for new religious or philosophical sanctions. Both the exhaustion of Ethical Socialism and the attempt to renew the utopian impulse in the movement can be explored in the career of A. R. Orage, editor of the *New Age*.

A. R. ORAGE: *The Transvaluation of Ethical Socialism*

Orage's early years present another example of a sensitive young man undergoing the painful struggle to redefine himself and his social place. His whole life, so a friend observed, was marked by a continuing quest for a "substratum of belief" through which he "could unlock all the doors of the universe" and achieve a personal integration.[83] His adoption of Ethical Socialism was one expression of the quest. And when in the years after 1906 the popular form of socialism began to lose its power, Orage, together with some colleagues on the *New Age*, attempted to revitalize its social vision.

Orage was born in a rural village near Bradford in 1873, the son of a failed farmer turned schoolteacher. As a young man he discovered in a Nonconformist Sunday School class the "splendours of language and the empire of the mind" revealed by Carlyle, Ruskin, Arnold, and Morris. The generosity of a local squire enabled him to attend a teachers' training college and take a position in elementary education in Leeds during the mid-nineties. After joining the local branch of the ILP he became one of its most popular speakers. He also contributed a bookish "causerie" to Hardie's *Labour Leader*, introducing his readers to contemporary thinkers and creative writers. His columns disclosed a mind soaked in the works of Plato, Emerson, and especially Whitman and Carpenter, whose writings seemed to him to provide "the finest philosophy the Western world has produced." In a letter to Carpenter he confessed his personal aspirations. "I want to go . . . into what inwardly I feel to be the deepest need of thousands like myself, the need for some formulation in one's soul for the more or less superficial and transitory beliefs."[84]

For a time theosophy provided the deeper faith he sought. During the late nineties, as the Socialist movement declined, Orage became a prominent speaker on the theosophical platforms of the north. Like Carpenter and a number of others within the Socialist movement, he was blending the mysticism of the East with the evolutionary optimism characteristic of late Victorian culture to provide a new foundation for personal and social hopes. Orage's position within the theosophical movement was, however, increasingly heterodox.[85] His continuing interest in Plato, particularly the Socratic dialogues, reflected a rationalist or critical bent which tended to drive Orage beyond fixed metaphysical positions.

In 1900 a chance meeting with Holbrook Jackson, a commercial traveler, Socialist, and aspiring writer, drew Orage to the work of Nietzsche. Two years earlier, in a lecture before the Fabian society, Hubert Bland had recommended Nietzsche as a "fine antidote to current sentimentality and to the modern tendency to carry morality into every sphere of life."[86] But the thought of Nietzsche did not, at least initially, bring a critical examination of Orage's ethically oriented socialism. Rather, he found in the German thinker's iconoclasm a new version of the radical rejection of contemporary civilization expressed in various ways by Morris, Carpenter, Bax, and Tolstoy. And Nietzsche's hope of transcending the present human condition through the ideal of the superman provided fresh meaning to the millennial hopes nurtured by socialism and theosophy. Indeed,

Orage gave a mystical turn to Nietzsche and set out in the early years of the century to blend the new ideas with beliefs derived from Carpenter and theosophy.

Nietzsche's emphasis on aesthetic values also helped inspire a new Socialist strategy. The Leeds Art Club, which Orage and Jackson formed in 1900, was designed to engender by aesthetic means "a social force capable of overthrowing the supreme evil of the age—plutocracy." The true route to socialism lay through cultural reforms or, as the club's syllabus stated, the creation of new standards "by means of which art and ideas may be judged each in their intimate bearings on life."[87] Orage and Jackson were joined in the venture by a young architect, Arthur J. Penty, who brought a concern with the relationship between the artist-craftsman and modern economic life drawn from Morris and Ruskin. The Leeds group was seeking to renew impulses in British socialism which had been largely eclipsed in the rise of the working class political movement.

For Orage the early years of the century were marked by a series of personal difficulties. His brilliant role in local Socialist and intellectual circles was more and more at odds with his position as an elementary schoolteacher. Moreover, his marriage was breaking up. Perhaps, as his biographer has suggested, Nietzsche's appeal to Orage lay in the latter's need to justify his break with conventional ethical values and refashion his moral standards. To worshipful young ladies in Leeds, a friend of these years recalled, Orage insisted that "every young man and woman should do precisely what he or she desires."[88] Late in 1905 he resigned his teaching position and set out for London, hoping to start a new career as a writer.

When Orage arrived in London he was still struggling to synthesize the disparate influences of socialism, theosophy, and Nietzsche. The struggle was apparent in three small volumes written during the next year or so, *Consciousness: Animal, Human and Superman; Friedrich Nietzsche, The Dionysian Spirit of the Age;* and *Nietzsche in Outline and Aphorism.*

The small volume, *Consciousness,* presented the possibility that men might attain a fully harmonious and unified mode of existence by means of a state of awareness as far above normal human consciousness as the latter was above "animal consciousness." Such a state, Orage argued, was anticipated in those "moments of ecstasy" found in aesthetic and religious experience. These experiences enabled people to overcome the antinomies and fragmentary nature of ordinary consciousness and grasp reality intuitively. They promised an escape from "our duality into a sphere where for an instant one becomes one of Plato's spectators of time and existence."[89]

Mystics of all ages, according to Orage, had sought this state. But the modern task was to develop "definite ecstatic faculties." Although he acknowledged the importance of traditional forms of religious discipline and purification, Orage denied that there was a "science of mysticism" and a single approach to the "modes of ecstasy." It was "presumptuous of anybody to lay down rules for the development of super consciousness." Orage went on to hint at new and more risky ways through nature. Modern men, he observed, were playing a "dangerous game" and the path ahead would be "strewn with the wrecks of the hasty, the superficial, and the over curious."[90] In Nietzsche's notion of the superman Orage saw "man made ecstatic" and "intensified." The superman was one who willed a higher state of consciousness. Orage claimed that Nietzsche was essentially a mystic; "behind his apparent materialism was a thoroughly mystical view of the world."[91]

Nietzsche's scathing indictment of modern European civilization extended and sharpened some of the ideas Orage had received from Carlyle, Ruskin, Morris, and Carpenter. But the indictment also came to bear on the moral and religious sentiments underlying Orage's socialism and, indeed, helped clear the ground for its reformulation. According to Nietzsche the sentiments of love and altruism were not enduring elements in human nature but rather expressions of a false consciousness. They were grounded in resentment, in feelings of weakness, and therefore decadent. They did not enhance life or release man's creative possibilities. Indeed, conventional moral values were "inhuman . . . petrified, the very instrument of society's destruction." The Socialist desire for a cooperative order was also anti-human. For it was "not in the nature of life to fulfill ideals." The "desire to have them fulfilled" or "the conviction that they will one day be fulfilled" expressed a will which had lost its way and no longer desired life. Man should not distort his nature through "conformity with abstract ideas" and morality; "actual man" was far "more valuable than ideal man." A noble existence was marked by unending conflict. Either men must openly accept the pain and the tragedy which such a life entailed or "conceal it from consciousness by means of soporifics and anodynes."[92]

The interpretation of modern life, which Orage drew from Nietzsche, threatened the basis of Ethical Socialism. Not only did the German thinker devalue the moral sentiments to which the Socialists appealed but he seemed to deny that the oppositions within human nature could be overcome. Still, Orage found in the concept of the Dionysiac a way of reconciling Nietzsche and socialism. For Nietzsche's gospel of Dionysus pointed to socially redeeming, indeed democratic, energies. Dionysus represented, according to Orage, the challenge of a "popular movement . . . elemental, irreligious, immoral, barbaric, and anarchic" to conventions which had lost their vitality; the "Dionysian will to renew" could be identified with socialism.[93]

Orage's blend of Ethical Socialism and Nietzscheanism was paradoxical but it was by no means unique in the movement. A similar attempt to introduce heroic vitalism or nonrational energies into socialism was evident in Shaw's dramatic work. The tendency also appeared in a number of Socialists drawn from the "professional proletariat." Edwin Muir recalled the mood and the need. "The idea of a transvaluation of values intoxicated me with a feeling of false power. I, a poor clerk in a beer bottling factory, adopted the creed of aristocracy . . . My Socialism and my Nietzsche were quite incompatible but I refused to recognize it. Nietzsche's ideas gave me exactly what I needed, a last desperate foothold on my dying dream of the future.[94]

For Orage in 1907, however, the Socialist dream was still vital; it simply wanted a new lead. And in the spring of that year Orage set out to provide it. He secured financial support from Shaw and a friend in the theosophy movement and purchased a nearly defunct weekly, *The New Age*. A number of the London Fabians, with whom Orage was now associated, were included among the paper's contributors. With Holbrook Jackson as coeditor, Orage was seeking to extend the mission begun in Leeds and nurture a Socialist vision which would enhance man's artistic and spiritual life as well as his economic and political well-being.

Initially the editors simply set out to make the *New Age* a lively forum for Socialist opinion on politics, literature, and art. They endorsed the policies of the Socialist and labor leaders in Parliament. And they welcomed the by-election victories of Curran and Grayson in the summer of 1907 in the confidence that the working classes were steadily being converted to socialism. In September, however, when the Socialists and labor men at the Kirkdale by-election were attacked on religious grounds, the *New Age* decided to take its stand with the "revolutionaries," since "nothing human was alien to Socialism." Indeed, Orage was now convinced that the movement had lost its way. In October he commenced a series of articles, "Towards Socialism," in which he attempted to redefine the Socialist mission.[95]

Orage sharply distinguished his socialism from the collectivism of the Fabians, or the "gospel of deliverance by contrivance." He was "appalled at the poverty of imagination" of those who viewed socialism as no more than a "redistribution of wages." "Every good Socialist," he declared, was a utopian, for Socialists were "temperamentally disposed to believe that the world and man can indefinitely be changed." "Once more," he concluded, "the genuinely Christian impulse is beginning to stir in men's minds and it is today and here that men intend to be in paradise."[96]

Orage still viewed the "Christian impulse" in terms drawn from Carpenter; its distinguishing feature was the sentiment of solidarity. Carpenter's influence was evident too in Orage's insistence that all instincts were holy and all repression immoral. And Orage carried over as well the hatred of commercialism and the ideal of the artist-craftsman found in Ruskin and Morris. Socialism would rescue men from "toil without the consent of the soul" and restore a "labor with delight." The man who was "happy in his work" was "already living . . . the life of a Socialist." In the light of this ideal the "ignoble life" of the present, with its "stupidity and ugliness," lost any valid claim on the individual. "To be anything less than wilful, rebellious and revolutionary is the mark in modern society of people with not sufficient imagination to hear the rattle of their own chains or insight enough to discover the Beast that devours them. All other sacrifice than spontaneous voluntary sacrifice is a degradation of man."[97]

Orage had lost, through the influence of Nietzsche, the metaphysical supports, both theosophical and evolutionary, on which he had relied. The universe lacked any "divine purpose," nature was "senseless," and man, therefore, must "fix his own end." Following Nietzsche, Orage now argued that life was an adventure with "no other purpose than experience." Men should resist any "defined and superimposed purpose" save that which they had developed for themselves. Nietzsche's aristocratic bent was also evident in "Towards Socialism." "Abolish poverty for us," Orage declared, "and our men of genius will begin that cyclopean task of building a civilization worthy of the conquerors of titans." But Orage was still attempting to reconcile the egalitarian values of socialism with Nietzsche's heroic outlook. In time a new enlightened democracy would emerge, in the light of which the present political system was a mere "infant."[98]

The faith expressed in "Towards Socialism" was personal. Orage did not attempt, in his editorial role, to propagate these views. By the end of 1907 he had assumed sole control over the paper and gathered an able group of writers, including G. R. S. Taylor, Sam Hobson, Arnold Bennett, L. Haden-Guest, and, less frequently, Shaw, Wells, and the Chestertons. To these writers the policies of the Socialist politicians were increasingly suspect. And during 1908 the *New Age* mounted a strong attack on the Labour Party and the ILP and called for a more vigorous assertion of Socialist principles. According to Orage the Socialists in Parliament lacked a plan of campaign. "The political socialist is a soldier in enemy country . . . Against [him] are set the traditions of a hemisphere and thousands of years of civilized life. At present, half of our members are romantically minded camp followers and sentimental sightseers. They will fly at the first sight of battle . . . [We] need to fight like the early apostles fought for Christianity (a far more cracked brain cause)."[99]

As debate within the movement intensified during the spring and summer of 1908, the *New Age* writers advanced the idea of "political catastrophism" as an "antidote to the prevailing intellectual idleness calling itself evolutionary socialism," and demanded a more dramatic form of leadership. "The ordinary man," Taylor wrote, "will never understand the science of Socialism for the same reason that he will never understand conic sections." But "he will take the same intense interest in Socialism that he takes in a football match, because his imagination is stirred by the sport of war. We must give the people inspiration as well as a program."[100] Taylor and the other *New Age* writers welcomed Grayson's scenes in Parliament because they provided inspiration of this kind.

Grayson's scenes were "Dionysian." They expressed the qualities of enthusiasm, passion, and recklessness which Orage identified with Nietzsche's mythic label for nonrational energies. Grayson, according to Orage, had attacked an enemy far more powerful than "Tory, Whig or Lord." "It is the paralyzing influence of immemorial gentility, produced by centuries of class rule that pervades every nook and cranny of the house, blighting enthusiasm, weakening resolve, and reducing good will to impotence without respect of persons—in short, it is the curse of tradition that stands in our way."[101] Orage invited Grayson to join him as coeditor and for three months, until he went off to write for the *Clarion*, Grayson added the excitement of his personality to the pages of the *New Age*. Its circulation jumped to an all-time high of twenty-two thousand and Orage became a figure of some influence within the movement. He may have developed political ambitions. During the early months of 1909 he took an active role in the efforts to provide, in the scheme for Socialist Representative Councils, a strategy designed to recover the movement's political initiative. Those who pushed the plan greatly exaggerated the capacity of the Socialists to secure independent political support. And for Orage, as for the other critics of ILP policy, the Edinburgh conference in the spring of 1909 represented a crushing defeat. Shortly after the conference, in fact, Hardie singled out the "irresponsible . . . disciples of Nietzsche" on the staff of the *New Age* as one source of the party's troubles.[102]

In the months which followed Orage reconsidered the relationship between the Socialist movement and politics. He became convinced that the capacity of a popular political party to absorb new ideas was limited; the Labour Party had "bitten off quite as much Socialism as it could chew." Indeed, Orage concluded that the "idealist theories and rather heterogeneous ideas" of the Socialists were liable to "hinder rather than help the cause of popular representation." It was time to free the Socialist movement from any close ties with party politics. Only if it separated itself from politics could the movement start afresh with a new strategy. Orage noted that the *New Age* had become steadily more aristocratic in its appeal; it was reaching leaders in "every party and creed." Dedicated Socialists should take up again a strategy of permeation, not in the Fabian sense of the term, but through preaching a "new gospel touched with spiritual fire."[103]

A new form of socialism could only be developed, according to Orage, if the movement was freed from its fatal addiction to "sentimentalism." And during 1910 and 1911 he attempted to carry further the work encouraged by Nietzsche of liquidating those moral and religious sentiments which had corrupted the Socialist cause. Most Socialists, he observed, were "simply frauds trading on emotional credit." They pretended to the "possession of feelings which, in fact, they never experience." They were "frustrated souls, self-cheated of self-knowledge" for they were strangers to the pain strong feelings brought.[104]

The task of escaping from the special sensibility underlying Ethical Socialism was much greater than Orage realized. But in the years ahead he set out with his colleagues on the *New Age* to reformulate the Socialist ideology. For many Ethical Socialists, however, the way to the new society no longer led into the political arena. They began to follow a number of new paths in their efforts to recover the distinctive aspirations of popular socialism. Yet, the exhaustion of Ethical Socialism had also left some of its adherents vulnerable once more to the metaphysical anxieties and the divided state so prominent among the early converts.

6

ETHICAL SOCIALISTS: THE RETREAT FROM POLITICS

IDDLE CLASS SOCIALISTS who were unwilling to see their hopes vanish through the workings of the political process were increasingly stranded after 1910. Forced to reassess the movement, they began to recover aspects of Ethical Socialism which had been set aside during the struggle to build a working class party. The social and aesthetic aspirations found in the writings of Morris, Ruskin, and Carlyle now regained something of their earlier vitality.

The shift in outlook was encouraged by widespread political disaffection among the workers after 1910, and by the growing popularity of Syndicalist and "industrial unionist" notions of social reconstruction. In a scheme for "national guilds," developed by Sam Hobson in the columns of the *New Age* during 1912 and 1913, the new ideas were blended with ethical and aesthetic impulses in British socialism. Guild Socialism, as the scheme came to be called, provided fresh inspiration for many who had become disenchanted with politics. It did not arrest for long, however, the process of ideological dissolution. Already, in fact, some of the Ethical Socialists were turning away from the goal of institutional reform and searching once more for an integrating faith. The search can be followed in the development of Orage. But it took various directions, as evident in the lives of three young men who entered the movement after the turn of the century—Eric Gill, Edwin Muir, and Herbert Read.

The Rejection of Collectivism: *Guild Socialism*

By 1910 the group around the *New Age* was almost completely estranged from the ILP and the Labour Party. Their paper, Orage conceded, was "practically boycotted" by those it had sought "disinterestedly to educate." Yet he welcomed the divorce. Since Labour Party leaders had rejected any clear Socialist identity, so too, Socialists could free themselves from their political obligations to the party and start afresh. "We cannot but feel that the New Age has received a call to be something more than the organ of a party which has already cast it off . . . From many quarters we have received the expression of what seems to be a widespread desire for some constructive suggestion . . . opening wider vistas . . . To that demand we hope to make a suitable reply."[1] The reply did not come for two years. But even before he took over the *New Age* Orage had been committed to a scheme of social reconstruction which ran counter to the collectivistic orientation of the ILP and the Labour Party. He had drawn his alternative conception of socialism largely from a friend in Leeds, Arthur Penty.

Penty had been a successful young architect when the demand for his work suddenly collapsed. To explain the break in the "economic continuity of my life," he attempted to understand the broader social setting within which it had occurred. "I had to turn myself inside out and learn to state in objective and impersonal terms, an experience that was subjective and personal." Through the guidance of Ruskin and Morris he traced his personal setbacks to long-range economic developments—the disappearance of the guild system, the growth of limited liability companies, and the unrestricted use of machinery. In the idea of a reunion of the artist and the craftsman, advanced by Ruskin and Morris, Penty found a fresh approach to social reconstruction. Yet, "systems and institutions," he concluded, were simply the visible expression of "active creative principles" and motives within men.[2]

In 1906, after moving to London, Penty presented his views in *The Restoration of the Guilds*. The small book was at once a fresh statement of the Socialist vision derived from Ruskin and Morris and an attack on the collectivist outlook which was coming to dominate all sections of the Socialist movement. The Collectivists, Penty argued, had mistakenly fixed on competition as the chief evil of capitalism; their concern with the well-being of the masses and with greater efficiency by means of a program of nationalization would "establish the worst features of the present system more securely than ever."[3] The true evil of capitalism, according to Penty, was commercialism, a term Morris had used to summarize such characteristics of modern society as the division of labor, mechanization, cheap and shoddy goods, the pursuit of money, and the low level of aesthetic tastes. Commercialism had destroyed craftsmanship and degraded the life of the worker.

For Penty, as for Ruskin and Morris, the medieval guilds had expressed a way of life in which commerce and politics were properly subordinated to the higher claims of religion and art, the principle of mutual aid prevailed, and each section of the community had its own appropriate duties and functions. To reverse the modern process of competitive growth, technology, ugliness, and money making, Penty looked to the trade unions, which already possessed many of the functions of the old guilds, as the "new center of order." The reform movement should shift its emphasis from politics to industrial activity.[4]

Penty did not utilize the economic analyses of the Marxists or the Fabians to build his case. Underlying his argument for restoring the guilds was an interpretation of history and a millennialist vision drawn directly from Carpenter. The "full significance" of his book, he stated in the preface, could only be grasped if it was "considered in conjunction with the theory of Edward Carpenter in *Civilization: Its Cause and Cure*." Penty was attempting to forge "the links required to connect the theory there enunciated with practical politics." *The Restoration of the Guilds* displayed, in fact, themes central to the writings of Carpenter—the need to simplify life in a radical way, the desire for a unified human existence based on the emotions, and the belief in the "unconscious wisdom" of the people. Penty also sounded the apocalyptic note present in Carpenter. A civilization which had "become so artificial" was "doomed to collapse through its total rottenness."[5]

Penty attributed the defects of his age mainly to an "internal spiritual decline." The separation of religion, art, and philosophy from life had "plunged society into the throes of materialism." Collectivism, he declared, was simply an attempt to "remedy the evils occasioned by the individual avarice of the few by an appeal to the avarice of the many—as if Satan could cast out Satan." Penty thus reasserted the moralistic impulse characteristic of Ethical Socialism.[6]

In his restatement of socialism Penty introduced an antidemocratic note absent from the writings of Morris and Carpenter. The new society based on guilds would "check the present anarchic tendencies of democracy" and free producers from the "demoralizing tyranny of an uninstructed majority."[7] Penty renewed the stress on hierarchy and subordination found in Ruskin. He expressed too the growing fears of working class domination evident among middle class Socialists.

The fears were apparent in the efforts of Penty and Orage to form a Guilds Restoration League in the summer of 1906. A draft of the objectives of the League, circulated to various Fabians and others, announced the desire to "give political application to the aims and objects of the Arts and Crafts Movement" and promote a common understanding with trade unionism. But Orage was convinced, as he told Wells, that the "real obstacle to middle class conversion to Socialism" was the fear that it might involve domination by trade union officials. While most artists and craftsmen supported the labor program on grounds of justice, he added, the collectivist formula would have to be modified to make room for aesthetic concerns.[8] The prospectus of the League combined "an economic and an artistic revolt."

The Guilds Restoration League consists of Socialists who, while agreed that the present Labour Programme is a necessary condition of the solution of the social problem in its material aspect, are nevertheless convinced that the final solution demands that provision shall be made for the imaginative and spiritual needs of mankind. And it affirms that the application of this principle to the problems of industrialism necessitates the Restoration of the Guild System as the only means whereby the integrity of the crafts may be secured.

Little came of the project to form the League. And when Orage restated the case for the guild system in the *Contemporary Review* during the summer of 1907, he protested against the "exclusive association of Socialism, which is no less than the will to create a new order of society, with the partial and class prejudice ideals of the working man." Orage had abandoned his earlier hope that the trade unions could be transformed into guilds. The natural attitude of the trade unions was simply collectivism, which expressed the "movement of revolt on the part of the wage labourers against the pressure of competitive individualism." The Socialists had been "generally blind to the danger of entrusting all their hopes to the Labour Party." "As a Socialist," Orage wrote, "I cannot forgive them their political ineptitude nor their betrayal (for it seems no less) of the interests of artists, craftsmen and imaginative minds generally." The lesson was clear. "A class that entrusts its well being to an inferior class is doomed to disappointment." As long as the trade unionist was committed to collectivism the artists and craftsmen would have "nothing to say to him." Indeed, the triumph of trade unions would mean the extinction of the creative spirit of craftsmanship. It was time, Orage argued, to end the close cooperation between the Socialists and the trade unions and consider separate political action.[9]

Orage's commitment to the guild ideal throws light on his role as editor of the *New Age* between 1907 and 1910. Despite his initially conciliatory attitude toward the Socialists in Parliament and the Labour Party, it seems clear, as his biographer observed, that he hoped to capture the Socialist movement and "lead it toward a different goal."[10] Penty was associated with the paper in its early months, contributing a series of articles on "The Restoration of Beauty to Life." And when Orage attempted, in the series of articles "Towards Socialism," to give a new philosophical orientation to the movement, the guild scheme was implicit. But during 1908 and 1909, as the *New Age* concentrated on political developments, this aim faded into the background.

The break with the ILP and the Labour Party made it easier for Orage to revive the guild ideal. Moreover the earlier hopes for a restored guild system and the growing suspicion of politics among Ethical Socialists were being reinforced by two new currents of thought—distributivism and syndicalism. During 1907 and 1908, G. K. Chesterton and Hilaire Belloc had engaged in a vigorous debate with Shaw and Wells in the columns of the *New Age* over the merits of collectivism. Though Chesterton and Belloc challenged the socialism of the Fabians from the standpoint of the traditional liberal concern for individual rights, they expressed a hostility toward the industrial order much like that of Carlyle, Ruskin, and Morris. And their proposed remedy—a decentralized distributivist state, made up largely of peasant proprietors—was congenial to those Ethical Socialists who looked with longing back to simpler social forms. Like many Ethical Socialists, the distributivists also challenged the emphasis of the Fabians and the Labour Party leaders on the material aspirations of the workers. Belloc used the phrase "servile state" to summarize the process by which the workers were sacrificing their freedom for welfare measures. By 1911 he was interpreting the new legislative proposals of the Liberals, particularly the National Insurance Bill, as a movement toward despotism. In the years just ahead Orage would adopt many of the arguments and much of the rhetoric of Belloc in his own running quarrel with the Socialist and labor politicians.

The Syndicalists and the industrial unionists also helped Orage and his associates redefine socialism. In the summer of 1910, after the Osborne decision had impaired the financial basis of the Labour Party, Orage noted the rapid spread of new concepts of working class organization and urged the trade unions to move back toward industrial activity. The Socialists would thereby be freed for new propaganda on a "vast scale . . . among all classes." Orage reinstated his earlier hope that the trade unions might play a crucial role in social reconstruction by assuming administrative responsibilities similar to those exercised by medieval guilds.[11]

Orage welcomed the syndicalist notion of a general strike as a necessary albeit "desperate remedy" for the workers. Its significance lay not so much in its material outcome as in its moral and spiritual effects. The workers would gain increased self-respect through their "willingness to stake everything" and, eventually, from "the conscious possession of power." But

Orage was also becoming convinced that Britain would be saved from the alternatives of industrial strife and a "plunge . . . into slavery by means of charitable legislation" only through some new plan for the national organization of labor.[12]

During the early months of 1912 Orage began to scout a new path for Socialists. Penty helped by contributing a series of articles in which he renewed his attacks on modern social and economic organization and attempted to counter criticisms of his scheme for restoring the guild system. He stressed once more the decay of social values and the destruction of aesthetic standards. Meanwhile, Orage was seeking a middle way between collectivism and syndicalism, convinced that the latter, with its "purely materialistic" and "single class principle," would "erect unions into tyrants." He advanced the idea of coresponsibility in which the "unions as corporate bodies and guilds are associated in joint responsibility with the owners of capital . . .

A fresh acceptance of the integral character of the unions and their right to an equal share in the responsibility of managing in the businesses their men are engaged in is the only concession the masters can make that will solve for our generation at least the problem of labor unrest . . . The true line of development of our trade unions is therefore most likely in the direction of the restoration of the essential features of the guild system, responsibility for skilled work of members, the disposition of its collective forces, and joint control with their clients (employers) of the whole range of industry.[13]

These ideas provided a background for the scheme of national guilds presented by Sam Hobson in a series of articles beginning in April. To the task of redefining socialism Hobson brought twenty years of experience with various groups in the movement as well as considerable knowledge of the world of commerce. In his attempt to work out the implications of the new approach to Socialist reconstruction, however, he diverged in important ways from the paths envisioned by Penty and Orage.

Hobson's role in the circle around the *New Age* was later

described in several novels, where he appeared as a cynical, rather disillusioned man of the world, and something of an adventurer, both in economic affairs and matters of the heart. Allusions to Hobson in the correspondence of prominent Socialists were at times darkly suggestive, though vague in nature. His autobiography, one of the most revealing accounts of the movement, discloses little of his personal life or even his ways of making a living. But it was this "strange and difficult man" who now took up the task of saving the Ethical Socialist vision from the compromises of the Labour Party politicians.[14]

In earlier years Hobson had sought to integrate the disparate impulses within the movement. Thus in a talk before the London Fabians in 1907, he attempted to bring the "ethical" and the "economic" sides of socialism back together. He noted the "bitter feud" between the "two temperaments" found in the ILP and the SDF, respectively, and argued that each point of view led to an impasse. The ethical emphasis of the ILP precluded "hard thinking" and it "infused into Socialist thought and action a purposeless opportunism that weakened the revolutionary fibre of the movement." Those who confined socialism to economics, however, missed "the human side of the problem" and created the impression that "we must submit to mighty and mysterious economic forces . . . that we are impotent to . . . modify." Hobson argued that ethics and economics were "rooted in identically the same impulse"; further thought would demonstrate that "whatever is economically necessary is ethically desirable and vice versa." Ethics was simply "the science of transforming our economic conceptions into a code of conduct." Hobson's language suggested both Marxist and anarchist influences. Socialism, he concluded, should intensify the class struggle "to the great end that it shall finally be dissipated and merge into a society reconstituted on the basis of mutual aid."[15]

Fabian development provided little place for such a conception, and Hobson resigned from the Society in 1909. He also became, like one of his fictional counterparts, "sick of the futilities and insincerities of politics." The "lesson we have learned from a decade of political labourism," he wrote late in 1911, "is that the industrial and economic situation remains profoundly unaffected by political action." And he warned those Social Democrats who were inclined, by means of the newly formed British Socialist Party, to return to politics "like a dog to its vomit," that they would "in a few years follow the old trail with the same disastrous results." Hobson was now committing himself more clearly than ever to what he called the camp of the revolutionist. The revolutionist was one who chose the "great game of life, which was an affair of the spirit," over the "rotten game" where one attempted to organize "imperfect man." Unlike mere reformers, who accepted the existing system, the revolutionary wanted to "get out of humanity all that there was in it." He was "quick to perceive that the formula and the phrases, the song and the music, the liberties and the law, that spring out of the revolution, speedily envelop the released prisoner in a new servitude." But Hobson had concluded that a revolutionary escape from the wage system required new forms of economic association, for "real power is to be found where wealth is produced." In the scheme for a national guilds system which Hobson elaborated in the *New Age* during 1912 and 1913, he offered a new synthesis of many of the elements making up the British Socialist movement.[16]

Hobson's attack on the wage system indicated the strong Marxist strain in his thinking. The Social Democrats had been correct in identifying the wage system as the "real enemy," for it enabled the employers to draw off surplus value and reduce the worker to a bare subsistence level of existence. More important, the wage system extruded the worker's personality from his labor and transformed it into a commodity like other "inanimate elements" in the productive process. The Social Democrats were also correct, according to Hobson, in relying on the class struggle to abolish the system. Indeed, the struggle between labor and capital would have to be "conducted on a war footing"; workers engaged in a strike should "disregard all legal obligations precisely as soldiers do in an enemy's country."[17]

Hobson described the end of the wage system in terms similar to those found in the early writings of Marx. The "return of labor to its natural habitat in the human body" would mean that where a man's labor goes "he will go too, entering into and owning its fruit. It will hence become a vital part of himself . . . the instrument of his destiny." Yet, this vision of human reintegration came not from Marx but from Ruskin and Morris. Hobson's socialism rested on an "aesthetic and ethical proposition," the belief that "innate passions" inclined man toward "honest production" and the "creation of beautiful things." Such impulses were, according to Hobson, thwarted by modern industry, for the accompanying drive toward specialization prevented most workers from learning a craft. It even appeared to Hobson that the "vast majority of manufacturers" were in a "gigantic conspiracy to crush out that very craftsmanship which is the life blood of their occupations." And he looked forward to a form of labor "as richly human as it was under the medieval guilds."[18]

These anti-industrial sentiments were deceptive. Hobson did not reject the major tendencies in modern economic life. The guilds which he hoped to substitute for the wage system had little in common with the regulative associations of independent craftsmen found in earlier times and idealized in the writings of Ruskin and Morris. The new guilds were as G. D. H. Cole described them, "vast democratically controlled agencies for the reorganization of industry."[19] They would be created by transforming existing trade unions into organizations which embraced skilled and unskilled workers, as well as the salaried groups of clerks and managers, within a given industry. The National Guilds were compatible with the dominant features of contemporary economic development—large-scale machine production, a complex division of labor, a dynamic technology, and international commercial relationships. Only those persons devoted to the creation of new ideas and inventions, such as writers, artists, pure scientists, and poets, would not be subjected to guild regulation.

Hobson accepted the syndicalist claim that political power was but the "shadow or reflection" of economic relationships and regarded the bureaucracy or civil service of the modern state as "essentially anti-democratic." The state retained, nevertheless, a fundamental role in the coming Socialist society; it would charter and equip the guilds, represent the community at large, and be the "final arbiter" in disputed matters. Hobson's

Fabian past was apparent in his reliance on the state to guarantee a fair and efficient distribution of goods and, through its educational function, to raise the level of citizenship. Something of the Fabian approach to politics was apparent in Hobson's contention that the public life had nothing to do with economic interests or crude ambitions; politics was at once the "science of social life" and a place where the "finer passions and ambitions of mankind" should find expression and satisfaction.[20]

Convinced that the Socialists had taken a "wrong turning" through their "adventure into politics" and their "agitation for mere nationalization," Hobson was seeking to awaken Socialists from "a decade of troubled sleep" and place the "pioneers once more on the march."[21] And so he did. In the years ahead his conception of guild socialism proved to be a rallying point for Socialists who were politically disenchanted.

The path opened up by Hobson diverged rather sharply from that envisioned by Penty. Even before Hobson's series of articles in the *New Age* was completed, Penty had returned to its columns with a revised version of *The Restoration of the Guild System*. While he did not attack Hobson directly, he criticized those who were advocating guilds "purely on the ground of political and administrative expediency" and insisted on the "desirability of maintaining in its integrity the old guild form." "When I advocate restoration I mean the guilds as they existed in Medieval Europe . . . associations of small masters where relations of personal devotion and service prevailed. Unless we can restore to society these personal and human ties then any restoration of the Guilds is purposeless." Small workshops, Penty conceded, might be compatible with machine production, but he rejected a system based on factories and commercial middlemen. Moreover, he opposed Hobson's stress on the class struggle and the resort to strikes and violence if necessary to break the hold of the wage system. Socialists should give priority to the education and personal reform of individuals.[22]

Hobson had made too many concessions to the modern world to suit Penty. But his ideas were adopted with enthusiasm by many *New Age* readers who had lost confidence in the ILP and the Labour Party. The guild idea also registered strongly on the Fabian Society. Here too disenchantment over the course of the Socialists in Parliament had prompted a new challenge to the Society's policies. It was led by G. D. H. Cole, who quickly became the leading spokesman for Guild Socialism.

Cole had been influenced initially by the writings of Morris and his claim that socialism represented a "completely alternative way of living."[23] He accepted many of the anti-statist views of the Syndicalists and the Distributivists, and, with the aid of Hobson's formulation, developed a rather similar conception of the future society in his book, *The World of Labour*, published in 1913. Here, and in later books, Cole made more room for Fabian elements in Guild Socialism; he rejected Hobson's sharp separation of the political and the economic, gave the state a greater role in the creation and coordination of the guilds, and reinstated Fabian notions of public ownership as a means of making the transition to the guild system. Early in 1915 Cole and other Fabians created, in the National Guilds League, a propaganda agency for the new form of socialism. Although the group broke with the Fabian Society in 1915 after failing to convert it to the guild idea, Cole and his associates retained the Society's commitment to careful social investigation. His subsequent elaboration of the theory of Guild Socialism was conditioned by his Fabian-like demand for empirical research and for practical proposals. And while the ethical and aesthetic aspirations underlying Cole's Guild Socialism tended to fade somewhat in later years, his career continued to express the contrary pulls of Fabianism and Ethical Socialism.

Hobson's subsequent development, less governed by Fabian constraints, reflected the decline of the guild extension of Ethical Socialism. He had left the country shortly after the publication of his articles on national guilds in order to take part in a business venture in Brazil. His return to England in the spring of 1915 coincided with the attempt of Cole and others to launch, in the National Guilds League, a vehicle for the ideas he had helped to formulate. And over the next several years, despite the damper which the war placed on schemes of social reform, Hobson participated in the work of the League and attempted to develop his concept of the guilds in the columns of the *New Age* and the *Guildsman*. However, his pessimistic assessment of the state of the movement was apparent in an article published in 1916. "What I wanted I still want; but I perceive that I desired something infinitely greater than the Socialist movement has in it to give. Socialism is now reduced to an affair of party politics—colored by a vague expectation that we can compel our bureaucracy to deal more humanely with labor than the present proprietors. Behind that thwarted revolution was a new spiritual vision, now blurred to all eternity."[24]

At the end of the war Hobson found an opportunity to apply his conception of the guild to actual economic developments. An acute national housing shortage, legislation which provided easy credit for housing construction, and Hobson's contacts with trade union leaders in Manchester, enabled him to create a builders' guild and attempt to demonstrate the virtues of the new Socialist approach to industrial life. Strong support for the experiment came from other Guild Socialists and for several years the National Guild of Builders carried the hopes of many of those who were seeking a noncollectivist route to a Socialist society.[25] The venture failed. Its demise was attributed to defects in Hobson's character, to poor management, and to the inherent difficulties of such an experiment in a capitalistic world. Yet, despite the failure, the ILP, struggling to recover its ideological identity, incorporated much of the guild scheme into its new constitution of 1923.[26]

In later years Hobson drifted to the fringe reform movements in British life, seeking to the end to find a new vehicle for the guild idea. But his death in poverty and obscurity in 1940 was in a way symbolic of the fate of the cause with which he had identified himself. Indeed, nearly twenty-five years earlier Hobson had written his own epitaph: "We will go down to our graves with our hunger unsatisfied, with a dull ache at the heart, because what we loved has not stood the test."[27]

ORAGE: *An Editor's Progress*

Hobson had answered the call for a new Socialist gospel. And the *New Age* served as an organ for this effort to revitalize the movement. But despite Orage's role in preparing the way for the guild idea, he did not contribute much to its elaboration. Indeed, the vagueness of his own contributions led one correspondent to attack him for his "complacent satisfaction with a phrase you have never bothered to think out."[28] Orage was, in fact, much less interested in the institutional issues raised by Hobson than in the ethical, aesthetic, and metaphysical questions which were arising once more along with the breakdown of the popular form of socialism.

For a time following his break with the ILP Orage had hoped for a "renaissance of political Socialism." Such a recovery would require that the Socialists free themselves from the trade unions. The Socialist "capture of the unions" had turned out to be a blunder, because the "class consciousness which the [Labour] party rejected in theory" had proven too strong. In excluding middle class intellectuals from positions of leadership, moreover, the party had lost its capacity to "face national problems" from an advanced viewpoint. The Osborne Judgment of 1909, which pronounced the financial contributions of the unions to the Labour Party illegal, seemed to Orage a "blessing in disguise," for it meant the "destruction of the existing Labour Party." Socialists could "resume their interrupted work of organizing men politically and resume their propaganda on a vast scale among all classes."[29]

The workers, according to Orage, should concentrate once more on economic organization. He welcomed the strategies of the industrial unionists and the Syndicalists. The general strike was an especially effective weapon for the working classes; it would enhance their self-respect by demonstrating their "willingness to risk everything." Still, industrial action by itself was "blind." It generated energy but the political activity of the Socialists was necessary to apply and give direction to the new force.[30]

Orage's advocacy of a new Socialist political initiative was misleading. He had no sympathy for conventional political activity; he rejected the view that parliamentary representatives should be engaged in the reconciliation of the diverse interests and aspirations of the various groups making up the nation. The true representative, according to Orage, did not speak on behalf of personal or sectional interests; he was "synthetic . . . He is the community individualized and acting as a single body." Plato's influence was apparent in Orage's conception of politics, but he also borrowed from the Fabians. He lamented the absence in the modern state of a "disinterested class of scientific statesmen supremely indifferent to anything but the highest welfare of society, a class let us say of Platonic guardians." Genuine politics was based on the capacity of enlightened men to discover the "true mind of the nation."[31]

Orage denied the legitimacy of the party system. He supported the proposal to pay members of the House of Commons because it would free them from the domination of the party. "The present demarcations, so irrational, so nebulous in theory, so gross in fact, will happily pass away." He looked forward to a time when every subject of legislation would be "placed above party." True legislation was "wholistic"; to alter marriage laws, for example, without dealing with the fundamental problem of capitalism was futile. Indeed, "true politics" would await the destruction of the wage system; the contemporary reforms of the Liberals were "mere plaster." Lloyd George's National Insurance Bill represented the "reductio ad tragicum" of a process that was carrying Britain to ruin. The bill, according to Orage, was "conceived in private iniquity, and brought forth in deception: it was cradled in lies and . . . fed on bribes and corruption." It expressed a vast conspiracy among capitalists bent on nurturing a proletariat which was "comfortable and bourgeois." In accepting "such gifts" the workers were forging new links in their own chains. Orage bitterly assailed Socialists who supported the "ameliorative revisionist Labour policy of recent years," for it was designed to make the wage system more bearable. He charged that Sidney Webb, despite his opposition to the Insurance Bill, was more responsible than any other individual for the "anti-Socialist, anti-national . . . and anti-human drift" of politics. But he reserved his harshest words for the leaders of the ILP and the Labour Party who, in their "invincible stupidity," believed that "wage slaves can get from the employers something for nothing."[32]

Behind Orage's bitter remarks lay a belief that the Labour Party had betrayed the high political calling to which the Socialists had summoned it. After "kicking everyone of brains out" of its councils, the party had failed to develop any "philosophy of society at large" and degenerated into a mere vehicle for class interests. Orage had welcomed the Osborne judgment because it was a belated recognition of the danger of "allowing a single class of citizens to elect and maintain members of Parliament pledged not to their constituents to do their best for public policy generally, but to the members of their organizations to do their best for them alone." Such a practice had led inevitably to a deterioration of the politician's moral character. Orage attributed the "dumb malignity" of the Labour Party leaders to the fact that they acted out of motives of interest rather than conviction. A "cynical cunning" had come to mark the local labor politicians as well. No wonder "higher minds were repelled" by politics. Its present tasks were "so evil that only evil men would undertake [them] with their eyes open."[33]

One regular contributor to the *New Age*, Ernest Radford, found the volte-face on the part of an avowedly Socialist journal "disgusting." He charged that Orage had lost all program and principle and reduced himself to belittling the "life work of men who are entitled to your respect." But Orage was simply making explicit attitudes and social values which had been largely suppressed during the period between 1907 and 1910. He was becoming convinced, moreover, that the "ruling classes" would either have to educate the public or "submit to a new barbarism." "We of the culture classes must insist that public opinion be as well informed, as serious and consistent as we are ourselves," but present politicians, he complained, found it easier to deal with the "inferior order of being that we call the mob or the people."[34]

The social education Orage wished to advance indicated his continuing debt to Ruskin, Morris, and Penty, and his hostility to the main social and economic trends in British life. True progress, he wrote, led back "toward simplicity." Sociologists should, therefore, be concerned mainly with the problem of the "spiritual unity of society," and to this end they should look not to reason or science as the chief guides but to "creative art."[35]

Orage shared the social nostalgia found in much of Ethical Socialism; his conception of the guild system was closer to that of Penty than to Hobson's. But he had become convinced by 1912 that the trade unions were moving toward the "restoration of the essential features of the guild system" and the "recapture" of their craft traditions. Like Penty and Hobson he believed that the degrading effects of the modern wage system could be traced to the "frustration of a natural instinct for pleasure" in work and "pride in creation." He even saw in the "spontaneous, unorganized, and irresponsible" character of the strike activity in the spring of 1912 evidence that it was "morally rather than rationally inspired." And Orage expressed the hope that he would "live to see each of the unions with its armorial bearings and its officers on state occasions in gorgeous heraldic display."[36]

Orage was not as enamoured with the medieval past as this suggested. He combined archaic social conceptions and imagery with arguments on behalf of the material well-being of the workers and national efficiency which suggested the influence of the Fabians. The central economic problem for the workers was still the recovery of surplus value, though the "comparative fixity of the wage fund" made this impossible until the profit system was destroyed.

Orage was breaking ever more sharply, not only with Socialist and labor politicians, but with British political institutions. He conceded that his political views were leading to a form of "impossibilism." In the "decline of a nation," however, the only remedy had frequently been "something which was practically impossible." He now urged Socialists to boycott elections.[37]

To support his hopes for a radically different society Orage began to resort to claims which lacked any basis in the objective world. Thus, during a lull in the industrial strife in 1912 he assured his readers that the working classes were being inspired by hidden forces. Beneath the ordinary "supraliminal" consciousness was a "subliminal" consciousness, making up four fifths of the collective mind of the workers.

It is from the sunken mind of the wage earners that impulses of a profound and spiritual character may be expected to come. And they may be expected to come at any moment . . . The nation is at a moment when a great and momentous decision is necessary— a decision which mere reason is incapable of making. Everything the nation as a nation holds dear is at the moment in imminent peril of being lost. The only question is whether the national sub-liminal consciousness of the working class will divine the issue and thrust into articulate consciousness a new and great spiritual res-olution.[38]

Orage also claimed that a new and still invisible body of committed workers would save the Socialist vision. Were he not assured that the "present leaders of the Trade Union move-ment" represented the "last of their imbecile race," Orage de-clared, he would despair of its future and that of the "nation at large." Fortunately, there was a new generation of working class leaders, laboring obscurely in the provinces, who had "sworn not only to forgo parliamentary honors," but "to de-liver their class from the bondage of wage slavery."[39] Having ceased to see any intelligible connection between the actual development of the working class and his hope for a radically different society, Orage was resorting to fantasy to connect the two realms. He was also reverting to his earlier state of self-division.

Reviewing Holbrook Jackson's *England in the Nineties*, published in 1913, Orage recalled the dual impulses which made up the "feel" of the early days of the ILP. "Our social reforming zeal," he wrote, was not allowed to interfere with the pursuit of personal moments of choice sensation "inspired by Pater." In time, however, it had been necessary to "choose between personal and social idealism." Those who chose the former, he observed, had suffered melancholy, decadence, suicide, or pre-mature death, while others, among whom he included himself, had "abjured Pater" and hedonism and "plunged into the waters" of democracy.[40]

Democracy, or the Socialist cause, had carried Orage onto the plane of political action, but he had never renounced the personal quest. He did not view that quest in the aesthetic form of Pater's disciples but in metaphysical terms. His attachment to Carpenter, to theosophy, and to the teachings of Nietzsche, indicated his continuing effort to ground his socialism in basic philosophical or religious claims. The attempt had been sus-pended during the years in which the political struggle occupied the *New Age*. But with the exhaustion of Ethical Socialism and his rejection of "machine politics" Orage resumed his personal search.

By 1910 Orage was writing an occasional column, "Unedited Opinions," in which he recorded his efforts to overcome "continuous doubts and self-divisions." He had, in fact, split his editorial work in two. He still presented his weekly commentary on public affairs in a column called "Notes." But the two columns lacked any intelligible relationship. "The mind facing soulwards," he confessed, "gives a different and conflicting account of the world from that of the sensible mind . . . looking towards the manifested world of matter."[41]

Orage left little doubt in his "Unedited Opinions" as to the relative claims of the two minds. The "real aspiration of man is to maintain" his soul, the "source of his being, its essence, spring, and ultimate reality," and "live more and more in its life." To become a genuine soul, moreover, it was necessary to shed the "successive veils of complexity and lies" in which "we are brought up." "I am angered past pity . . . when I reflect on what it costs to disentangle one's soul . . . in the jungle of modern thought." Orage was convinced that spiritual integrity required a rejection of the "distinguishing characteristics of the modern world." The "true mark of the soul" consisted of its refusal to submit to the demands of "opportunism" and "practicality." Orage was retreating to a subjective realm where the self might contemplate an absolute perfection. And his "unedited self," or the spontaneous workings of his imagination, exercised a growing command over his political and social commentary.[42]

Orage provided a revealing account of the movement of his imagination in a series of stories published between 1910 and 1913, called "Tales for Men Only." Here he expressed hopes which he could no longer identify with the Socialist movement. The stories dealt with a small group of artists and philosophers who were seeking spiritual perfection through the formation of a "single group mind" or "collective soul." It would represent a "new order of being, a sort of living genius from which each of us may draw according to his need, and of which each of us forms, as it were, a limb or power." The artist exercised the crucial role in leading mankind along the "path to perfection."

"The artist," Orage wrote, "was the arrow, humanity is the bow. It is his aim and humanity's hope that he may be shot beyond the world." Although Orage had now rejected Nietzsche as a philosophic guide, his continuing influence was evident in the reaffirmation of the possibility of a superman. Even the political world might be made "safe" by his genius. "His concealed and esoteric influence, working behind the scene of men's minds, would actually control the scene on which the marionettes of the popular stage dangled in self-satisfaction."[43]

The quest for spiritual perfection was, as the title of Orage's stories indicated, "for men only." Several of the tales dealt with the author's efforts to prevent a female interloper from contaminating the group with sentimentality and philanthropic goals. Since sex was a woman's "whole existence," and her femininity was "unalterable," women were incapable of entering the "pure companionship of liberated intellects." Candidates for membership in the group were allowed "one single preliminary adventure among women" but no more. Nor was homosexuality an alternative, for the suppression of sexual desire was a prerequisite for true culture. The blatant mysogyny of the tales was also expressed at this time in the *New Age's* violent opposition to the suffragette movement. Women, according to Orage, had "deliberately given up civil responsibility" for the "economic security of the home." When, in 1913, the House of Commons rejected a bill to give women the vote, Orage expressed regret that the door was simply "banged in their faces" and not "bolted and barred."[44]

Such an outburst, together with the attitudes expressed in the tales, suggested Orage's failure to establish relationships of genuine mutuality with those around him. To his mistress of these years, looking back bitterly across a broken relationship, he seemed to suffer from "egomania" and "periodic fits of curious mental illness." Orage's own contention in 1911 that sex had no more significance than any other physical appetite, and certainly had no relationship with love, was perhaps a sign of the rift within. So too were his relationships with the younger men who entered the *New Age* circle. He sought, one of them observed, only disciples. Another noted that Orage carefully fabricated the "personality that he turned to the world." And

Hobson observed after his death: "With what supple ease and so resolutely did you screen your inner life from all of us."[45]

Orage's editorial style reflected his unwillingness to engage in give and take. Rarely did he acknowledge any element of truth in the position of his opponent; his style was personal and polemical. Despite the *New Age's* hospitality to new trends in art and literature, Orage did not encourage any genuine dialogue on fundamental social and cultural issues. Toward rival journals and the press in general he adopted a posture of sharp hostility. "Is it conceivable," he asked, "that we can write of the British press except in terms of hatred and contempt?" At times a paranoid strain was evident. Disturbed by the absence of public notice of the *New Age*, he charged that other editors and leaders of the government were boycotting the paper while "reading it in private." No wonder an outside observer remarked on the caustic bitterness and malevolence of the *New Age*. And G. D. H. Cole, the young Fabian convert to Guild Socialism, lamented the paper's "somewhat indiscriminate propensity to denunciation" and its tendency to "resent criticism of every sort."[46]

The style also reflected, however, the paper's dedication to the cultural mission announced in the "tales for men only." Something of this mission had been present in the *New Age* from the beginning. The paper had aligned itself initially, through Arnold Bennett's reviews, with the realist trend in contemporary literature.[47] An appreciation for the work of Wells, Galsworthy, Bennett, and to some extent, Shaw ran parallel to the *New Age's* support for the Labour Party. But following the break with the Labour Party and state socialism, the paper's outlook on art and literature shifted. The writings of the realists came under ever sharper attacks. Indeed, Shaw wrote to Orage to ask him where the *New Age* was going and then complained that he had "collected a set of the most stupid writers in England." Meanwhile, the readers of the paper were being introduced to post-realist or post-impressionist styles in European art by an able group of critics including Ashley Dukes, Huntley Carter, T. Sturge Moore, and Walter Sickert. By 1913 Orage could claim that they were developing "as serious and well considered principles in literature as we have in economics and politics." In time, he promised, "every part of the *New Age*" would "hang together," for the "literature we . . . love is associated with the forms of society we would assist in creating."[48]

No such synthesis of economics and literature, or politics and culture, emerged in the pages of the *New Age*. Its hospitality to the cultural *avant garde* tended, rather, to produce a highly eclectic fare. Nor did Orage's renewed interest in the socially redemptive functions of the arts connect him with the dominant tendencies in British cultural life. Despite some sympathy for Symbolist and Expressionist styles in the arts, he was hostile to the emerging modernist sensibility. He dismissed Yeats and the Irish School as banal and absurd; he denounced the Futurist painters as decadent, and attacked Ezra Pound, together with the Imagist poets generally, despite their prominent role in the *New Age*, as enemies of the paper on its literary side.[49]

Still, Orage believed that the artist should light the way to a higher level of human existence. Novels should be heroic rather than representative; they should "set the fashion in manners, conduct, character, and style." Drama, he argued, should be religious and present episodes in "the life of the soul" and the subconscious.[50]

For guidance in judging art and literature Orage had turned, under the influence of T. E. Hulme and other *New Age* writers, to classical models. As early as 1911 he had disavowed the romantic "delusion of indefiniteness" in favor of the Classical and Christian belief that man was a "fixed species" living in a universe of fixed truths. Orage retained, however, a romantic belief in the redemptive role of the artist, for the artist was engaged in the "imaginative perfection of nature" and called men to realize the ideal possibilities which lay behind appearances.[51]

Orage attempted, in his role as critic, to stand above the caprices of his time and judge current writers in terms of the established laws of literature" and general "moral laws." And in his column, "Readers and Writers," begun in 1913, he developed a capacity for stylistic analysis and a disinterestedness which influenced a number of younger British writers. His disinterestedness arose, however, out of his deep estrangement, not only from contemporary social developments, but from modern cultural trends as well. On those rare occasions when he judged specific literary works as a whole, in contrast to his more limited stylistic critiques, he was inclined to denounce rather than praise. By 1918 he had concluded that his age lacked the "settled background" of fact and imagination necessary to produce true art and was, therefore, hopelessly decadent. His cultural criticism was marked by a growing sense of futility.[52]

Orage's attempt to find in the realm of culture a corrective to the "spiritual anarchy" of the age and a source for social reconstruction served simply to increase his own state of division. His eighteenth century literary standards bore no intelligible relationship to the guild idea which the *New Age* was promoting in economic and political affairs. Orage made no attempt to integrate the two concerns. Moreover, by the end of the war both his metaphysical and his social views were undergoing basic changes.

Orage's commitment to Guild Socialism was weakened by his acquaintance with a new social prophet, Major C. H. Douglas. The ensuing "duel . . . for his soul" between Douglas and Penty ended with the victory of Douglas. The "Social Credit" scheme championed by Douglas provided a fresh approach to social reform; it promised a "social dividend" or "an annual share in the communal production" for every citizen by means of the manipulation of modern mechanisms of credit and currency. But the narrowly rationalistic terms to which Douglas reduced the social problem were increasingly remote from Orage's metaphysical quest.[53]

Orage's personal search during the war years can be followed in his "Unedited Opinions." He had turned again to the Eastern religious traditions for knowledge of ways to develop new spiritual faculties and achieve a full and harmonious expression of one's "illuminated instincts." The major Hindu epic, the *Mahabharata*, seemed to him to offer a wisdom which lay beyond the human plane. In May 1913 he expressed his desire to raise sufficient funds to send every reader of the *New Age* a copy of the book.[54]

Orage was encouraged in his renewed quest for higher levels of consciousness by the theories of the psychoanalysts, which the *New Age* helped introduce into Britain. In confining themselves "to the body," however, the psychoanalysts were limited, according to Orage, to the "lesser mysteries" and concerned with "generation" rather than with the "greater mysteries" and the "regeneration of the soul." For guidance into the greater mysteries Orage had turned in 1915 to Dimitri Mitrinovic, a member of the Serbian legation in London and a prophet-like figure, whose gospel was inspired by the writings of Christian mystics in the Eastern Orthodox tradition and by the Vedantic scriptures. Mitrinovic introduced his followers to spiritual exercises designed to lead mankind "back through the ages to the state of complete organic harmony which it enjoyed before the fall." Under the name Cosmoi, he wrote a series of articles for the *New Age* which developed the theme of the coming unity of the human race as one great self-conscious mind.[55]

But Orage did not rest in the teachings of Mitrinovic; he was discovering in the doctrines of G. I. Gurdjieff, through his disciple, P. D. Ouspensky, a more compelling cosmology. A friend who accompanied him to the meetings held by Ouspensky recalled the "profound emotional unheaval" and the despair experienced by the editor as the new prophet "swept all his theories and views more or less disdainfully aside." "I may find," Orage told him, "that all I have regarded as the real 'me,' the literary man, the artist, the philosopher, all is artificial. Perhaps my real bent is cobbling old boots." Gurdjieff's message reinforced Orage's growing disillusionment with "the purely literary and intellectual life," and his belief that since it "was leading me nowhere . . . I had to begin all over again." Not only did the new prophet explain the "fallen state," the cosmic source of the split characteristic of human existence, but he offered a method through which one could achieve complete harmony and self-perfection. It entailed the destruction of the "accidental personality" imposed by society or civilization and the recovery of an essence or "Objective Conscience, buried deeply within us." Beneath "the surface of things" was "hidden the oneness of all that exists."[56]

In 1921 Orage's life reached, under the impact of the new gospel, a breaking point.[57] He cut his ties with the *New Age*, entered Gurdjieff's institute near Paris, and undertook the training designed to purge his former self and lead to a new state of being. A year later, having absorbed the teaching of his new master, he traveled to New York to serve as Gurdjieff's chief apostle in America.

From his new religious perspective Orage criticized the various beliefs—social, ethical, and aesthetic—which he had held earlier. Just as the guild idea had been abortive when transplanted out of its "original setting" in medieval religious life, so too the Social Credit scheme of Douglas had proved to be impotent without a "change of heart." Nor could any system of morality which made the individual responsible only to his neighbor or to society provide a sufficient basis for reform. As for the confidence Ruskin and Morris placed on the power of beauty to advance social justice, it too was mistaken; the growth of the individual's artistic tastes was more likely to diminish "social feelings." Only religion, defined as "the attempt to establish an ideal and conscious relation between man and God," supplied the factor necessary to save mankind from the "extremes of imbecility and madness."[58]

In the course of his discipleship in America Orage, according to his friends, "died to an old self" and discovered a new mode of life resting on the belief that the "essence of things" lay in the inner realm of the "fantastic." His friends noted that Orage had lost his "mental arrogance" and his feeling that "he had to give an answer to every question." The "new man," Philip Mairet observed, was "less brilliant than the old" but he was humbler and wiser.[59]

The close association with Gurdjieff did not last. The circumstances of their separation—of Orage's voluntary "defrocking" before his group in New York—remain unclear.[60] But in 1930, after marriage and the birth of a son, he returned to England. A year later he gathered a number of his former colleagues around him in a new literary venture, the *New English Review*.

As editor of the *Review*, Orage took up once more the cause of Social Credit. But he remained committed to the ideas of Gurdjieff and the *Mahabharata*, convinced that they held the promise of a cultural renewal in Europe "comparable to that of the Renaissance." It was clear, however, that the divisions of earlier years had not been overcome. To one of his former colleagues he now seemed a "pathetic figure . . . leading an advanced army that had long since fallen in the rear." A year or so before his sudden death in 1934, Orage confessed that his "years of search and research" had yielded no answers to the question of the "meaning and aim of existence."[61]

Others shared Orage's belief that the politicians had betrayed the Socialist cause. And the decline of the movement plunged them, like Orage, back into the condition of division which had, for a time, been overcome by socialism. In their renewed efforts to deal with that condition they tended to accentuate certain features of Ethical Socialism at the expense of others. The disintegration of the popular form of the Socialist ideology can be examined further in the lives of Eric Gill, Edwin Muir, and Herbert Read.

Beyond Ethical Socialism: *The Ways of Gill, Muir, and Read*

Eric Gill, like many of the young middle class adherents of socialism, had turned to the movement after suffering the loss of a well integrated existence. His father, an Anglican clergyman, had passed from Congregationalism through Methodism to the established church and, in 1897, to a position at Chichester cathedral. For young Gill Chichester seemed, in retrospect, a world where "life and work and things were all in one and one in harmony." But when, in 1903, he went to London to train in an architectural firm, Gill recalled, "my whole world disintegrated." A "perfect specimen of the earnest and enthusiastic boy from the provinces," he had entered a "world which was almost entirely without moral certainties." During the period of "all around iconoclasm" which followed, Gill became an agnostic and "in a vague unattached way a Socialist."[62]

Socialism was for Gill a way of expressing his revolt against the chaos and ugliness of industrial civilization. Already influenced by the writings of Carlyle, Ruskin, and Morris, he could not easily submit to the demands of an architectural office where designs for churches and other buildings were being turned out in more or less mechanical fashion with no concern for the feelings or creative possibilities of builders or workmen. The work violated Gill's emerging sense of vocation; it required a "detachment of mind" and meant a "lack of integration." But Gill escaped from the dilemma. His skill as a stone letterer opened up an alternative livelihood and a path to independent artistic expression.[63]

Meanwhile he had joined the London Fabian Society. For a time he supported Wells in his challenge to the older leaders and then he worked with Orage and Jackson through the Fabian Arts Group in an effort to "deprive Fabianism of its webbed feet." Gill also contributed articles dealing with arts and crafts to the *New Age*. He had become convinced, like many of the Socialists inspired by Ruskin and Morris, that their successors in the arts and crafts movement had taken a "false track." In their efforts to overcome the separation between design and execution these reformers had mistakenly confined themselves to the task of educating the upper classes. They had made no impact on the workers who were, he believed, the source of true aesthetic values.[64]

Gill saw the trade union movement as a force capable of overcoming the deficiencies of the arts and crafts approach to reform. The trade unions were, he claimed in 1909, essentially "organizations of producers," seeking to "gain control of their conditions of industry." Although they had concentrated on demands for fair wages, the unions could liberate the "real craftsmen class" from the "degradation of wage slavery." All that was needed was security and a reasonable livelihood for the laborers to do the "good work" which was the "foundation of art." Art, after all, was simply the "well doing of what needs doing."[65]

Gill thus shared the tendency of aesthetically oriented Socialists to view the trade union movement and the Labour Party as forces which would advance the struggle of Ruskin and Morris against commercialism. By 1910, however, he had concluded that the Socialist and labor politicians were not concerned with the quality of production. They were "so moved by the outcrying of the underfed," so obsessed with the "interests of owners and exploiters," that they imagined "things could be righted by the making of laws." Gill concluded that the "politics of the Victorian era" had been "one long series of attempts by legislators to patch up and keep together a state essentially unsound." Later he attributed the hope of Socialists for "salvation through parliamentary action" to a "blissful ignorance." Lacking any "experience of actual political life," they were "unaware of its meanness and corruption, its fraudulence and hypocrisy," and the "corrupt and career seeking of trade union secretaries" and the labor men in Parliament.[66]

As Gill lost confidence in political methods he became convinced that religion provided the key to the revival of the arts. The "spirit of commercialism" and the conception of the world "as a place of trafficking without rhyme or reason" could be attributed to the "decay of the power of religion." For the old inspiration, men had substituted "knowledge of material facts" and "control over the forces of nature." The work of men had become as a result mechanical and degrading, and society in general had been deprived of "any common aim, any unity of experience and endeavor, any national, all-embracing inspiration."[67]

Religious and artistic activity were, according to Gill, intimately connected. The artist was the true "voice of God," he was "prophet and priest." He "united man with God" by creating images and instilling a spirit of worship and understanding. Indeed, works of art were the "only real products of the human race." Like Shaw, from whom he likely derived the notion, Gill had come to regard man, and particularly the artist, as the vehicle for the developing "consciousness of God."[68]

Gill's association with the Fabian Society did not survive the change in his outlook. In January 1911 he resigned, explaining to Pease that he had become skeptical of the possibility of "any real improvement in social conditions through legislation." The Fabian approach to reform, he declared, was like a "cart without horses." And he scolded Pease for his "notorious hatred of artists" and his failure to recognize the necessity of religion.[69]

To his close friend, William Rothenstein, he expressed his new religious yearning in terms both ecstatic and vague.

It is really too splendid if it's true . . . [the] possibility that religion is about to spring up again in England. A religion so splendid and so all embracing that the hierarchy to which it will give birth, uniting within itself the artist and the priest, will utterly destroy our present commercial government and our present commercial age. If this is true it is grand, if not then we are of all men most miserable.[70]

Gill claimed later that Nietzsche had helped draw him back toward a "spiritual basis" of life; *Thus Spake Zarathustra* was at this time one of his "most cherished books." Indeed, having been freed from conventional morality by this "sacred scripture," he had engaged in an extra-marital adventure which seemed, in retrospect, a "turning point." For the experience led him to reaffirm his love for his wife and young family. Nietzsche's ideas, Gill concluded, supplied only "mental pabulum"; they did not provide a "practical rule of life."[71]

Gill's changing outlook was also influenced by his experience as a craftsman. His first attempt at stone carving in 1909 had produced a "small revolution" in his view of life; the effort to fashion a nude female figure connected in a new way his erotic imagination and his manual skills. And as he extended his activity into sculpturing Gill uncovered depths of experience which, he believed, had been hidden from William Morris and his followers. Their work now seemed to him to be "lacking in guts"; they were not on "speaking terms with the devil." Strong sensual drives were being released along with Gill's developing artistic powers. His move toward an "all embracing eroticism," as a friend later described it, was only partially checked by his recovery of religious faith.[72]

In the Catholic church Gill found a way of unifying his seemingly divergent impulses; his new faith also indicated a way of transcending the existing economic system. If he was correct in tracing "all the ills of modern industrialism" to the loss of religion, he wrote Rothenstein, he was "duty bound to join the church." He had concluded, in fact, by the spring of 1911, that the Catholic church represented the only way of raising "citizenship to a higher power." Indeed, the church, he now felt, "should rule the world like a government." To a Catholic friend from whom he was seeking advice, Gill summarized his views.

> Since the age of seventeen or thereabouts I've wandered among the "new arts" and the "new religions," and the new politics too, and have been as enthusiastic as could be expected. But I've got through the Arts and Crafts, I've got through the Socialisms, and I've got through the new theologies. At the same time there is something in them all which is right. They are all revolts against the present devilish state of England. It seems to me from what I can learn and also guess that the Roman Church is the right answer to modern England and also to Morris and also to Wells and Shaw and also to the Campbellites and Besantites and Anglicans and the rest.

Early in 1913 Gill was received into the Catholic church.[73]

Gill had moved his family to Ditchling, a rural village in Sussex, during 1911. Here, with other Catholic craftsmen who settled in the area, Gill began to develop the idea of an artistic and religious community. He continued to condemn the factory system of production "without reservation" and, like the Guild Socialists, argued that the control of industrial organization and machines should "be in the hands of the workers." But the "impious muddle" into which men had fallen could only be overcome by a revolution. Palliatives served, in their "impatient compassion . . . to augment and prolong the evil." Still, Gill conceded that the existing system had acquired an almost irresistible momentum. To the author of a book on the scientific management of industry, he wrote:

> I fully admit you are on the rising tide . . . [but] in the end your side will not win because it bases itself on a false estimate of human nature. We say that normally (though certainly not at present or even generally) a man finds his greatest interest and pleasure and enthusiasm in his work, the work by which he earns a living. You aim at the opposite. You, as far as England and indeed the whole of modern civilization is concerned, will win . . . But the weakness of your position is that you do not in your heart believe that the factory system of production (I say nothing about machinery) is the best system.[74]

The war reinforced Gill's belief that a "revolution was coming" and, indeed, gave to his outlook an apocalyptic quality. A new state, he maintained, could only be built "on the ruins of a Godless civilization" if "we all become Christians" and adopt "poverty, chastity, and obedience" as ruling ideas. Unless personal relations and political life were reconstructed in terms of common agreement about the nature of man, the future held only deepening confusion and disintegration. Gill also sought to disengage himself further from the prevailing social order. Concerned because the income received from his stone carvings made him "absolutely dependent . . . on the few and cultured," he undertook to "insure against the future" by "learning to live as much as possible upon my own resources as a small landed proprietor."[75]

Gill attempted to create at Ditchling a new kind of community—"a cell of good living in the chaos of this world." Other Catholic families joined him to form in 1921 a "little guild of Christian craftsmen" under a religious rule derived from the Dominican order. The "Guild of St. Joseph and St. Dominic," he claimed, was "primarily a religious fraternity for those who make things with their hands." Their work would be done not only in order to produce goods for use but because it was intrinsically satisfying; the workers would own their workshops as well as the products of their labor. By means of this experiment and his writings Gill was seeking to guide the coming revolution in "a direction consonant with the fundamental facts of human nature and man's essential perfection." It was, admittedly, a "forlorn hope," but "not nearly so forlorn" as the efforts by legislators and art associations to "whitewash the sepulchre."[76]

Within three years the Ditchling Guild had split into two camps. The causes of the break are not clear but they lay to some extent in differing conceptions of the nature of communal responsibilities, and perhaps even more in Gill's desire to widen his distance from the conventional world. For some time he had dreamed of a "Ditchling over the mountains" and in 1924 he relocated his family and several others in an abandoned Benedictine monastery in the Black Hills of Wales. This new attempt to live according to the principles and beliefs which inspired "the pre-industrial world" lasted until 1928 when the community found a new and somewhat tamer retreat in Buckinghamshire. From these rural settings, comparatively "untouched by men of business," Gill could, however, accept commissions for his work and move from time to time back into the wider world of men and affairs. And while he came to accept to some extent the coexistence of two worlds—a world of machine minders, on the one hand, and his own world of humane labor, on the other—Gill believed until his death in 1940 that a civilization in which "things [were] grasped and possessed" was doomed. Only when men recognized their goods as "beings manifesting Being himself" could they "recover something of our lost equanimity, our lost integrity, our lost innocence."[77]

Human integrity could be regained, according to Gill, only by returning to the religious beliefs and social forms of the past. In Gill's life the social nostalgia which the Ethical Socialists had carried over from Morris, Ruskin, and Carlyle unfolded with a relentless logic. Unlike Morris, however, who relied on aesthetic feelings, or the natural pleasure of individuals in their work, Gill had reaffirmed religious faith as the sole basis for the good society. He could conceive of social reconstruction only in terms of a "unanimous state" where men were agreed on fundamental questions. But his utter rejection of modern economic and political institutions meant that he was in the end a "Christian exile" in a "strange land."[78]

Gill's journey ended, so his friend Father d'Arcy concluded, with ideas which had "no edges, and no relations and no background."[79] Edwin Muir, in contrast, arrived at a certain kind of reconciliation with the world around him. But no figure recorded so fully the state of anguish he experienced during the decline of his Socialist hopes. Muir was one of those "unusually articulate and conflict ridden" persons who brings "issues of general significance to a more vivid, intense, and clarifying focus."[80] The extraordinary psychological penetration of his autobiography, together with his early poetry and prose and his three novels, provides a unique account of the struggles of a young man in the professional proletariat to overcome by means of socialism the acute state of social alienation and self-division.

As a young man Muir had suffered the traumatic loss of a

well integrated way of life and had been plunged into a mode of existence filled with a sense of nameless anxieties and menace. He experienced the condition described by Ludwig Binswanger as the "distancing and devaluation and depletion of the world's abundance of life, love and beauty."[81] His Socialist commitment served as one of the strategies by which he sought to sustain an increasingly precarious self.

The Isle of Wyre in the Orkneys, where Muir was born in 1887, was a rural community still little touched by the major economic and social changes of nineteenth century Britain. Muir spoke of himself as having been born in 1751 and then making, at the age of fourteen when his family moved to Glasgow, a historical leap of one hundred and fifty years. Later the event seemed a "fall" from the harmonious order of his childhood—the cooperative ethos of the farmers, the intimate relationship with nature and animals, and the encompassing imagery and symbols of Bible and legend were irretrievably shattered. Muir recalled his sense of a broken world and the impact of the series of family deaths which followed the move to Glasgow. "All that time seemed to give no return, nothing but loss; it was like a heap of dismal rubbish in the middle of which, without rhyme or reason, were scattered four deaths. I climbed out of these years like a man struggling out of a quagmire but that rubbish still encumbered me for a long time."[82]

Wrenched out of the secure grooves of his childhood, thrown into the chaos of Glasgow, and seared by the family tragedies, Muir faced the task of rebuilding his world and bringing other persons, the physical environment, and his sense of self, into a more or less harmonious relationship. Although he obtained a series of clerical positions in the years ahead they did not provide any satisfactory basis for reordering his life. Filled with dejection at the prospect of becoming an "ageing round backed clerk," he constructed an inner realm of meaning to compensate for the dull routines of the office. "I lived two lives," he recalled, a "private life of intellectual discovery, and another in which the name of a book never escaped my lips and I was careful to behave like everyone else."[83] From his reading Muir was slowly and painfully finding symbols with which to build a new world.

Socialist ideas played a central role in this process of reconstruction. Muir was converted to socialism after reading Blatchford's *Britain for the British,* joined the Clarion Scouts, and became active in the Glasgow ILP. In later years he described the new sense of security he experienced in his first May Day parade.

> It was as though he had stepped out of a confused and distracted zone into calm and safety, as though the procession had protectively enfolded him, lifted him up and set him down again on the farther bank of a tranquil river among this multitude who like him had reached the favoured land; and the people who passed on the pavement with averted or hostile or curious eyes, on their way to church or merely out for a walk, had no longer any power over him; for they were still wandering out there in exile, out there on the pavement and he was safe, at home and free. Yet one thing still troubled him: that he was in the last line of the procession, so that the threatening world yawned at his very heels; but when a new contingent from the Kingston ILP marched up and stationed itself behind him his security became perfect; he was embedded in fold after fold of security . . . Even when the procession . . . crumbled . . . into isolated souls again . . . the spell did not lose its power and [he] wandered from platform to platform, where Socialist orators . . . spoke of the consummated joys of the future society where all people would live together in joy and love.[84]

Within the Glasgow Socialist movement Muir gravitated to a group calling itself the "intellectuals." Made up of "schoolteachers, civil servants, shop assistants, commercial travelers," and others, the members followed the latest literary and philosophical tendencies and discussed the ideas of such figures as Ibsen, Shaw, Wells, Carpenter, Nietzsche, Bergson, and Sorel. Muir also became a regular reader of the *New Age*, sharing its "contempt for sentimentality" and its "crushingly superior and exclusive . . . tone."[85]

Having reordered his life around an extravagant version of the Socialist future, Muir was highly vulnerable to the changing fortunes of the movement. And as the political prospects of the Socialists faded in the period after 1910, he began to experience in a new and severe way the anxieties which had tormented him earlier. Heinrich Heine's poems, which had become the main support for his "lyrical faith in the future," his "state of euphoria," now evoked feelings of dejection and thoughts of death. A poem dealing with death "seemed specially meant for me"; it expressed his deepening sense of isolation and separation. "I identified myself with the dead man who knew so well he was dead. Something in myself was buried and I was only half there as I worked in the office . . . I felt I had gone far from myself; I could see myself as from a distance, a pallid, ill nourished, vulnerable young man in a world bursting with dangerous energy."[86] Muir began to write poetry at this time and an early effort, "A Chronicle of Woe," mirrored his mood. Ostensibly concerned with the life of a laborer who, unable to find work, killed himself, the poem conveyed Muir's own sense of being an outcast in a hostile and menacing world, and perhaps his own "longing for sweet oblivion."[87]

Muir eagerly embraced the Guild Socialist ideas through which Orage and the New Age group were attempting to revitalize their ethical and aesthetic hopes. And during the war years he contributed to the movement's new organ, the Guildsman, published in Scotland. He worried, however, lest the efforts of the trade union leaders to secure material gains for the workers might endanger the process of industrial reorganization. One of Muir's first poems, "Address to Wage Slaves," published in the New Age in 1913, warned the workers to ignore "selfish counsels" and resist the temptation to "embrace a generation's comfort at the expense of servitude for ever for your children." The very future of civilization was at stake in their struggle.

> Not for yourself ye fight, mankind awaits
> Impatiently your holy proclamation
> And cannot stir until your fight is won
>
>   . . . . .
> Ye slaves supine, for only you, weak will'd
> Can burst the manacles which strictly bind
> Civilization in her sordid round
> The chains which fetter her encompass you
> The gloom which hides her face is for your shame
> Free but yourselves; and liberated, she
> Will move in triumph to her sacred ends.[88]

Still, Muir's "illusive world," as he said later, was "beginning to crumble." He wrote to Orage for advice. When the editor suggested that he immerse himself in the writings of a great thinker, Muir chose Nietzsche and found in the "fantasy of the superman" a "last desperate foothold for my dying dream of the future." But his rekindled devotion to remote possibilities made ever more tenuous his contact with real problems and real individuals. "My belief in the future, which once made me love mankind, now showed itself to be inhuman; but as I loved it above everything else I clung to it and let humanity go . . . Suffering had no place in the vision of mankind to which I clung."[89]

Nietzsche's philosophy did little to arrest Muir's renewed personal crisis. It deepened in 1914 when he took a clerical position in a boneyard outside Glasgow. In this new, often nauseating environment, his sense of estrangement from his physical surroundings, a periodic experience in these years, became more intense. He was filled with simultaneous feelings of separation and yearning. "It was as if I could grasp what was before my eyes only by an enormous effort, and even then an invisible barrier, a wall of distance, separated me from it." His very existence seemed to be imperiled. "Dread raised its walls around me, cutting me off; for even while I yearned for those things I felt a menace in them, so that the simplest object was dangerous and might destroy me . . . A jagged stone or a thistle seemed to me bursting with malice, as if they had been put in the world to cut and gash." Muir's relations with other persons was marked by a similar ambivalence. He alternated between a "desperate pursuit of company" and complete withdrawal. "I was more sociable and more lonely than I had ever been before." His inability to establish relationships of mutual trust was reflected in the number and transience of his "absent minded affairs" with women. Indeed, he developed a technique for "shutting the door . . . at once" whenever "he felt his deeper feelings in danger of coming up." Muir's world had become dangerously impoverished; both persons and things were losing their particularity and their value. "I moved," he recalled, "in a crystalline globe, a bubble, insulated from the life around me, yet filled with a desire to reach it, to be at the very heart of it and lose myself there." He was still, however, engaged in a strenuous effort to hold a personality together by force of will and Nietzschean ideas.[90]

The strain was apparent in the poems and prose pieces which Muir contributed to the *New Age* in these years under the pseudonym Edward Moore. So too was the shape of the personality he was projecting by means of these verbal stratagems. It was a personality frozen into a stance of unrelenting hostility toward the contemporary social and cultural worlds. Remnants of his Socialist ideology still entered into his indictment; man's enslavement to the industrial system and to machines meant that "economic emancipation must come first." But he was occupied mainly with the "spiritual aridity of modern life" and the "general dissolution of traditions" and values. Much of his critical wrath was directed against the literary realists—Bennett, Shaw, Galsworthy, Wells, and others—for their "crude and shallow" imitation of life. His chief target, however, was Christianity, with its leveling doctrine of original sin, and its moral derivatives of humanitarianism.[91]

The hand of Nietzsche lay heavy on this critique; it also shaped Edward Moore's vision of a new innocence in which the separation between instincts, morality, and reason would be overcome and mankind would once again enjoy a "good conscience." But while Christianity must be surpassed on man's road toward a "new sensuality and a new spirituality," man could not return to the simple harmony of the pagan world.

Spiritual humility, wherever it has spread, has continually weakened man by introducing within him a disrupting conflict. But it has also made life subtler and deeper; it has enlarged the inward world of man, even if it has straitened the world outside. So that when we return—as we must—to the Pagan ideal of "expression," our minds should be richer than those of the Pagans, for man has now more to express.[92]

If the main bent of Nietzsche's thought consisted of the acceptance of life in all its tragedy and suffering, Muir, or Edward Moore, was not a genuine disciple. His aphorisms were pervaded by the hope of a final resolution of man's "disrupting conflict." Indeed, men still possessed an "unconscious," a realm of innocence, beyond the reach of morality and intellect. Here lay the source of a creative love and joy in the things of the world which anticipated the "rapture of new life."[93] No statement could express more clearly Muir's sense of his own deficiencies or the way in which he was seeking to insulate himself against any bruising contact with real life by means of a screen of words and extravagant ideals. There was in fact a glaring contradiction between his aphoristic affirmations of love and beauty and his own life, which, as his friends recalled, was marked at this time by panic-stricken flights from the potentialities of human intimacy and by an adamant refusal to surrender for one moment to the aesthetic pleasures.

Paradoxically, the publication of Muir's aphorisms in book form in 1918, as *We Moderns*, stripped him of these elaborate verbal defenses. Having "flapped bravely enough in the void," he recalled, he now found himself "naked." He discovered how "genuinely unhappy" he was and at the same time experienced a strong sense of sin and guilt. This state also opened a "possibility of amendment."[94]

Liberation from his tightly repressed state came initially through the love of the woman who became his wife, Willa Anderson. Their developing friendship broke through the strategies to which Muir had resorted in his fear of self-disclosure. Marriage also drew him to London in 1919. The impersonality of the metropolis reinforced Muir's "feeling that I did not really exist," but the change also brought a new circle of friends. He became assistant editor of the *New Age*, although he resisted Orage's pull toward discipleship. Recognizing something of his personal difficulties, Orage arranged for Muir to meet one of England's pioneer psychoanalysts, Maurice Nicoll. For many in the *New Age* circle the Freudian concept of the unconscious seemed to "throw new light on every human problem" and promise a way of transforming the "whole world of perception." Muir's sessions with Nicoll were at once painful and liberating. The "dead memories of shame and grief" he had "shovelled underground . . . broke through" his resistance and made "great breaches and gashes . . . which I desperately tried to close up again and preserve intact my old flattering image of myself." But the image and the "whole world of ideas" Muir had laboriously built up did not survive the analysis. The superman, the main support of that world, "took himself off without delay" after a dream in which Nietzsche appeared in a crucifixion scene, suffering and triumphant.[95]

Muir's Socialist faith was also ebbing. By the end of the war he had lost his confidence in the proletariat as the savior of mankind. A poem, "Caliban," lamented the fate of laborers who "no longer love anything, not even themselves." His Guild Socialism, he recalled, had now come to occupy "only a clean dry place . . . [in] my mind." In 1920 he noted the materialistic outlook which had changed the spirit of socialism during the previous ten years, and he placed much of the blame on Blatchford's creed, with its determinism and its denial of "the evil in man." It was time, he added, "to call things by their own name" and recognize the need of the workers for goals beyond self-interest.[96]

Later, Muir analyzed the decline of his Socialist faith. He described his ideology as a "How," in which the older religious notions of salvation, of heaven and immortality, had been restated in secular and evolutionary terms. As such, the "How" was "so great that it seemed to fill all space and time, and ward off the 'annihilating experience' of the 'Why,' " or ultimate questions about human existence. Then came the "hour of doubt."

Thus there may fall on the believer a fear which the How, in spite of all its majestic inclusiveness, is impotent to relieve. And it is not merely the fear that can be caused by the recognition that the How, the pseudo-Why, is itself in process of changing, so that one has none but shifting ground beneath one's feet . . . No, it is a far deeper and yet vacant fear, the fear that if one were to comprehend the How from beginning to end, seeing every point in the universal future as luminously as the momentary and local point at which one stands, and seeing oneself with the same clarity as part of that whole, the universe might turn out to be merely a gigantic crystalline machine, before which one must stand in blank contemplation, incapable any longer of looking for a Why in it, so finally, though inexplicably, would that one thing be excluded by the consummated How.[97]

Insofar as socialism absorbed one's whole existence and became a "pseudo-Why," it seemed to Muir, looking back, to narrow the boundaries of life. It also tended, in his analysis, to deny the more intimate aspects of the self and human relationships. Hence his fictional portrayal of a Socialist friend who visited the family when Muir's brother, "Tom," was dying.

> He was indifferent to everything "personal" and scarcely found any interest in himself except for the fact that he was an advocate of Socialism . . . He felt at a loss in this atmosphere where the personal had unaccountably grown to such dimensions, overshadowing and bleaching all color out of the general, and making even the most clinching argument hollow and unreal . . . He could feel his authenticity oozing out of him . . . so that when he sat in the kitchen with Mrs. Manson and Jean and Mansie and Tom, sometimes he could hardly convince himself that he was there no matter how hard he talked. Nor indeed was he actually there to them except as a troubling succession of words.

Muir concluded that the future envisioned in his socialism consisted simply of "what is left when man eliminates from himself all that is displeasing, unclean and painful." The residue was merely a "human semblance, deprived of all attributes save two, shape and color; a beautiful pallid abstract of the human form." When the Socialist's "dreamed-of-heaven" faded, Muir recalled, the old "sense of separation," the "old dread of chaos returned." There came too a new longing for a "whole and perfect" world outside time.[98]

Muir's account of the dissolution of his Socialist faith was written some years later. In 1921 he and his wife had left England to live abroad and support themselves by means of literary work. During the years ahead, spent for the most part in Czechoslovakia, Austria, and Italy, he continued what his wife described as an effort to liberate "his true self."[99] His development was mirrored in his literary essays, his poetry, novels, and a series of translations of continental writers. Indeed, Muir's own experience of the cruelties and terrors of life probably gave him easier access than most to the work of those figures—Franz Kafka and Hermann Broch—who expressed most powerfully the social and cultural disintegration under way in central Europe between the wars. But by means of his own dreams and fantasies Muir also learned to come to terms with his earlier life. The process of reconciliation was guided in part by Nietzsche and the idea of eternal recurrence. In his novel, *Poor Tom*, he described a crucial moment in his journey. As he stood, in the guise of his fictional self, Mansie, looking at his dead brother, he "wanted to experience again, like someone learning a lesson, all that he had already experienced; for it seemed a debt due by him to life from which he had turned away, which he had walked around until his new road seemed the natural one, although it had led to places where all life was frozen to rigidity."[100]

As the old fears and hostilities melted down, Muir found, in Michael Hamburger's words, that "a truthful and thorough going subjectivity turns out to be the opposite." "The self of Muir's poetry is so thoroughly stripped of circumstance, pose and vanity as to be depersonalized."[101] The faithful recapitulation of his fall from the innocence of his childhood brought a new objectivity; increasingly he identified his own experiences with those of mankind in all times and places. In the symbolism and mythology of the Bible and the Greek world he found the means to clarify and express his developing perceptions of life. And he gradually returned to a more traditional conception of human existence in which the individual was engaged in a "fundamental moral struggle within."[102]

During the thirties Muir reaffirmed his Socialist faith, convinced once more that "capitalism prevents us from being human."[103] And his later poetry displayed a continuing sensitivity to political realities in a world of mass persecution and totalitarianism. But socialism and politics now occupied limited areas in Muir's view of life. He warned again, as in his earlier analysis, against the tendency for ideologies, including socialism, to view life wholly in temporal and utilitarian terms. Ideologies, and the works of the artistic imagination as well, were properly subordinated to a religious view of existence.

Along his way Muir had discovered that he believed in immortality, that he was a Christian. And in the doctrine of the Incarnation he found a means of understanding what he had come to see as the inextricable mingling of good and evil in life. Muir did not, in the end, overcome the oppositions and divisions with which he had struggled; he accepted them as ineluctable features of the human condition.[104]

In a brief memoir of Edwin Muir shortly after the latter's

death in 1962 Herbert Read noted their "deep affinity of origin and experience." He pointed to their similar childhoods in remote farming communities in the north, their traumatic removals to large cities at the age of fifteen to work as clerks, and their common enthusiasm for socialism and the ideas of Nietzsche. Both men also came under the influence of Orage and the *New Age*, contributed to its columns, and identified themselves with Guild Socialism. But during the war years, according to Read, their paths diverged. While Muir escaped the army because of physical disabilities, the war seemed to Read looking back as a time in his life that divided "innocence from experience, faith from disillusionment, hope from frustration." And he saw in Muir's later "intimations of immortality" and a "real self" beneath the "personality molded by will and time" a "class of experiences to which the war had left me sardonically indifferent." [105]

Read did not see very deeply into their divergent developments. Not only did his remarks tend to deny his own lifelong quest for a truer self beneath the plane of consciousness, but they belied the essential continuities in his own outlook. Despite his experiences in battle in France, Read emerged from the war with his prewar attitudes and commitments largely intact. Nothing in his wartime experience was comparable to the shattering experiences through which Muir had passed. Indeed, Read retained to a much greater extent than Muir the "first intuitive attachments" of childhood; "bright points of ecstasy" from that "lost realm," he observed, remained with him to some extent throughout his life and continued to influence his remarkable range of activities as a poet, art critic, and social visionary.[106]

Born on a farm in northern Yorkshire in 1893, Read suffered a rupture with a unified world at the age of nine when his father died and he was sent off to a boarding school. A further move to Leeds in 1908, and a job as a bank clerk increased his sense of estrangement. But family resources still permitted Read to look forward to a university education. After entering the University of Leeds in 1911, however, he turned away from the paths toward conventional careers in order to follow the intellectual adventure on which his reading had already launched him. The writings of Blake "shook me to the depths of my awakening mind . . . scattered the world of my objective vision and left me floundering in subjective fantasies." Nietzsche influenced him even more profoundly and produced a "decisive crisis"; for "at least five years he, and none of my professors or friends, was my real teacher." Read also experienced "vague political stirrings" in his university years and turned to the writings of the Socialists. He found the thought of the "humanitarians"—Morris, Tolstoy, Kropotkin, Carpenter—"more inspiring than Keir Hardie and Ramsay MacDonald." To these influences he soon added those of Proudhon, Max Stirner, Ibsen, Shaw, and Marx. But a pamphlet by Carpenter, *Non Governmental Society*, seemed to him to affect him most deeply; later he would trace his conversion to anarchism to the reading of this essay.[107]

Read was constructing his new mental world out of disparate materials. But he moved naturally into the stream of Ethical Socialism flowing through the movement in the West Riding. One expression of that movement was the Leeds Arts Club. Read joined it and through several of the members became acquainted with Orage. He followed the lead of the *New Age* in its attempt to renovate the Socialist movement. Although Read accepted Carpenter's vision of a society in which power and control would be decentralized, he did not believe that it was "immediately realizable." Moreover, he had been influenced by the economic determinism of contemporary Marxists and had come to doubt the efficacy of moral ideas. He was also attracted to the concept of national guilds advanced by the *New Age* as a way of reconciling the collectivist and Syndicalist forms of the Socialist movement. The trade unions, he wrote in the *New Age* in 1915, would provide the "units on which the future society will be built." And he argued that the creation of the guilds would mean that the "decisive features of production would no longer be monetary but rather aesthetic." The "ethical superiority" of this motive would enable men to realize the "cooperative ideal which was the golden dream of William Morris" and transform work into "something like artistic joy."[108]

Yet, by the time Read entered the army in 1915 he felt a

growing tension between his Socialist commitment and his personal ethical and aesthetic bent. He began to fear that the utilitarian aims of democracy might be "fatal . . . to spiritual superiority" and the "ideal of the superman." Read, like Orage, opposed the National Insurance Act because it threatened the "essential affirmation" of man—his "right to choose."[109]

For a time Read found in the writings of Georges Sorel a way of holding the two sides of his life together. Translated into English by T. E. Hulme in 1916, Sorel's *Reflections on Violence* seemed to Read to promise a "new individualism" and a "new socialism." The French thinker, Read declared in a *New Age* article, recognized that the Socialist revolution projected by Marx had been endangered by schemes of social amelioration which arrested the process of class polarization. To remedy the "social rot" Sorel had reinstated the "value of psychological activity" in the Socialist movement and, "the supreme value of heroic action" by affirming anew the collective myth of revolution. In emphasizing the place of violence Sorel had also pointed to a possible relationship between the war and the Socialist goal. Read argued that the war was nurturing a new spirit of heroism within the working class while at the same time sharpening class conflicts and thus bringing "Marx's hypothesis" of a "fatalistic revolution well within sight . . . [of] fulfilment." He professed his own readiness to "fight for Socialism . . . all the better for being an old soldier."[110]

Until the end of the war Read continued to see the guilds as the next stage in the development toward socialism. The guild or the "group system," he wrote in the *Guildsman* in 1917, was the proper unit of social reconstruction. Through the emphasis on "function" the groups would "eliminate state power," overcome its "abstractness" and remoteness and restore the "actuality which is the individual's salvation." By means of the guilds, moreover, "the State becomes the organism of the spiritual unity of mankind, the mother of a new race, the patron of a new art, the threshold of a new age."[111]

For Read the hope rapidly faded in the postwar years. Later he saw the "progressive retreat of Socialism based on freedom" before the growing power of the state as the decisive event of the twentieth century. But well before the collapse of Guild

Socialism Read had turned away from the movement in order to cultivate art as the chief redemptive force in life. In 1916 he proclaimed his faith in aesthetic activity. "Art is to my mind of such fundamental value that it should color one's whole outlook on life. It gives the world a fuller richness, a greater spiritual value; and to the individual it gives a sense of joy in things. Allied to love, it is a complete philosophy of life . . . Art unites us with something vaster—with the whole cosmic process."[112]

While still in the army Read, and a friend, Frank Rutter, started a new journal, *Arts and Letters*, to advance the redemptive mission of art. As a young poet he was already employing the imagist techniques being developed within the *New Age* circle. In the effort to find the "exact word" and "render particulars exactly," Read, like the other Imagists, was reacting against an excessively conventionalized poetry. His artistic attitudes, moreover, increasingly gave the lead to his political views. In 1918, after reading Thoreau's *Walden*, he declared himself an anarchist.

It [*Walden*] is a revolt of the individual against the association, which involves him in activities which do not interest him, a jumping to the ultimate anarchy which I have always seen as the ideal of all who value beauty and intensity of life. "A beautiful anarchy," that is my cry. I hate mobs—they fight to kill—build filthy cities—make horrible dins. I begin to think that their salvation and recreation is none of my concern.[113]

Read had not abandoned his hope for a fundamental transformation of society. The purpose of *Arts and Letters*, he declared, was to "return to the Socialism of Morris in preference to that of Karl Marx" and "insist on the primacy of beauty, even in economics." Although the new literary venture estranged him from Orage for a time, Read agreed to write the *New Age's* main literary column, "Readers and Writers," during 1921. And when Orage decided to give up the paper to follow the mystical path, he asked Read if he would take over the editorship. Read rejected the offer but in the years ahead, as art critic, poet, essayist, and educational reformer, he carried on the search for integrating principles in cultural and social life.[114]

Amid the dissolution of Ethical Socialism, Read was returning not only to the ideas of Morris but to the earlier romantic sources. He reasserted the claim of Shelley that the poet was, by virtue of his imaginative gifts, both seer and lawgiver. Through his apprehension of the image, the poet possessed a mode of cognition superior to that expressed by the analytical methods of reason or science; only the poet gained access to "reality in its nakedness." Read found fresh support for the claims of the Romantics in the writings of Bergson, Whitehead, Freud, Jung, and in the art of the Surrealists. Jung's argument that the fantasy-making activity of the poet was of "more-than-individual use" encouraged Read to give poetry a "kind of universal integrative function" formerly provided by myth or religion.[115]

During the mid-thirties Read renewed the "romantic assault on reality." He launched a fresh attack, from his neo-Romantic position, on British moral and social convention. Beneath the more or less stable "set of ideas and reactions," or "character," which the individual derived from society, lay a truer self or "personality" capable of existing "without division or inner revolt." From the Surrealists, in particular, Read drew assurance that the unconscious offered access to a superior reality closed off from ordinary consciousness and providing a corrective to the "massive self-deceptions" of normal life. It was from the "intimate, internal world" on the other side of consciousness that "true order issues."[116]

The creative artist, and especially the poet, was for Read the mediator between mankind and the deeper, hidden, saving realities. Aesthetic experience provided contact with the "very structure of the universe" and disclosed principles of conduct which represented a "complete alternative to the religious ethic." In place of "man-made systems" and ideologies, the artist brought the true principles of order present in nature. But nature's order was not absolute. In the dialectical relationship between the "active fantasy" of the artist and the "sensational and social world of action," the aesthetic faculty retained the power to bring new worlds into existence.[117]

Read presented his emerging aesthetic philosophy of life, as well as an account of his inner journey, in a fantasy published in

1935, *The Green Child*. The story also explored the opposing sides of his own personality. His active political side was expressed in the effort of his hero, Olivero, to build a perfect social order in the interior of South America. Approaching the political realm as an artist, for whom material resources and human beings were "so much plastic material for creative design," Olivero developed a "machine of government . . . working without friction of any kind." Although in form a benevolent dictatorship, this utopia realized aims which were central to Morris and much of Ethical Socialism. Read portrayed a simple way of life based on the "cultivation of the earth," free from the disruptions of the "commercial spirit" and, indeed, from all "immoral and anti-social tendencies."[118]

Yet, the very perfection of the social order over which Olivero presided induced a spiritual unrest. The "absence of conflict, of contending interests, of anguish and agitation," drove him back into the depths of his own consciousness. He ended his exile and returned to his native Yorkshire to resume his search into the deeper mysteries of the self. Entering the subterranean world of the "Green People," Olivero gradually left behind all earthly interests, passions, and sentiments, and indeed, all the distractions of consciousness as well. And he advanced by means of the study of the forms, properties, and structures of crystals, the "most esteemed science" of the Green People, to an ultimate experience of aesthetic pleasure. He also gained a full comprehension of the natural order and the power to create new structures. But having passed beyond the "illusions of selfhood," Olivero was also ready for a death in which he became at one "with the physical harmony of the universe."[119]

Read's autobiographical fantasy revealed the shape of a life which was circling back on itself. Insofar as Read found meaning in his journey he found it in his memories of childhood. The true basis for the good life lay in the "innocent eye" of his early years and in the farmer's "intuitive sense of reality and right and wrong." To recover his own relationship with nature Read moved back to his native village in 1949 and began to work seven acres of land.[120]

Read's struggle to "complete the divided self" had led back

to the harmony of his earliest years. Until the end of his life he insisted that "our alienation and fears" would be overcome only "if we could return like prodigal children to the contemplation" of the beauty of the world. But his journey had separated him more and more from the development of British institutions. His last years were marked by deepening pessimism and despair. Even the modern artists, to whom he had looked for redeeming truths, were surrendering to the general loss of form and descending into nihilism. "Spiritually, the world is now a desert," he wrote in 1962. And he warned that mankind, lacking any "direct contact with the organic rhythms and balanced processes of nature," would "walk like blind animals into a darker age than history had ever known."[121]

Gill, Muir, and Read followed different paths away from the Socialist movement and they arrived at different places. But each carried forward aspirations which had come together for a time in Ethical Socialism. The rapid breakup of these aspirations within the context of political action had released elements of the popular form of socialism for a more or less independent development.

Ethical Socialism had gained much of its support through its capacity to articulate conventional working class interests and to legitimate them in terms of prevailing moral and religious values. It served as an instrument to advance previously established notions of class interests within industrial society. The development of the Labour Party, dominated numerically and financially by the trade unionists, gradually diminished this source of support for the movement.

For many of its adherents, particularly in the lower middle class, Ethical Socialism was not so much an instrument to advance well defined interests as it was the promise of a social order radically different from that of capitalism. That promise was often vague; it drew on Marxist, Fabian, Christian, and Romantic ideas. But the distinctive aspiration within Ethical Socialism, emerging in the thought of Carlyle and Ruskin, continuing in the writings of Morris, Carpenter, and Blatchford, the propaganda of Hardie, Glasier, and Grayson, and the work of the *New Age* group, was profoundly nostalgic. The main spokesmen for Ethical Socialism looked back to pre-industrial social institutions and values. This regressive bent reached a climax in the circle around Orage and the *New Age*; indeed, the social and political attitudes displayed there had elements in common with elitist views which were beginning to crystallize in new right wing ideologies on the continent in the years before World War I.

The two older forms of Socialist ideology in Britain—Social Democracy and Fabianism—were undergoing parallel processes of decomposition in the period after 1910. Here, too, efforts to develop effective political strategies served to separate out and disperse aspirations which had been synthesized in socialism. But in contrast to Ethical Socialism, the Marxism of Hyndman and the Fabianism of Webb tended to favor the development of industrialization and political integration through representative institutions. In coming to terms with that development, however, the Social Democrats and the Fabians gradually cut themselves off from vital elements in the Socialist ideology.

PART FOUR

THE TRIUMPH
OF PARLIAMENTARY
POLITICS OVER
SOCIAL DEMOCRACY
AND FABIANISM

7

THE BRITISH MARXISTS: FROM SOCIAL DEMOCRACY TO COMMUNISM

THE DISARRAY WITHIN the ILP and the exhaustion of Ethical Socialism gave the Social Democrats and the Fabians an opportunity to assume the initiative within the movement. During the years after 1906 groups within each of the older Socialist organizations developed new strategies to meet the changing political situation. In reexamining their political roles, however, the Social Democrats and the Fabians reopened old conflicts and began to lose their ideological coherence.

Social Democratic leaders were convinced that the troubles within the ILP demonstrated their own wisdom in withdrawing from the political alliance with the trade unionists. They eagerly supported the dissident Ethical Socialists in their struggles against the Socialist and labor politicians. Moreover, the split in the ranks of the ILP encouraged the SDF to resume its efforts to achieve Socialist unity. During 1911 and 1912 they succeeded in drawing elements from each section of the movement into a new British Socialist Party.

The hopes which Hyndman and his colleagues placed in the new party proved to be short lived. Not only did it fail to unify the various groups but the Social Democrats themselves were increasingly divided. Disagreements about the correct Marxist approach to international conflict and new disputes generated by the war broke apart the organization Hyndman had built. The process of ideological decomposition was completed by the

Bolshevik revolution and by the emergence of the new Communist model for a revolutionary Marxist party.

PLOUGHING THE POLITICAL SANDS, 1906-1910

Ten Social Democrats stood for Parliament in 1906 and all save Will Thorne, who did not face Liberal opposition and was supported by the LRC, were defeated. Hyndman came close, losing a three-cornered contest at Burnley by less than three hundred votes. He viewed his failure to enter the House of Commons as a "disaster for the movement" for it seemed to him to leave the small group of Socialist MP's without strong leadership. Still, the emergence of a Labour party in Parliament demonstrated that the workers were waking up. And Hyndman saw in the enthusiasm at labor and Socialist meetings "strong evidence of the growth of genuine Socialism in Great Britain."[1] Although a new effort to take the Federation back into the alliance with the trade unions was defeated at the annual conference in March, the Social Democrats adopted a more conciliatory attitude toward the other sections of the movement.

At the local level the SDF's policies had usually been more flexible than the rhetoric of its leaders might suggest. Several score of its members were now sitting on local government bodies, elected in nearly all cases with broad labor and Socialist support. Many Social Democrats were active in trade unions. Even Quelch, a vigorous opponent of the political alliance with the unions, conceded that union membership was a "practical admission of the class struggle." A few years earlier he had become chairman of the London Trades Council, dominated for some time by Social Democrats, and in that capacity Quelch attended the annual conferences of the Labour Party where he led a small group advocating a militant policy. Moreover, the SDF still pressed for piecemeal reforms, particularly in the areas of education and housing, and amid worsening unemployment after 1907 again took the lead in demanding measures of relief.[2]

Social Democrats continued to subordinate the practical side of their program to their larger mission; they were confident that they alone were scouting the future course of the working classes and, indeed, the nation.

Should we mix with the slow moving crowd, trudging along, abating our pace, in order to keep company with the rest, stopping and halting wherever they choose? Or should we rather dash forward, place ourselves in front and explain to the crowd the meaning and significance of the road, the aim of the journey, and in general act as guides. The first means being led by elemental forces, the second means leading and guiding them. The ILP chose the first, the SDF the second.[3]

Such an outlook permitted slight tolerance for the dilemmas of the labor and Socialist men in the House of Commons. During 1907, as the impotence and the caution of the Labour Party members became evident, the Social Democrats reverted to a role that was mainly critical. The deepening disarray within the ILP seemed to vindicate their more principled position. Rothstein, in fact, claimed that the rebellion within the ILP was "due to the SDF's willingness to stand outside and retain its freedom to agitate and criticize." For a number of Socialists, disillusioned with the politics of the Labour Party, the policy of the SDF exercised a growing appeal. It was, however, a policy which was more reactive than creative; it was shaped less by theory than by the rising currents of discontent within the Socialist and labor movements.

Hyndman's version of Marxism was still the main source of the Social Democratic ideology. The SDF executive was not, as Rothstein suggested, "completely under the sway" of Hyndman, for he was more inclined to follow a path of political accommodation than the majority of his colleagues. But he had regained much of his earlier ascendancy in the life of the party, while its administrative machinery was controlled by men who had learned their Marxism from him. Even Rothstein conceded that Hyndman was, "for all his exasperating defects, by far the ablest man in the movement."[4]

Hyndman's Marxist faith, restated in a series of lectures in the autumn of 1907, had lost little of its rigidity. He insisted again on the scientific validity of Marx's theory of value, the inexorable unfolding of economic processes which were destroying capitalism, and the approach of a time when mankind would consciously control the "forces around us" to secure the "happiness of all." The utilitarian tone was characteristic, for Hyndman viewed human motivation largely in terms of pleasure and pain. And he fixed on those features in Marxism which reinforced his commitment to mankind's increased material well-being through a more rational and efficient productive process and through greater equality in the distribution of wealth. He vigorously denied frequent charges that he had come to socialism from Tory surroundings. "I was always a Radical," he wrote Kautsky, "until I became a Socialist."[5]

Hyndman's Marxism remained fixed within a strong nationalistic framework. Socialism provided the only way "to save the advanced nations" from the "dreadful anarchy of the class war." His nationalism did not preclude a strong sympathy for the exploited peoples of the British Empire, nor a strong commitment to international cooperation. But legitimate national interests must be defended. And Hyndman's growing sense of the menace which Germany posed to Britain's position led him to undertake a vigorous personal campaign, both in *Justice* and in the non-Socialist press, on behalf of military preparedness. His advocacy of a "citizens' army" and a big navy outraged many of his Social Democratic colleagues and damaged the party's relationship with the German Socialists. Defending himself against charges of chauvinism in a letter to Kautsky, he wrote of the fatuity of "those who advocate disarmament by one power while another Imperialist power is arming to the teeth as Germany is."[6]

Hyndman did little to discourage the tendency for Social Democrats to identify themselves with the rising current of antipolitical feeling within the movement. Indeed, this feeling reinforced the catastrophic strain in his Marxism; the prediction of a cataclysm ahead was one way of dealing with the great discrepancy between his Socialist faith and anticipations on the one hand and British social development on the other. Hence the eagerness with which Hyndman and other Social Democrats welcomed Grayson's defiance of the Labour Party executive. Grayson's victory at Colne Valley, according to *Justice*, "completely justified our position." He fought for "straight, pure, uncompromising, revolutionary Socialism." The readiness of the Social Democrats to embrace the new popular spokesman for

Ethical Socialism indicated that their desire to preserve the integrity of Marxist theory was less compelling than ties created by a common opposition to the Labour Party. During 1908 Social Democrats joined dissident elements in the ILP, and other Socialists, in supporting unauthorized candidates in Dundee, Pudsey, and Newcastle. The results were disappointing but Social Democrats could claim that they had secured a "clean vote."[7]

Grayson's scenes in the House of Commons were cheered by most members of the SDP and occasioned sharp attacks on Parliament by Hyndman and others. As presently constituted, Hyndman declared, Parliament was a "miserable fraud." It could best be used, he argued, by "honest men of the working class . . . as a platform for rendering the conduct of public business impossible until the needs of the workers are dealt with seriously." Quelch denounced Parliament as an institution designed to "safeguard and consolidate the capitalist class" and he urged the Labour Party to emulate the obstructionist tactics of the Irish members. During 1909 the anti-political strain in Social Democratic propaganda increased. Lloyd George's budget of that year was described by Hyndman as "not even partially Socialist in its tendency" despite its progressive tax features. And the new proposals for the relief of destitution— the Minority Report of the Webbs, and the schemes for social insurance advanced by the Liberals—were dismissed as mere "tinkering devices."[8]

The growing antagonism toward the Labour Party and reformist political activity did not go unchallenged within the SDP. Social Democrats who were critical of their party's policies had been supplied with ammunition from Marx and Engels in March 1908 when MacDonald published in the *Socialist Review* selections from their correspondence in the early eighties where the work of Hyndman was strongly attacked. This condemnation of Social Democratic strategy was renewed inside the party by J. B. Askew. "That the Socialist movement should be brought into conflict with the Labor movement," he wrote, "must be unthinkable to anyone . . . to whom the theory of the class war represents a living reality and not a mere phrase." "Could we make a more complete confession of our moral bankruptcy than by saying that it is impossible for us despite our numbers and our education in the principles of Socialism, to prevent a movement arising among the ranks of the trade unionists for independent political action, from drifting into a mere appendage of the Liberal Party?" Social Democrats, according to Askew, should recognize the semi-class consciousness of the Labour Party and the trade unions and make them more amenable to socialism by identifying it with "their daily struggle" rather than with a "far off ideal."[9]

Askew's critique was supported by the Lancashire section of the party. Dan Irving contended once more that the Social Democrats were losing their savor because they were "isolated from the lump" and John Moore complained that their "absurd position" had led to "political death in Rochdale, Blackburn, Clitheroe, and other places where formerly we were strong." From Scotland too, where the SDP was slowly recovering from its losses to the schismatic Socialist Labour Party, the ablest Social Democratic leader, John Maclean, reported that his branch unanimously favored reaffiliation with the Labour Party.[10]

Rothstein answered this new challenge to the SDP's policy. While conceding that the party had departed from the "theoretically correct" position of going "hand in hand with the masses," he claimed that such a policy would not have succeeded with the British workers.

> By no permanent and intimate cooperation with the masses such as was urged by Marx and Engels could the Socialists have hoped to "revolutionize them from within." On the contrary, what would have been achieved was merely the adaptation of the Socialists to the mental level of the masses, which spelt not confusion, not theoretical unripeness, but Liberalism . . . A certain modicum of impossibilism was in those days not only inevitable but really necessary if the Socialist movement was to subsist . . . And what was true twenty-five years ago is but a shade less true now.

Marx, and especially Engels, he added, were "real past masters in going wrong in their opinions of men and concrete issues."[11]

Efforts to alter the SDP's increasingly intransigent course

during 1908 and 1909 were defeated; the party's uneasy balance between reformist and "impossibilist" tendencies was again, as in the eighties and the early years of the century, in jeopardy. Although Hyndman and Quelch reaffirmed from time to time the need to build a parliamentary Socialist party, they were also tempted to swim with the new tide of political disenchantment. For many Social Democrats the temptation was greatly increased by the outcome of the general elections in 1910.

Seven Social Democratic candidates stood for Parliament in January 1910. The results were disheartening. Not only did the party fail to win any seats but its electoral support declined. Social Democratic leaders saw the Liberal Party as their main antagonist, for most of the workers had obviously preferred its "half loaf . . . to the whole loaf of the Socialist common-wealth." They directed most of their anger, however, at the Labour Party. Its "utterly ruinous incapacity" had "frittered away" the "unceasing, gratuitous and self sacrificing work of the Social Democrats." Hyndman claimed that the Labour Party had "discouraged the workers in the belief in independent action," and Quelch described it as a Frankenstein monster "destroying the class consciousness which gave it life." The only consolation to be drawn from the election, according to an editorial in *Justice*, was the thought that the Labour Party had "committed suicide" and left the way clear for the consolidation of all Socialist forces "under the banner of uncompromising Social Democrats."[12]

Still, it was time, as Quelch put it, to take stock. And while he quickly concluded that the problem lay "deeper down than our own errors or mistakes," others were judging the work of the party more harshly. Herbert Burrows, one of the founding members of the SDF, who had suffered a humiliating defeat in a London constituency, declared that they had been "ploughing the sands politically for thirty years" and were bankrupt. A similar verdict was expressed in the "ominous resignations" of "cherished members," including Askew, who moved over to the ILP. The SDP, he declared, had "misunderstood the theory of Marx in its political aspect" for Marx taught that "we must look to the organized proletariat as the main source of our strength."[13]

He defended the ILP's continuing attempt to convert the trade unions to independent political action as the way to socialism. Askew's parting shot drew from Hyndman his clearest statement of his relationship to Marx and Engels.

> I am a little tired of having Marx and Engels eternally trotted out as political popes who ought to direct our action even from their graves. Marx was as all the world now knows, the greatest genius in political economy and sociology of modern times, and Engels was only second to him . . . I may fairly claim to have done more than any man living to spread knowledge of their theories among English speaking peoples. Their vilification of myself has never checked me for one moment in this useful work . . . These great men were not, however, great in practical affairs and their judgement of character was notoriously bad . . . I do not pretend to put myself on a level as a thinker with Marx and Engels but I do say that in English affairs I have proved to be right and they have proved to be wrong. Let us be content to admire them for the magnificent life work they did and to learn from them the theoretical basis of scientific socialism. "Texts" from Marx like texts from Paul of Tarsus are not much use to us in the practical social work of today.[14]

The SDP's practical social work, however, was very much in question. And after a second crushing defeat at the polls later in 1910 the self-examination of the Social Democrats began in earnest. Hyndman, taking a leaf from Bax, now contended that the "unconscious and uncontrollable material" factor was ready at hand but the "psychological factor of realizable idealism" was still almost wholly lacking. And he attributed this backwardness to the British educational system. Some Social Democrats blamed the party's propaganda. By "painting the political canvas with the lurid colors of obvious and feeble exaggeration," one member noted, they had become divorced from reality. Others attacked the doctrine of scientific determinism or the "damnable dogma of inevitability"; it "paralyzes our energies" and "dampens our enthusiasm."[15]

Most of the Social Democratic analyses came down in the end to the "bourgeois conventionalism" of the workers. Indeed, one of the London leaders, a journalist and former Fabian,

Victor Fisher, ventured the "heretical assertion" that the "middle class proletariat . . . thousands of underpaid clerks, shop assistants, commercial travellers, etc.," constituted at the moment a "more promising Socialist material . . . than the average manual worker."

The virility and independence of the working class brain has been on trial in the policies and methods of the Labour Party . . . The Labour Party represents . . . their stodginess, their lack of imagination, or inspiration, their innate Puritanism, their gospel grinding and Bible thumping, their profound ignorance of the international movement, their ingenuousness in falling under the hypnotic power of New Liberalism, their incapacity to realize an ethic and a power of their own . . . The working class do not possess a tittle of the imagination or mental elasticity of their middle class adherents or inspirers [within the movement].[16]

Electoral failures, anger over the compromises of the Labour Party, and growing doubts about the Federation's traditional policies were driving some Social Democrats away from political action. During 1910 and 1911 an unprecedented wave of strike activity and the rapid growth of trade union membership seemed to promise a way out of their impasse. British Marxists were drawn to the ideas and methods of the "industrial unionists" and the Syndicalists.

AN ALTERNATIVE PATH: *The Socialist Labour Party*

The industrial strategy had been pioneered in Britain by the SDP's schismatic offspring, the Socialist Labour Party. In the period after 1906 the new party, centered in Scotland, remained small, embracing a dozen or so branches and a few hundred members. It continued to draw its ideological inspiration from the writings of De Leon and his chief British disciple, James Connolly. And through the articles and discussions in its monthly paper, the *Socialist*, and its distribution of new translations of Marxist works, the party helped open new possibilities for British Socialists.[17]

To read the *Socialist* and the SLP pamphlets is to enter a distinctive world of discourse. Here the practical measures proposed by the other Socialist organizations, including the SDP, were ruthlessly discarded.

> One question is sufficient to brush aside any claim that may be made in this connection. In what position will this leave the worker once it is carried into law? Does he still remain a commodity? Is he still compelled to take his labor power into the market to sell for a subsistence wage? Is he still compelled to devote all his life and energies to producing surplus value for the capitalist? If the answer is yes—then the position of the revolutionary worker is clear. He will say, capitalism is always capitalism no matter what superficial modifications take place in its outside structure . . . I shall lay my axe to the root of the tree.[18]

The leaders of the SLP were determined to avoid any entanglement in the institutions on which the SDP, for all its growing intransigence, continued to rely. They believed that the SDP and the ILP had failed because they lacked "that degree . . . of submission to principle that constitutes a revolutionary Socialism."[19] The "great secret of success" lay in "obedience" to the laws taught by science. In the SLP the drive toward ideological purity which arose periodically among Marxists was being carried forward in an especially rigorous manner. Indeed, the most dedicated members of the party were approaching, in language and behavior, the goal of Marxists like Bax, for whom Socialism entailed a totally new outlook on life.

Circumstances in Scotland favored this radical spirit. Not only were the Scottish Socialists relatively free of the strong English loyalties which conditioned and restrained Hyndman's Marxism, but they drew added emotional impetus from separatist political aspirations. Economic developments in the north also contributed to their feelings of social estrangement. Technological backwardness and comparatively archaic patterns of industrial organization meant that the impact of new and more rational economic methods was especially severe, particularly among the engineering trades which supplied the bulk of the working class Socialists in the manufacturing centers. Religious traditions in Scotland were also important. Here, as in other regions where Ethical Socialism took deepest root, the cast of mind and the sentiments nurtured by churches or chapels in the middle classes and working classes alike, left their stamp on the new ideology even as the converts were being drawn away from their old religious moorings. And while the ILP, with its ethically charged propaganda, appealed more effectively to this sensibility than the SDP or the SLP, the greater doctrinal rigor of the Marxist parties held a special attraction for those who had been reared in a Calvinist culture. A number of the young converts in Scotland during the early years of the century, like many in the earlier generation of British Socialists, only gradually surrendered their view that religious orthodoxy was the chief enemy of the workers.[20]

The "impossibilism" of the SLP expressed a state of mind in which the desire for an integral system of doctrine overwhelmed any inclination to achieve immediate benefits for the working classes. Objective interests, in any conventional sense of the term, gave way to essentially subjective considerations. Such a mentality assigned an extraordinary efficacy to clear principles. Thus the SLP leaders claimed that their party was "a centering point of an almost spontaneous growth of revolutionary sentiment . . . owing purely and simply to [their] genuine revolutionary principles." Hence their vigilance against any disposition of their members to touch the "pitch" which had "defiled" the ILP and the SDP. They expelled one member for taking part in the work of a Clarion van, an "instrument of middle class domination," and they denounced another for giving hospitality to a former SLP leader who had been thrown out of the party for compromising its principles.[21]

Preoccupied with the task of keeping the Marxist system of meanings pure, the SLP leaders devoted most of their energy to attacks on other Socialist groups. The Social Democrats were the chief enemy. The rather limited efforts of Quelch and others to reach the trade unionists were denounced as a form of "Fabianism," for any attempt to "permeate with Socialism, organizations which are structurally rotten" was "chimerical." As for the Labour Party and its "ILP and Fabian allies," they were "simply the hangers on of capitalism . . . waiting doglike for the crumbs that fall from the master's table." Indeed, those Socialists who attempted to advance the cause by means of non-Socialist organizations invited a withering moral denunciation. "Their natural villainy assumes an ever blacker hue in contrast to the noble principles to which they pretend allegiance."[22]

Still, as one *Socialist* writer observed, the party's "political puritanism" and its work of "exposure" was barren unless it was followed up by constructive policies. The SLP's strategy was, in fact, a logical outgrowth of its ideological posture. For it aimed at the construction of institutions which would give objective form to Marxist-inspired proletarian aspirations. De Leon still provided the chief guidance. He had fixed on the Marxist claim that political institutions were merely the reflex of the productive process and he carried out the logic of this position. His disciples in the SLP followed suit and relegated political action to a secondary place. They saw themselves as propagandists devoted to the work of creating industrial unions which would parallel and completely replace the existing structure of trade unions. In time, when this form of unionism found expression in the political field, "as it surely will," it would absorb "all other Socialist and labor parties," for it would express "the needs, the hopes, the aspirations and the will of the working class." After overthrowing the "class state, the united Industrial Unions" would furnish the "Administrative machinery for . . . the Socialist Commonwealth." In the meantime the SLP would function chiefly as a propaganda body.[23]

The shift toward industrial unionism as the "foundation on which the party is built," quickly produced conflicts within the SLP. One group in the party concluded that political action should be repudiated altogether. After failing to win their case at the annual conference in 1906, they created a parallel organization—the Advocates of Industrial Union—to advance their policy. The SLP leaders continued to defend the need for the "revolutionary struggle in the political field" but the presence of a second organization, with much the same membership, and committed mainly to industrial action, dramatized the divergence and generated continuing tensions. The Advocates accused the SLP leadership of trying to use their platform for political purposes while they in turn were labeled hyper Marxists, sectarians, and anarchists.[24]

The kind of ideological purity which the SLP sought was elusive and, indeed, illusory. The very effort to agitate brought its members into dangerous proximity with tainted groups and bourgeois institutions. New difficulties arose within the party during 1908 and 1909 over the issue of unemployment. An editorial in the *Socialist* warned against taking part in unemployment demonstrations on the ground that they built up "hopes that can only end in disappointment." In "giving way to sentiment," moreover, there was the danger of the "revolutionary mission being delayed." Nevertheless, an SLP branch in Bury cooperated with other Socialist groups in a protest on behalf of those without work, and Neil Maclean, the party's national secretary, joined other Socialists in Edinburgh to urge the city council to provide work or maintenance. Although the party's executive defended these actions, a referendum of the members forced it to reverse itself and expel Maclean.[25]

Viewing the SLP's troubles from America, one of its founders, James Connolly, attributed its failure to realize the "future we mapped out" to its uncritical emulation of De Leon's methods. "You worshipped an idol and you will have to suffer for your idolatry," he told C. Carstairs Matheson, editor of the *Socialist*. And he urged his British colleague to "shake yourself clear in time." Connolly, in fact, left the American SLP during the course of 1909. Although he agreed with its growing emphasis on an industrial strategy, he did not repudiate political action. Moreover, his experience in Britain and America had convinced him that the "developing class consciousness of the labor movement in Great Britain is healthier and more potent for good than the 'cleverness' of a sect which insists on cutting the umbilical string" connecting it with the workers.

I have come to the conclusion that while our position is absolutely sound in theory, and might be sound in practice if adopted by men of large outlook, yet its practical immediate effects have been the generation of a number of sectarians, narrow minded doctrinaires, who have erected Socialism into a cult with rigid formulae which one must observe or be dismissed. From which I draw the frank conclusion that our position . . . needs the corrective of association with Socialists of a less advanced type. In short, I believe that our

proper position is in the general . . . Labour movement as friends
and *helpers*, rather than in a separate organization as hostile critics
and enemies.[26]

The British SLP refused to depart from its narrow path. It
continued to put candidates up for seats in municipal elections
but it sought votes only from "those who endorse our principles." Leaders of the party were convinced that the defeats suffered by the ILP and the SDP in the general elections of 1910
could be attributed to their "advocacy of reforms." For reforms
"lead away from Socialism . . . [down] the path of ignorance
and disappointment and of death to the Socialist ideal." Indeed,
they believed the election demonstrated that the Labour Party,
along with the trade unions and Reformist Socialism, was
"dying a natural death." The prospects of their own party, a
Socialist editorial declared, were "never brighter than they are
today."[27]

The industrial unrest which spread across Great Britain
during 1910 gave some substance to the SLP claim that the
Socialist and labor political strategy had been mistaken. The
wave of strikes, starting among the miners and spreading to the
seamen, dockers, and transport workers, indicated growing
working class disaffection with political action and with the
traditional trade union methods as well. For a time the SLP
drew new strength from this mood of disenchantment. In November 1910 the *Socialist* announced that its circulation had increased by a thousand during the year, that the party had enrolled a hundred and fifty new members and increased the
number of branches to nineteen. The Advocates of Industrial
Unionism also gained ground and, at the giant Singer Sewing
Machine factory near Glasgow, developed sufficient strength to
test its strategy. Here the drive to rationalize the productive
process by means of American managerial techniques, together
with a weak and fragmented labor organization, made the
SLP's scheme for a union organized on industrial rather than
craft lines especially relevant. In March 1911, after a woman
worker had been dismissed, the SLP men succeeded in shutting
down virtually the entire factory.

The strike soon collapsed and four hundred of the most

militant of the workers were discharged. Many of these men subsequently carried the new idea of industrial unionism into the factories, workshops, and shipbuilding firms of the Clydeside. But, as Walter Kendall observed, the SLP's "revolutionary disdain for the petty details" of trade union organization and its "contention that wage struggles could never materially benefit the worker's lot," suggested its inability to "function as anything more than a propagandist sect."[28]

The SLP had owed much of its limited appeal to its comparative freedom from the kind of compromises characteristic of the other Socialist bodies. It continued to be fed in large part by Socialists who had become impatient with the opportunism of the SDP and the ILP leaders. The hope of transcending the existing order of life might even draw the SLP Marxist to the ideas of Nietzsche. Thus a writer for the *Socialist* urged his readers to join with Nietzsche and "turn a deaf ear to [such] slave moralists" as Hardie, Snowden, and MacDonald, and "with all the stern and uncompromising determination that Nietzsche so admired, scorning as Marx says, all half measures, weaknesses, and meannesses, make a complete clearance of our despicable oppressors to the end that we may be free to develop Overmansward."[29]

The propaganda of the SLP helped prepare the ground for the new industrial strategy which, amid the growing sense of economic injustice and political disenchantment among some sections of the workers, made rapid headway after 1910. But the party's outlook—its adamant refusal to engage the actual concerns of the workers—disqualified it for giving new leadership to the labor and Socialist movements. Leadership for the new industrial oriented agitation came instead from two Social Democrats—Guy Bowman and Tom Mann.

THE CHALLENGE OF SYNDICALISM

Mann, a leading Socialist propagandist in Britain during the eighties and nineties, had returned in the spring of 1910 after nearly a decade of work for the labor movements in Australia and New Zealand. More recently he had been influenced by the writings of De Leon and particularly by Connolly's pamphlet, *Socialism Made Easy*. Bowman, who had served as manager of the Social Democratic press, had discovered in the ideas and methods of the French Syndicalists a fresh approach to socialism. In May he persuaded Mann to travel to Paris with him to explore the French movement. Not long after they returned the two men set out, by means of a weekly paper, the *Industrial Syndicalist*, to reeducate the British workers. The "French policy," Mann had decided, "will serve us best."[30]

Mann, who soon came to dominate the new agitation, denied that syndicalism was necessarily anti-political, but he criticized the British workers for their "absurd respect for parliamentary methods." Through organization in the economic sphere and the use of the techniques of industrial combat developed by the French, the workers could "bring about such changes as they desire by direct action without the intermediation of any other institution." They had come to "realize the full meaning of economic determinism." It was time, therefore, to "build up the fighting forces of the proletariat in workshops, factories, mills, and mines."[31]

Mann was neither doctrinaire nor sectarian in his outlook. As in his earlier work for the Socialist movement, he employed ideas to awaken the workers to a new sense of grievance, or to new social possibilities, without much concern for theoretical issues. Although he spoke of the "curse of sectional unionism," and deplored the "dispersal of energies" involved in organization by trade or craft, he hoped to win over the old unions and amalgamate them in new federations. To the leaders of the SLP Mann's work seemed a betrayal of the cause of industrial unionism. He was simply "carrying the old spirit" of trade unionism into a "broader structured organization."[32]

The nonsectarian, yet revolutionary, rhetoric of Mann, together with his tactical flexibility, was well suited to the mood of the miners, seamen, dockers, and transport workers who, during 1910, 1911, and 1912, were locked in bitter struggles with their employers. Indeed, that mood was often anti-ideological—hostile to the Socialist proposals of the ILP, the Fabians, and the Social Democrats, and disposed to reduce all issues to immediate economic considerations. Mann's agitation during 1911 and 1912 was fed in part by the indignation generated in the drive toward greater efficiency within a number of British industries. Greater mechanization and other forms of economic rationalization were eliminating many of the skills on which the craft unions rested.

Syndicalism may have discarded, as one historian suggests, its "mythopoetic and heroic aspects . . . as it crossed the channel." But for British Socialists who had lost confidence in the work of the ILP, the Fabians, and the SDP, the new strategy, constructed out of American and French experiences, served to revitalize hopes for a radically different social order. It seemed "clearer and more precise than anything I had heard from the other Socialists," a young engineer recalled. "It invested the daily work of the trade unions with . . . a purpose that made it worthwhile." Not only did Mann quickly gain a significant following within the SDP but the Syndicalist agitation won the support of dissident members of the ILP like Smart, who had concluded that the Socialist vision had been pushed aside by electioneering tactics. Through industrial organization, according to Smart, they could check the drift toward a form of collectivism controlled by the "officials of a class state" and build up a "communal . . . order within the shell of the old." And Edward Carpenter, a prophetic figure in the early development of Ethical Socialism, enthusiastically welcomed the new strategy.

Socialism has no doubt taken us a long way in the right direction . . . But we are now beginning to see that its path is in danger of wandering through some ugly swamps of bureaucracy, officialism, and over government, and that it may be difficult to get safely through along that line . . . Syndicalism is going to restore . . . guilds in a form suited to modern conditions and everyone who values what may be called real culture, and the restoration of beauty and joy in daily life, must surely welcome the movement and lend a helping hand.[33]

Industrial syndicalism provided a new meeting ground for Social Democrats and Ethical Socialists who had lost faith in the ILP. This blurring of organizational loyalties encouraged SDP leaders to make a new effort to realize their longstanding goal of Socialist unity. At the party's annual conference in April 1911, the delegates voted to convene a unity conference later in the year. To Hyndman it seemed a way of consolidating Socialist forces and "bringing the ILP into line." Support for the Social Democratic initiative came from several of the leading ILP rebels. In August Grayson announced that the "psychological moment" for a new party had arrived and he formally resigned from the ILP. He was soon joined by Smart and Leonard Hall, a recent member of the ILP national council, and several of the *Clarion* leaders. Although Blatchford had stated a year earlier that it was time to "form a new party and begin all over again" he was now engrossed in his literary work and he declined to take an active role. "I am in the garden," he said, "because the bulk of the army I helped to enlist has been marched into the enemy's camp by the leaders." But other *Clarion* men—Tom Groom and Fred Hagger—worked with Grayson to prepare for the conference. Grayson was, in fact, bent on heading a distinctly *Clarion* group within a new federated party.[34]

The unity conference, which was convened in Manchester at the end of September, drew delegates from all sections of the movement.[35] While the bulk of the ILP rank and file remained loyal to their party leaders, thirty-six of its branches sent forty-one delegates. Thirty-two others came from *Clarion* groups and sixty more from various Socialist societies. The largest bloc of delegates, eighty-six, came from seventy-seven branches of the SDP. Occasioned in large part by a deepening disillusionment with labor politics, the conference proceedings also reflected the new hopes aroused among Socialists by the growing militance of the workers and Syndicalist propaganda. The major debates revolved around the question of whether priority should be given to an industrial or a political strategy and, indeed, whether the reform proposals hitherto advanced by the Social Democrats were still relevant. Despite SDP opposition the delegates carried a motion that social reforms must be deleted from the party's program. But a move to commit the new party mainly to the struggle in the industrial field was defeated.

The Manchester conference provided a tentative basis for the regrouping of British Socialists. The SDP leaders pledged themselves to dissolve their branches upon ratification of a constitution, and a provisional executive, representing each of the major sections, was given the task of preparing for a founding conference in the spring. The administrative structure of the SDP remained intact and served as the mechanism for reorganization; Grayson had been out-maneuvered by the Social Democrats in the struggle to shape the new party.

The unity conference had done little, however, to resolve the disagreements among the Socialists. Social Democrats soon attempted to correct the impression that the deletion of palliatives precluded the support of "measures to protect the health and lives of the workers." Hyndman, in somewhat tortured reasoning, distinguished palliatives designed to make the present system "more tolerable" from genuine "stepping-stones" toward a Socialist society.[36] But the continuing force of the older Socialist disagreements as well as the new divisions created by the challenge of syndicalism were evident in the weeks which followed the conference.

Smart brought the disagreements out into the open in November when he charged that the continued adherence of the Social Democrats to schemes for nationalization was at odds with the "spirit of revolutionary socialism revealed at Manchester." He went on to urge the various sections of the new party to scrap their "worn out mental rubbish in the form of creeds, dogmas and shibboleths." He claimed that the ILP men had "thrown off the creed" that socialism is to be won by the education of the trade unions and other working class organizations; the Fabians in their midst had abandoned their method of "permeating the orthodox political parties." The SDP, therefore, should get rid of its "ghostly phrases" and throw such notions as the class war and "capitalist collapse . . . to the scrap heap." But Smart proceeded to reassert his own belief in the "ethical and religious transformation of society into a cooperative commonwealth" as the main idea of socialism. And he argued that "class conscious people are never Socialists for the faith of the latter rose above such narrow-minded considerations. There were, he maintained, "as many Socialists . . . in proportion to numbers . . . among commercial travelers as among carpenters and joiners."[37]

Social Democrats reacted sharply. "What are we left with

as a basis" for a revolutionary objective, asked Tom Kennedy, the SDP's national organizer. And he declared that the "theory and practice of the class struggle must stand as a vital principle for the guidance of the workers." Another respondent observed that the "half starved clerks and authors, wretchedly paid journalists and commercial travelers" who made up the middle class Socialists were still after all motivated by economic interests and were part of the class war. Quelch too insisted that class consciousness was the "essential mental equipment of the working class Socialist." Though he conceded that a "wide tolerance" was needed if they were to "organize the floating Socialist sentiment in the country into a consolidated revolutionary force," Quelch reaffirmed the Social Democratic conviction that the emancipation of the workers would have to be the "work of the working classes themselves."[38]

Meanwhile, Hall was vigorously championing the cause of industrial action. "I am convinced that the far most valuable service the Socialists can do is to . . . push for all we're worth the idea . . . of the general strike as the most potent line of the Socialist Revolution." He expressed his puzzlement at the "chilling reserve or antagonism" to industrial propaganda on the part of a "certain section of the politically militant Socialists." In a pamphlet prepared for the founding conference of the British Socialist Party in the spring of 1912, Hall argued that political action was secondary. "Any effective parliamentary Socialist force must be the reflex and be kept the instrument of a wide awake social revolutionary public opinion and a powerful and aggressive industrial organization outside . . . Sinking fratricidal traditional sectionalism and suicidal craft snobbery . . . in favor of fraternal guilds of the workers, we shall . . . develop the embryo of the communal organization of the nation for which Socialists are working."[39]

In their efforts to spread their sails to catch the gusts of disaffection emanating from the ILP and the new winds of syndicalism, the SDP leaders were endangering their historic commitment to political action. Even as they sharpened their attacks on the trimming tactics of the ILP and the Labour Party in the years after 1907, Hyndman, Quelch, and others had continued from time to time to warn against anarchism and "impossibilism" and reaffirm their belief in parliamentary methods. The party's main response to the electoral defeats during 1910 had been a demand for a more democratic political order by means of a single annual parliament, proportional representation, and the introduction of initiative and referendum procedures.

By the early months of 1912 Hyndman had begun to regret the efforts of Social Democrats to tap the new spirit aroused by the industrial agitation. Privately, he referred to syndicalism as "reactionary rubbish" and a "backward form of anti political anarchism." Its promised "short cut to victory," he believed, was "likely to lead to deeper disasters." Soon Hyndman had concluded that the "sentimental anarchist," such as Mann or Grayson, was a "worse enemy to Social Democracy than either the "Liberal Socialists or the Labour Socialists." Mann, in fact, had already parted company with the SDP because of the "fictitious importance which it attached to parliamentary action."[40]

Social Democrats could not easily turn their backs on the new combativeness among the workers which, in the spring of 1912, brought a national coal strike. According to Rothstein they were witnessing the "birth pangs" of the "new consciousness" they were seeking to create. Though not "equivalent to Socialist consciousness," he wrote, the Syndicalist spirit provided its condition. They should, therefore, "intensify it, widen it, and deepen it." The SDP organizer in London, E. C. Fairchild, agreed. The "spirit that animates the workers," he declared, was far more important to the Socialist than the form of organization. The strikes were producing a "condition of mind" on which Socialists could build.[41]

At the founding conference of the British Socialist Party in May 1912, the Social Democrats were still conciliatory toward the industrialist group and they acknowledged the equal importance of the unions and the party in the struggle of the working classes. But Hyndman and his associates were now firmly in command of the new party and easily defeated Hall's efforts to identify it more closely with the industrial revolt. They also inserted into the party's program proposals for a minimum wage and an eight hour day, and measures to help the unemployed, which had been advanced earlier by the SDP. But the conference indicated, as one observer concluded, that "a great battle was to be fought" between those who favored direct action and the strike, and the "conservative advocates of political action."[42]

During the months following the conference, as the challenge of the Syndicalists inside and outside the party continued, the opposition of Hyndman and the older Social Democratic leaders to the industrial strategy became explicit. Speaking in the name of the BSP executive in September, the Hyndman group denounced the Syndicalists and reaffirmed the primacy of political action. Hall and Smart, both members of the executive, protested this "uncalled for attempt . . . to reimpose papal dogmas and creeds." But they were more and more isolated. Even the Birmingham section of the BSP, which had provided the strongest support for Hall, was increasingly torn between the advocates of political and industrial tactics. The division there was to some extent along class lines. According to one observer the members who were most in favor of Syndicalism were "either middle class people who would not be seriously put out by a strike or clerks and shop assistants who are too indifferent to join a trade union."[43]

In the period before the second annual conference of the BSP in May 1913 the Social Democratic leaders vigorously denounced the "pernicious and disruptive" influence of the Syndicalists and called for the election of an executive which would be united "on all essentials."[44] The conference was poorly attended and marked by "obstructionist tactics and behaviour." The absence of Hall, Smart, and most of the *Clarion* and ILP elements meant that the BSP was becoming little more than a new version of the SDP.

In their efforts to assimilate the movement toward industrial action, the Social Democrats had seen the new party become "the asylum of all the outcasts of the political and industrial organizations of the country." Anarchists, Syndicalists, industrial unionists, and other "impossibilists" all "sought to capture it, with the result that our branches and conferences have become bear gardens and dog kennels." In the years ahead the BSP leaders would continue to worry about the "parasitical growth" of syndicalism and attack the "anarchist enemy within the gate." But they had reaffirmed the party's commitment to politics. Moreover, the desertion of the ILP rebels, the *Clarion* element, and the industrialist group helped the reformist wing within the party regain the initiative. The election of Dan Irving as chairman of the BSP at the spring conference in 1913 was one sign of the altered outlook. The time had come, Irving observed, to "consider things less in the abstract and more in relation to the actualities of our existence."[45]

Further encouragement for a reformist course came from the International Socialist Bureau in the summer of 1913. Having accepted the British Labour Party as a member of the International, the continental Socialist leaders proposed that the Social Democrats meet with the ILP and the Fabians in order to seek a basis for unity. Irving supported the proposal, and J. Hunter Watts, a founding member of the SDF and frequent member of the executive, pushed the idea in the columns of *Justice*. He called on the party to "extricate itself from the prison of the past" and become a "powerful factor in the political world." And he added:

> It was of the greatest importance a quarter of a century ago to differentiate ourselves from major parties and utopian socialists, who imagined they could regenerate society by establishing a higher code of morality . . . The ILP supplied a long felt want [in organizing] the large body of British men and women who ape the foibles and prejudices, even if they do not claim to be members, of the lower middle class. Today there is little to distinguish the two Socialist organizations.[46]

It was time, according to Watts, to reaffiliate with the Labour Party.

A vigorous debate on the question was soon under way. Were they prepared, Quelch asked in a lead editorial in *Justice*, to "haul down the flag?"[47] During July and August the columns of *Justice* presented a lively exchange of views. The death of Quelch in September, however, removed the strongest opponent of reaffiliation. And when a Socialist Unity conference was convened in December by the International Socialist Bureau, Hyndman was present to express the increasingly

conciliatory attitude of the BSP executive. Though still determined that their candidates should fight elections under a
"Labour and Socialist" banner, the Social Democrats agreed to
Webb's proposal that the matter be referred to their respective
organizations. Subsequently neither the ILP nor the Fabians
accepted the idea, but the Social Democratic leaders were now
firmly committed to the idea of seeking Socialist unity within
the framework of the Labour Party.

It was not easy to convince the bulk of the BSP members to
change course. After a heated debate at the 1914 conference, a
referendum was held. The proposal to reaffiliate carried only by
a four to three margin and ten branches, including several of
those which had come over from the ILP, left the party in
protest. Meanwhile, the new spirit of Socialist unity was finding
expression in a series of joint propaganda meetings featuring
Hyndman, Hardie, and the Webbs or Shaw. During 1914
Hyndman appeared at both the ILP and the Fabian conferences
as a "fraternal delegate." Addressing the Fabians in the summer,
he emphasized the importance of forming close links between
the middle class and working class sections of the Socialist
movement.[48]

The outbreak of the war delayed the reaffiliation of the
Social Democrats to the Labour Party. Not until 1916, when the
Labour Party held its next conference, was the BSP accepted
into the alliance. Meanwhile, the war had intensified old conflicts among Social Democrats and generated new disagreements. Indeed, the experiences of wartime renewed the inherent
tendency of British Marxism to divide into incompatible modes
of action. Marxists in Britain faced once more the choice
between a fuller involvement in existing political institutions
and a new effort to transcend the structures of national life.

World War I and the
Fragmentation of Social Democracy

Many Social Democrats did not sympathize with
Hyndman's advocacy of military preparedness or, indeed, share
his commitment to the British nation. Scottish branches of the
BSP were much less responsive to patriotic appeals, while the
increasingly articulate émigré element within the party also

lacked strong feelings of nationalism. They brought to the BSP an internationalist outlook which appealed to a substantial number of the younger recruits. By 1910 Hyndman's position was being sharply attacked in the letter columns of *Justice* and in resolutions presented to the annual conference. At the 1911 conference Hyndman and his supporters barely avoided passage of a resolution in favor of decreased military expenditures and a less assertive foreign policy, only to see it adopted after a referendum of the branches. The move toward a showdown on the matter was checked by the drive toward Socialist unity and the emergence of the even more divisive issue of industrial unionism. But once the priority of the political strategy was reestablished within the BSP, questions of military and foreign policy, sharpened by growing international tensions, became critical. At the annual conference in 1913 the critics brought the BSP to the edge of disruption. The Hyndman group attempted to rope off the armaments issue as nonessential to the Socialist cause. But this Fabian-like maneuver was unsuccessful; a split was avoided only by Hyndman's announcement that he would refrain from public statements which would "prejudicially affect the party." Through timely concessions the older Social Democratic leaders had "kept positions inside the party which a more forthright stand might well have lost."[49]

The London leadership was losing its traditional control over the policies of the party. In 1912 the delegates at the annual conference had decided to elect half the members of the executive on a district basis, and thus prevent, as the sponsors of the proposal argued, "domination by a small handful of men who were in some cases out of touch with the rank and file."[50] The death of Quelch in 1913 and his replacement as editor of *Justice* by H. W. Lee, the party's long time secretary, also loosened the hold of the Hyndman group. The new party secretary, Albert Inkpin, was not closely identified with the older leadership. During 1914 demands for membership control over *Justice* and the party's electoral campaigns, were further signs that Social Democrats were no longer traveling in the tightly run ship of the past.

The outbreak of the war seemed to represent the "shock from without" which Hyndman had seen from time to time as the prerequisite for Socialist advance in Britain. The international conflict confirmed his warnings about the German menace and, he believed, plunged the nation into a life and death conflict. Yet, Hyndman also thought that the exigencies of wartime would force the British government to "accept Socialist measures."[51] So he eagerly threw himself into the activities of a new body, the War Emergency Workers' National Committee, which brought Socialists and labor leaders together to protect the interests of the working classes. The committee's work will be discussed in the next chapter, but it made possible the kind of engagement with pressing national problems toward which Hyndman's form of socialism had always inclined him.

Hyndman was joined in his patriotic stand by most of the veteran Social Democratic leaders, including Irving, Watts, Lee, Kennedy, and even Bax. Three years earlier Bax had proclaimed his "absolute indifference to national interests" and, indeed, his "secret wish to see the British people punished and humiliated" for their "dastardly role" in the Boer War. Now he concluded that the nation was engaged in a "just cause" against the "Prussian military system." And he bitterly attacked the German Social Democrats for supporting their government.[52]

Under the impact of the war the older BSP leaders accentuated the nationalistic element in Hyndman's socialism. Not all members accepted this. Some Social Democrats felt that the party's support of the nation was too weak, while others saw it as a betrayal of the revolutionary cause. Hyndman's synthesis of Marxism and nationalism was breaking down. Several members of the party began to discard their Socialistic commitment in order to follow the call of patriotic feelings. Others dismissed the claims of the nation in order to concentrate on Socialist objectives.

The ultra-patriotic wing of the BSP was led by Victor Fisher. A year or so before the war, in explaining his decision not to stand again for the party's executive, Fisher had noted the failure of the Social Democratic attempt to realize the goal of Socialist unity. And he had gone on to lament the more subtle failure to "find an adequate means of unity among the various sections" making up the BSP. With the outbreak of the war Fisher discovered fresh inspiration for socialism in what he called the "eternal idea of nationality." "Let us accept it and with Socialist enthusiasm refashion and remold it." Social Democrats would thus free themselves from the "monster" created by "our own imagination—the Economic Man." In the spring of 1915 Fisher organized the Socialist National Defense League to promote Socialist measures in the war effort and "counteract the peace-at-any-price policy of the anti-national element in the Socialist and Labor movements." He enrolled several prominent Social Democrats, including Irving, Bert Killip, and J. F. Green and the two leading figures on the *Clarion*, Blatchford and Thompson, as well as a number of independent Socialists like H. G. Wells, Ben Tillett, and Steward Headlam. In its efforts to mobilize the workers behind the war effort, the League received financial support from Viscount Milner and it evolved, through several organizational changes, into the National Democratic Party. In the general election at the end of the war the party returned ten candidates to Parliament, one of whom, Green, defeated MacDonald at Leicester. Along the way the party had discarded most of its socialism and developed an outlook close to that of the Conservative Party. Fisher, Green, and Blatchford, in fact, all entered the ranks of the Conservatives.[53]

An even stronger challenge to Hyndman's synthesis of Marxism and nationalism, and to his continued dominance over BSP policy, came from those for whom the Socialist cause transcended the war effort; the military conflict, they believed, could be traced to the contradictions within capitalism. This Internationalist group in the BSP, concentrated in the London and Glasgow branches, now renewed its earlier effort to gain control of the party. It was guided in part by the attempt to formulate a new international Socialist policy at a conference in Zimmerwald, Switzerland, in September 1915. The delegates at Zimmerwald had rejected Lenin's argument that Socialists should devote themselves mainly to efforts to overthrow the capitalist system in favor of a manifesto which called for negotiations to end the war. But the Zimmerwald manifesto foreshadowed a break with the prewar Socialist leaders of the Second International, most of whom, like Hyndman, were occupied with the wartime goals of their respective nations.[54]

For a year and a half following the outbreak of the war the prowar and internationalist sections of the BSP avoided a clear confrontation. But during 1915 the columns of *Justice* mirrored the growing bitterness of the dispute; efforts by the executive to find a compromise policy simply antagonized both sides. Finally, the refusal of Lee to moderate the strong patriotic line of *Justice* led Fairchild, the London leader of the opposition, to start a rival paper, the *Call*, in February 1916. In the weeks which followed the two papers appealed to the members for support. "Either the BSP remains true to its international Socialism and goes the way indicated at Zimmerwald," Fairchild wrote, "or it ceases to be Socialist and joins the . . . imperialist trumpeteers." Meanwhile in the columns of *Justice*, Lee, Irving, and Watts attacked the anarchistic tendencies creeping "parasitically over the Socialist movement."[55]

At the BSP conference in Sheffield in April 1916, Hyndman and his supporters were quickly defeated. In a stormy scene, during which Hyndman was denied an opportunity to speak and heard himself described as a "political instigator," he led twenty or so delegates out of the meeting hall. The rout of the prowar group was completed in the subsequent elections for the party executive as Internationalist candidates took all the seats on the executive save one. Hyndman and the old Social Democratic leadership had, in effect, been expelled from the organization they had largely built.[56]

Hyndman was seventy-four in 1916; most of his supporters were only a decade or so younger. But they set out to "begin the Socialist movement here anew." In June they formed the National Socialist Party, a title which expressed their conviction that "both the BSP and the ILP have cut themselves adrift from the people of these islands."[57] With Joseph Burgess, the former ILP leader, as national organizer, the new party claimed more than forty branches by the end of 1916. Although its leaders rejected an invitation from Fisher to join forces with the Socialist Workers Defence League, the new party pursued a strongly patriotic line. While they sought to reaffirm the traditional Social Democratic policy, they were, in fact, breaking with their past and entering more fully into the mainstream of British political life.

The BSP, meanwhile, was seeking new direction. Although they failed to win control over *Justice*, which became the organ of Hyndman's party, the new BSP leaders held onto the party headquarters and administrative machinery, and a substantial majority of the branches and membership. And they developed a policy some place in between Hyndman's avowed support of the war and the "revolutionary defeatism" sought by some members of the BSP. Under Fairchild's leadership the party's executive drew back from the proposal, advanced by the Bolsheviks at Zimmerwald, to establish a new Socialist International, and looked to a restored International Socialist Bureau to negotiate peace terms. They also refused to disavow their reaffiliation with the Labour Party, despite the latter's participation in the wartime coalition government.

The new leaders of the BSP were reaffirming central features of the Social Democratic position which the Hyndmanites, in their patriotic zeal, were tacitly abandoning. Convinced that the party lacked the popular support necessary for any practical action on behalf of Socialist objectives, they resigned themselves to a policy of waiting. "We are right but we are before the time when our views of Socialism and democracy shall be applied," Fairchild had written earlier, and in the war years he continued to see the main task of the party as that of educating the workers. Harry Quelch's son, Tom, who had remained in the BSP, echoed the earlier views of Hyndman and Bax. "Economic conditions are ripe for revolution," he wrote, but Social Democrats still faced a "lack of understanding and class consciousness on the part of the workers."[58]

The reorganized BSP tended, in fact, to slip back into the state of immobility which had characterized the SDP. Unable to choose between a policy of genuine political participation on the one hand, and outright anti-nationalistic and revolutionary action on the other, the party looked to a revitalized Socialist International to resolve its dilemma. While the veteran Social Democrats, led by Hyndman, were finding new purpose in the nation's wartime struggle, the BSP leaders continued to guard the integrity of their Marxist doctrines. In seeking to maintain this middle position, however, they became more and more vulnerable, like the SDP earlier, to the pressure of outside forces.

Not all members of the BSP favored such a passive role. Even before the break with the Hyndmanites a number of Social Democrats wished to strike off on a more militant course than that envisioned by Fairchild. The outcome of the war, so the party's leading figure in Scotland, John Maclean, declared, was "no concern of the workers, one way or another." Their chief task was to "sharpen the class struggle and make ourselves ready for revolutionary action." Indeed, developments in wartime, particularly along the Clydeside, renewed the continuing tendency among British Social Democrats toward fragmentation or "leftward differentiation."[59]

Recent studies have done much to clarify the complex mixture of ideological influences and working class grievances which characterized the Clydeside during war.[60] Although the ILP was by far the largest of the Socialist organizations in the area, and led the way in agitation against the war, it was less successful than the two Marxist bodies, the BSP and the SLP, in relating its Socialist ideology to the new situation. In the grievances of the engineering workers especially, "rooted in a craft tradition which was disintegrating under the impact of war," lay the material for a revolutionary agitation.[61]

Before the war many of the traditional skills of the engineering workers were being rendered obsolete by technological changes and a greater specialization of labor. The craftsman's versatility and capacity for initiative and judgment, formerly demanded in the engineering trades, were being eliminated by a process of economic rationalization. Although the powerful Amalgamated Society of Engineers had generally succeeded in preserving the privileged position of its members, the Union's "wages strategy . . . made no allowances for the technological dynamism of the industry." Wartime needs for greater productivity increased the anachronistic state of this section of British industry. The position of the engineers was threatened, first by a process of "dilution," whereby women and unskilled workers performed many of their old tasks, and second, by demands for modes of industrial discipline which clashed with the traditional liberties and the customs of the craftsmen. The difficulties of the engineers were increased by the reluctance of their trade union leaders, strongly committed to the nation's war effort, to resist these developments. The growing breach between the officials of the engineering unions and the rank and file made room for a Socialist appeal more closely attuned to the immediate concerns of the workers.[62]

In the collision between the craft traditions of the engineers and the drive toward economic rationalization, much more was at stake than the maintenance of wage levels. The engineering workers were struggling, so James Hinton has argued, against a development which "threatened not only economic security but spiritual values which lay at the heart of their world outlook." They were facing the loss of a way of life which had conferred social status and self respect.[63] Here was one important source of the special militancy which characterized the industrial strife along the Clydeside during the war. Here too was promising ground for the Socialist appeal on behalf of a transformed society.

Socialist efforts to win over the Clydeside workers were concentrated on the shop stewards, who had emerged, even before the war, as spokesmen for the engineers, often in opposition to the increasingly centralized and remote union leadership. The new pressures of wartime increased the opposition and transformed the Shop Stewards' movement into a rival of the official union organization. And through the formation of the Clyde Workers' Committee in October 1915, the shop stewards in the area gained the unity necessary to offer significant resistance to the new industrial policies being imposed by the employers and the government.[64]

The Clyde Workers' Committee became, during the closing months of 1915, the scene of a struggle between the BSP and the SLP to give the engineering workers a new lead and a social vision which transcended their immediate concerns as craftsmen. Although the committee was dominated by members of the SLP, still committed to a strategy of industrial unionism, they were countered by the most gifted and influential of all the Scottish Marxists—the BSP leader, John Maclean. The fortunes of Social Democracy in the Clyde Valley during the war years, and indeed, the development of the revolutionary wing of the BSP generally, were so closely bound up with the work of Maclean that his career requires brief examination. Maclean was, according to one historian, the "dynamo that powered the revolutionary movement on the Clyde."[65]

Maclean's early development reflected many of the forces which shaped the growth of socialism in Scotland.[66] Born of working class parents, strongly influenced by one of the most extreme of the Calvinist dissenting bodies, the Original Secession Church, he entered a path of hard earned education and self-improvement which led into the lower professional class. After study at the Free Church Teaching College in 1900, Maclean accepted the first of a series of teaching positions in the area around Glasgow. Meanwhile, participation in a mutual improvement society, the Progressive Union, enlarged his cultural awareness and also led him to adopt secularist and atheistic views. For a time Maclean, like many young Socialist converts, saw organized religion as the chief enemy of the working class. He had become a Socialist after reading Blatchford's *Merrie England*, but soon found in *Capital* a belief system which he held the rest of his life. In 1903 he joined the only branch of the SDF in the Glasgow area which had survived the breakaway to the SLP, and during the years ahead he did more than any other person to renew the growth of Social Democracy in Scotland. Convinced, like the Social Democratic leaders, that a genuine Socialist party presupposed the education of the workers in Marxist theory, he conducted highly successful classes in Marxist economics. And he found in a young bank clerk, James MacDougal, an associate who could supplement his educational work. By means of these classes and his summer propaganda campaigns throughout Scotland, Maclean did much to educate a new generation of Socialist leaders, a number of whom were teachers like himself. While many of his students backed off from his "dialectical materialism," in favor of the ethical idealism of the ILP, they often carried something of his Marxism and much of his militance into the wider Socialist movement.

Maclean's loyalty to Hyndman was broken by the latter's zeal for military preparedness. By 1910 he was working with the Internationalist wing of the BSP in an effort to counter nationalistic sentiment and loosen the hold of the older leaders on the party's policies. He also took an active part in the new surge of industrialist agitation, seeking far more than most Social Democrats to integrate Marxist theory with the immediate struggles of the workers. Although Maclean rejected the call of those who wished to abandon politics for an economic strategy, he made room in his Marxism for the idea of industrial unionism.

After the outbreak of war Maclean quickly assumed a leading role in the struggle against the government's policies. Although the BSP branches in Scotland were divided over the war, Maclean gradually won over the majority to his position. Meanwhile, at the national level, he joined Fairchild, Rothstein, and other Internationalists within the BSP in attacking Hyndman's policies. When Bax exhorted Social Democrats to hate the Prussian state system, Maclean replied that "our first business is to hate the British capitalist system." The war demonstrated, he argued, the folly of mere reformism and the need for a genuine revolutionary policy. Working class control of the factories by means of industrial unions would make possible the takeover of the "rapidly expanding State machinery for the fundamental reorganizing and unifying of the whole of the process of production and exchange."[67]

The Clyde Workers' Committee presented a new opportunity for Maclean to connect his Marxist-inspired agitation against the war with the economic grievances of the working classes.[68] He and MacDougal were warmly welcomed into the weekly meetings of the committee and granted full rights to participate in the discussions. The committee was headed by one of his own students, William Gallacher, but the efforts of Maclean to guide it toward a revolutionary strategy were unsuccessful. Most of the members of the committee were preoccupied with the struggle of the engineers against dilution and, insofar as they contemplated a larger mission, were drawn more to the industrial strategy of the SLP. Indeed, the participation of Maclean in the meetings of the CWC ended in December 1915 after one of his associates attacked the committee for its refusal to take a stand against the war and its failure to rise above narrow economic considerations.

The defeat of the Social Democrats left the field clear for the SLP men on the committee to push their strategy of workers' control through industrial action. They had now abandoned the De Leonist policy of dual unionism in favor of the Syndicalist effort to capture the old unions from within. But the SLP group also failed to make the committee a militant force for socialism. They were hampered by the government's decision in 1916 to expel the most important leaders of the Shop Stewards' movement from the Clyde area. However, neither in Scotland, nor in the industrial areas of England into which the Shop Stewards' movement spread in these years, were its leaders able to overcome the essentially archaic aspirations of the skilled engineers and unite all sections of the workers on behalf of a vision of Socialist transformation.

Having failed to win the Clyde Workers' Committee over to his revolutionary version of Social Democracy, Maclean returned to the work of education and propaganda. In March 1916, however, his vigorous attacks on the government's plan for national conscription brought the powers of the state down upon him and he was arrested on charges of sedition. A few weeks later he was sentenced to three years of penal servitude. His imprisonment, coming at the time when the Internationalist wing of the BSP was taking control of the party away from the Hyndmanites, made it easier for Fairchild and the new leaders in London to pursue a moderate and pacifist policy.

While the leaders of the BSP continued to look to international Socialist initiative for negotiations to end the war, they also drew closer to the ILP. Common opposition to the war tended, as at the time of the Boer War, to overcome ideological disagreements. But this move toward Socialist unity angered those BSP members, particularly Rothstein and Tom Quelch, who shared Maclean's desire for action designed to hinder the nation's war effort and prepare the workers for revolution. During the second half of 1917 Rothstein and Quelch were urging the party to enter actively into the Shop Stewards' movement, now spreading beyond Scotland into Sheffield, Manchester, and other industrial centers, and to seek to translate the economic grievances of the engineering workers into revolutionary political demands. Rothstein saw the possibility of organizing the masses for a definite resistance to the war by means of a general strike in munitions factories and related industries.[69]

The political upheavals in Russia during 1917 sharpened this new division among the Social Democrats. BSP leaders, along with all sections of the Socialist movement, welcomed the March revolution in Russia and joined the ILP in organizing a conference at Leeds in July to celebrate and discuss the event. But groups within the BSP drew different lessons from developments in Russia. To Fairchild it provided new hope that a peace treaty might be negotiated by a restored Socialist International. The uprising in Russia, however, also reawakened the old fears among Social Democrats that the workers might undertake revolutionary action without the necessary training and discipline in Socialist principles to accomplish their emancipation.

Rothstein, Quelch, and Maclean—released from prison in June 1917—believed, on the other hand, that the Russian experience had vindicated their call for a more militant strategy. They welcomed the Bolshevik seizure of power in November as a sign that the general collapse of capitalism was imminent. Indeed, the Bolshevik revolution worked as a catalyst among British Marxists, breaking down old combinations and helping new ones to form. It also initiated the final stage in the decomposition of the Social Democratic tradition in Britain.

The growing tension within the BSP was evident at the next annual conference, held in London in the spring of 1918. The delegates gave unanimous support to a resolution expressing complete agreement with the Bolshevik "measures for the reorganization of Russia under the control of the working classes." But the impact of the Bolshevik revolution was most evident in the subsequent debates about the BSP's affiliation to the Labour Party, its relationship to the other Socialist bodies, and its attitude toward the Shop Stewards' movement and its industrial strategy. Thus, Maclean, speaking to the question of continued affiliation, warned against sacrificing "all for unity," and he noted that their comrades in the workshops had been forced "to throw over" the official trade union leaders in order to "develop a movement on revolutionary principles." "The Labour Party was bound up at the present time with capitalism, and fighting Socialism. The whole of Society was in the melting pot; we had a chance of developing a force and organization that would sweep away the Labour Party on one side and develop the workers' class consciousness, industrially and politically." Fairchild strongly opposed this view. "Whether we liked it or not, the Labour Party, including ourselves, was the political movement of the working classes . . . The besetting sin of the Socialists of this country was their passion for formal logic. They talked of revolutionary propaganda and tactics, but the things they called by these names did not really make for revolution."[70]

The Russian Revolution had provided, so one delegate claimed, "a rallying point for all sections and had shown us the way" to socialism.[71] It was a path which (given their interpretation of events in Russia) drew these Social Democrats away from the party's traditional political strategy. During the months following the conference Fairchild and his supporters continued to defend that strategy, arguing that the BSP's main task was still that of building a strong party by educating the workers in Marxist principles. To that end they urged closer ties with the Labour Party and the ILP. They were, however, being stranded by the new tide of opinion within the BSP.

Unity negotiations between BSP representatives and SLP leaders during the autumn and winter of 1918 indicated that the two bodies were, under the influence of the Bolshevik revolution and their shared experiences in the Shop Stewards' movement, converging in their outlooks. They were finding a common ground in the notion of soviets, springing up spontaneously in workshops and factories out of the "revolutionary instincts" of the masses, and opening a new path to a Socialist society. To join the BSP on this ground, the SLP had to give up the De Leonist concept of national industrial unions in favor of local committees representative of workers from all the industries. But they could see in the Bolshevik achievement a confirmation of the SLP view that "the old concept of the political state had to go by the board."[72] During the early weeks of 1919 leading figures in the SLP—Tom Bell, Arthur Macmanus, J. T. Murphy, and William Paul—succeeded in altering their party's position and bringing it close to that of the left wing of the BSP.

The BSP conference in April 1919, demonstrated that "Sovietism . . . had captured the party and its leaders." Formation of the Communist International a month earlier had confronted British Marxists, along with European Socialists generally, with a choice between traditional Social Democratic policies and a Leninist strategy. Voting at the conference, and a subsequent referendum of the branches, left no doubt about the BSP's eagerness to follow the Bolshevik lead. Fairchild, and the party's treasurer, Alexander, continued for some months to fight for the older Social Democratic commitment to a parliamentary party. The new leaders, Fairchild charged, wished to "start afresh as though there had been neither Parliament nor trade unions in British history." But the BSP's acceptance of the Soviet as the "only possible agency for the Socialist revolution" marked, in Hinton's words, "the decisive break with the Social Democratic orthodoxy and constituted the ideological basis for the formation of a unified revolutionary party."[73]

The regrouping of British Marxists around the Communist banner proved to be a difficult and protracted affair. Despite their ideological reorientation, the BSP leaders were reluctant to cut their ties with the Labour Party, seeing the party as a promising field for revolutionary agitation. To the members of the SLP, however, this residual opportunism presented a major obstacle to reunion. Indeed, the issue helped reactivate the kind of conflict which had disturbed the SLP throughout its history and, in fact, initiated a new series of schisms. The SLP as a party backed off from the plan for unity and retreated into sectarian isolation. But it contributed the key leaders to the Communist Party of Great Britain, officially founded in August 1920.

Members of the BSP made up the bulk of the supporters of the new party. In choosing this ideological and strategical reorientation, they had discarded Hyndman's form of Marxism for that of Lenin. And while the new Communist Party was, as Kendall has argued, an "artificial creation" owing its existence and much of its substance to outside influences, it simply perpetuated one side of the Social Democratic tradition in Britain. For Social Democracy had always been something of "a stranger in its own country."[74] With the rejection of the political strategy to which Hyndman had tied the Social Democrats, the ever present aspiration within that tradition to transcend the structure of British institutions was released once more. The Bolshevik model, together with the industrial strategy advanced by the Shop Stewards' movement, had revived hopes for a radically new kind of society. As in Russia, working class associations in the factories, the shops, and the mines, and a spontaneous uprising of the masses would inaugurate a genuinely Socialist order.

The Russian revolution had rekindled the apocalyptic expectation present in much of British Marxism. But this expectation was reawakened at a time of growing frustration within the revolutionary wing of the movement. As negotiations toward the new party proceeded during 1918 and 1919, the possibility of substantial support among the working classes for the new strategy was evaporating. The renewed Shop Steward offensive along the Clydeside had floundered once more on the shoals of craft exclusiveness, and the movement "vanished like the dew." Moreover, at the end of the war the workers of the Clyde and elsewhere in Britain quickly lost the economic and political leverage they had acquired during a time of labor scarcity and demands for a high level of production. Perhaps, as Hinton has argued, the Bolshevik use of the soviets gave British Marxists a belated understanding of the theoretical implications of their own wartime experiences. But the belief among British Marxists in the imminence of revolution suggested that they were also moving into a world of fantasy. They were employing, as Hinton observed, Sovietism as a "revolutionary myth to cover their retreat from the factories."[75]

The dilemmas of wartime and the lure of the Bolshevik model had virtually completed the fragmentation of the Social Democratic tradition in Britain. The Marxist drive toward a radically new social order—which had drawn some Social Democrats to the archaic utopia of Morris, others to the industrial vision of De Leon, and still others to French syndicalism—had finally found a more durable form in the type of organization Lenin had fashioned out of the ruins of tsarist Russia. British Marxists misunderstood the nature of the Bolshevik achievement; they did not grasp the crucial role of Lenin's vanguard party. But from distant events, arising out of different historical experience, they had found a new hope.

Social Democrats who rejected the Bolshevik inspiration

were increasingly isolated in these years. And the further decomposition of their ideology can be followed in the lives of the two leading Marxist opponents of the Communist succession—Maclean and Hyndman. If Maclean's tragic end suggested the personal and social impasse into which British Social Democracy might lead, Hyndman's later development revealed the working out of some of its latent possibilities.

THE END OF SOCIAL DEMOCRACY:
The Two Ways of Maclean and Hyndman

"The message," so a fellow Socialist wrote of Maclean, "became his personality."[76] This remark captured the extraordinary quality of dedication in the Clydeside leader. No figure in the movement during these years placed his life so fully in the service of his Socialist ideology or paid so high a price for such a surrender of self.

From the time he entered the movement Maclean emphasized the Social Democratic mission of developing a Socialist consciousness among the workers. Working class education, he insisted, was as important as working class association. Maclean did not ignore the struggle for immediate ends; he participated in industrial disputes, in the Scottish Cooperative movement, in demonstrations on behalf of the unemployed; and he conducted a vigorous agitation against the war. But he saw these activities as the growth points of a working class thoroughly informed by Marxist principles. And through his classes in Marxian economics he attempted to give the workers a systematic alternative to conventional social wisdom or the "mere system of apologetics" taught in the universities.[77] In his way Maclean was seeking to free the working classes from what Antonio Gramsci called the cultural hegemony of the bourgeoisie.

Maclean's educational efforts culminated during the war years in the development of the Scottish Labour College. Inspired in part by Maclean's popular classes in and around Glasgow, in part by Ruskin College and its Marxist offshoot, the Central Labour College in London, the new school was to be "financed and controlled by the working class" and was to train them for "the battle against the masters." Its curriculum was based on Marxist economic doctrines. By the end of the war it had opened its doors to day students and claimed three full time tutors, including Maclean and his chief disciple, MacDougal.[78]

During the war years the ideological and strategic framework within which Maclean carried on his educational mission was gradually altered. Before the war he had shared the basic Social Democratic goal of building up a parliamentary party by grounding the workers in Marxist doctrines. He had also urged his colleagues to return to the Labour Party, convinced that it offered the most promising vehicle for Socialist advance. Maclean, like Hyndman, saw the party's role as that of preparing the workers to take power when the anticipated breakdown of capitalism occurred. But he also maintained, until the end of his life, that the change could be accomplished in a peaceful way; the term revolution did not necessarily imply violence and bloodshed.

The developments of wartime—Hyndman's intense patriotism, the renewed debates within the BSP, the upsurge of industrial militance along the Clyde, and his own arrests and imprisonments—drove Maclean toward an increasingly militant position. For Maclean, as for many British Marxists, a decisive shift in outlook came with the revolution in Russia. He quickly became a strong champion of the Bolshevik government. Lenin, in fact, identified him as his leading supporter in Britain. Maclean was named one of the honorary presidents of the First All Russian Congress of Soviets and appointed Russian Consul in Scotland. During the winter of 1917-18 he conducted a vigorous campaign to bring the "message of the Russian Revolution to every working class center in Scotland." When in March he was chosen by the Labour Representation Committee of the Gorbals division of Glasgow to stand as its parliamentary candidate, Maclean declared that the House of Commons should be superseded by a soviet. And at the end of the month he told the delegates at the BSP's annual conference that they "were in the rapids of revolution." He called on them to emulate the Bolsheviks by concentrating their efforts on the "unofficial . . . shop steward movement" within the trade unions and to be ready "to seize the opportunity at any moment to down capitalism." Two weeks later he was charged with sedition and, after a trial enlivened by his passionate denunciations of capitalism, he was sentenced to five years in prison.[79]

Released a few weeks after the end of the war, Maclean immediately resumed his agitation. He did not repudiate political activity, or even urge the BSP to pull out of the Labour Party, but he was looking more and more to industrial action, and the formation of "one big union," as the way to advance the cause of the revolution. During the first six months of 1919 he believed that a revolution might be imminent. He threw himself into the struggle of the Clydeside workers to gain a forty hour week, hopeful that it would ignite the industrial masses generally and enable the Socialists to "take control of the country." After the strike failed he urged his colleagues to seize on the unemployment problem as a "way to get the masses on the move." Meanwhile, as a member of the BSP executive, he had joined those who were seeking to redirect its policies along Soviet lines. When Fairchild defended the traditional Social Democratic political strategy at the spring conference, Maclean charged that he had "gone over to the enemy."[80]

Maclean soon diverged from the new leaders of the BSP. Something of the old suspicion of Scottish Social Democrats toward the "London juntas" was apparent here, but Maclean had also come to distrust the influence which Rothstein, by virtue of his close ties with the Bolsheviks, was exercising on the party's development. Moreover, his experience in the Clydeside strike early in 1919 and his propaganda tours in England, had convinced him that the workers south of the border had not joined the Scottish workers in the "swing to the left." Maclean had begun, in fact, to follow the path of his friend, Connolly, who had fused his socialism with the struggle for Irish independence. In the course of 1919 Maclean drew close to those who were reviving the cause of Scottish nationalism. Meanwhile, he was constructing, by means of Marxist doctrines, a picture of postwar international conflicts which gave Scotland a crucial role in the coming showdown of imperialistic powers. Maclean had come to feel that Scotland required its own revolutionary party.[81]

As the BSP moved during 1919 and 1920 into the Communist Party of Great Britain, Maclean, was "gently splipped

. . . out." His attacks on the London leaders and on Bolshevik interference, together with his commitment to a separate Communist party for Scotland, led to his exclusion from the process of Marxist reorganization. But well before the August conference which gave birth to the new party, Maclean was charting an independent course in the columns of his revived paper, the *Vanguard*. His course still owed much to the Bolshevik example. He rejected the older Social Democratic view that no revolution could succeed until "the vast majority of the wage earners were conscious socialists," in favor of the possibility, demonstrated by the Bolsheviks, of activating the "revolutionary impulse of the masses" in the midst of a social breakdown. But he also urged his fellow Marxists, after the manner of Georges Sorel, to formulate a program for the workers which no capitalist government could concede and which would "necessarily bring a clash with the dominant class." Such a program, he argued, might so arouse the workers in a crisis "that by effective spontaneous action, they would sweep the capitalists out of power."[82]

Maclean set out in the autumn of 1920 to organize a Scottish Communist party, convinced that the London Communists had been corrupted and that Lenin, who supported them, did not understand the British situation. In Maclean's reading of the international developments the key to the situation was an alliance between Scottish and Irish workers to destroy the "greatest menace to the human race"—the British Empire. "We on the Clyde have a mighty mission to fulfill. We can make Glasgow a Petrograd, a revolutionary storm center second to none. A Scottish breakaway at this juncture would bring the Empire crash to the ground and free the waiting workers of the world."[83]

Maclean's efforts to gather Marxist forces in Scotland into a separate Communist party were thwarted by Gallacher, recently returned from Moscow and a conversion to Leninism, who brought to bear the full prestige and authority of the Bolshevik leader. Maclean then turned to the SLP as the "most distinctive Marxian organization in Scotland," hopeful that it would "drop the rope a bit."[84] But the SLP leaders were unwilling to sacrifice their branches in England and Wales in order to establish a Scottish party. Although Maclean joined the SLP he did not remain a member for long.

Having abandoned Social Democracy and having failed in his attempt to "get the clear headed and honest Marxist Revolutionaries in one camp,"[85] Maclean was increasingly isolated. His isolation became virtually complete in May 1921 when he was arrested again for seditious activities and sentenced to a prison term. Except for a two month period in the autumn, he remained in prison over the next seventeen months.

He emerged in October 1922 to find his followers scattered, demoralized, or captured by the Communist Party. The militant spirit along the Clyde had died down or been absorbed by the revitalized Labour Party. The Scottish Labour College, to which he had devoted so much of his energy, was moving away from its Marxist base into the more moderate orbit of the ILP. But Maclean was still as determined as ever to form a Scottish revolutionary party and establish a Scottish Workers Republic. And to this end he entered a series of municipal and parliamentary election contests in the months ahead, using the political platform not "to talk on rents, taxes, or capital levy," but "on questions of trade and the world political and economic complications." Even if elected to Parliament, he told his audiences in the Gorbals constituency, he would stay in Scotland to advance the work of the revolution. In February 1923, he formed the Scottish Workers Republican Party to do battle with the "pinks" of the ILP and the Communist party. He was convinced that the Communists were fading out and clearing the ground for a "real fighting party independent of outside dictation and finance."[86]

Maclean's antagonist, Gallacher, claimed later that Maclean was increasingly prey to hallucinations induced by the ordeals of prison life. There is little sign of mental derangement in Maclean's letters to his family and friends at this time. But the letters present a picture of social development which was more and more remote from the behavior of the Scottish working classes. Thus Maclean continued through the summer and autumn of 1923 to believe that his new party was "steadily sweeping over Glasgow," that capitalism was "slipping and plunging to its well merited doom," and that the "people will come to me for guidance" in a crisis. Indeed, amid the ruins of his Social Democratic faith he continued to hold fast to the notion of an approaching social cataclysm generated by imperialistic rivalries.[87]

Through his fierce attachment to the revolutionary hope, Maclean withdrew during his last years into a virtually solipsistic state; he gradually lost the personal and institutional ties which give shape and stability to most lives. In 1919 his wife had left with the two children, unable to bear any longer the hardships resulting from his work for the cause. The exchange of letters during 1922 and 1923, in which they struggled to find the terms for a reunion they both desired, reveal the intensity of his commitment to the Socialist revolution and her fear that it was destroying him. At one point, Maclean confessed that illness and poverty "just about make one sink into one's self and cut entirely with the rest of the world." For a moment it seemed possible that he might resume his teaching career and a normal life for the family, on condition that he give up political activity. But he refused to turn back. "My only hope for economic security at present is from the masses . . . If I go down, I want to go down with my flag at mast top. Nothing on earth will shift me from that."[88]

And so he remained, as Sylvia Pankhurst described him, enduring "the bare and lonely life of an ascetic . . . doing his own cooking and housework." To the cause of the revolution he had literally delivered over his self, becoming in the process indifferent to elementary considerations of dress and physical well-being. He was so shabby, his daughter recalled, "that I was ashamed to walk down the street with him." In November, as he was campaigning again for the Gorbals seat, the end came. Weakened by malnutrition, having given his only overcoat to a needy comrade, he was stricken by double pneumonia and died at the age of forty-four.[89]

Some years earlier Philip Snowden had described Maclean as "a fool of colossal dimensions." His colleagues in the Clydeside were more likely to view him as a martyr or a saint. The terms suggest that Maclean had, in the course of his life, moved beyond the plane of conventional social or political evaluation. Certainly his popularity in the Clydeside, his continuing power to draw large audiences, bore little relationship to the practical results of his labors. By virtue of the steadfastness of his revolutionary passion, and his sacrifices, he had come to symbolize deep aspirations among the Scottish lower classes. Indeed, Maclean's force as a symbol increased after his death. In later years his blend of social radicalism and nationalistic feeling took on, in retrospect, epic dimensions and provided fresh inspiration for many including the major poetic voice of a new Scottish nationalism. "One of the few true men of our sordid breed," Hugh MacDiarmid wrote of Maclean, "A flash of sun in a country all prison grey." [90]

No such resurrection followed the death of Hyndman in November of 1921. In later years most British Marxists would execrate him, while for Socialists generally his career offered little more than a case study in the dangers of dogmatism and autocratic leadership. Hyndman's activities and reflections during his last years disclose, however, another side to the development of British Social Democracy. If Maclean's isolation and his premature death can be seen as one denouement of that tradition, the accommodation of Hyndman and his disciples to British political institutions represents another.

Following his break with the BSP in 1916, Hyndman and a number of the older Social Democratic leaders had set out again, by means of the National Socialist Party, to propagate their Marxism. Over the next several years the new party enjoyed a modest growth, claiming upwards of fifty branches and two thousand members. Its leaders identified themselves with the British war effort and kept up a running criticism of the pacifist or antiwar activities of the ILP and the BSP. In 1918, when the Labour Party adopted a program with a clear statement of Socialist goals, the National Socialist Party applied for membership and was accepted. A year later the party's name was changed to the Social Democratic Federation. Its leaders were seeking, in the face of the Communist claim to the Marxist succession in Britain, to reassert "the fundamental principles of Social Democracy."[91] But Hyndman and his colleagues had in fact given up the intransigence of that tradition in order to enter more fully into the political process.

The shift in outlook and strategy was apparent in the wartime activities of Hyndman himself. His participation in the War Emergency Workers' National Committee indicated both his eagerness to translate Socialist principles into practical measures for social amelioration, and his willingness to employ existing administrative agencies for that purpose. Hyndman also sought to use the committee to advance bolder Socialist ideas. When the government inaugurated a policy of military conscription during 1916, he introduced a scheme for the "conscription of riches" which entailed the nationalization of much of the country's economy. His plan was quickly countered by Webb's more modest proposals for the taxation of war profits and for new forms of public controls. But a curious kind of cooperation had replaced the old antagonism between the two Socialist leaders. "I bring out a root and ground revolutionary proposal and set it well before them, " Hyndman observed, and that "puts them in a fright . . . Then Webb comes in with his proposal, only a few degrees milder than mine; and they are so relieved that they pass it unanimously." Actually, Hyndman was developing a Fabian-like faith in the advance toward socialism by means of incremental changes in existing governmental policies. During the months following the end of the war, as the committee's representative on the government's Consumer Council, he struggled to ensure its permanence as an agency for the protection of the living standards of the lower classes. It might serve, he observed, as a "nucleus for social reorganization."[92]

Hyndman's intense patriotism no doubt helped dissipate the militant spirit which had frequently characterized his leadership before the war. But it did not alter his fundamental commitment to Marxism. "The historic and economic theories which you and I" share, he told an American Marxist in 1917, "remain quite unshaken." And he still saw, in the "aimless drift" of the public authorities and the economic hardships of the working classes, sure signs that the capitalistic order was nearing its final collapse.[93] He continued to waver, however, as in earlier years, between the hope that the British could effect a peaceful transition to socialism and the fear that a violent upheaval was imminent.

Still, the failure of Social Democratic ideas to make substantial headway among the workers had led Hyndman to reflect more and more on the defects of his position. Before the war he had believed that economic developments would inevitably engender the outlook appropriate to a Socialist order and, indeed, displace all older systems of belief.

> The Religion of Socialism will yet succeed in bringing together in one conscious material creed the many races and societies that make up the civilized world . . . [Science] affords one clear and reasoned explanation of the constitution of the kosmos from ether and the gasses to Man; and thenceforth throughout the millions of years of Man's development, attaining at least to its full fruition in the Golden Age of Scientific Communism . . . We form a part, a sentient and at last a controlling part, of the evolution of life through the ages.

In 1913 he reaffirmed his belief in the "irresistible movement of economic and social purpose, independent alike of morality and religion."[94]

Under the influence of Bax, however, Hyndman had made more room for the play of human consciousness and will than most contemporary Marxists. He believed that Bax, the "only original thinker now in any country," was capable of formulating a new philosophical synthesis. "I have been bullying Bax," he wrote Shaw in 1914, "into doing really well that ground work of a Socialist philosophy which he partly carried out in his 'Roots of Reality.' " Bax did not finish the task. And in later years Hyndman saw in the absence of an *Aberglaube*, or an inspiring metaphysical principle, a key to the failure of Social Democracy. "I used to think," he told his comrades, that "Social Democracy would take the place of religion, but now I see that human beings want something more. Religious belief in some shape or another will be necessary for hundreds of years yet and we shall have to find it somehow." He had begun to fear, in fact, that a "mere material education" might "lead to scientific barbarism" unless augmented by a "higher social ideal." At times he even contemplated the possibility of a national "change of heart," or a "mass revelation," presumably generated by a profound social crisis.[95]

Hyndman's suggestion that the absence of a religious or metaphysical dimension to Social Democracy had significantly, perhaps fatally, limited its appeal, did not, however, modify his utilitarian interpretation of Marxism. From the beginning, despite his friendship with Bax, Hyndman had resisted efforts to expand the Socialist ideology into a total philosophy of life and challenge moral and religious conventions. Suspicious of moralistic, religious, and aesthetic appeals, skeptical of the efforts of Morris and others to transform the nature of the productive process, he remained committed to changes which could be carried out within the industrial and parliamentary systems. Hyndman's socialism was, despite its Marxist inspiration, much like Webb's Fabianism. What he called the coming science of sociology presupposed the conceptions of self-interest and general well-being implicit in existing political institutions.[96] When Hyndman attacked British political leaders, as he did with unrelenting ferocity, he pointed to their inefficiency, their failure to coordinate the various governmental agencies, and above all, their inability to ensure an adequate distribution of goods and services to all sections of the community.

Wartime developments accentuated these features in Hyndman's Marxism. Separated from revolutionary Marxists through the disputes generated by the war, Hyndman and his supporters increasingly stressed those features of national development that were leading toward socialism. Moreover, the Hyndmanites were falling back, like Maclean in a different context, on nationalistic feelings in order to reenergize their Socialist ideology.

Hyndman's growing commitment to reformism was reflected in his hostility to Bolshevism. Though initially prompted by his fear that the revolution in Russia would weaken the allied war effort, he was also convinced that "Lenin and company" had forced the pace of political change in a disastrous manner. "Nothing will persuade me," he wrote Shaw in 1920, "that people can make twelve o'clock at eleven, in economics, and sociology, by dogmatism, corruption, and wholesale butchery." Hyndman firmly opposed those Socialist and labor leaders in Britain who hoped to emulate the Bolsheviks and achieve public ownership through a general strike or other forms of direct action. Given the low level of understanding among the workers, such actions were "more likely to result in anarchy and civil war, followed by a military dictatorship." The best chance for a peaceful transition to socialism lay in a further democratization of the political process and the convergence of the monopolistic forms of advancing capitalism with the expanding forms of working class economic association.[97]

Hyndman was reassured by the development of the Labour Party at the end of the war. Its acceptance of a new constitution and policy statement in 1918, though pushed through by the "wire pulling triumvirate of Henderson, MacDonald, and Webb," was a great step forward. Here we have "a series of Socialist measures," he observed, for which Social Democrats "have worked for nearly forty years." The sight of labor leaders who had been "mere Liberal Capitalist tools yesterday, passing as great Socialist authorities," amused him and aroused some envy. "We did the work, they take the credit." And while he concluded before long that the Labour Party still lacked "a genuine Socialist inspiration," he remained convinced that "we must stick to that line."[98]

Hyndman's optimism gave way, as in earlier years, to moments of deep pessimism. In this "queer, apathetic, ignorant old country," he told Shaw in 1920, it might take "a century or so to prove to Englishmen the scientific truth of Marx's analysis." And yet, when he saw signs of an "approaching cataclysm," he did not welcome it. Although he had done his utmost over the years to promote "an outbreak of the class war," he had also struggled, in his own mind, to avert it. Such a claim might have seemed strange to many of those he had drawn into the ranks of the Social Democrats. But from his initial warning to British political leaders in 1880 about the dangers of revolution, he had been dedicated mainly to the task of modernizing and strengthening the British nation. Unlike those Marxists who hoped to exploit the domestic and international disorders caused by the war to foment revolution, Hyndman held ever more firmly to parliamentary institutions.[99]

In following the path of political accommodation, Hyndman was not applying his form of Social Democracy in an idiosyncratic manner. Much the same outcome was apparent in the development of the party which carried forward the work of propagating his Marxist ideas. In the postwar "coupon" election, eleven members of the National Socialist Party stood for parliamentary seats and, aided by the strong tide of patriotic feeling within the electorate, six of these Social Democrats were returned. Over the next several years five additional members, standing once more under the banner of the Social Democratic Federation, and firmly attached to the Labour Party, were elected. To the official historian of British Social Democracy it seemed as though the Federation had exchanged roles with the ILP; as the latter adopted an increasingly critical stance within the Labour Party during the twenties, the members of the Federation were attempting, like the Fabians, to serve as a moderate Socialist leaven.[100]

In the postwar years the Social Democrats continued their efforts to raise the "standard of Socialist consciousness amongst the working class." But they had now renounced the "attempt to be the vanguard" in favor of being a "loyal soldier in the working class army."[101] Their old role as vanguard, and the call to revolution, had been taken over either by the rejuvenated ILP or by the Communist Party. Having submerged itself in the working class political movement, the SDF had lost any distinctive ideological basis for its existence and entered a course leading to its extinction.

8

THE
FABIAN CONVERSION
TO PARTY POLITICS

SHORTLY AFTER THE general election of 1906 H. T. Muggeridge told the London Fabians that the "appearance of a Socialist and Labour Party on the political stage" threatened to leave the Society in the "shadows. . . hugging the delusion of the efficacy of its long exploded methods."[1] Fabians in general were not so ready to concede that their methods were outmoded. But in the period following the general election the earlier conception of the Fabian mission, developed mainly by Webb, was under renewed assault from several distinct groups within the Society.

None of the attacks succeeded in altering the Fabian policy. And by the spring of 1907 Webb was insisting once more that the proper role for the Fabians lay behind the political scene in efforts to apply their ideas in such areas as "labor legislation, local government, and educational administration." In England, he maintained, more was done in politics "whilst ignoring elections and parties than by or with them."[2] Yet, even as Webb reaffirmed his position he was being drawn into a course of action which carried him and the Fabians as well away from the Society's traditional policy. His wife's work on the Royal Commission on the Poor Laws led to a public campaign which forced the Fabians to redefine their place in British political life.

The work of redefinition took nearly a decade. It also served, like the parallel efforts among the Ethical Socialists and the Social Democrats, to separate out some of the motives and aspirations underlying Fabianism. The decline of the Fabian form of socialism was mirrored in the later development of Shaw who gradually abandoned his old role in the life of the Society. And the final stages of the decline unfolded in the lives of the Webbs themselves.

FABIAN DISSENTERS, 1906-1908

Accounts of the Society in these years have usually focused on the campaign of H. G. Wells to reorient the Fabians. But Wells did not, as one member, Henry Macrosty, observed, create the "new leaven within the Society." He simply "voiced it" more effectively than anyone else.[3] Before long the singularity of Wells became apparent and those who had rallied around him turned back to their disparate forms of opposition to the Society's policies. The "episode of Mr. Wells," as Pease called it, served, however, to clarify the tensions within Fabianism.

During 1906 the Fabian leaders faced three distinct challenges to their policies. One section of the membership, led by Muggeridge and R. C. K. Ensor, argued that the Fabians should draw closer to the ILP and the Labour Party. The "root of the matter," Muggeridge declared, was "whether the Fabian Society should remain a learned body apart from the real life of the nation or whether it would become in a real sense the guide, philosopher, and friend of the unpolished but live movement of the people." It was time, he argued, for the Fabians to abandon permeation and run candidates under the auspices of the Labour Party. Some support for this position came from Hubert Bland, who had long questioned the wisdom of Fabian efforts to permeate all parties. His tract, "Socialism and Labour Policy," published during 1906, called on the Labour Party leaders to distinguish themselves more sharply from the Liberals by adopting the Fabian program for guaranteeing employment and a minimum standard of living. The Fabians, he argued, could provide a "broad-minded criticism" and enable the new party to rise above sectional conflicts and appeal to the "many and varied interests of the average electors."[4]

A second group, led by Sam Hobson and Cecil Chesterton, urged the Fabians to strike out on their own politically.

Influenced no doubt by Hobson's quarrel with the ILP, they were convinced that the growing power of the trade unionists within the Labour Party threatened Socialist goals. To these members the general election had demonstrated an "astonishing growth of Socialist sentiment" and the possibility of "a solid Socialist party" in many constituencies. Nor were they worried lest the Fabians compete with the ILP. "When middle class Socialists do join the ILP," Hobson observed, "a few months exhaust their patience of the red tape that chokes the organization and they sigh for some more active body of Socialists whose methods are more fluid and less mechanical." Convinced that loyal "parallel action" was possible, he called on the Society to employ its resources to create "a Socialist party in which the middle classes can play their natural and rightful part." Shaw too began to favor such a venture; he was increasingly worried lest middle class Socialists be caught in an economic squeeze between "labor and plutocracy."[5]

A third attempt to reorient the Fabians came from Orage and Holbrook Jackson, newly down from Leeds where their Leeds Art Club had suggested another road to socialism. The Society's difficulties, Jackson told Pease, could be traced to its "altogether too narrow view of the Fabian work." Fabians should renew the mission of William Morris and seek to create "a definite Socialist attitude" in the areas of art and philosophy as they had already done in politics and sociology. To implement this idea Jackson and Orage organized the Fabian Arts Group early in 1907. "It would make an appeal to minds that remained unmoved by the ordinary Fabian attitudes and provide a platform for the discussion of the more subtle relations of man to society which had been brought to the front in the work of such modern philosopher artists as Nietzsche, Ibsen, Tolstoy and Shaw."[6]

These challengers to Fabian policy found in H. G. Wells a vigorous leader. In February he had renewed his own criticism of the Society's work in a talk, "Faults of the Fabians," which seemed to encourage each section of the dissenters. He scolded the Fabians for their preciousness and their timidity; he called on them to expand their organization and their propaganda work; and he urged them to play a more active role in political life. He also argued that in London, at least, "the hope of Socialism rested on the middle classes," or "that indeterminate class" made up of teachers, students, journalists, clergymen, public officials, poor doctors, and others in the professional groups. And Wells went on to claim, as he had earlier, that socialism was religious. The Fabians should cultivate their natural ties with the "ethical societies that are scattered around London."[7]

Later in 1906, in a lecture, "Socialism and the Middle Class," Wells challenged the wider Socialist movement to reconsider its goals. He disparaged the "administrative socialism" of the Fabians, dismissed the "sentimentalized" versions of the ILP and the *Clarion*, condemned the narrow economic outlook of the Marxists, and called for a socialism appealing to the "creative and imagination-using professions." Socialism represented, according to Wells, a "profound change in the circle of human thought and imagination." In a published version of the talk Wells urged Socialists to enlarge their scope by reexamining the institution of marriage and by investigating the special problems of women in society. "The appearance of the feminine mind and soul in the world as something distinct and self conscious, is the appearance of a distinct new engine of criticism against the individualist family . . . [and] the once, ascendant male." Wells was confident that plain speaking on these issues would "grip the middle class woman and the middle class youth of both sexes . . . and enormously enlarge and stimulate the Socialist movement."[8]

Following his talk in February the Fabian executive gave Wells virtually a free hand in organizing a special committee to propose changes in the Society's policies. The committee's report, presented in the fall, endorsed Wells' basic demands. It recommended that the Fabians expand their Socialist mission to include both a "more ample and beautiful life" and "overt forms of political action." The influence of Wells was especially evident in two proposals—to replace the existing Fabian executive with a directorate and to add to the Society's "basis" a clause favoring the substitution of "public for private authority in the education and support of the young."[9]

These proposals threatened the framework within which the Fabians had worked. The authoritarian notion of a directorate capable of providing the Society with what Wells called a single "mind" clashed with its pluralism and its democratic modes of procedure. Although the Fabians, as Shaw told Wells, did not believe in government by the people they were fully committed to "government by consent of the people." The membership would never accept dictation from above. The second proposal—to commit the Fabians to the public maintenance of children—was even more explosive. It seemed clear to several members that Wells was seeking to connect socialism with unconventional views of sexual relations; they threatened to leave the Society if the clause were added to its "basis."[10]

The manner in which Wells conducted his campaign also endangered the life of the Society. Unwilling to limit his critique to questions of policy, he engaged in personal attacks on the older leaders. Indeed, Hobson soon warned Wells that his "constant girding at the Executive and imputation of motives" was "making matters difficult and embarrassing" his supporters. But Wells proved incapable of setting aside the personal feelings of hostility and resentment generated in the dispute and confining himself to the issues. Perhaps, as Beatrice Webb observed, it was "the first time he had tried to cooperate with his fellow men." Shaw, meanwhile, was urging Wells to study the "habits of the human political animal" and learn to suppress his personal sense of grievance. Otherwise, he observed, Wells would simply be "unfit for public affairs."[11]

Such advice was lost on Wells. Not only did he refuse to accept the kind of self-limitation demanded by Fabian methods, but he was still committed to a view of the Society's role in British life which broke sharply with its past. By the time of the showdown meeting in December 1906, this was apparent to both Shaw and Webb. The recommendation of the Special Committee, Webb declared, meant a "complete reversal of the principles which had made the Society what it was." And Shaw, who assumed the major responsibility of defending the existing policies, concluded that the rebels were demanding the "annihilation" of the older leadership. He assured the members that this would in fact be the outcome if Wells carried his proposals.[12]

The basic questions of policy raised by Wells and the other

dissenters were not debated at the December meetings. Not only did Wells estrange a number of his influential supporters by his behavior, but he allowed Shaw to maneuver him into a position in which the members were forced to choose between a vague promise of new leadership and the "old gang." Yet Wells's humiliating defeat did help to clarify the two main challenges to the policies of the Society. During the early weeks of 1907 one group of Fabians continued to urge the members to seek a direct political role, while a second group attempted to persuade the Society to broaden its Socialist mission.

Wells increasingly identified himself with the second position. In April, under the auspices of the Fabian Arts Group, he led a discussion, in which Shaw, Edward Carpenter, Beatrice Webb, and others participated, on the problem of nurturing the moral qualities required by a Socialist society. "If we can't elaborate a system of personal discipline," he declared, "it seems to me that Socialism must remain a dream." And he argued, somewhat along the lines of A Modern Utopia, that a "religious Socialist movement . . . powerful enough to stir men's hearts" presupposed a "system of private devotions" and even "some sort of simple ritual." Meanwhile Wells was continuing his efforts to expand the Fabian basis to include a proposal for "state maintenance of motherhood." Shaw warned him that he should stay within the proper scope of the Society. "All the rest that you have to say you must say in your books, as I say what I have to say in mine. It is quite useless to try to expand the Fabian spout to take all your output."[13]

By the spring of 1907 Wells recognized that his conception of socialism was incompatible with any direct political role. Between a Socialist party and a Socialist movement, he acknowledged, there was a fundamental conflict. The party represented a "series of more or less hopeful" steps in the Socialist direction and was "sustained by interests not ideas." The movement drew its adherents from all sections of society and embraced a whole new view of life.

Essentially the movement is an attempt to create a force of conviction in the community, and essentially political activity is an attempt to utilize the forces in a community. The one thing accumulates force, the other spreads it. In political campaigns one leaves the clear ground of creative design for a jungle of expediency . . . Socialism is not a substitute for old party principles. It opens new ground. Socialism is the development of a scheme where there has been a void. It can be superimposed on many existing systems of ideas.

Wells now urged the Fabians to pull out of the "chances, tactics, and personalities of factions altogether and to remain a factory of ideas and suggestions." As if to proclaim his own freedom from party attachments, Wells shocked many of his fellow Socialists in April 1907 by publicly supporting a Liberal party candidate over a Socialist at a Manchester by-election.[14]

To Webb this "complete jump around" on politics seemed to show a "lack of courtesy or loyalty to his late colleagues on the special committee." And Chesterton concluded that Wells had "gone over bag and baggage to the permeators." But Wells had touched an important new current of aspiration within the Society. It was especially evident among the younger members, now organized as the Fabian Nursery. To this group Wells delivered three lectures in the fall of 1907, "First and Last Things," in which he "gnawed away" once more on religious and metaphysical questions. The lectures offered little that he had not presented in his earlier writings. And they exhibited again his contradictory claims that moral and religious beliefs were created "exactly as an artist makes a picture," while history revealed an objective social and political movement bringing a "collective consciousness . . . a collective will, and a collective mind."[15]

Wells elaborated his view of the Socialist mission more fully in New Worlds for Old, a book later described by G. D. H. Cole as the "most influential piece of Socialist propaganda in Britain since [Blatchford's] Merrie England."[16] After pointing out the limitations of each of the main forms of British socialism—the Marxism of Hyndman, the "administrative socialism" of the Fabians, and the moral idealism derived from Morris and Tolstoy—Wells presented his own form, "constructive socialism." He included the central Socialist notion of public ownership and called for the "substitution of the spirit of service for the spirit of gain in all human affairs." But the chief task of Socialists was to develop a new synthesis of "thought, art, literature, and will" out of their "dispersed, indistinct and confused utterances." Socialists would either "beget the whole Public Opinion of tomorrow or fail." Wells likened the existing public mentality to the "very divided mind" of an individual; his description suggested his own sense of the divided state experienced by many of the middle class converts to socialism.

> It is without clear aim; it does not know except in the vaguest terms what it wants to do; it has impulses; it has fancies . . . In addition it is afflicted with a division within itself that is strictly analogous to that strange mental disorder which is known to psychologists as multiple personality . . . In its essence the Socialist movement . . . is an attempt in this warring chaos of a collective mind to pull itself together, to develop and establish a governing idea of itself.[17]

Wells was still determined to make the problem of sexual relations, the movement's "most jealously guarded secret," a central concern of the Socialist inspired "collective mind." And this aim separated him further from conventional political activity. His advocacy of "easy love making," ever more obtrusive in his novels, was being used by the fall of 1907, much like Blatchford's atheism, to discredit Socialist and labor candidates at the polls. Forced to concede the political liabilities of this notion, Wells took refuge in the view that ideas presented in works of art should not be criticized from the "standpoint of morality." He publicly denied any intention of attacking the institutions of marriage and the family. It was, as he confessed later, a moment in which his "conciliatory strain" overcame his convictions. For he had concluded that sexual love was the "cardinal fact" of man's emotional life. Although Wells was not familiar with Freud's notion of the unconscious, his description of the mental hinterland was strikingly similar. "For most of us there is no jail delivery of those inner depths, and the life above goes on to its honourable end . . . [In] the cavernous hidden life . . . things may be prowling that scarce ever peep out to consciousness except in the gray half light of sleepless nights." The Socialist movement could not, Wells believed, ignore such a fundamental aspect of life as sexual relations or the related problem of procreation. His desire to "sexualize Socialism" was expressed somewhat indirectly in his attempt to incorporate a proposal for the public maintenance of children into the Fabian basis. But in the fall of 1908 Wells admitted defeat. He resigned from the Society, observing that it had missed a great opportunity for "a propaganda to the British middle classes on Fabian lines."[18]

Wells attempted in the most autobiographical of all his novels to sort out his experiences within the Fabian Society and clarify his view of the relationship of socialism to politics. *The New Machiavelli* recorded his gradual discovery of the gulf between his outlook and that of the Webbs. "It wasn't clear at first how we differed (or) . . . easy to define the profound antagonism of spirit . . . The shapes of our thought were the same, but the substance quite different. They wanted things more organized, more correlated with government and a collective purpose, just as we did, but they saw it not in terms of a growing collective understanding, but in terms of functionaries, legislative changes, and methods of administration." The Fabian leaders, he concluded, threatened to deliver men over entirely to a "sham expert officialdom."[19]

Through his hero, Remington, Wells also indicted the British political system. Abandoning the distinction he had made earlier between parties and movements, he envisioned politics mainly as a contest of ideas and personalities. And as Remington discovered that the parliamentary process was virtually impervious to his noble principles and unreceptive to his bold proposal, for the "public endowment of motherhood," Wells' own sense of frustration seemed to explode in angry assertions about the unreality of politics. The "actual players on the stage of politics," he wrote, were not in touch with the "permanent reality" in human affairs. They were "vulgar self seeking careerists," engaged in "shallow attempts at fixing up." Remington, in fact, reduced the problem of government to that of finding men of character who could stand above the "dog fight" and rescue society from its hopeless muddle and chaos. And after giving up on the Socialists and the Liberals successively because of their "narrow economic preoccupations," he turned to the Conservatives in the hope that a comprehensive reform might come through a renovated aristocracy. But in the end, after an adulterous relationship had made it impossible for him to pursue his political career and his grand social design, the hero concluded that those who "think without fear and speak without discretion" must remain "unrecognized and un-rewarded." They would share the "common lot of those who live by the imagination and follow it now in infinite loneliness of soul."[20]

Wells' depiction of Remington, ending in sentimentality and self-pity, suggested that he had never grasped the essential characteristics of the political realm, that he remained locked within a sphere of primary imaginings. Remington was, in fact, a projection of the Wells who, in his dealings with his Fabian colleagues, as in his most intimate relationships with his wife and other women, was unable to accept the actual world of other persons or social institutions. To ransack Remington's soul, one critic observed, was to discover an inner self which was primitive and anarchistic, unable to obey laws or follow rules, and "loyal to instincts" alone.[21]

The hero of The New Machiavelli could only conceive of a link up between his ideas and the world of public affairs through a national catastrophe. A "chastening war," he de-clared at the end of the novel, would be necessary to rescue Britain from her "apathy of soul." In the years ahead Wells continued his own search for a governing idea and found it in the "notion of a racial mind," together with its corollary of a world state. But his grand abstractions bore little relationship to the development of British institutions. For evidence of the "essential soundness" of his view of the "governing order of the future" he would point in later years to the successes of the Fascists and the Communists.[22]

The spectacular passage of Wells through the Fabian Society has obscured the most significant debate among the Fabians in these years. Early in 1907 a number of the Fabians took up one of the main recommendations of the Special Com-mittee and urged the Society to discard the strategy of permea-tion and run its own parliamentary candidates. Although Muggeridge and Ensor were still seeking a policy of closer cooperation with the ILP and the Labour Party, Hobson, with some support from Shaw, maintained that it was time to organize a distinct Socialist party. In February a new committee was appointed to consider ways of "increasing Socialist representation in Parliament."[23]

Nearly a year later the committee's report on political policy was discussed at a large meeting of the Society. After a vigorous debate, marked by counterattempts to loosen and tighten Fabian ties with the Labour Party, the members resolved to start a fund to "promote Socialist candidates for Parliament," while allowing local Fabian societies to decide the terms of the candidacy. This policy of local option was confirmed at the annual conference of the Fabians in August 1908. In December, however, Hobson reopened the question with a motion that the Society end its affiliation with the Labour Party and direct its energies to the "upbuilding of an avowed Socialist party." Shaw countered with a proposal that the Fabians renew their efforts to push the Labour Party toward a clear Socialist program. After Shaw's motion carried and the executive refused Hobson's demand for a referendum of the membership, the latter resigned. He attacked the executive for its "unreasoning dislike" of a "more distinctly Socialist movement" and charged that it had gone back on its earlier commitment, expressed in its response to the report of the Special Committee, to the idea of a new Socialist party.[24]

By 1909 the dissenters had admitted defeat. Wells and Hobson had resigned and those who shared their desire for a broader Socialist mission or a new Socialist party had shifted their efforts to the pages of the *New Age*. In the years just ahead the main challenge to the old leadership would come from Fabians who wished to identify the Society exclusively with the Labour Party. In time they succeeded, but only after the Webbs had concluded that the old strategy of permeation was bankrupt.

THE POLITICAL EDUCATION OF THE WEBBS

Sidney Webb's conception of the Fabian mission had survived the challenges of Wells and others. And his influence, exercised partly through Pease, as secretary, and less consistently through Shaw, remained dominant in the affairs of the Society. He was seeking again to direct the Fabians toward disinterested inquiries into social problems which could be utilized by the leaders of either of the major parties. Compared to this work, Webb believed, elections and parties were "quite subordinate—*even trivial*—parts of political action."[25]

The Webbs had followed their investigation of the trade unions with a painstaking examination of the growth of local government, employing, as Webb told Wallas, Darwin's "monograph on barnacles" as their model.[26] By means of the minute study of actual social institutions they hoped to produce an *Origin of Species* for society and provide a solid foundation for the work of the politician. While the latter defined the basic goals of society through his representative function, the social scientist indicated the ways in which the goals could be implemented. But this distinction between ends and means had been virtually erased in Sidney's conception of socialism. For it assumed that British institutions were moving inexorably toward a collectivist or Socialist order. Moreover, he doubted the capacity of the ordinary citizen for the "intellectual apprehension of socialism" and, indeed, its necessity. It was sufficient for the people to have a "consciousness of consent" to the collectivist measures developed by politicians and administrators.

Webb's skepticism about the desirability of a high degree of popular participation in political life earned him the distrust of many Socialists and Liberals. Thus a writer for the organ of the Liberal radicals, the *Nation*, after blaming Webb for the failure of Wells' "gallant effort to pump oxygen" into the Society, went on to attribute a sinister design to the Fabian leaders. "The creation of a highly centralized machine, so delicately specialized in structure and so intricate and secret in its workings as to be incapable of any real control on the part of the electorate, appears to be the conscious program of Mr. Webb and his associates. Skilled political engineers are to operate the machinery of government."[27] Actually, Wells was more vulnerable to the charge than Webb, but the Fabian bent toward social engineering was being viewed with suspicion by many social reformers.

The Webbs were moving, as Ensor observed, "from the front stairs to the back stairs of politics" in these years. Sidney still sat on the London County Council but the bitter disputes engendered by the education acts had estranged him from the Radicals. Although he held his seat amid the general rout of "progressive" candidates in 1907, he no longer found the work fruitful and declined to stand in 1910. The Webbs were, however, on good terms with many of the leaders of the new Liberal government. And as the Liberals began to seek new approaches to social problems they turned to the Webbs for advice. The dinners and discussions at the home of the Webbs drew cabinet ministers and undersecretaries, including R. B. Haldane, John Burns, Reginald McKenna, and Winston Churchill, and political leaders of lesser rank. Winston, so Sidney reported after a dinner in 1908, was "eager to assure me that he was willing to absorb all the plans we could give him."[28]

Beatrice Webb's appointment to the Royal Commission on the Poor Laws had also opened up a channel for influencing public policy in a crucial area of Fabian concern. She used this official reexamination of the prevailing system of public relief for the poor to raise fundamental questions about the nature and causes of poverty in British society. Through skillful questioning of witnesses and the marshalling of additional evidence gained from independent inquiries, she attempted to differentiate various categories of poverty, point to their underlying economic and social causes, and lead the commission toward a comprehensive plan for the prevention of destitution. Such a scheme, to be financed through a progressive tax system, would incorporate many of the ideas presented in the Fabian tracts, including the basic goal of a national minimum standard of living for the disabled and able-bodied alike, as well as provisions for health care and protection against unemployment.

At the end of July 1907 she still believed that "the course of events in the Commission . . . is working up towards my solution." But during the next few months, as she developed a plan for a comprehensive centralized scheme that would replace the Poor Law machinery, she succeeded only in creating a solid majority against her. Not satisfied with dragging "the whole

Commission so far in my direction," she decided to go forward alone and present by means of a "Minority Report" a bold scheme for the prevention of destitution. By January 1908, the Webbs were "working like blazes" and, as Sidney put it, preparing "to go full tilt at the walls of the confounded old Elizabethan Jericho, which we must destroy."[29]

This was a fateful decision. It led to a basic change in the relationship of the Webbs and, in time, of the Fabian Society, to the political process. Beatrice had decided to "look elsewhere for my forces and to undermine and circumvent the commissioners' will by calling on those forces." During the early months of 1909, following the completion of the report, she began to create a propaganda organization, "The Committee for the Break-up of the Poor Law," later changed to the "Committee for the Prevention of Destitution," to carry the cause to the people and bring the pressure of public opinion to bear on the liberal government.[30]

The decision to fight openly and to go "straight for our object" of cleaning up the base of society was, so far as one can see, a joint decision on the part of the Webbs. Sidney, according to Beatrice, had "no kind of qualms." But in the ensuing campaign Beatrice assumed the leadership in the public life of the Webbs; at the same time the campaign undermined the Fabian policy developed by Sidney. The attempt to mobilize public opinion discredited by Webbs' claim to scientific detachment or disinterestedness on social questions. Moreover, it brought their Socialist commitment into the open and separated them from the political forces on which they had relied up until this time.[31]

Initially Beatrice saw the campaign as an exercise in permeation on a grand scale. Through hundreds of public lectures, numerous tracts, newspaper articles, and personal contacts with influential individuals, the Webbs and those they had enlisted in the campaign set out to alter the nation's attitude toward the problem of the poor. "We are, in fact, creeping into the public mind," Beatrice wrote in September 1909, "before anyone is aware of it." She carefully disassociated the campaign from socialism in order to appeal to those of "intelligence and good intention" of all political persuasions. They wanted to reach persons who "might not join the Fabian Society."[32]

Yet, Fabians played central roles in the campaign. Beatrice, in fact, saw a symbolic meaning in the committee's "little office wedged between" the offices of the Fabian Society and the London School of Economics. It represented a middle ground between aroused Socialism, and non partisan research and administrative technique." But her attempt to establish a middle ground between her Socialist commitment and "non partisan research" simply demonstrated their connection and the impossibility of achieving through this "triangular activity" a "rapid but almost unconscious change in the structure of society." Indeed, very quickly the Webbs were involved in a struggle for political power.[33]

In their efforts to outflank the majority on the Poor Law Commission and summon the power of public opinion, the Webbs had challenged the position of administrators and political leaders. "You have declared war," a prominent civil servant told her, "and war it will be." And at a dinner party in October Churchill told Beatrice that she "ought to convert the cabinet" and "leave the work of converting the country to us." Having failed to anticipate the reaction of politicians to their incursion into the field of popular agitation, the Webbs were surprised by the antagonisms aroused in their customary political circles. Shortly after the beginning of their campaign Beatrice noted, "We have been strangely dropped by the more distinguished of our acquaintances and by the Liberal ministers in particular." It took some time for her to realize that they could not exercise a "behind the scenes influence over statesmen, civil servants, and newspaper editors, while" engaging in "public propaganda of projects which these eminent ones may view with hostility or suspicion."[34]

In the contest for the "mind of the people," the Webbs could not match the political skills of Churchill and Lloyd George or the resources available to the government. Nor did the Webbs anticipate the effort of the Liberal leaders to find other solutions to the problem of destitution. Even before the Webbs had begun to write their report, Lloyd George and Churchill were exploring the scheme of social insurance introduced earlier into Bismarckian Germany.

Not only had the Webbs cut themselves off from the politicians but they raised in the course of their campaign the kind of philosophical or ideological issues the Fabians had attempted to avoid. While the Minority Report was designed to appeal to persons of varied social outlooks, it envisioned a new relationship between the individual and society. The report demanded that public assistance be tied to the obligation to become better citizens. Hence the provision for the forcible detention in training centers of individuals who refused to seek employment. "With what we may call the 'industrial malingerer' there will be other remedies. With the cooperation of the National Labour Exchanges he can be given successive chances of employment; and, after a certain number of trials, his repeated return will be a cause for his judicial commitment to a Detention Colony." When Lloyd George asked Beatrice to comment on a plan for insurance against unemployment, to be financed by contributions from the individual worker, the employer, and the state, she promptly rejected the idea. The "fatal defect" of such a plan, she said, was the suggestion to the person aided that "they had a right to the allowances whatever their conduct."[35]

The report assumed a highly organic conception of society. In place of the atomistic picture of social relations found in classical liberalism or the modified individualism of more recent liberal thought, it called for the kind of mutual obligation between the individual and the community which, in Beatrice's words, was characteristic of "the nobler aspects of the medieval manor." Beatrice, at least, was dropping the guise of scientific disinterestedness and making explicit her hope for a higher form of citizenship. She was not content, as she told Churchill, to secure simply a change in the law; she was determined to convert "the country to the philosophy of our scheme."[36]

Shaw warned Beatrice "not to underestimate the enormous weight of Benthamite-Whig objection to your scheme as destructive of liberty." Liberal leaders were, in fact, quick to recognize this issue. Masterman, for example, was "horrified at Mrs. Webb's zeal for disciplining people," while John Burns, a Liberal cabinet minister and former Social Democrat, assured H. G. Wells that he would save the country from "the new helotry of the service state run by the archivists of the School of Economics." Churchill, who with William Beveridge was developing the Liberal government's approach to the problem of unemployment, based on the principles of compulsory insurance, expressed even more clearly the conflicting views in a discussion of the issue of malingering. The advantage of the insurance principle, he explained, lay in its freedom from any concern "with the character of an individual, with ethics, or with sentiment," and its reliance simply on the average reasons for unemployment, whether arising from personal failings or the forces of the market. "I do not like mixing up moralities and mathematics . . . Our concern is with the evil not the causes. With the fact of unemployment, not with the character of the unemployed." Churchill's distinction was invalid, for no approach to the problem could be simply mathematical. But the Liberal morality did not demand that the individual achieve a new standard of citizenship.[37]

Beatrice Webb admitted later that it would have been wiser politically to join forces with the majority of the commissioners and simply seek the abolition of the Poor Law. But she was still intrigued with the possibility of "making a political movement without being in politics or desiring to be in politics." As late as March 1910 she remained convinced that the Webbs were "making the bed [the Liberals] will have to lie in." Again she greatly underestimated the political adroitness of the Liberal leaders. Once they had fixed on their insurance scheme, they were able to win over most of the labor leaders by safeguarding the interests of the trade unions and the Friendly Societies. MacDonald quickly grasped the situation and aligned most members of the parliamentary Labour Party with the Liberals. By the closing months of 1910 the Webbs had become pessimistic about the prospects of their campaign.[38]

As the Liberal leaders piloted their insurance scheme through Parliament, Sidney was inclined to make the best of it and trust later legislation to correct its defects. He was reverting to his cautious, pragmatic approach to reform. But Beatrice could not reconcile herself to the measure and continued to hope for its defeat. Although it involved a significant transfer of wealth from the rich to the poor, it represented merely a "mechanical" approach to the problem of destitution and lacked the necessary guarantees against malingering. She was now convinced, moreover, that "the issue has become so much bigger" than the Minority Report. The conflict with the Liberals had thrust the whole question of socialism out into the open. In the Insurance Bill she saw, as Mary Hamilton put it, "some of the things they wanted done," being done, "in a fatally wrong way—a way that blocked future advance on the right line." The "issue is fairly joined," Beatrice observed, "complete state responsibility with a means of prevention, or partial state responsibility by a new form of relieving destitution."[39]

"Sidney and I *are* Socialists; there is no denying the fact," she wrote in her diary in May 1910. And she attributed the Liberal opposition to the Minority Report in part to the "return of active fear of Socialism" and the identification of the Webbs with the Socialist movement. The Liberal politicians were to some extent seeking to head off socialism. "With a stake in the country in the form of insurance against evil days," Churchill declared, the "workers will pay no attention to the vague promises of revolutionary Socialism." Indeed, insofar as the Liberal bill rested on an ideological basis, it reaffirmed the principles of individual self-reliance and the free market. At the same time the Liberals were demonstrating, by means of the contributory principle and subsidies to the Friendly Societies, that substantial gains in social security and, indeed, the attainment of the national minimum might be achieved without traveling the collectivistic road envisioned by the Fabians. The Insurance Bill signaled, as A. M. McBriar concluded, the "defeat of more fundamental socialized change by a galvanized Liberalism."[40]

At the end of 1910 it was apparent that their campaign had led the Webbs into a *cul de sac*. Beatrice reassured Sidney that "we were right to undertake the task" and expressed her confidence that "the education of the country with our ideas goes on." But they were discouraged over the results of the campaign, and resentful toward the "contemptible lot" in the Liberal cabinet. To Beatrice at least, it was also clear that they could no longer carry on their research and their political work in different "departments simultaneously." "We always did know that agitation would interfere in more ways than one with our scientific research. But it is clear to me that the time has come for agitation and that we have to go through with it. Public opinion is in a ferment and we are the only people with

sufficient knowledge and a sufficiently comprehensive philosophy. We have got to use ourselves up in this [work]." Already
she was considering how she might redirect the energies of the
three or four thousand persons mobilized in the campaign into
the Socialist movement. Rapid progress toward socialism, she
had observed in September 1910, would probably require a
Socialist party. And in January 1911 she confessed that despite
Sidney's misgivings and continued preference for quiet research, they would have to "throw themselves into the democratic movement" and "offer ourselves as officers in the larger
crusade to conquer the land of promise." Their first task, she
concluded, was to "revivify the Fabian Society."[41]

The Fabian Society was now in a parlous state. Shaw
charged at this time that the Webbs had thrown the Society
"aside as useless" in their campaign. To other Fabians the campaign had demonstrated that the strategy of permeation was
bankrupt and they now renewed the effort to identify the Society more closely with the Labour Party. Responding to a new
effort in this direction during 1910, R. C. K. Ensor presented,
on behalf of the executive, an analysis of the Society's political
policy over the years. He called attention to the continuing
tension between those favoring permeation and those who
hoped to form "a separate political party for Socialist purposes." And while Ensor defended the Fabian policy of developing proposals for all political agencies, he conceded that this
policy might be transitional and pass away.[42]

When in the summer of 1911 the Webbs left on a year long
trip around the world, the Fabians were beginning to reconsider
the whole question of political strategy. Pease steadfastly defended the old policy, convinced that the Society's role in the
Minority Report campaign had been an unfortunate departure
from its traditional path. A number of the younger Fabians
were now eager to commit the Society fully to the Labour
Party. But the deepening crisis in Fabianism, brought to a head
by the Minority Report, can be explored in the development of
Shaw. For Shaw had come to question the Fabian approach to
socialism. He was abandoning his old role as Webb's publicist
and the chief mediator in the affairs of the Society, and the tight
compartments into which he had separated his work as a Fabian

reformer, and his activity as an artist and social prophet, began to break down.

Shaw: *The Triumph of the Prophetic Mission*

Shaw continued, in the years after 1906, to serve as a spokesman for Webb's views or, as he told the latter, to play "Tyndall to your Helmholz." In his Preface to a new edition of the *Fabian Essays* he reaffirmed his belief that the Society's goal was simply to introduce "design, contrivance and coordination . . . into the present industrial scramble for private gain." And he conceded that Wells was correct in describing the Fabian "specialty" as "administrative Socialism exclusively."[43]

But Shaw had questioned from time to time the Society's strategy of permeation. In 1902 he told Beatrice Webb that the Fabians should "collar the ILP and the rest of the Labor fragments" and "not waste another five minutes on permeation." And even as Shaw took the lead in defending the old policy against Wells he was trying to convince Webb that they had reached the "psychological moment" for launching a Fabian parliamentary party. Shaw's advocacy of such a party, incorporated into his reply to the report of Wells' Special Committee, was to some extent a tactical move. "By springing to the front and snatching the flag from the hands of Hobson and Taylor," he told Webb, "we shall dish the rebellion completely." But during 1907, after the repulse of Wells, he continued to support the idea of a new Socialist party. Grayson's dramatic victory at the Colne Valley by-election in the summer seemed to Shaw to offer a fresh opportunity for "suspended Socialism . . . to precipitate itself in a political party." The Fabians, he wrote Pease, "*must* back it [the Colne Valley group] . . . for all it is worth."[44]

Meanwhile Shaw had grown skeptical about the role of the Labour Party. As early as 1903 he had warned MacDonald that the growing influence of the trade unionists in the LRC was leading to the "inevitable expulsion" of the Socialists. "If we drift as we are doing now, nothing will happen except that the Fabian, S.D.F., and I.L.P. will be banished exactly as the Trade Unionists formerly banished the Positivists; and the L.R.C. will then discover that it has no reason for maintaining a separate existence from the Parliamentary Committee of the Trade Union Congress." The success of the labor candidates in the general election led Shaw to claim, with slight justification, that the Fabians had "made the Labour Party." But soon he was deploring the tendency for the ILP and the Labour Party to "boycott middle class men such as Stanton Coit and Stephen Sanders, in favor of trade union candidates." Shaw had begun to fear that the party's narrow concentration on working class interests was squeezing the Socialists politically between "labor and plutocracy." In a fit of exasperation during the fall of 1907, he publicly repudiated the Labour Party and predicted that it would sink deeper and deeper into reaction.[45]

Shaw's public statements could not always be taken at face value. In political affairs, as in his drama, he was often bent on defeating normal expectations. No wonder Webb complained of a lack of constructiveness in Shaw. "He fails to 'catch hold' of the ordinary man—just as a locomotive engine when its wheels revolve fast without biting the rails" fails to make "the train progress."[46] The metaphor was doubly revealing.

After 1910 Shaw continued to urge the Fabians toward an independent Socialist party. He strongly opposed those within the Society who, following the resignations of Wells and Hobson, renewed the attempt to identify the Fabians exclusively with the Labour Party. Their offer of "intellectual patronage" to labor, Shaw told them, was a dream; it would simply make the Fabian Society an "appendage of the Labour Party exactly as the Labour Party used to be an appendage of the Liberal Party." In 1911, after reviewing the development of Fabian policy, Shaw asserted that it was now clear that "the Labour Party would not and could not be a Socialist Party." Given its pre-emption of all "winnable labor seats," Fabians should get into Parliament by any means possible—as Liberals, Conservatives, or independents—and then "form the nucleus of a Socialist party." The creation of such a party, Shaw contended, "was the next business of the Society."[47]

. The other side of Shaw's attempt to keep the Fabians out of the embrace of labor was an effort to revitalize the Society's sense of its Socialist mission. He watched with growing doubts as the Webbs diverted much of the Fabian energy during 1909 and 1910 into their campaign for the Minority Report. According to Shaw the Webbs were reducing socialism in the public eye to mere social reform. Convinced that the Society was "no longer pioneering in the old Fabian fashion," Shaw urged on Webb the need to "explode on the public" a more extreme proposal.[48]

Shaw was not the only member of the "old gang" to question the Fabian course. Although Bland had been a strong opponent of any strategy which would "spread the Socialist attack over too wide a front," he was firmly committed to the destruction of the capitalistic order. By 1910 he was convinced that the Fabians had been side-tracked and needed to find a "new line of march." Unless the Society could be moved "onto the main line again," he told Shaw "it had better die peacefully and die soon." A year later Bland told a Fabian branch in the north that "palliative measures have come in the way of our direct march" and "put the ends of Socialism further off, until at last we to all intents and purposes lost sight of them altogether." And in his final appearance at a Fabian meeting in July 1912, he restated his belief that the Society "had diverged from the course originally planned for it." It had ceased to work for the "extinction of private property in land and for the transfer to the community of such industrial capital as can conveniently be managed socially." Bland also criticized those who would identify the Fabians exclusively with the Labour Party. "If the Labour Party is the vanguard of progress," he said, "our place is ahead of the vanguard . . . with the scouts, with the pioneers."[49]

Partly under Bland's promptings, Shaw attempted at the end of 1910 to give the Fabian Society "something to live for" and "enable it to become once more the political pacemaker of England." His lecture, "Equality," in which he advocated the absolute equality of incomes, was designed to identify the Society with a fresh goal "not in sight twenty five years ago." It was, he claimed, "the most important departure in Socialism since Karl Marx." A touch of absurdity clung to the proposal, as Shaw recognized, but it was a genuine attempt to reinstate the ideal of the classless society. The doctrine of equality, he told a friend, was "the only form in which Socialism is interesting and . . . convincing."[50]

The Fabians did not rally to the support of Shaw's proposal. Perhaps the lack of response, perhaps too Shaw's feeling that any bold departure from the old policies would have to be the work of younger leaders, convinced him that he should reduce his role in the Society. In March 1911 he informed Pease that he and Bland had decided not to stand for the executive at the coming elections. Their resignations, along with those of several others of the "old gang" were necessary, Shaw argued, to save the Society from "fossilization" and, in Bland's words, to bring in new blood. Shaw remained an active Fabian but his relationship to the Society, and to the Webbs, was changing; he had ceased to be a reliable supporter of the old policies.[51]

A "growing estrangement" with Shaw was apparent to Beatrice Webb during the spring of 1911. The spontaneous give and take between Shaw and her husband was gone. And over the next few years, despite her periodic hopes of recovering something of the complementary relationship "of our respective minds," Beatrice found him less and less useful as a colleague; he had become "perverse, irate and despotic" and "bored with the old questions." During these years Shaw was busy with the production of his plays—now enjoying extraordinary popular and financial success—and, for a time, distracted by his infatuation with Mrs. Patrick Campbell, a sure symptom, according to Beatrice, of his "intellectual deterioration." But Shaw was departing from the main line of Fabian development. And as he did so the old separation between his activity as a Fabian reformer and his work as an artist began to disappear. He was, as he told Beatrice in 1911, increasingly preoccupied with "remoter solutions that I can impose upon the Fabian Society," and less inclined to pass his ideas through the "clogged and muddy filter" of the Publications Committee.[52]

Shaw's quest for "remoter solutions" led into a further exploration of the issues which had become dominant in *Major Barbara*. "Most of his intellectual energies" after 1906, Erich Strauss observed, were absorbed in the study of the place of religion or religious emotions.[53] The plays of these years were concerned in large part with the problem of conversion. But the development of Shaw's ideas on religion can be followed more clearly through his addresses in places set apart both from the theater and from the Socialist rostrum. He expounded his faith in the "life force" most systematically in pulpits or on non-political platforms.

Shaw believed that the main philosophical supports for the Socialist movement—Darwinism and Marxism—had "banished mind from the universe," together with the qualities of will, rationality, and imagination, on which human progress depended. And his interest in religion expressed his deepening conviction that the Socialist movement needed to "recover spiritual energy." His experience in "various forward movements" had persuaded him that persons who had no religion were "cowards and cads." Individuals gained a "fuller consciousness of moral responsibility" through the assurance that they were part of a meaningful cosmic process; religious faith instilled "courage and self-respect."[54]

Shaw's religious lectures developed the idea, presented in *Man and Superman* and *Major Barbara*, of a spiritual force at work in the universe using man to realize its purposes. Such a notion drew Shaw close to the immanentist theology within British nonconformity, and he found R.J. Campbell's pulpit at City Temple a particularly congenial setting for his discussions of the life force. The new theologians, Shaw said, had discarded the old notion that creation was begun by a perfect being and they recognized that "the force behind the universe was working up through perfection and mistakes to a perfectly organized being having the power of fulfilling its highest purposes." Shaw was recapturing in his own terms the millennial vision of human reintegration. "In a sense there is no God as yet achieved, but there is that force making God, struggling through us to become an actual organized existence, enjoying what to many of us is the greatest conceivable ecstasy, the ecstasy of a brain, an intelligence, acutely conscious of the whole, and with executive force capable of guiding it to a perfectly beneficial and harmonious end." Human beings, and particularly the artist of genius, were experiments in the making of God, or the integrated "higher organisms" of the future. [55]

This millennial-like vision, hitherto confined to Shaw's plays, was being transferred to a realm of public utterance, where it presented an implicit challenge to his practical Socialist work. Shaw was exposing his Fabianism to a more fundamental criticism than that expressed in his call for an equalization of incomes. In the period after 1911, as the Fabians attempted to develop a new political policy, Shaw was increasingly concerned with the task of introducing new values and ideals into economic and political institutions. "Unless we develop our spiritual life," he wrote in 1913, there was no hope for "economic Socialism." He warned of a "fatal separation" between "power and culture" in England; the flight of the leisured and cultured classes from public affairs had delivered control of the state over to "barbarians" and "upstarts from the counting house."[56]

Not only was Shaw attempting to enlarge the Fabian conception of socialism but he had ceased to share Webb's confidence in the state as an instrument of socialization. Hence his insistence on the distinction between "collectivism" and socialism and his sympathy for the new group of Fabian rebels, inspired by Guild Socialist ideas, who mounted a fresh attack on the Society's policies during 1912 and 1913. Shaw supported Cole's motion at the annual meeting in July 1912 to commit the Fabians "primarily to research and thereby make available for propaganda the most recent developments in industrial and Socialist theory." The motion, which lost by a single vote, was designed according to Beatrice Webb, to alter the basis of the society and bring "a new propaganda and a new doctrine."[57]

Shaw contributed generously to the financing of the *New Statesman*, launched in 1913 by the Webbs to promote Fabianism. But he was soon at odds with the paper's editor, Clifford Sharp. Shaw refused to adapt his articles to the "corporate" Fabian line and Sharp concluded that Shaw was "hopelessly out of touch with practical economics and practical politics."[58]

Shaw was more supportive of the Fabians and the Webbs than these episodes suggest. Although he had ceased to serve on the Society's executive, he did act as chairman of the new Fabian Research Department where Cole and the rebels were dominant, and in that capacity resumed for a time his old role as conciliator. He also took part in the annual Fabian summer schools and the Society's new annual fall lecture series. At times his relationship with the Webbs recovered something of its old intimacy. After a ten day walking and motoring tour with Shaw in the north of England late in 1914, Beatrice conceded that he "has kept the crucial purposes of Socialism before us as distinguished from the machinery for getting it."[59]

World War I reinforced Shaw's sense of the dangerous drift of British life. It also served to weaken further his commitment to those institutions on which the Fabians relied. His essay, "Common Sense about the War," demonstrated his extraordinary detachment from the patriotic passions which stormed around him. But his major play in these years, *Heartbreak House*, suggested that detachment was giving way to despair. It also indicated a further loss of the self-restraint which had kept his political and artistic work in separate spheres. The dreamlike, almost surrealistic techniques of the play permitted a release of attitudes and feelings which were less controlled by the dramatic aims or conscious beliefs evident earlier. Indeed, his optimistic faith in the life force gave way to a picture of the human condition which approached nihilism. No wonder one student of Shaw has seen in *Heartbreak House* the "full emergence" of ideas "essentially antithetical to his Fabianism."[60]

Yet, *Heartbreak House* also indicated that Shaw was seeking an integral conception of his work as artist and reformer. Something of his sense of what his Fabian commitment had cost him was suggested in the cry of the central character, Shotover: "We kill our better self every day in order to propitiate" the powers that be. But Shaw was now resurrecting his "better self," for *Heartbreak House* exhibited, as one critic observed, the "sudden upsurge of the Victorian prophet in Shaw." And he was no longer willing to limit his prophetic role to the province of art.[61]

Shaw's new sense of an ethical and religious mission was evident in the spring of 1918 when he joined Webb and Henderson in a series of lectures dealing with the prospects of the Labour Party. His willingness to participate in the series, which reflected the new bonds between the Fabian Society and the Labour Party, indicated the strength of Shaw's old loyalties. But his lecture, "The Climate and Soil of Labour Culture," demonstrated that Shaw had left the ground of practical politics for a different vantage point.[62]

Shaw conceded in his lecture that the prospects for labor's political advance were bright. The experiences of the war had accelerated the march toward a collectivist state. But such an outcome held more menace than promise. Shaw denied that the nationalization of the means of production, distribution, and exchange constituted socialism; it was simply "an indispensable material condition of its realization." Socialism, in fact, had already been "extensively side tracked ." In words reminiscent of William Morris, Shaw warned of the efforts to build, in the form of a "proprietary socialism," a "half-way house so comfortable that we shall never get the worker past it."[63]

Party politics, according to Shaw, provided no protection against this outcome; rather, it intensified the danger. The "electoral agents" into whose hands parties tended to fall, were the "most hopelessly demoralized" element in society. True socialism would not be the work of the "so-called practical" reformer but of a new kind of statesman, educated not only in economics and sociology but in metaphysics. Such a pioneer, however, was still "as a lonely man in a strange land amid a hostile people."[64]

Shaw noted the failure of previous movements of thought, including utilitarianism and Fabianism, to be "assimilated by the English people." The ideas of the *Fabian Essay* had "dropped like stones in the sea." Shaw granted that the initial Fabian indifference to Morris, Carlyle, and Ruskin, and the Society's hostility to art and metaphysics had been "right at that time." Now a "Reformation far more radical than Luther's" was needed. "Socialism must have a positive religion, characteristic of and proper to the epoch which it is to inaugurate, with articles of faith and commandments based on it and accepted as the foundation of the Socialist state." Socialism had ceased, in fact, to be Shaw's main goal; it had become clearly subordinated to his concept of creative evolution. [65]

Shaw was now sixty-four; perhaps a prophetic role seemed more appropriate at this point in life than the work of the practical reformer, or, indeed, that of the ordinary artist. At any rate in his next major play, *Back to Methuselah*, finished in 1920, theatrical conventions served as the means for developing his metaphysical views. Shaw described the play as the "beginnings of a new Bible." And one critic has seen in the work Shaw's "subtlest thoughts and his widest and deepest and most steadfast look at the human situation."[66]

Back to Methuselah was also a confession of ideological bankruptcy. Although the play made room for Shaw's earlier commitment to Fabian reform and incorporated a Socialist stage in man's future evolution, it assumed that existing human beings were incapable of building a decent social and political order. The accumulating problems of civilization were beyond mankind's moral and intellectual powers. Social redemption, therefore, could only be conceived in terms of a radical transformation of human nature, or through the evolution of a new species endowed with a capacity for greater physical longevity and higher qualities of will, imagination, and intelligence.[67]

Shaw had left behind not only the Fabian form of socialism but all political and artistic activity insofar as it was occupied with real men and women in history. In his conception of the evolutionary process artists were simply agents in an ascending scale of consciousness, while politicians, mercilessly satirized in the second section of *Back to Methuselah*, disappeared from the human scene. The play culminated in a vision of life in which the old divisions were overcome. In Shaw's paradise human reintegration was realized in ecstatic intellectual experiences.

Shaw's paradise lay so far in the future as to have slight relevance to the immediate problems of British political life. Following the war he continued to identify himself to some extent with the Fabian approach to social reform. But his reach for remoter solutions increasingly dominated his political judgments. And his judgments were shaped by the heroic conception of life which had become dominant in his plays. What in earlier years had represented the exercise of his artistic imagination, safely confined within dramatic conventions, was now directed toward the actual realm of public affairs, where it found expression in a growing contempt for democratic forms and an admiration for the "heroic" leaders emerging in Italy, Germany, and Russia. Shaw's admiration for the dictators signaled his repudiation of the institutional processes and values Fabian socialism had assumed.[68] Meanwhile the Fabian Society had come to terms with the British political system.

FABIANS AND THE LABOUR PARTY

Before the Webbs departed on their world tour in the summer of 1911 Beatrice observed that the Fabians would have to find a "new impetus" or "die of indifference." The failure of their campaign for the Minority Report, the social legislation of the Liberals, and the withdrawal from the Fabian executive of Shaw, Bland, and others of the older leadership had, in fact, placed the Society's future in doubt. But the uncertain state of the Society also presented a new opportunity for leadership. And shortly after the Webbs' departure the Fabians received a manifesto from a self-constituted Reform Committee which urged them to abandon the strategy of political permeation and identify themselves exclusively with the Labour Party. The old policy, according to the reformers, had given the Liberals a "specious popularity," deprived the Labour Party of needed qualities, and retarded the growth of socialism. "It will not be possible to convert all classes in the country to a belief in Socialist principles if the Labour Party which, after all, is the chief vehicle of Socialist achievement, is allowed to remain simply an expression of working class discontent. The Labour Party would be greatly benefited by the inclusion in its midst of individuals with a fresh outlook, a broader vision, a different education, and a greater sense of proportion." The committee recommended that the Fabian Society commit its resources entirely to the Labour Party in order to develop a party "composed of all classes" and exercising a national appeal.[69]

The Reform Committee was made up of younger Fabians, several of them converts of Wells, who had passed through the Fabian Nursery and taken active parts in the campaign on behalf of the Minority Report. Henry Schloesser, the committee's chairman, had represented the Society at the annual conference of the Labour Party earlier in the year after Shaw had assured him that the experience would "cure my romantic notions."[70] Instead, it convinced Schloesser that the Fabians should emulate the ILP and enroll as members only those who were loyal to the Labour Party.

The reformers pressed their case with vigor and produced the "most serious division in the Society since the Wells controversy." But at two critical meetings—a general membership meeting in February 1912 and the annual conference the following July—they were defeated, as the Fabians reaffirmed the right of the members "to fight for Socialism as they pleased."[71]

Still, the Fabians were beginning to realize that their Socialist commitment was incompatible with a nonpartisan approach to politics. Moreover, their creation of a parliamentary electoral fund in 1908 had tightened their bonds to the Labour Party. In the general election of January 1910 the Society had sponsored three parliamentary candidates—William Sanders, Harry Snell, and Will Crooks—each of whom was identified with the Labour Party. Indeed, the victory of Crooks represented the first success for a parliamentary candidate financed by the Fabians. But at that election the cross purposes within the Society were made evident when its most prominent Liberal, Leo Chiozza Money, found some Fabians supporting his opponent, Herbert Burrows, a Social Democrat. After protests to the members, Chiozza Money withdrew from the Society's executive though he remained a Fabian.

The Fabians were also developing closer relationships with the ILP. Although the Reform Committee had failed to win its main objective it had secured passage of a motion to create a joint standing committee of Fabian and ILP representatives for the purpose of Socialist propaganda. In the summer of 1911 the two organizations joined in holding a large meeting in London to protest against the Insurance Bill, and during the fall they shared responsibility for a series of lectures on socialism.

The Webbs received a running commentary on these developments from Clifford Sharp, their most faithful ally among the younger Fabians. Described by Beatrice as a "hard-minded conservative collectivist," Sharp conveyed, through his letters, the state of uncertainty among the Fabians. At one point he concluded that the Society was "played out," no longer capable of responding to a set of political conditions quite different from the circumstances within which it had risen. But he also noted the growing desire among Fabians to find a more positive relationship with the Labour Party and with the "real semiconscious aspirations of the working classes." Sharp appealed to the Webbs to rescue the Fabians from their state of drift.

"Everybody is as it were waiting for a lead," he wrote in March 1912, and he assured Beatrice that the "executive would be clay in the hands of a dictator."[72]

The Webbs returned in April to find that the social and political climate had greatly altered during their absence. Lloyd George had clearly "trumped the Labour Party" by passing the National Insurance Act, while the new tide of industrial unrest and the spread of Syndicalist ideas had called into question the Socialist commitment to parliamentary politics. Yet, the growing cooperation between the Fabian Society and the ILP also gave promise of a more effective Socialist leadership within the labor movement. The Webbs wasted little time, in fact, before taking up the new tasks that presented themselves. Sidney was soon sitting on the joint committee with the ILP and Beatrice became a member of the party. Meanwhile she was "winding up the national committee" and entering fully into the affairs of the Fabian Society for the first time. There "seems to be a clear call for leadership in the Labour and Socialist movement," she wrote, and "we find we must respond."[73]

It was a complex task. The simultaneous moves toward a closer relationship with the Labour Party and a reassertion of the Socialist aims of the Society inevitably generated new conflicts among the Fabians. When, at the annual conference in July, Sidney supported those who favored closer ties with the Labour Party, he provoked a counterattack from members led by Cole, who favored disaffiliation and an independent Socialist policy. In Cole's version of Guild Socialism the ethical and aesthetic idealism of Morris as well as his hostility to conventional political action was returning to challenge the basis of Fabianism. Over the next several years this new threat from the left complicated the efforts of the Webbs to develop a coherent policy for the Society.[74]

The Webbs attempted first to answer the claims of the Guild Socialists and the Syndicalists that they had found, in industrial organization, the key to social reconstruction. Sidney had abandoned his earlier opposition to trade union participation in politics as long as they acted "with caution." And while the Syndicalist claims on behalf of the workers seemed to the Webbs, in the summer of 1912, a dangerous revival of revolutionary and class war ideas, they saw in the new movement signs of a "real and persistent" desire for participation by the workers in industrial decisions, "of which Collectivism has to take account." Beatrice took the initiative in setting up a Fabian Committee of Inquiry on the Control of Industry. It was, she observed, a reply to those who claimed that the Society was "not living up to the reputation of the Fabian Essays."[75]

The committee quickly became a battleground between those who supported the traditional Fabian emphasis on the needs of the consumer and those, led by Cole, who gave priority to the role of associations of producers in the reconstruction of society. In time the inquiry, or the Fabian Research Department which grew out of it, was captured by Cole and his associates and became virtually autonomous.

Meanwhile, the Webbs were helping to strengthen Fabian ties to the other Socialist bodies. Cooperation with the ILP dispelled some of the Fabian scorn for its mode of Socialist enthusiasm and led the Webbs to acknowledge the party's value. It did not produce "parliamentary leaders," but it could advance the work of "education and propaganda among the rank and file, and among the trade union . . . officials."[76] Sidney also played an important part in the process, initiated by the International Socialist Bureau, through which the Fabians and the ILP developed more harmonious relations with Hyndman and the British Socialist Party. When representatives of the three bodies sat down together in March 1913 he served as chairman.

Increased solidarity among the Socialists, however, jeopardized the Fabian effort to play a more influential role within the Labour Party. Attempts in this direction had not been encouraging. Beatrice Webb had wondered, while still on the world tour, whether they should become involved in labor politics in view of the prominence of their old antagonist, MacDonald. And several months after returning to England she conceded that they still had no relationship with the Parliamentary Party, which was "drifting into futility" under a leader who had "ceased to be a Socialist." A meeting with a group of Labour MP's in December 1912 did little to improve the situation. The politicians were fearful lest collectivist proposals arouse excessive hopes in the rank and file. Only after the

Webbs threatened to take their legislative proposals to Liberal or Tory members did Henderson, leader of the group, adopt a more receptive attitude. Not much came from this meeting, however, and a subsequent plan for joint propaganda work by the Fabians, the ILP, and the Labour Party fell through when the labor leaders demanded that the two Socialist bodies simply place themselves at the party's disposal.[77]

As part of their effort to give new leadership to the Socialist and labor movements, the Webbs launched the *New Statesman* in the spring of 1913, with Sharp as editor. The paper, he declared in the opening issue, was committed to the "world movement toward collectivism." But he claimed that it would be "bound by no ties of party, class, and creed," and would approach "economic, social, and political issues in the same spirit [as the] chemist or biologist."[78] The Webbs immediately undermined the claim by starting a series of articles, "What is Socialism," in which they presented the most comprehensive statement thus far of their vision of social reconstruction. The series also exhibited Beatrice's attempt, growing out of the defeat of the Minority Report campaign, to develop the ethical implications of socialism.

The articles recapitulated the major features of Fabian socialism. They restated the central Fabian demand that the "enormous tribute . . . which is taken by the private owners of . . . exploitive capital" should be reclaimed for the purposes of the whole community. Taxation by the state, conceived as the servant of all consumers, would enable it to redistribute wealth and secure a national minimum standard of living for all. Although the Webbs made room for proposals for the nationalization of certain industries, the "main sphere of Socialist action" still consisted of the extension of local government or municipal enterprise. Here too was the primary realm for the application of scientific method, or "systematized common sense," on which the Webbs relied. Socialists, they insisted, were simply interpreting the "growing science and experience of the world."[79]

The Webbs did not abandon their consumer and distributive orientation or their confidence in governmental authority, but they were sensitive to the growing fears of the "servile state" and to the demands for a wider basis of participation in economic decisions and political power. "Thus the Socialist State, far from being a centralized and coercive bureaucracy, presents itself to us as a highly diversified and extremely numerous set of social groupings in which, as we ourselves see it, governmental coercion, as distinguished from National and Municipal Housekeeping, is destined to play an ever dwindling part." Indeed, they employed Guild Socialist arguments on behalf of producer associations to counter Syndicalist demands for working class control. By advancing the claims of the "virtually new class of minor professionals," or the "black coated proletariat," making up perhaps two-ninths of the population, the Webbs were also challenging Marxist and Syndicalist notions of working class solidarity. The voluntary groupings of the "greatly swollen brain working professions" and the "vast armies of salaried executants and assistants" were crucial parts of the spontaneous undergrowth of social tissue on which the Webbs relied to check the downward thrust of the state.[80]

Among these social groupings, the trade unions remained crucial. Indeed the Webbs' praise of the unions was extravagant. "There is nothing in the short and simple annals of the poor that transcends in nobility and spiritual beauty the unselfish devotion, the long unremunerated work, the heroic self denial, and even the willing sacrifice of self and family, which abounds among the unrecorded incidents of trade union history . . . In these humble organizations are evolving all the moral and intellectual qualities that participation in the work of government demands."[81]

The moral and intellectual qualities the Webbs sought, however, were associated with the professional sectors of the middle class. They believed that the values characteristic of the "brain-working" groups would spread through the manual workers and make the motive of public service the "predominant spring of action" in society. The articles restated the hope for a higher form of citizenship which had become explicit in the campaign on behalf of the Minority Report. To base social change simply on the desires of the individual consumer would do no more than advance the "material comfort of the race." Indeed, the Webbs were augmenting the traditional Fabian concern with the distribution of wealth with aspirations found in Ethical Socialism. They repeated the Ethical Socialist demand that organized religion be rescued from its "alliance with plutocracy" and declared that socialism alone could "stem the tide of secularist materialism." To be truly effective, the "re-organization of persons and things" must be "the outward and visible manifestation of an inward and spiritual grace." Socialism presupposed a "radical change of heart" and a "revolution of social purpose."[82]

Statements of this kind can safely be attributed to Beatrice and they belied her claim that she was "parasitic on Sidney" in her public writings. Comments on religion were, to be sure, no more than "our private imaginings" and subject like everything else in the Socialist state to the commands of its citizens. But the series "What is Socialism" suggested the continuing tension within the partnership of the Webbs and the desire of Beatrice to transcend the terms of Sidney's Fabianism. She was impatient with purely "technical questions" and "piecemeal social engineering." And while she continued to insist on the distinction between the scientist, as one who worked out the means of achieving social goals, and the idealist, as one who sought to convert the people to new values, her own work suggested the fallacy of the distinction. Her deepening involvement in the affairs of the Fabian Society was inspired by the hope for a higher personal and social ethic.[83]

Fabian socialism had emerged only through the abandonment of the utopian hope for a radically new form of human community. The articles, "What is Socialism," implicitly challenged Sidney's conception of the Society's role and indicated the degree to which his wife had drawn him away from his earlier position. For the articles represented a joint effort to revitalize the Society's mission by broadening the Fabian "basis."

The old policy was still strongly represented in the figure of Pease, the secretary. Sharp had already concluded that he was a bar to any policy of revitalization. And Beatrice observed in 1914 that he was "more and more Liberal and 'official labor' in his outlook" and "contemptuously indifferent to International

Socialism and to 'Radical' movements at home." A legacy from a rich uncle enabled Pease to retire from his position in 1914 and helped clear the way for a bolder conception of Fabianism.[84]

The main difficulty in the way of a more vigorous assertion of the Society's socialism, however, still lay in the Fabian courtship of the Labour Party. Most of the trade union officials remained hostile to any attempt to identify the Labour Party with a systematic Socialist program. Indeed, Webb and the other Fabian leaders were so wary of damaging their relations with the labor politicians that they did not even urge their members to adopt the proposal, designed to advance Socialist unity, that Labour Party candidates be allowed to stand under a Labour Socialist banner. Support for the idea within the Society came from Cole because he believed it would hasten "the disruption of the Labour Party."[85]

Fabians and other Socialists who were seeking to use the Labour Party to advance their cause were, as Beatrice Webb recorded in her diary during 1914, in a "quandary." "They have pledged themselves to working class representation as part of the process of making the manual laborer conscious of his disinherited position . . . But they are by their adhesion to the present Parliamentary party bolstering up a fraud—pretending to the outside world that these respectable but reactionary trade union officials are the leaders of the Social Revolution."[86] A year later she observed that the outlook for the labor movement "could hardly be blacker" because its leaders were incapable of thinking out "any coherent policy."[87]

World War I brought a new opportunity to develop a coherent policy for labor. On the War Emergency Workers' National Committee, formed to protect the interests of the working classes during the military struggle, labor and Socialist leaders found a new ground for cooperation. The Socialists, including Hyndman and Webb, worked with trade union officials on behalf of the lower classes in such areas as food, health, employment conditions, housing, and relief. Few could match Webb's skill in dealing with the administrative and legislative problems arising in these areas. Through his ability to draft reports, prepare resolutions for the labor members of Parliament, devise solutions to specific administrative difficulties, and mediate between the diverse views of his colleagues, he "rapidly established his intellectual ascendancy within the Committee."[88]

It was much the same kind of ascendancy he had established earlier within the Fabian Society. By carefully limiting the work of the committee to those practical matters on which agreement, or at least consensus, was possible, he avoided the divisive issues raised by the Socialist ideology and the war. Marxists, Fabians, and "labourist"-oriented trade unionists, as well as ILP pacifists and prowar working class leaders, joined in the activity of the committee.

Beatrice Webb described her husband's role at this time as that of an "unpaid civil servant to the Labour Party." And so he was insofar as he accepted the constraints imposed by the dominant interests and powers of the trade unionists and the labor politicians. In this new context he was resuming the line of advance which had been interrupted by the campaign for the Minority Report. The War Emergency Committee opened up fresh possibilities for introducing collectivist measures into existing administrative and political agencies. Webb's work on the committee called in particular on his skill in transforming "a moral question into a purely technical one." But in such a transformation the values built into existing institutions were implicitly carried over into the technical solution.[89]

During the course of the war the members of the committee began to formulate the hopes of labor for a better society. In 1916, after the government adopted a policy of compulsory military service, the committee members responded with a call for the "conscription of riches." Indeed, Hyndman immediately translated the phrase into a "root and branch revolutionary proposal" to transfer to the government much of the wealth in private hands, and to establish public control over crucial sectors of economic life. However, Webb's counter plan, which retained the Socialist goal of public ownership, but placed primary emphasis on the need to tax surplus wealth for purposes of social welfare, was adopted by the committee. His plan was an important step in the formulation of a new Labour Party program. Already, in fact, Webb was redirecting his main energies into the work of the Labour Party executive, which he had joined in 1915 as the delegate from the Fabian Society. And when, in the summer of 1917, Arthur Henderson resigned from the wartime coalition government, Webb was well placed to work closely with him in redefining the role of the Labour Party in British political life. During the fall Webb served with Mac-Donald and others on the committee appointed to write a new constitution for the party. Under Clause IV of the constitution, ratified the following spring, the Labour Party officially adopted the Socialist objective of "the Common Ownership of the means of production."[90] But the clause did not indicate any substantial conversion of the trade unionists to socialism or any reduction of their influence within the party. Indeed, the massive growth of the trade unions during the period between 1911 and 1918 had helped them to increase their control over the Labour Party.

The insertion of the Socialist clause was the outcome of several concerns—Henderson's desire to counter the Bolshevik appeal to European Socialists, the need to differentiate the Labour Party more clearly from the Liberals, and a recognition by the trade unionists that "a sop to the professional bourgeoisie" in the form of the Socialist objective was necessary to widen the appeal of the party beyond the working classes. Thus Ross McKibbin, in his study of the party's development in these years, concluded that the Socialist clause served an "umbrella function; it was an acceptable formula in a party where there was otherwise little doctrinal agreement." The new constitution "confirmed the triumph of the unions and the defeat of the Socialists."[91]

Whether the opposition between the trade unionists and the Socialists was as sharp as the statement suggests may be questioned pending further study of the major unions involved. But the setback to the Socialist cause within the Labour Party had been clear for some time to the leaders of the ILP. Its relationship with the Labour Party, already badly strained by 1914, had worsened during the war. The ILP's pacifist stance had enabled it to attract a new group of middle class recruits but a larger number of working class adherents had fallen away. And the increased prominence of the middle class element in the ILP, particularly in its London branches, served to heighten the long-standing suspicion of many trade union politicians toward the "missionary intellectuals" of the Socialist movement. By

1916 the ILP men in the House of Commons had ceased to attend meetings of the Parliamentary Labour Party. And at the Labour Party's next annual conference the delegates reduced the influence of the ILP by taking away the power of the Socialist societies to appoint representatives to the Labour Party executive.

The Labour Party's new constitution represented a further defeat for the ILP. By giving fresh impetus to the growth of the local branches of the Labour Party it greatly reduced the importance of the ILP's propaganda and organizing role. Moreover, the incorporation of a Socialist objective in the constitution and in the Labour Party's new statement of purpose, "Labour and the New Social Order," suggested, as R. E. Dowse observed, that the ILP had lost "one of its most important reasons for continued life." "Left without the task of converting the younger party to Socialism," its leaders were no longer sure of its identity and purpose.[92] At the same time the ILP had been displaced in the upper counsels of the Labour Party by Webb and the Fabian point of view.

At the end of the war Beatrice Webb saw her husband, in his new role as "chief adviser" to the Labour Party, as a "man of destiny creating . . . the most powerful organized political force in the United Kingdom excepting the State." Noting the disarray among the Liberals, she claimed that the Labour Party, "with its completely Socialist program and its utopia of the egalitarian state," was the "only alternative" to a Conservative government. The Fabian Society now revised its "basis" to affirm its new role as a "constituent of the Labour Party." A number of the Fabians were following Webb's lead and assuming important roles as chairmen or secretaries of the party's advisory committees. They were becoming a kind of civil service for the party.[93]

Having given up the belief, central to Fabianism, that Socialists could stand above the political battle and offer their services disinterestedly to enlightened politicians and administrators, the Fabian Society had found new energy and direction by attaching itself to the advancing political power of the workers. Although the Fabians could claim, with some justification, that they had helped the Labour Party broaden its appeal beyond the working classes, the development of the Society in the postwar years indicated the price it had paid for its new political role. The revival, in terms of new members and propaganda activity, which the Fabian leaders anticipated, did not materialize. The energies of the Society's most active members were absorbed in the work of the Labour Party while potential recruits were either drawn to local branches of the party or to the more distinctively Socialist bodies—the re-vitalized ILP and the Communist Party. Whether measured by the quantity of its Socialist publications or by its capacity for new ideas, the Society failed to recover the vitality of earlier years.[94]

For some time after the war Sidney Webb, having re-affirmed much of his Fabianism within the context of the Labour Party, remained confident that Britain was moving irresistibly toward a system of public ownership, economic equality, and more thoroughly democratic control. As a member of the Royal Commission to investigate the depressed condition of coal industry shortly after the war, he drafted a scheme for nationalizing the mines, convinced that it would begin a "landslide towards public control." And as a member of Parliament, and a cabinet member in the Labour government of 1924, he found new scope for his skills in committee work and administrative invention. After 1925, when he ceased for a time to occupy a high place in the Labour Party, he lost his confidence that it was the best vehicle for socialism. He returned, so his wife suggested, to his earlier belief that "Fabian permeation of other parties was a more rapid way" to the egalitarian society than the "advent of a definitely Socialist Government." But as late as February 1931 he still believed that socialism "will make itself," that Britain would "slip into the egalitarian state" as it did "into political democracy—by each party, whether nominally Socialist or anti-Socialist, taking steps" in that direction.[95]

Beatrice, meanwhile, had lost her faith in the Fabian approach to socialism, whether through the advance of the Labour Party or the workings of British political institutions. At the end of the war she had resumed the task, undertaken in the *New Statesman* articles of 1913, of working out the details of the Socialist society. During 1918 and 1919 she drafted two sections of the project which were then worked over by her husband and Shaw. In *A Constitution for a Socialist Commonwealth* the Webbs presented a scheme for democratic controls extending beyond the political realm into social and economic affairs. *The Decay of Capitalist Civilization* analyzed the economic failings of capitalism and indicted the profit system. Beatrice believed that the latter would "give a lift to the Fabian Society and its doctrines." But she was increasingly distressed by the narrow outlook and the intellectual defects of the typical trade union leader; she had begun to feel that the Labour Party might be "too good for its ostensible constituents." And she worried lest the party achieve political power "before the labour movement has found its soul." During the early twenties the gulf between her Socialist hopes and the development of the Labour Party widened. By 1924 she had concluded that the Socialists in the Labour Party were suffering from "a policy of inverted permeation." They were not converting the party to their Socialist views; rather, they were being captured by the "philistine citizen." Although she claimed from time to time that MacDonald had "guyed . . . the Fabian policy of permeation," she had ceased to place much hope in political activity, or even in those administrative solutions which had occupied the Fabians. What mattered more and more to her were "states of mind" and the need for a "new rule of life." How was it possible to shift "social institutions off the basis of the brutal struggle for existence and onto that of fellowship?" How could Socialists nurture the spirit of service and the commitment to scientific reasoning that their form of society required? Once more she was seeking a higher form of citizenship, based on an ethic of service and the discipline of science.[96]

When, in 1931, MacDonald and Snowden abandoned the Labour Party to help form a National Government to deal with the economic crisis, Beatrice viewed their defections as the "final and most violent symptom of the disease from which the Labour Party was suffering." The new crisis in the life of the party seemed to her the natural outcome of a spiritual failure. And she welcomed the subsequent electoral defeat of the Labour Party because it provided a new opportunity to develop "the faith, the code of conduct, [and] the knowledge needed for an egalitarian state." The defeat also gave impetus to her growing faith in Russian communism and her belief that the Bolsheviks had discovered the "spiritual power" lacking in the "paper constitution" of the Webbs. The Communist party in Russia was nurturing a new spirit of service and a dedication to scientific method; it had found a remedy for the "catastrophic failures of the motive of pecuniary self interest" in capitalistic societies.[97]

Sidney Webb attempted to moderate his wife's enthusiasm for Russian communism. But both were seeking fresh inspiration for socialism in developments outside of British life and, at the same time, confessing the bankruptcy of their Fabianism. Earlier they had lost the Fabian faith in the power of disinterested intelligence to penetrate the parliamentary political process; now they had ceased to believe that the process itself was moving inexorably toward a Socialist society. And like the Ethical Socialists and the Social Democrats who refused to accept the extinction of their vision through the journey into politics, the Webbs sought other paths.

In the end the Webbs joined those Fabians who, over the years, had become skeptical of the Society's policies. The early defections of Annie Besant and Clarke, the subsequent resignations of Wallas, Wells, Hobson, and Cole, and the gradual disenchantment of Olivier, Bland, and Shaw testified to the persistence of aspirations which Sidney Webb's Fabianism did not acknowledge. The aspirations varied. But their continuing force indicated that Fabian socialism was sustained by hopes for a social transformation far more radical than anything expressed in the Society's policies. As one after another of the Fabian leaders concluded that their hopes could not be realized through existing institutions, the Socialist ideology which had connected their dreams to political action faded out.

CONCLUSION

BRITISH SOCIALISM FOUND support in those
sections of late Victorian and Edwardian so-
ciety which were especially vulnerable to the disrupting effects
of economic change, to the anxieties resulting from social
mobility, and to the uncertainties produced by a deepening
religious and cultural crisis. But middle class and working class
recruits tended to come to the Socialist movement with different
aims. Those from the "professional proletariat," in particular,
were seeking new guidelines in a world that had become
problematical; working class supporters, in contrast, usually
entered the movement with well defined places in society and
specific grievances. Skilled workers for the most part, they
joined the movement mainly in order to advance or protect
interests which had already been articulated by their trade
unions.

To recognize the different social backgrounds and the
different motives of the Socialists goes far to explain what has
seemed to some a paradox in twentieth century Britain—the simultaneous consolidation of the Labour Party and the decline
of the Socialist movement. The journey into politics served to
separate the dominant interests of the working class leaders
from the Socialist commitment to a radical transformation of
society. Socialists were increasingly caught in a dilemma; they
were forced to choose between their social visions on the one
hand and the immediate possibilities for political action and

careers opened up by the Labour Party on the other. In the political setting the various forms of the Socialist ideology either disintegrated or were divorced from the labor movement only to dissolve into sectarianism and private fantasies.

During the period covered by this study British society was moving, however fitfully, toward new forms of national integration. The social welfare legislation of the Liberals, the greatly increased strength of the trade unions, the extension of the franchise to include all the workers, and the emergence of the Labour Party as the second major party were removing many of the grievances which had fed the Socialist movement. The social spaces into which the Socialist ideology could penetrate were shrinking.[1]

The Socialists contributed, unwittingly, to the process through which the working classes were being integrated into a capitalistic system. They did much to awaken the lower classes politically. Yet, by helping to create, in the Labour Party, an effective vehicle for representing working class interests in the existing order, the Socialists undermined their own cause. As the trade union leaders secured fuller access to Parliament, the instrumental function of socialism and its popular appeal declined. The marginal members of the middle classes, who had supplied much of the propaganda and organizing energy of the movement, were increasingly isolated. They might attempt to recapture their Socialist visions in the Community Party or, for a time, in the revitalized ILP. But by the early twenties, as the movement's earliest historian recognized, socialism was "no longer a cause, a new order of society to be set up, but a program of social reform."[2]

Developments in Great Britain since 1920 have given little reason to alter this judgment. Despite periodic attempts to rejuvenate the Socialist hope for a fundamental transformation of society and to gain mass support, the great majority of the working classes have accepted the policies of the Labour Party politicians and the dominant trade union leadership.[3] The Labour Party has continued to be a barrier to the growth of a stronger Socialist commitment. No wonder some Marxists have now, as in earlier years, rejected the Labour Party as a possible vehicle for socialism.[4]

Different perspectives yield different explanations for the failure of socialism to become a transforming power in British society. Conservative and liberal social thinkers point to the achievements of welfare capitalism or to the theoretical and practical difficulties associated with such Socialist ideas as egalitarianism, public ownership, or worker control. Those of radical social persuasions attribute the absence of mass support for socialism to the pervasive and subtle repressions of the capitalistic order or to the lingering benefits of the "imperial state." But the main features of the Socialist failure to become a decisive force were established in the early decades of the century. To this period we can still look for an understanding of the nature of the Socialist appeal and its decline.

The Socialist movement was a discordant blend of the utopian and the practical. Although much of its inspiration can be traced to the social estrangements and the ontological anxieties of marginal individuals and their struggles to find a "new life," socialism gained a significant following only through its capacity to express working class interests. Separated from the ground of immediate practical concerns, the Socialist visionaries lost their strength. But insofar as the Socialists concentrated on the advance of trade union interests they cut themselves off from the deeper inspiration of the movement.

Political practice broke the tension which was essential to the growth of the movement. It brought the Socialists up against intractable economic, social, and cultural forces and compelled them to choose between aims that had become incompatible. Each of the major Socialist groups—Marxists, Fabians, and Ethical Socialists—suffered a fatal sundering of the two drives.

Hyndman had attempted by means of his peculiarly English interpretation of Marxism to balance the two sides of that system of thought. In the end, however, under the pressures of wartime, he and his followers made their peace with the dominant institutions in British life and tacitly allowed the Socialist hope to fade. But almost from the beginning Hyndman's practical leanings had been challenged by Marxists who sought to preserve the Socialist promise of radical change. The aesthetic vision of Morris, the persistent demands of Bax for new metaphysical anchorage, the sectarian zeal of the SLP, the lonely and self-destructive vigil of Maclean, and the remote, unbending stance of the British Communists, all testified to the continuing force of the Marxist vision. They also bore witness to the failure of the Marxist form of socialism to find points of growth in British life.

The Fabians, under the leadership of Webb, had excluded from their official policies the radical hopes present in the early years of the Society. But Fabian attempts to influence public life "without being in politics" demonstrated the fallacy of Webb's confidence in the power of disinterested intelligence and narrowed the Society's work to the terms set by the Labour Party. Although Wallas, Shaw, and others explored anew the problem of social or "spiritual energy" and sought to recover the aim of a transformed society, the Fabian Society too lost touch with its deeper aspirations.

Ethical Socialists expressed most fully the utopian impulses within the movement. They were, therefore, most susceptible to the disenchantment produced by politics. The process was reflected in Blatchford's naive attempt to provide a new metaphysic, in the increasing emptiness of Grayson's rhetoric, in the unconscious duplicities of Glasier and Hardie, and in the political practices of MacDonald and Henderson. The rapid collapse of Ethical Socialism exposed some of its adherents once more to the existential anxieties which had for a time been resolved by their ideological commitments. But efforts to renew the hope for a transformed life, whether in Guild Socialism or through the religious quests of Orage and others, were increasingly divorced from the struggle to advance the labor cause.

The Socialist ideology was not inextricably tied to the new political organization of the working classes. The connection was fortuitous; it reflected a particular set of historical circumstances. Individual Socialists—Shaw, Wells, Hobson, Orage, and others—came to recognize, in fact, the threat which the Labour Party posed to their goals and contemplated ways of rebuilding the movement on different social foundations. Indeed the tendency for disappointed Socialists to seek support outside the working classes for their hopes of radical change was a European-wide phenomenon in the years after World War I. The ties between Socialist disenchantment and new political initiatives on the extreme right or left proved relatively weak in Great Britain. But the British were not completely immune to the new and dangerous constellations of forces to which the disintegration of the Socialist movements contributed.

What persisted through all stages of the British Socialist movement was a hope that was not bound up with a particular class or set of interests. The inner dynamic of socialism was supplied in large part by those adherents who had been loosened from conventional interests; a deep commitment to socialism presupposed, as Marx had recognized, a strong sense of social and cultural disinheritance. But such a condition was more characteristic of marginal members of the middle classes than it was of working class leaders.

Socialists greatly exaggerated, however, the extent to which they had broken with tradition. To a later generation the Socialist visionaries, Bax and Carpenter, Shaw and Wells, Orage and Hobson, seem incorrigibly Victorian. For all their iconoclasm they displayed attitudes central to the Victorian sensibility—a strong belief in progress and an extravagant confidence in the transforming power of ideas and moral sentiments. The Socialists also reinstated the millennial impulse which, in attenuated form, underlay these attitudes. But they expressed too the fear, growing throughout the nineteenth century, that older social, ethical, and aesthetic values were being destroyed by the development of industrial capitalism.

Ideologies by their very nature induce a certain blindness to their origins. Only through a radical simplification of reality do ideologies command the surrender of self and gain the energies necessary to sustain a movement. But ideologies occupy, as the development of British socialism indicates, a middle position in life. They mediate between elemental levels of human motivation and deeply embedded habits of mind, on the one hand, and the challenges presented by traumatic historical change, on the other. The power of ideologies to call forth and direct new human energies, however, is closely connected with a besetting peril—the temptation to offer total solutions to the problems of life. Insofar as ideologies claim to resolve existential dilemmas or provide complete explanations of the social process, they assign absolute value to that which is historically contingent. In doing so they lead inevitably to disillusionment.

Yet, to acknowledge the inherent limitations of ideologies, and to recognize the ways in which socialism expressed late Victorian social and cultural dilemmas, is not to dismiss the movement as a passing moment in modern British history. Many of the issues with which the Socialists struggled remain relevant nearly a century after they began their work. Only those who are convinced that the modes of individualism, competition, production, and consumption associated with corporate capitalism are suited to the emerging shape of human problems will deny the significance of the Socialist effort to chart a different path into the future.

The Socialist effort has, however, reached an impasse. As one leading Marxist observed, the "historical forces and mechanisms on which Socialists relied . . . are not working as they were supposed to" and Socialists "no longer know how to get from the old to the new."[5] The bewilderment of Socialists is mitigated somewhat by the confused state of social thought generally but it seems clear that they must reconsider the nature of their ongoing journey. Certainly in a world marked by the loss of strong and satisfying bonds between private and public spheres of life, ideologies, as systematic efforts of mind and imagination to envision a better society, will remain a part of the modern human adventure. And whatever the deficiencies of the theories and strategies of the Social Democrats, Fabians, and Ethical Socialists, their struggles still hold much to instruct those who seek the road to socialism in a new time.

NOTES
UNPUBLISHED SOURCES
INDEX

NOTES

INTRODUCTION

1. Peguy's famous distinction appears in his "Notre jeunesse," *Cahiers de la Quinzaine*, 11.12 (Paris, 1910).

2. Heinz Hartmann, *Ego Psychology and the Problem of Adaptation*, tr. David Rapaport (London, 1958), p. 17.

3. My use of the concept of ideology has been influenced greatly by Clifford Geertz, "Ideology as a Cultural System," *The Interpretation of Cultures* (New York, 1973). Geertz presents a defense of ideology as a nonevaluative, analytical concept. After discussing the two main approaches to ideology, interest theory and stress theory, Geertz calls for a deeper understanding of the "process of symbolic formation" or the ways in which ideology provides information and meaning as distinguished from its social and psychological functions.

1. THE "DIVIDED CONSCIOUSNESS" AND THE EMERGENCE OF BRITISH SOCIALISM

1. Percival Chubb to Thomas Davidson, May 25, 1882, Thomas Davidson papers, Yale University Library, New Haven, Conn.

2. Ibid., April 5, 1883.

3. Ibid., April 1, May 25, 1882.

4. Ibid., July 6, 1883. For a psychoanalytical approach to this state of mind see Roy Schafer, "Ideals, the Ego Ideal, and the Ideal Self," in R. R. Holt, ed., *Motives and Thought* (New York, 1967), pp. 129-174.

5. William Clarke to Thomas Davidson, Jan. 22, 1883, Davidson papers. Clarke's career is examined by Peter Weiler, "William Clarke: The Making and Unmaking of a Fabian Socialist," *Journal of British Studies*, 14 (November 1974), 77-108. Also see H. Burrows and J. A. Hobson, eds., *William Clarke: A Collection of His Writings* (London, 1908).

6. Clarke to Davidson, June 12, 1882, Jan. 12, 1883, Davidson papers.

7. The phrase "identity crisis" is usually associated with the work of Erik Erikson and the view of human development presented in his book, *Childhood and Society* (New York, 1950). For later refinements and applications of the concept see Roy Schafer, *Aspects of Internalization* (New York, 1968), pp. 39-41; Fred Weinstein and Gerald M. Platt, *Psychoanalytical Sociology* (Baltimore, 1973), p. 69; and Kenneth Hoover, *A Politics of Identity* (Urbana, Ill., 1975), pp. 133-162. Much of the analysis in R. D. Laing, *The Divided Self* (London, 1960), seems to fit the crises of Chubb and Clarke. For a sociological and psychoanalytical interpretation of the problem as a consequence of modernization, see Fred Weinstein and Gerald Platt, *The Wish to be Free: Society, Psyche and Value Change* (Berkeley, 1969).

8. Chubb to Davidson, April 11, 1884, Davidson papers.

9. Clarke to Davidson, Dec. 12, 1884; Chubb to Davidson, Jan 12, 1882.

10. Clarke to Davidson, Jan. 22, 1883; Chubb to Davidson, April 11, 1884, May 25, 1882, Feb. 4, 1884, ibid.

11. Clarke to Davidson, Nov. 17, 1883, ibid.

12. For recent accounts of the break see Willard Wolfe, *From Radicalism to Socialism* (New Haven, Conn., 1975), pp. 151 ff., and Weiler, "Clarke," p. 87.

13. Chubb to Davidson, April 1, 1882, March 4, 1889, Davidson papers.

14. Chubb's work in the American Ethical Culture movement is discussed in Howard B. Radest, *Toward Common Ground: Ethical Societies in America* (New York, 1969), pp. 136-138, 158-159.

15. Clarke to Davidson, Jan. 13, 1883, Dec. 12, 1884, Davidson papers.

16. Clarke to Henry Demarest Lloyd, Oct. 22, 1884, Henry Demarest Lloyd papers, State Historical Society of Wisconsin, Madison. See also Weiler, "Clarke," p. 94.

17. William Clarke, "The Fabian Society," *New England Magazine*, 10 (March 1894), 99.

18. Weiler, "Clarke," pp. 83-89, 96-97; William Clarke, *Walt Whitman* (London, 1892), pp. 116-117.

19. Weiler, "Clarke," pp. 101, 107.

20. Shaw's early years are treated most fully in B. C. Rosset, *Shaw of Dublin* (University Park, Pa., 1964). Shaw himself provides a revealing account of this period of his life in the Preface to *Immaturity* in the *Collected Writings* (New York, 1939), I. Also see George Bernard Shaw, *Sixteen Self Sketches* (New York, 1949). The quotations are drawn from the preface to *Immaturity*, p. xlvii, and the *Collected Letters of George Bernard Shaw*, I, *1874-1897*, ed. Dan Laurence (New York, 1964), p. 19.

21. This is the conclusion of R. F. Dietrich, *Portrait of the Artist as a Young Superman: A Study of Shaw's Novels* (Gainsville, Fla., 1969), p. 52. See also Claude T. Bissel, "The Novels of George Bernard Shaw," *University of Toronto Quarterly*, 17 (October 1947), 38-51.

22. Erik Erikson uses this stage of Shaw's development to illustrate his concept of the identity crisis in *Identity, Youth and Crisis* (New York, 1968), pp. 142-150. Erikson does not recognize the tentative nature of Shaw's "solution" or the way in which his divided state becomes an important source of his artistic activity. Shaw's passage into the Socialist movement corresponds to Robert Merton's classic account of the way in which resentment may give way to rebellion and organized political action. See Robert Merton, "Social Structure and Anomie," *Social Theory and Social Structure* (New York, 1962).

23. See the analysis in Dietrich, *Portrait of the Artist*, pp. 71, 19.

24. Shaw, *Immaturity*, p. 51.

25. Dietrich, *Portrait of the Artist*, p. 83; Shaw, Preface to *Immaturity*, pp. xviii, xxxvi.

26. Dietrich, *Portrait of the Artist*, pp. 52, 151.

27. Shaw, Preface to *Immaturity*, p. xxxvi; *Sixteen Self Sketches*, p. 83.

28. Shaw's development during the eighties is described in detail by Wolfe, *From Radicalism to Socialism*, chs. 4, 8.

29. Quoted by Martin Meisel, "Shaw and Revolution: The Politics of the Plays," *Shaw, Seven Critical Essays*, ed., Norman Rosenblood (Toronto, 1971), pp. 112-113.

30. H. J. Perkin, *The Origin of Modern English Society, 1780-1880* (Toronto, 1969), p. 346.

31. Ibid., p. 404.

32. John Saville, "The Ideology of Labourism," in *Knowledge and Belief in Politics*, ed. Robert Benewick, R. N. Berki, and Bhikhu Parekh (New York, 1973), pp. 214 ff.

33. Trygve R. Tholfsen, *Working Class Radicalism in Mid-Victorian England* (New York, 1977), pp. 243, 283.

34. Eric Hobsbawm, *Labouring Men* (New York, 1967), p. 304.

35. Studies of the ideological propensities of the lower middle class have dealt mainly with German materials and the background to National Socialism. For a discussion of the relevant literature see Arno Mayer, "The Lower Middle Class as Historical Problem," *Journal of Modern History*, 47 (September 1975), 409-436. Mayer describes it as the "up and down escalator 'par excellence' of a society that is in motion." See also the older study which employs Max Scheler's analysis of "ressentiment"—Svend Ranulf, *Moral Indignation and Middle Class Psychology* (New York, 1938). Perkin views this section of Victorian society as "a Protean class which could assume the guise of any other class at will" but whose professional members were also inclined to exalt their own social ideal of service. See *Origin of Modern English Society*, pp. 220 ff., 252 ff., 428 ff. John Rex maintains that the distinguishing feature of the "petite bourgeoisie" is the absence of "any real social and political identity as a class" and its incapacity for "collective action." *Sociology and the Demystification of the Modern World* (London, 1974), p. 131. Also see Thomas Luckman and Peter Berger, "Social Mobility and Personal Identity," *European Journal of Sociology*, 5(1964), 331-344. Geoffrey Crossick concludes that "increasing status anxieties . . . involved for some a turn to socialism" but that the lower middle class was mainly a conservative force. See his essay, "The Emergence of the Lower Middle Class in Britain," *The Lower Middle Class in Britain, 1870-1914*, ed. Geoffrey Crossick (London, 1977), pp. 30-32.

36. Weiler, "Clarke," p. 90; Stanley Pierson, *Marxism and the Origins of British Socialism* (Ithaca, 1973), pp. 161-169.

37. Lister's relationship to the movement is summarized in his obituary, *Halifax Courier and Guardian* (Oct. 14, 1933), and a description of a Socialist gathering at Shibden Park by Dr. J. Johnson appears in the Alfred Mattison papers, Brotherton Library, Leeds; Clifford Geertz, "Ideology as a Cultural System," *Ideology and Discontents*, ed. David Apter (New York, 1964), pp. 47-66. Also see the discussion by Abner Cohen, *Two-Dimensional Man* (Berkeley, 1974), pp. 23-25, 80-82.

38. Philip Rieff, *The Triumph of the Therapeutic* (New York, 1968), p. 73;

René Wellek, "Romanticism Reexamined," *Romanticism Reconsidered*, ed. Northrop Frye (New York, 1963), p. 129.

39. Among the many treatments of this period I have found the following recent studies most helpful: M. H. Abrams, *Natural Supernaturalism* (New York, 1970); Lionel Trilling, *Sincerity and Authenticity* (Cambridge, Mass., 1972). See also the opening chapter of Hillis Miller, *The Disappearance of God* (Cambridge, Mass., 1963). For a sociological analysis of the rupture between the "private" and the "public" see Peter Berger, Brigitte Berger, Hansfried Keller, *The Homeless Mind* (New York, 1973).

40. Abrams, *Natural Supernaturalism*, p. 212. The loss of the relationship between poetry and public affairs during the eighteenth century and the Romantic struggle to recover it is analyzed by Thomas Edwards, *Imagination and Power* (Oxford, 1971).

41. Sheldon Wolin, *Politics and Vision* (Boston, 1960), p. 341.

42. Masao Miyoshi, *The Divided Self: A Perspective on the Literature of the Victorians* (New York, 1969), p. 107; E. D. H. Johnson, *The Alien Vision of Victorian Poetry* (Hamden, Conn., 1963), pp. 29, 38-39, 215-219. For Arnold see also Robert Langbaum, *Mysteries of Identity* (New York, 1977), ch. 2.

43. Johnson, *Alien Vision*, p. 215.

44. Peter Gay uses the phrase, "hunger for wholeness" in his *Weimar Culture* (New York, 1970), ch. 4. The Bradbury quotations are from his study, *The Social Context of Modern English Literature* (New York, 1971), chs. 3, 4. For George Moore's attempt to reconcile the divergent tendencies toward "fantasies and dreams" on the one hand and the "tangible realities of contemporary experience" on the other, see Graham Hough, "George Moore and the Nineties," *Edwardians and Late Victorians*, ed. Richard Ellmann (New York, 1960), pp. 1-27. Tendencies toward the "schizophrenic" condition and "solipsism" are discussed in John Vernon, *The Garden and the Map: Schizophrenia in Modern Literature and Culture* (Chicago, 1973), and Alan Kennedy, *The Protean Self* (New York, 1974). See also Wylie Sypher, *Loss of the Self in Modern Literature and Art* (New York, 1962).

45. The best study is Chushichi Tsuzuki, *H. M. Hyndman and British Socialism* (London, 1961). For a treatment of the general response of the British to Marxism see Kirk Willis, "The Introduction and Critical Reception of Marxist Thought in Britain, 1850-1900," *Historical Journal*, 20.2 (1977), 417-460.

46. Marx's judgment of utilitarianism appears in *The German Ideology*. The relevant pages are reprinted as an appendix in Sidney Hook, *From Hegel to Marx* (Ann Arbor, Mich., 1962), pp. 315-322; Wolfe, *From Radicalism to Socialism*, pp. 93 ff.

47. Henry Collins, "The Marxism of the Social Democratic Federation," in *Essays in Labour History, 1886-1923*, ed. Asa Briggs and John Saville (London, 1971), pp. 47-69.

48. This aspect of Marxist thought is stressed in Leszek Kolakowski, "The

Myth of Human Self Identity," in *The Socialist Idea*, ed. Leszek Kolakowski and Stuart Hampshire (New York, 1974), pp. 18-35.

49. Chubb to Davidson, Feb. 4, 1883, Davidson papers; Stanley Pierson, "Ernest Belfort Bax; The Encounter of Marxism and Late Victorian Culture," *Journal of British Studies*, 12 (November 1972), 39-60.

50. See Stanley Pierson, *Marxism and the Origins of British Socialism* (Ithaca, 1973), pp. 75 ff.

51. The development of Morris and the Socialist League is treated most fully in Edward Thompson, *William Morris: Romantic to Revolutionary* (London, 1955).

52. Henri De Man, *Psychology of Socialism* (New York, 1928), p. 133.

53. For the development of Fabian ideas see Wolfe, *From Radicalism to Socialism*; A. M. McBriar, *Fabian Socialism and English Politics, 1884-1918* (Cambridge, 1962); Norman and Jeanne MacKenzie, *The Fabians* (New York, 1977).

54. Sidney Webb, *English Progress towards Social Democracy* (London, 1888), p. 10.

55. Quoted by Meisel, "Shaw and Revolution," p. 113; George Bernard Shaw to H. M. Hyndman, June 22, 1888, holograph copy in Shaw papers, British Museum, London.

56. Shaw to Hyndman, June 22, 1888, Shaw papers.

57. George Bernard Shaw, ed., *Fabian Essays* (London, 1948), p. 96; Burrows and Hobson, eds., *William Clarke*, p. 202.

58. Tract 70, *Report on Fabian Policy* (London, 1896), p. 1; Shaw's letter to the members, Oct. 6, 1896, urging them to resist the effort to withdraw the tract from publication. Shaw papers.

59. For an account of this transformation of Socialist ideology see Pierson, *Marxism and the Origins of British Socialism*, pp. 140-173.

60. See Stanley Pierson, "Edward Carpenter: Prophet of a Socialist Millennium," *Victorian Studies*, 13 (March 1970), 301-318.

61. See Laurence Thompson, *Robert Blatchford* (London, 1951).

62. See Pierson, *Marxism and the Origins of British Socialism*, pp. 174-214.

63. Quoted in Francis Johnson, *Keir Hardie's Socialism* (Leicester, 1922), p. 8.

64. Recent treatments of ideology have distinguished between its "instrumental" and "expressive" functions. See, for example, L. B. Brown, *Ideology* (London, 1973), pp. 117-129. Also see Cohen, *Two Dimensional Man*, pp. xi, 26 ff., and Geertz, "Ideology as a Cultural System," pp. 52 ff.

65. The early development of the ILP is examined in Henry Pelling, *The Origins of the Labour Party*, rev. ed. (Oxford, 1965).

66. Quoted in Anne Fremantle, *This Little Band of Prophets* (New York, 1966), p. 129.

67. J. C. Kenworthy, *The Anatomy of Misery*, 2nd ed. (London, 1900), p. 91; Robert Blatchford to A. M. Thompson, 1894, Robert Blatchford cor-

respondence, Manchester Central Reference Library, Manchester.

68. For MacDonald's early development see David Marquand, *Ramsay MacDonald* (London, 1977).

69. Quoted by Fremantle, *This Little Band of Prophets*, p. 133.

70. For the background and formation of the Labour Representation Committee see Frank Bealey and Henry Pelling, *Labour and Politics* (London, 1958), pp. 30 ff., and Philip Poirier, *The Advent of the Labour Party* (London, 1958), pp. 77-99.

71. Tsuzuki, *Hyndman*, pp. 105-106.

72. Shaw to Beatrice Webb, July 30, 1901, Passfield papers, British library of Political and Economic Science, London.

73. H. M. Hyndman to Karl Kautsky, Feb. 22, 1902, Kautsky correspondence, International Institute for Social History, Amsterdam; *Labour Leader*, June 16, 1900; Cecil Chesterton, *Gladstonian Ghosts* (London, 1904), pp. 51, 43.

74. Hubert Bland to Edward Pease, Oct. 17, 1899; S. G. Hobson to Sidney Olivier, Oct. 24, 1901, and Hobson's "Draft Resolution" for the meeting of Dec. 8, 1899; Sidney Oliver to Edward Pease, Oct. 16, 1899; "Reply" by the majority of the Executive Committee. All in the Fabian papers, Nuffield College, Oxford.

75. H. M. Hyndman to Edward Carpenter, Sept. 16, 1900, Edward Carpenter papers, Sheffield Public Library; Shaw to Beatrice Webb, July 30, 1901, Passfield papers.

2. Ethical Socialism, 1900-1905

1. John Penny in the *Labour Annual* (Liverpool, 1901), p. 24.

2. Frank Bealey and Henry Pelling, *Labour and Politics* (London, 1958), pp. 8 ff.

3. *Clarion*, April 30, 1898; H. A. Clegg, Alan Fox, and A. F. Thompson, *A History of British Trade Unionism since 1889*, I (Oxford, 1964), 377. Some working class leaders "disliked the ILP because of the large middle class element." See Frederick Rogers, *Labour, Life and Literature* (London, 1913), p. 210. On the ILP recruitment in London see Paul Thompson, *Socialists, Liberals and Labour* (London, 1967), pp. 230 ff.

4. Harold Laski in the *Daily Herald* (May 17, 1937).

5. Biographical details may be found in Colin Cross, *Philip Snowden* (London, 1966), and Snowden's *Autobiography*, 2 vols. (London, 1934). The quotations are from the *Autobiography*, I, 19, 47.

6. Snowden, *Autobiography*, p. 60.

7. Quoted in C. E. Bechofer-Roberts, *Philip Snowden* (London, 1929), pp. 10-11.

8. Anthony Farley [S. G. Hobson], *Letters to My Nephew* (London, 1917), pp. 261 ff.

9. Philip Snowden, *The Christ That Is to Be* (London, 1904). There is an angry reply by H. S. Wishart, a Marxist member of both the SDF and the ILP, *Christ: The Greatest Enemy of the Human Race* (Bradford, n.d.).

10. Snowden, *Autobiography*, I, 82; *Yorkshire Post* (May 17, 1937).

11. See Philip Poirier, *The Advent of the Labour Party* (London, 1958), pp. 163 ff. The Taff Vale case and its political consequences are discussed in Bealey and Pelling, *Labour and Politics*, pp. 55-72. See also Henry Pelling, "Trade Unions, Workers, and the Law," *Popular Politics and Late Victorian Society* (New York, 1968), pp. 63-81, and Clegg, Fox, and Thompson, *History of British Trade Unions*, chs. 8, 9.

12. *Clarion*, March 21, 1902 (a week later, however, the *Clarion* noted a *Daily News* report that Snowden had made a public profession of his Socialist faith); H. M. Hyndman to Gaylord Wilshire, March 2, 1902, H. Gaylord Wilshire papers, microfilm copies in British Library of Political and Economic Science, London.

13. The Clitheroe division, located on the border of the West Riding, was one of the few Nonconformist strongholds in Lancashire. Snowden had lived in the constituency for ten years and his close identification with the Temperance movement further enhanced his appeal. An examination of the economic, political, and religious situation in the area may be found in Bealey and Pelling, *Labour and Politics*, pp. 98-124. For the changing political outlook of the trade unionists see P. F. Clarke, *Lancashire and the New Liberalism* (Cambridge, 1971), pp. 90 ff.

14. *Labour Leader*, July 26, 1902.

15. The basis for working class Toryism in Lancashire is discussed in Clarke, *Lancashire and the New Liberalism*, pt. 2. Crooks' campaign in London is described in Poirier, *Advent of Labour*, pp. 168-169.

16. J. Bruce Glasier to Keir Hardie, May 15, 1903, Glasier correspondence, Archives of the Independent Labour Party, Bristol.

17. Quoted in Bealey and Pelling, *Labour and Politics*, p. 155. See also Poirier, *Advent of Labour*, pp. 196-207. Glasier to Hardie, Glasier correspondence. See also A. W. Purdue, "Arthur Henderson and Liberal, Liberal-Labour, and Labour Politics in the Northeast of England, 1892-1903," *Northern History*, 9 (1975), 195-217.

18. John Saville, "The Ideology of Labourism," in *Knowledge and Belief in Politics*, ed. Robert Benewick, P. N. Berki, and Bhikhu Parekh (London), pp. 213-226.

19. The struggle between the Socialists and the Lib-Labs is discussed in Clegg, Fox, and Thompson, *History of British Trade Unions*, pp. 372-383. See also Clarke, *Lancashire and the New Liberalism*, p. 336.

20. Arthur Henderson to J. R. MacDonald, Nov. 3, 1905, Labour Party Letter Files, Transport House, London. The crucial role of Shackleton and Henderson in consolidating the forces of labor in Parliament is stressed in Clegg, Fox, and Thompson, *History of British Trade Unions*, pp. 388 ff.

21. Godfrey Elton, *James Ramsay MacDonald* (London, 1939), p. 135.

22. *ILP News*, February 1902.

23. J. R. MacDonald to Ward (Sheffield L. R. C.), Sept. 30, 1903, Labour Party Letter Files.

24. Accounts of the negotiations and the agreement may be found in

Bealey and Pelling, *Labour and Politics*, pp. 125-159, and Poirier, *Advent of Labour*, pp. 175-195. See also the analysis of the results in Clarke, *Lancashire and the New Liberalism*, ch. 12, and A. K. Russell, *Liberal Landslide: The General Election of 1906* (Newton Abbot, Eng., 1973), pp. 44-46. Gladstone's memorandum on the agreement describes it as an "act of friendship and without any stipulation of any kind." The memorandum is reprinted in Kenneth O. Morgan, *The Age of Lloyd George* (London, 1971), pp. 139-140.

25. The best biography of Hardie is Kenneth Morgan, *Keir Hardie* (London, 1975). Hardie's parliamentary work in these years is discussed in Frank Bealey, "Keir Hardie and the Labour Group," *Parliamentary Affairs*, 11 (1956-57), 81-93 and 220-233. See also the assessment in Clegg, Fox, and Thompson, *History of British Trade Unions*, I, 372.

26. *Labour Leader*, Nov. 30, 1901, Jan. 4, 1902, May 25, 1901, Sept. 9, 1904.

27. Ibid., Sept. 20, 1902; Glasier to Hardie, March 11, 1903, Glasier correspondence.

28. Keir Hardie, "The International Socialist Congress," *Nineteenth Century*, 56 (October 1904), 570.

29. Ibid., p. 564; Keir Hardie, *Speeches and Writings* (Glasgow, n.d.), p. 115.

30. For biographical details see Laurence Thompson, *The Enthusiasts* (London, 1971), and Stanley Pierson, *Marxism and the Origins of British Socialism* (Ithaca, 1973), pp. 141-146.

31. Glasier to Hardie, March 3, 1895, April 3, 1903, May 2, 1900. Glasier correspondence.

32. *Clarion*, Nov. 3, 1900; Glasier to Hardie, n.d., Glasier correspondence; Glasier to Blatchford, Oct. 23, 1901, Robert Blatchford correspondence, Central Reference Library, Manchester.

33. *Labour Leader*, Nov. 21, 1903; *ILP News*, Dec. 1903.

34. Glasier to Carpenter, June 17, 1903, Edward Carpenter papers, Sheffield Public Library, Sheffield.

35. *Labour Leader*, April 2, 1904.

36. Glasier to Hardie, Sept. 2, 1904, Glasier correspondence; Thompson, *Enthusiasts*, ch. 7.

37. J. R. MacDonald, "The People in Power," *Ethical Democracy*, ed. Stanton Coit (London, 1900), p. 61.

38. *Labour Leader*, Aug. 9, 1902.

39. See David Marquand, *Ramsay MacDonald* (London, 1977), ch. 5.

40. *Speaker*, Aug. 27, 1904; Glasier to Hardie, Sept. 8, 1904, Glasier correspondence.

41. *Labour Leader*, March 12, 1904. MacDonald became editor in February. Marquand, *Ramsay MacDonald*, p. 87.

42. "Prospectus of the Socialist Library," in the Introduction to Enrico Ferri, *Socialism and Positive Science* (London, 1905); *Labour Leader*, April 14, 1905.

43. J. R. MacDonald, *Socialism and Society* (London, 1905), pp. 98, 62.

44. Ibid., pp. 82, 125-128, 69.

45. Ibid., pp. 124, 37.

46. Ibid., pp. 138, 143. See also his article, "The Second Ballot in Party Government," *Independent Review*, 5 (1905), 24.

47. MacDonald, *Socialism and Society*, p. 160. For a discussion of MacDonald's rhetoric and its political function see Rodney Barker, "Socialism and Progressivism in the Political Thought of Ramsay MacDonald," *Edwardian Radicalism, 1900-1914*, ed. A. J. A. Morris (London, 1974), pp. 131-147.

48. Hardie, "International Socialist Congress," p. 559.

49. *Clarion*, Oct. 6, 1900.

50. Ibid., Dec. 13, 1901. The SDF statement is printed in the *Clarion*, Dec. 27, 1901. The fullest account of the episode is in Thompson, *Enthusiasts*, pp. 124-128.

51. *Labour Leader*, March 29, 1902; *Clarion*, April 11, 1902.

52. Glasier to Lizzie Glasier, April 3, 1902, Glasier correspondence.

53. See Hobson's autobiography, *Pilgrim to the Left* (London, 1938).

54. James Firth (Secretary of Rochdale Trades Council) to J. R. MacDonald, Dec. 28, 1902, and Aug. 26, 1903, Labour Party Letter Files. See also Clarke, *Lancashire and the New Liberalism*, p. 315.

55. *Labour Leaders*, Feb. 7, 28, 1903.

56. Ibid., March 14, 1903; Glasier to Hardie, March 2, 1903, Glasier correspondence.

57. *Labour Leader*, July 15, 1904.

58. Ibid., Aug. 5, 1904.

59. *Speaker*, Sept. 3, 1904.

60. Glasier to Lizzie Glasier, Dec. 2, 1905, Glasier correspondence.

61. *Labour Leader*, Jan. 12, 1906.

62. Blatchford to Glasier, Christmas, 1901, Glasier correspondence.

63. *Clarion*, Oct. 7, 21, 1899; Glasier to Hardie, Nov. 23, 1900, Glasier correspondence.

64. *Clarion*, Aug. 17, 1901, May 5, 1900, January 28, June 10, 1899.

65. Ibid., May 17, 1900, Aug. 24, 1901; Glasier to Blatchford, late 1901, Glasier correspondence.

66. Robert Blatchford, *Britain for the British* (London, 1902), chs. 1, 19.

67. *Clarion*, June 20, 1902.

68. Alexander M. Thompson, *Here I Lie* (London, 1937), p. 107; *Clarion*, Aug. 11, 1900, Aug. 6, 28, 1898.

69. *Clarion*, Dec. 19, 1902.

70. Ibid., Feb. 13, 1903; Blatchford to Thompson, early 1903, Blatchford correspondence. Blatchford expressed his fears to Hardie in two letters in March, 1905, Glasier correspondence.

71. Blatchford to Thompson, spring 1903. Blatchford correspondence; *Clarion*, Oct. 28, 1904.

72. Robert Blatchford, *Not Guilty* (New York, 1908), pp. 3, 129.

73. Ibid., pp. 2, 138, 37, 1, 182; *Clarion*, Feb. 27, 1903.

74. Blatchford, *Not Guilty*, pp. 104, 2.

75. G. K. Chesterton, *Autobiography* (New York, 1936), p. 182.

76. G. K. Chesterton, "The Eternal Heroism of the Slums," in *The Religious Doubts of Democracy*, ed. George Haw (London, 1904); Chesterton, *Autobiography*, p. 183.

77. George Lansbury, "Why I Returned to Christianity," *Religious Doubts of Democracy*, p. 8; Percy Redfern, *Journey to Understanding* (London, 1946), p. 118. See also Redfern's essay in *Religious Doubts of Democracy*.

78. *Labour Mail* (Birmingham), December 1906.

79. *Clarion*, Sept. 28, 1906, Jan. 29, 1904, Oct. 12, 1906, Oct. 21, 1903.

80. Glasier to Lizzie Glasier, Sept. 1, 1905, Glasier correspondence.

81. Graham Wallas to George Bernard Shaw, Dec. 13, 1908. George Bernard Shaw papers, British Museum. Blatchford's influence is also noted by Susan Budd, "The Loss of Faith: Reasons for Unbelief among Members of the Secularist Movement in England, 1850-1950," *Past and Present* (April 1967), pp. 109-110.

82. *Clarion*, June 27, 1907.

3. SOCIAL DEMOCRATS AND FABIANS

1. H. M. Hyndman to A. M. Simons, Oct. 5, 1902, Simons correspondence, Wisconsin State Historical Society, Madison; Hyndman, "Socialism and the Future of England," *Cosmopolis*, 9 (January 1898), 34, 26, 43.

2. Hyndman, "Socialism and the Future of England," pp. 28, 25, 43.

3. The role of Hyndman and the SDF in the LRC is described in Chushichi Tsuzuki, *H. M. Hyndman and British Socialism* (Oxford, 1961), pp. 105-106, 135-136.

4. Ibid., pp. 134 ff.; Hyndman to Edward Carpenter, Sept. 16, 1900, Edward Carpenter papers, Sheffield Public Library.

5. See Hyndman's letters in *Challenge*, Aug. 19, 1901, and in *Wilshire's Monthly Magazine*, Oct. 11, 1901. Copies of these issues are included in the H. Gaylord Wilshire papers. Microfilm copies in British Library of Political and Economic Science, London.

6. Social Democratic Federation, *Report of the Annual Conference*, 1901. See also Communist Party of Great Britain, "Some Dilemmas for Marxists," *Our History*, 4 (Christmas 1956), 4; Quelch's "Introduction" to his translation of Marx's *Misery of Philosophy* (London, 1900), p. iv; and his article in the *Social Democrat*, May 1902.

7. The essay, "The Materialist Doctrine of History," was reprinted in Bax, *Essays in Socialism, New and Old* (London, 1906). See also Kautsky's reply in the *Social Democrat*, August 1902.

8. *Justice*, May 26, 1900; Bax, *Outspoken Essays on Social Subjects* (London, 1897), p. 257; *Essays in Socialism*, p. 101.

9. Bax, *Essays in Socialism*, pp. 24, 29.

10. See Hyndman's letter in *Challenge*, Aug. 19, 1901, included in the Wilshire papers; Rothstein to Karl Kautsky, Dec. 8, 1902, Kautsky correspondence, International Institute for Social History, Amsterdam.

11. Rothstein, "The Eclectic Theory of History," *Social Democrat*, 9 (November 1905), and 7 (June 1900). See also Walter Kendall, *The Revolutionary Movement in Britain, 1900-21* (London, 1969), pp. 12-13.

12. Rothstein to Kautsky, Sept. 15, 1901, Kautsky correspondence.

13. Bax, *Essays in Socialism*, pp. 257, 252.

14. T. A. Jackson, *Solo Trumpet* (London, 1933), p. 56.

15. The origin of the Socialist Labour Party is discussed in Kendall, *Revolutionary Movement in Britain*, pp. 14-22, 65ff; D. M. Chewter, "The History of the Socialist Labour Party in Great Britain from 1902 until 1921," B. Litt thesis, Oxford, 1966. See also C. Tsuzuki, "The Impossibilist Revolt in Britain," *International Review of Social History*, 1 (1956), 377-397, and Raymond Challinor, *The Origins of British Bolshevism* (London, 1977), ch. 1.

16. Tom Bell, *Pioneering Days* (London, 1941), p. 45; *Socialist*, September 1904; C. D. Greaves, *The Life and Times of James Connolly* (London, 1960), p. 128.

17. *Socialist*, August 1905, September 1904. See also Paul Thompson, *Socialists, Liberals, and Labour* (London, 1967), pp. 191-192.

18. Jackson, *Solo Trumpet*, p. 59; *Socialist*, August 1905.

19. *Socialist*, November 1907, January 1906.

20. James Connolly to J. C. Matheson, Nov. 19, 1905, Aug. 22, 1904, June 10, 1906, James Connolly papers, National Library of Ireland, Dublin.

21. T. A. Jackson, *Dialectics: The Logic of Marx and His Critics* (London, 1936), p. 401.

22. Social Democratic Federation, *Report of the Annual Conference*, 1904.

23. The basis of the Social Democratic appeal in Lancashire is discussed in P. F. Clarke, *Lancashire and the New Liberalism* (Cambridge, 1971), pp. 40 ff.

24. Social Democratic Federation, *Report of the Annual Conference*, 1905.

25. Hyndman to Wilshire, April 4, Nov. 18, 1905, Wilshire papers.

26. The figures for the decline are drawn from the report of the "Special Committee," presented by L. Haden Guest in 1906. Copy in Fabian Papers, Nuffield College, Oxford; Sidney Webb, "Lord Rosebery's Escape from Houndsditch," *Nineteenth Century and After*, 50 (September 1901), 347; R. C. K. Ensor, "Permeation," in *The Webbs and Their Work*, ed. Margaret Cole (London, 1949), p. 68.

27. Edward Pease to H. G. Wells, Jan. 10, 1902, Wells papers, University of Illinois Library, Urbana.

28. Sidney Webb to Edward Pease, Aug. 25, 1895, Passfield papers, British Library of Political and Economic Science, London.

29. Sidney and Beatrice Webb, *Industrial Democracy* 2nd ed. (London, 1911), p. 597.

30. Ibid., pp. 15, 40.

31. Discussions of national reintegration in terms similar to those used by the Webbs can be found in Rheinhard Bendix, *Nation Building and Citizenship* (New York, 1964), ch. 3, and T. H. Marshall, *Class, Citizenship and*

Social Development (New York, 1964), ch. 4.

32. Webb, *Industrial Democracy*, p. 822.

33. Ibid., pp. 838, 538, 832-833.

34. Ibid., p. 70.

35. Ibid., pp. 844, 598, 850.

36. Eric Hobsbawm, *Labouring Men* (New York, 1967), p. 301. The ways in which the Webbs departed from a strictly descriptive or inductive method and, particularly in the final section of *Industrial Democracy*, introduced subjective and deductive elements, is discussed by T. S. Simey, "The Contribution of Sidney and Beatrice Webb to Sociology," *British Journal of Sociology*, 7 (January 1961), 106-123.

37. Webb, "Lord Rosebery's Escape," pp. 373-374.

38. George Bernard Shaw to Sidney Webb, July 26, 1901, *Collected Letters of George Bernard Shaw*, II, *1898-1910*, ed. Dan Laurence (London, 1972), p. 230; Beatrice Webb, unpublished diaries, 20, New Year's Day, 1901, and 23, Oct. 14, 1902, Passfield papers.

39. Ensor, "Permeation," p. 65; Beatrice Webb, *Our Partnership* (London, 1948), pp. 224-229. The relationship of the Webbs to the Liberal imperialists has been discussed in several recent studies. See Bernard Semmel, *Imperialism and Social Reform* (New York, 1960), chs. 3, 6; G. R. Searle, *The Quest for National Efficiency* (Berkeley, 1971), pp. 122 ff.; Bernard Porter, *Critics of Empire* (London, 1968), pp. 109-123.

40. B. Webb, *Our Partnership*, p. 292; B. Webb, unpublished diaries, 24, Oct. 16, 1904, Passfield papers.

41. Fabian educational policy is criticized by Brian Simon, *Education and the Labour Movement, 1870-1920* (London, 1965), pp. 223 ff. See also the discussion of the evolution of the Labour Party's policy in Rodney Barker, *Education and Politics, 1900-1951* (Oxford, 1972).

42. Robert Morant to Sidney Webb, April 8, 1904, Passfield papers. See also A. V. Judges, "The Educational Influence of the Webbs," *British Journal of Educational Studies* 10 (November 1961), 33-48.

43. B. Webb, *Our Partnership*, p. 223.

44. Notes for the lecture, entitled "Education," are in the Wallas papers, British Library of Political and Economic Science, London. For the intellectual development of Wallas see Martin Wiener, *Between Two Worlds* (Oxford, 1971), and Reba Soffer, *Ethics and Society in England* (Berkeley, 1978), ch. 9.

45. An unpublished lecture on the church is in the Wallas papers.

46. See the review by Wallas of M. I. Ostrogorski's *Democracy and the Organization of Political Parties* in the *Independent Review*, November 1903; B. Webb, unpublished diaries, 21, Dec. 9, 1901.

47. Notes for a lecture at South Place Ethical Society, October 1901, Wallas papers.

48. Webb to Wallas, Jan. 10, 1904; Wallas to Webb, March 5, 1905, Passfield papers.

49. J. H. Muirhead, *Reflections by a Journeyman in Philosophy on the Movements of Thought and Practice in Our Time*, ed. John Harvey (London,

1942), p. 94; B. Webb, *Our Partnership*, pp. 241 ff.; Graham Wallas, *Men and Ideas* (London, 1940), p. 106; Mary Peter Mack, "Graham Wallas' New Individualism," *Western Political Quarterly* (March 1958), 17.

50. George Bernard Shaw, *Sixteen Self Sketches* (New York, 1949), p. 131; *Collected Letters of George Bernard Shaw*, I, 258, 726, II, 156.

51. Shaw, *Collected Letters*, II, 427.

52. Ibid., p. 230. The division and tension is explored in several studies. See James Hulse, *Revolutionaries in London* (London, 1970), pp. 192 ff., and Martin Meisel, "Shaw and Revolution: The Politics of the Plays," in *Shaw: Seven Critical Essays*, ed. Norman Rosenblood (Toronto, 1971), pp. 106-134. Erich Strauss, *Bernard Shaw: Art and Criticism* (London, 1942), sees in "Candida" the "disintegration of Shaw's complete personality into Artist and Socialist who, henceforth, up to the war, followed different paths" (p. 85).

53. Shaw's relationship to Morris is discussed in Hulse, *Revolutionaries*, pp. 122-130. Shaw states his view of the artist in his essays, "The Board School," and "Tolstoy on Art," in *The Collected Works of George Bernard Shaw* (New York, 1930), XXV, 268-273, XXIX, 273.

54. See "A Symposium on the Problem Play," in *Shaw on Theater*, ed. E. J. West (New York, 1958), pp. 64-65.

55. Shaw, *Collected Works*, I, 632.

56. See "A Dramatic Realist to His Critics," in West, *Shaw on Theatre*, pp. 18-41; Strauss, *Shaw*, p. 14.

57. See the essay, "Manchester Still Expiating" (1898), *Collected Works*, XXV, 329.

58. The development of Shaw's metaphysical beliefs is discussed in J. Percy Smith, *The Unrepentent Pilgrim* (Boston, 1965), pp. 129-164. "What he wanted," according to Smith, "was a credible cosmic perspective and a frame of reference for the discussion of moral and social questions."

59. See Strauss, *Shaw*, pp. 41 ff., and Hulse, *Revolutionaries*, ch. 8.

60. Shaw, *Collected Letters*, II, 427, 100; Beatrice Webb, unpublished diaries, 24, March 7, 1904.

61. Shaw, *Collected Letters*, II, 368.

62. Shaw, *Collected Letters*, II, 368; Hulse, *Revolutionaries*, pp. 193-194.

63. Shaw, *Man and Superman*, in *Collected Works*, X, 198.

64. Beatrice Webb, *Our Partnership*, p. 256; S. Webb to Pease, July 7, 1902, Fabian papers, Nuffield College, Oxford. Shaw had already advanced the idea of breeding a new race of men in *The Perfect Wagnerite* (1898).

65. Shaw, *John Bull's Other Island*, *Collected Works*, XI, 181.

66. For recent analyses see Louis Crompton, *Shaw the Dramatist* (Lincoln, Neb., 1969), ch. 7; Margery Morgan, *The Shavian Playground* (London, 1972), ch. 8; Charles Berst, *Bernard Shaw and the Art of Drama* (Urbana, Ill., 1973), ch. 6; Maurice Valency, *The Cart and the Trumpet* (New York, 1973), pp. 247-265; and Rose Zimbardo, ed., *Major Barbara: A Collection of Critical Essays* (Englewood Cliffs, N.J., 1970). A penetrating Marxist critique of the play and an interpretation of its place in Shaw's Socialist development is presented in Strauss, *Shaw*, pp. 57 ff.

67. Valency, *The Cart and the Trumpet*, pp. 262, 275-276.

68. Shaw, *Major Barbara, Collected Works*, XI, 213.

69. Ibid., pp. 328, 347. Shaw removed the term "democratic" from the version in the *Collected Works*.

70. Ibid., p. 349.

71. Ibid., pp. 321, 340, 246.

72. Ibid., p. 330.

73. Thus Robert Brustein, *Theater of Revolt* (Boston, 1969), concludes that the "Shavian soul" is a "sunlit soul, empty of menace, without fatality" (p. 206).

74. Morgan, *Shavian Playground*, p. 157; *Labour Leader*, Dec. 2, 1904. See also Robert Whitman, *Shaw and the Play of Ideas* (Ithaca, 1977), ch. 4.

75. Shaw, *Collected Letters*, II, 536.

76. H. G. Wells, *Experiment in Autobiography* (New York, 1934), p. 439.

77. Ibid., pp. 43, 147-148. For the early development of Wells see Norman and Jeanne MacKenzie, *The Time Traveller* (London, 1973), chs. 2, 3, 4.

78. Wells, *Experiment in Autobiography*, pp. 142, 204.

79. MacKenzie, *Time Traveller*, p. 55.

80. Quoted by Lovat Dickson, *H. G. Wells* (New York, 1969), p. 47. Fred Weinstein and Gerald Platt, *The Wish to be Free: Society, Psyche, and Value Change* (Berkeley, 1969), p. 142; MacKenzie, *Time Traveller*, p. 118.

81. The early writings are examined in Bernard Bergonzi, *The Early H. G. Wells* (Manchester, 1961).

82. Ibid., p. 145.

83. Dickson, *Wells*, p. 92.

84. H. G. Wells, *Anticipations: The Works of H. G. Wells* (New York, 1924), pp. 72, 81, 228, 88.

85. Ibid., pp. 155, 124.

86. Ibid., pp. 256, 250, 257-258.

87. Ibid., pp. 260-262.

88. B. Webb, unpublished diaries, 27, Aug. 22, 1909, Passfield papers; Wells, *Anticipations*, p. 227.

89. Wells, *Anticipations*, pp. 124, 241-248, 256, 124, 253. An interpretation of the plight of the ego caught between wishes and "learned prohibitions," and the possible outcomes is offered in Weinstein and Platt, *The Wish to be Free*, pp. 38 ff.

90. Webb to Wells, Dec. 8, 1901, Wells papers, University of Illinois Library, Urbana.

91. For a perceptive discussion of Wells' "otherworldly bent" see Van Wyck Brooks, *The World of H. G. Wells* (New York, 1915), p. 36. The paper, "Locomotion and Administration," is included in Wells, *Works*, IV, 283-304.

92. The reaction of Beatrice Webb to Wells is discussed in MacKenzie, *Time Traveller*, pp. 170-172.

93. Wells, *Experiment in Autobiography*, pp. 510-511.

94. The correspondence between Wells and Shaw is cited and discussed in MacKenzie, *Time Traveller*, p. 186.

95. Wells, *A Modern Utopia*, *Works*, IX, 50, 161, 204. Freud notes the tendency for modern artists to split up their ego by self-observation into many component egos, and in this way to personify the conflicting tendencies in their own lives. See his essay, "The Uncanny" (1919).

96. Wells, *A Modern Utopia*, *Works*, IX, 93, 10.

97. Ibid., pp. 235 ff. According to Freud an author may "dwell in his own soul and look upon people from the outside," divide them sharply into types, and completely disregard the "manifest variety" of human beings. See "The Relation of the Poet to Day Dreaming" (1908).

98. Wells, *A Modern Utopia*, *Works*, IX, 115, 155, 32, 92.

99. The paper, "Scepticism of the Instrument," is included in *Works*, IX, 333-354.

100. Wells, *A Modern Utopia*, p. 246.

101. MacKenzie, *Time Traveller*, p. 129.

102. MacKenzie, *Time Traveller*, pp. 194-195, and Olivier to Wells, May 29, 1905, Wells papers.

103. The paper, "Misery of Boots," originally published in the *Independent Review*, December 1905, is included in *Works*, IV, 390-414.

104. S. G. Hobson to Wells, Nov. 10, 1905, Wells papers.

4. ETHICAL SOCIALISM, 1906-1908

1. John Paton, *Proletarian Pilgrimage* (London, 1935), p. 199.

2. For the strength of the Social Democrats see the *Socialist Annual* (Liverpool, 1909), p. 51. The ILP figures are drawn from the reports of the annual conferences. The peak *Clarion* circulation was reported in the issue of May 15, 1908.

3. *The Socialist Movement in Great Britain*, reprinted from the *London Times*, Jan. 3-19, 1909 (London, 1909), p. 54.

4. William Gallacher, *Revolt on the Clyde: An Autobiography* (London, 1936), p. 6.

5. *Albany Review*, September 1907; John Trevor, *The One Life* (Horsted Keynes, Eng., 1909).

6. Laurence Thompson, *Robert Blatchford* (London, 1951), p. 183. The *Sorcerer's Shop* was printed in serial form in the *Clarion* during 1906 and published in book form the following year. One student of utopianism, V. DuPont, viewed the book as the "best utopia in dialogue form since Plato." Quoted by Frederik Polak, *The Image of the Future* (New York, 1961), I, 358.

7. *New Age*, July 11, 1909; Edwin Muir, *An Autobiography* (New York, 1954), p. 113.

8. Victor Grayson was the most prominent of those who rejected the pulpit for the Socialist platform in the first decade of the century but others included Ernest Bevin, W. C. Anderson, J. T. Murphy, J. F. Green, and A. J. Cook. Some local leaders of the ILP, particularly in the mining areas, continued to serve as lay preachers but the contribution of such men to the growth of the movement has been exaggerated. The *Clarion* is the best source for news of the Labour Churches in these years. The Bradford experience is

reported in the *Clarion*, Feb. 9, 1906. See also Fred Reid, "Socialist Sunday Schools in Britain, 1892-1939," *International Review of Social History*, 11 (1966), 18-47.

9. *Clarion*, July 20, 1906.

10. Wells' influence is stressed in G. D. H. Cole, *History of Socialist Thought* (London, 1953-60), III, *The Second International, 1889-1914*, pt. 1, pp. 203-204.

11. Glasier's series of articles, later revised and published as the *Meaning of Socialism*, appeared in the *Labour Leader* during the spring of 1906. For the quotation see the issue of March 30, 1906. Keir Hardie, *From Serfdom to Socialism* (London, 1907), p. 89.

12. J. R. MacDonald to R. C. K. Ensor, Oct. 12, 1908. Ensor papers, Corpus Christi College, Oxford; Minutes of the National Administrative Council of the ILP, March, 1909, Archives of the Independent Labour Party, Bristol.

13. The results of the electoral agreement with the Liberals in Lancashire and Yorkshire are discussed in Philip Poirier, *Advent of Labour* (New York, 1958), pp. 253-257. See also P. F. Clarke, *Lancashire and the New Liberalism* (Cambridge, 1971), pp. 313-320; A. K. Russell, *Liberal Landslide: The General Election of 1906* (Newton Abbot, Eng., 1973), pp. 46-47; and Henry Pelling, *Social Geography of British Elections* (New York, 1967), pp. 288-307.

14. *Huddersfield Worker*, Jan. 5, 1907.

15. *Labour Leader*, Nov. 30, 1906; Glasier to Hardie, June 1, 1906, Glasier correspondence, Archives of the Independent Labour Party, Bristol.

16. Russell, *Liberal Landslide*, p. 47; Keir Hardie, "The Moral of Huddersfield," *Independent Review*, January 1907.

17. The fullest account of Grayson's life is Reginald Groves, *The Mystery of Victor Grayson* (London, 1946). Although Groves uses the story of Grayson to engage in polemics against the Labour Party, his book is based on extensive interviewing. Also see the campaign biography, Wilfred Thompson, *The Life of Victor Grayson* (Sheffield, 1910).

18. Percy Redfern, *Journey to Understanding* (London, 1946), p. 166. Redfern roomed with Grayson in Manchester at this time.

19. See Henry Pelling, *Popular Politics and Society in Late Victorian Britain* (London, 1968), pp. 136-137; Sam Eastwood to J. R. MacDonald, Dec. 10, 1906, Labour Party Letter Files, Transport House, London; D. F. E. Sykes, *The History of Colne Valley* (Slaithwaite, Eng., 1906), p. 356; *Huddersfield Worker*, Jan. 5, 1907.

20. *Huddersfield Worker*, Feb. 2, July 6, 1907; Ernest Lockwood, *Colne Valley Folk* (London, 1936), p. 143.

21. See the correspondence between Sam Eastwood and J. R. MacDonald, May, June, December 1906 and June 1907, Labour Party Letter Files. See also the minutes and correspondence of the N.A.C. of the ILP, February and July 1907, ILP Archives; Glasier to Lizzie Glasier, July 5, 1907, Glasier correspondence. The episode is described in Ross McKibbin, *The Evolution of the Labour Party* (Oxford, 1974), pp. 49-50.

22. Report by Snowden and James Howard, April 24, 1907, Labour Party Letter Files.

23. MacDonald to Edward Whiteley, July 10, 1907; MacDonald to Victor Grayson, June 27, 1907. Ibid.

24. Grayson to MacDonald, no date. Ibid.

25. *Yorkshire Factory Times*, July 10, 1907; Thompson, *Grayson*, p. 81.

26. *Huddersfield Worker*, July 27, 1907.

27. *Nation*, Aug. 3, 1907; W. T. Stead in the *Review of Reviews*, quoted by Lockwood, *Colne Valley Folk*, p. 78; *Daily Express*, July 20, 1907, and succeeding issues.

28. *Labour Leader*, July 26, Aug. 9, 1907; Annie Cobden Sanderson to MacDonald, July 25, 1907, Labour Party Letter Files; *Huddersfield Worker*, July 27, Aug. 3, 1907.

29. *Yorkshire Factory Times*, July 26, 1907.

30. One prominent example was John Glasse, minister of the Greyfriars church in Edinburgh, and a good friend of William Morris. He wrote several pamphlets for the movement, including *The Relationship of the Church to Socialism* (Edinburgh, 1900). See Hardie's tribute to Glasse in David Lowe, *Souvenirs of Scottish Labour* (Glasgow, 1919), p. 110. A report of Glasse's farewell sermon and a reminiscence appears in the *Christian Commonwealth*, Dec. 1, 1909. The contributions of clergymen to the movement are described most fully in Peter d'A. Jones, *The Christian Socialist Revival, 1877-1914* (Princeton, 1968).

31. Quoted in Sidney Dark, ed., *Conrad Noel: An Autobiography* (London, 1945), p. 128.

32. The formation of the community is described in G. L. Prestige, *Life of Charles Gore* (London, 1935), pp. 110, 145. See also C. S. Philips et al., *Walter Howard Frere: A Memoir* (London, n.d.), p. 44. For a report on the conference see *C. R.: A Chronicle of the Community of the Resurrection*, no. 14 (1906), and *Labour Leader*, May 11, Oct. 12, 1906.

33. Widdrington's account of the origins of the League appeared in *Commonwealth*, April and July 1927. Also see *Christendom*, March 1946, and Dark, *Noel*, p. 55. The League's activity is discussed in Jones, *Christian Socialist Revival*, pp. 225-292.

34. F. Lewis Donaldson, *Socialism and the Christian Faith* (London, n.d.), p. 7.

35. *The Optimist*, July 1911, p. 131; *Commonwealth*, April 1927. See also the sermons by Donaldson in W. Henry Hunt, ed., *Churchmanship and Labour* (London, 1906).

36. *Labour Leader*, June 28, 1907; *Yorkshire Factory Times*, July 26, 1907.

37. *Labour Leader*, June 22, 1907.

38. Sykes, *Colne Valley*, p. 234; Frederick R. Swan, *The Immanence of Christ in Modern Life* (London, 1907), pp. 109-110, 228-229; *Huddersfield Worker*, March 30, 1907.

39. *Huddersfield Worker*, March 23, 1907; Aug. 29, 1908; Sept. 14, 1907.

40. Ibid., Jan. 18, June 6, 1908.

41. They included *How I Became a Socialist*, I and II (Oxford, 1908), and *The Messiah Cometh Riding upon the Ass of Economics* (Huddersfield, 1909). See also *Christian Commonwealth*, Dec. 4, 1907. The quotations are drawn from *The Messiah Cometh*, pp. 9, 15, 18, and *How I Became a Socialist*, II, 29.

42. Arthur Porritt, *The Best I Remember* (London, 1922), p. 121.

43. *Labour Leader*, Jan. 18, 25, 1907.

44. Fenner Brockway, *Inside the Left* (London, 1942), p. 16; R. J. Campbell, *The New Theology and the Social Movement* (Liverpool, 1907).

45. R. J. Campbell, *Christianity and the Social Order* (London, 1907), pp. 118, vii, 126.

46. *Christian Commonwealth*, Feb. 10, 1909.

47. Ibid., Dec. 8, 15, 1909; Feb. 7, 14, April 5, 18, 1907. Shaw delivered several addresses in connection with the "new theology" movement. See *Christian Commonwealth*, Nov. 29, 1906, and May 23, 1907.

48. *Labour Leader*, July 10, 1908.

49. The Labour Party's work in Parliament is examined in H. A. Clegg, Alan Fox, and A. F. Thompson, *A History of British Trade Unions since 1889* (Oxford, 1964), I, 588 ff. See also J. H. S. Reid, *The Origins of the British Labour Party* (Minneapolis, 1955).

50. The resolution, introduced by Ben Tillett, was interpreted as a direct attack on the ILP. *Labour Leader*, Feb. 8, 1907.

51. Ibid., May 3, 1907.

52. Ibid., May 10, 17, 1907. H. T. Muggeridge criticized the ILP at this time for its intellectual sterility and failure to "throw any new or helpful light upon the difficulties with which our fellow Socialists on local bodies, in Parliament, or on the platform, are struggling in their efforts to apply our principles."

53. J. R. MacDonald, *The New Unemployed Bill of the Labour Party* (London, 1907), p. 15.

54. The development of the Socialist and trade unionist approach to the problem is discussed in José Harris, *Unemployment and Politics* (Oxford, 1972), pp. 239 ff., and Kenneth D. Brown. *Labour and Unemployment, 1900-1914* (London, 1971), pp. 37-84.

55. Hansard, *The Parliamentary Debates*, 4th ser., vol. 186 (March 13-March 27, 1908), cols. 32-35, 86, 63.

56. Ibid., cols. 18, 50, 57.

57. Ibid., cols. 22, 77-78.

58. *Labour Leader*, May 3, 1907; quoted by Brown, *Unemployment and Politics*, p. 117.

59. *Huddersfield Worker*, Oct. 26, 1907; *Labour Leader*, May 17, 1907.

60. *Labour Leader*, May 17, 31, 1907.

61. Ibid., May 24, 1907.

62. Stanley Salvidge, *Salvidge of Liverpool* (London, 1934), pp. 76-79. Clarke, *Lancashire and the New Liberalism*, pp. 45-52, places the episode within the larger context of Liverpool and Lancashire politics.

63. Blatchford's *Merrie England* evoked several counterattacks which relied rather strongly on religious arguments. See, for example, the anonymous series, *England's Ruin or John Smith's Answer to Mr. Blatchford's Plea for Socialism in "Merrie England,"* nos. 1-6 (London, 1894-96). By 1910 the Anti-Socialist Union had issued nearly one hundred tracts attacking socialism. Many of these linked socialism with atheism. See especially *The Case against Socialism: A Handbook for Speakers and Candidates*, London Municipal Society (London, 1908). The quotation is drawn from Joseph Rickaby, *The Creed of Socialism* (Bristol, 1910), p. 6. See also Kenneth Brown, "The Anti-Socialist Union," *Essays in Anti-Labour History* (London, 1974), ch. 10.

64. *Justice*, Oct. 19, 1907.

65. *Clarion*, Oct. 4, 1907; *New Age*, Oct. 3, 10, 1907.

66. *Labour Leader*, Oct. 4, 1907.

67. *Yorkshire Factory Times*, July 10, 1907; Frank Smith to Glasier, late 1907 or early 1908, Glasier correspondence. T. D. Benson, ILP treasurer, also expressed his fear that they were "sacrificing the general propaganda power of the party." *Labour Leader*, April 19, 1907.

68. Independent Labour Party, *Report of the Annual Conference*, 1908.

5. THE EXHAUSTION OF ETHICAL SOCIALISM

1. See the preface by Morris in Frank Fairman, *Socialism Made Plain* (London, 1889), and George Bernard Shaw, "The Illusions of Socialism," *Forecasts of the Coming Century*, ed. Edward Carpenter (Manchester, 1897), p. 160.

2. Robert Michels, *Political Parties* (New York, 1962), Collier ed., tr. Eden and Cedar Paul, p. 365. The personal animosities among the ILP leaders are described in Roland Kenney, *Westering* (London, 1939), pp. 120 ff. See also Laurence Thompson, *The Enthusiasts* (London, 1971), pp. 166 ff., 180-181, and Glasier's letters to his sister Lizzie in the Glasier correspondence, Archives of the Independent Labour Party, Bristol. The changing orientation of the political parties in these years is discussed in P. F. Clarke, *Lancashire and the New Liberalism* (Cambridge, 1971).

3. *Huddersfield Worker*, May 2, 1908.

4. *Labour Leader*, May 8, 1909; *Huddersfield Worker*, May 30, 1908.

5. *Huddersfield Worker*, May 23, Dec. 19, 1908.

6. *Labour Leader*, May 1, 1908.

7. *Justice*, Sept. 19, 26, 1908.

8. J. R. MacDonald to members of the National Administrative Council, n.d., James Ramsay MacDonald papers, Public Record Office, London.

9. *Labour Leader*, June 26, July 10, 1908.

10. Ibid., Sept. 18, 1908.

11. Ibid., July 10, Sept. 25, Oct. 9, 1908.

12. *Huddersfield Worker*, Sept. 26, 1908.

13. Will Thorne, *My Life's Battles* (London, 1925), p. 126; Hansard, *The Parliamentary Debates*, 4th ser., vol. 194 (Oct. 12 to Oct. 26, 1908), cols. 495-497, 631-634.

14. *Clarion*, Oct. 23, 1908; *Justice*, Oct. 31, 1908; *New Age*, Oct. 24, 1908. Plimsoll was the leader of a campaign to protect merchant seamen from unsafe ships. His scene in the House of Commons on July 22, 1875 was a notable precedent for others seeking to dramatize an issue through the disruption of parliamentary procedures. J. Fenner Brockway, *Inside the Left* (London, 1942), p. 24, tells of the excitement with which a Socialist meeting in London received the news of Grayson's scenes.

15. *Labour Leader*, Oct. 23, 30, 1908; J. R. MacDonald to Sam Gordon, Oct. 20, 1908. Labour Party Letter Files, Transport House, London.

16. Hardie to Glasier, Dec. 28, 1908. Glasier correspondence; Henry Pelling, *A Short History of the Labour Party* (London, 1965), p. 21. Also see H. A. Clegg, Alan Fox, and A. F. Thompson, *A History of British Trade Unions since 1889* (Oxford, 1964), I, 388-390, 406 ff.

17. Glasier to Lizzie Glasier, Oct. 30, 1908. Glasier correspondence; *New Age*, Oct. 29, 1908; *Labour Leader*, Dec. 18, 1908; *Christian Commonwealth*, April 7, 1908.

18. *Huddersfield Worker*, May 9, 1908; *Labour Leader*, Dec. 27, 1908.

19. *Huddersfield Worker*, Feb. 13, April 10, 1908; *Labour Leader*, March 5, 1909.

20. *Labour Leader*, April 16, 1909.

21. *Christian Commonwealth*, April 21, 1909. The use of the resignation to reinforce the power of the leadership is discussed in Michels, *Political Parties*, pp. 83-84.

22. *Labour Leader*, April 23, 1909.

23. Ibid., April 23, 30, 1909.

24. See the discussion of the Labour Party's parliamentary activity in Clegg, Fox, and Thompson, *A History of Trade Unions*, pp. 388-405.

25. *Christian Commonwealth*, April 28, 1909.

26. MacDonald published the letters at the suggestion of Max Beer, the London correspondent for *Vorwarts*, who had little sympathy for the British Social Democrats. See also *Labour Leader*, April 9, 1909; Keir Hardie, *My Confession of Faith in the Labour Alliance* (London, 1909), p. 13; and Glasier's articles in the *Labour Leader* during January 1909.

27. *Justice*, Sept. 3, 1910.

28. R. E. Dowse, *Left in the Centre: The Independent Labour Party, 1893-1940* (London, 1966), p. 19. The number of branches dropped from 887 to 672 between 1909 and 1914; affiliation fees fell off nearly 30 percent. For the declining commitment in the branches see *Huddersfield Worker*, Oct. 24, Dec. 12, 1908.

29. See Ray Gregory, *The Miners and British Politics, 1906-1914* (Oxford, 1968); Clegg, Fox, and Thompson, *A History of Trade Unions*, pp. 415-422; *Labour Leader*, June 14, 1914.

30. Leonard Hall et al., *Let Us Reform the Labour Party* (London, 1911). Hall, the son of a doctor, had worked as a journalist and labor organizer. At the time of his death he was described by Smart as "not made for civilization. His temperament would have forced him into a more adventuresome life had

not the Socialist movement provided him with an outline for his energies . . .
He held that rebellion . . . is always right, even if its theories are wrong."
Justice, July 6, 1916.

31. For the later development of the ILP see Dowse, *Left in the Centre.*

32. John Bruce Glasier, "Diary," Dec. 12, 1908, in possession of Malcolm
Glasier.

33. Hardie, *Confession of Faith*, pp. 12-13.

34. Hardie's attack on Leonard Hall in the *Labour Leader*, June 4, 1909,
led one veteran leader, Fred Hughes, to criticize Hardie for his lack of "fair
play and decency in discussion." See *Labour Leader*, June 11, 1909. Smart's
comment appears in the *Huddersfield Worker*, May 1, 1909; the epitaph for
Hardie in the *New Age*, April 1, 1909.

35. Kenneth Morgan, *Keir Hardie* (London, 1975), p. 234. For the views
of Hardie's colleagues see Glasier to MacDonald, Sept. 1, 1908, MacDonald
papers; Thompson, *Enthusiasts*, pp. 168, 172; T. D. Benson to MacDonald,
Sept. 1, 1908, MacDonald papers.

36. The episode is discussed in Morgan, *Hardie*, pp. 234-236; Thompson,
Enthusiasts, pp. 178-187; R. J. Holton, "Daily Herald v. Daily Citizen, 1912-
1915. The Struggle for a Labour Daily in Relation to the 'Labour Unrest,' " *International Review of Social History*, vol. 19 (1974), pt. 3, pp. 347-376.

37. See Kenneth Morgan, "The New Liberalism and the Challenge of
Labour: The Welsh Experience, 1885-1929," *Essays in Anti-Labour History*,
ed. Kenneth D. Brown (London, 1974), pp. 159-182. See also G. R. Williams,
"The Welsh Religious Revival, 1904-5," *British Journal of Sociology*, 3 (September 1952), 256-258.

38. See Fenner Brockway's remarks in *Christian Social Reformers of the
19th Century*, ed. Hugh Martin (London, 1927), p. 242.

39. *Labour Leader*, April 9, 1914; Glasier, "Diary," Jan. 22, 1909.

40. Glasier to MacDonald, Dec. 1, 1909, MacDonald papers.

41. Glasier, "Diary," Dec. 28, 1908, Jan. 22, 1909.

42. *Labour Leader*, April 9, 1909.

43. Glasier, "Diary," Feb. 14, 1909; Thompson, *Enthusiasts*, p. 165.

44. Glasier to MacDonald, Sept. 30, 1911, MacDonald papers.

45. J. Bruce Glasier, *The Meaning of Socialism* (Manchester, 1919), p.
224.

46. For a balanced account of MacDonald's role see David Marquand,
Ramsay MacDonald (London, 1977), chs. 6, 8.

47. *Labour Leader*, May 21, 1909. MacDonald's view of the relationships
of the ILP and socialism to the political process can also be found in his regular
column, "Outlooks," in the *Socialist Review*. In his *Socialism and Government* (London, 1909), MacDonald distinguishes between a Socialist party and
a party traveling toward socialism and suggests that the latter was more effective.

48. MacDonald to J. Phipps, Nov. 4, 1908, Labour Party Letter Files;
Labour Leader, May 21, 1909.

49. Russell Smart to MacDonald, n.d. 1909, MacDonald papers; Mac-

Donald to R. C. K. Ensor, June 22, 1909, Ensor papers, Corpus Christi College Library, Oxford.

50. Henderson's work is discussed in Ross McKibbin, *Evolution of the Labour Party, 1910-1924* (Oxford, 1974), p. 234.

51. The "containment" policy of the Liberal party is discussed by Neil Blewett, *The Peers, the Parties, and the People: The British General Elections of 1910* (Toronto, 1972), ch. 12. MacDonald's policies are assessed by Ross McKibbin, "James Ramsay MacDonald and the Problem of the Independence of the Labour Party, 1910-1914," *Journal of Modern History*, 42 (June 1970), 216-235.

52. T. D. Benson to MacDonald, Jan. 26, 1911, MacDonald papers. For a discussion of the different roles of the political leader see Samuel Beer, *British Politics in a Collectivist Age* (New York, 1965), pp. 105-108.

53. C. L. Mowat, "Ramsay MacDonald and the Labour Party," *Essays in Labour History*, 1886-1923, ed. Asa Briggs and John Saville (London, 1971), pp. 129-151; W. C. Anderson to MacDonald, Aug. 3, 1910, March 31, 1911, MacDonald papers.

54. *Huddersfield Worker*, Oct. 30, 1908.

55. In August 1907 Grayson was reported to have urged strikers in Belfast to use broken bottles against the police. He claimed later that he had been misquoted. As a result of the dispute he was strongly criticized by the Huddersfield branch of the National Union of Journalists. For details see *London Times*, Aug. 15-22, 1907. Victor Grayson, *The Destiny of the Mob* (Huddersfield, n.d.), pp. 9-10.

56. *Manchester Evening Chronicle*, March 2, 1908. See also Grayson's article, "Confessions of a Bon Vivant," *Labour Leader*, March 13, 1908, and S. G. Hobson, *Pilgrim to the Left* (London, 1938), p. 114.

57. *New Age*, April 4, Oct. 10, 1908.

58. *Clarion*, Sept. 25, 1908; Wilfred Thompson, *The Life of Victor Grayson* (Sheffield, 1910), p. 162.

59. H. M. Hyndman, *Further Reminiscences* (London, 1912), pp. 281 ff.; Hobson, *Pilgrim to the Left*, p. 115.

60. *Huddersfield Worker*, Feb. 13, 1909.

61. The disagreements within the Colne Valley Labour League are aired in the letters of Ben Riley to MacDonald during 1908 and 1909, MacDonald papers.

62. *Clarion*, March 18, 1910.

63. See Reginald Groves, *The Mystery of Victor Grayson* (London, 1945). See also Hobson, *Pilgrim to the Left*, pp. 114 ff.

64. *Huddersfield Worker*, Oct. 24, 1908; Karl Mannheim, *Ideology and Utopia* (London, 1936), p. 196.

65. Percy Widdrington in *Commonwealth*, July 1927.

66. *The Optimist* (July 1908), pp. 212 ff. Later in 1908 this Anglican paper became the *Church Socialist Quarterly* and the official organ of the League.

67. *Church Socialist Quarterly*, January 1910, January, April 1911; *Commonwealth*, July 1927.

68. For biographical details see Maurice G. Tucker, *John Neville Figgis: A Study* (London, 1950), and the introductory essay by G. R. Elton in J. N. Figgis, *The Divine Right of Kings* (New York, 1965).

69. J. N. Figgis, *The Gospel and Human Needs* (London, 1907), p. x.

70. Ibid., pp. 47, 72.

71. Ibid., pp. 9, 11; J. N. Figgis, *Civilization at the Crossroads* (London, 1911), p. 70.

72. Ibid., p. 88.

73. J. N. Figgis, *Churches in the Modern State* (London, 1913), pp. 31-33. For an analysis of the social philosophy of Figgis see Henry Magid, *English Political Pluralism* (New York, 1941).

74. *Christian Commonwealth*, June 23, 1909.

75. Ibid., May 19, 1909.

76. Ibid., Oct. 9, 1910. See Campbell's presidential address in this issue.

77. R. J. Campbell, *A Spiritual Pilgrimage* (London, 1916), p. 153. See also the article by one of Campbell's close associates, K. C. Anderson, "The Collapse of Liberal Christianity," *Hibbert Journal*, January 1910.

78. There are two studies of Forsyth: Robert M. Brown, *P. T. Forsyth: Prophet for Today* (Philadelphia, 1952), and William Bradley, *P. T. Forsyth* (London, 1952).

79. P. T. Forsyth, "Calvinism and Capitalism," *Contemporary Review* (July 1910), p. 77.

80. P. T. Forsyth, "The Insufficiency of Social Righteousness as a Moral Ideal," *Hibbert Journal* (July 1908), pp. 609-611, 603.

81. Ibid., p. 601; P. T. Forsyth, "A Holy Church: The Moral Guide of Society," *Congregational Year Book* (London, 1906), p. 31.

82. P. T. Forsyth, *Socialism: The Church and the Poor* (London, 1908), pp. 27-29, 56.

83. J. Middleton Murry, *New English Weekly*, 5 (Nov. 15, 1934); for biographical background see Philip Mairet, *A. R. Orage: A Memoir*, rev. ed. (New York, 1966); Wallace Martin, *The New Age under Orage* (Manchester, 1967); Tom Gibbons, *Rooms in the Darwin Hotel* (Nedlands, Western Australia, 1973), ch. 4; Samuel Hynes, *Edwardian Occasions* (New York, 1972), pp. 39-47.

84. *Labour Leader*, Jan. 18, 1896; Orage to Edward Carpenter, Feb. 3, 1896, Edward Carpenter correspondence and papers, Sheffield Public Library, Sheffield.

85. Orage's relationship to the theosophy movement and his intellectual development in these years is discussed in Gibbons, *Rooms in the Darwin Hotel.* See also Wallace Martin, ed., *Orage as Critic* (London, 1974), pp. 6-7.

86. *Fabian News*, July 1898.

87. Mairet, *Orage*, p. 22.

88. Charles Frederick Kenyon, *Set Down in Malice* (New York, 1919), pp. 130-132.

89. A. R. Orage, *Consciousness: Animal, Human and Superman* (London, 1907), pp. 76, 83.

90. Ibid., p. 85.

91. A. R. Orage, *Nietzsche in Outline and Aphorism* (London, 1907), p. 123. The impact of Nietzsche on Orage is discussed in David S. Thatcher, *Nietzsche in England* (Toronto, 1970), pp. 243-264. See also Patrick Bridgwater, *Nietzsche in AngloSaxony* (Leicester, 1972), chs. 7, 10.

92. A. R. Orage, *Friedrich Nietzsche: The Dionysian Spirit of the Age* (London, 1906), pp. 28, 59.

93. Orage, *Nietzsche in Outline*, pp. 20, 47, 89, 43.

94. Edwin Muir, *An Autobiography* (London, 1954), p. 126.

95. *New Age*, Oct. 3, 10, 1907.

96. Ibid., Oct. 10, 1907.

97. Ibid., Nov. 14, 1907.

98. Ibid., Oct. 3, Nov. 7, 1907.

99. Ibid., April 18, May 2, 1908.

100. Ibid., June 13, 1908.

101. Ibid., Oct. 24, 1908.

102. Hardie, *My Confession of Faith*, p. 14.

103. *New Age*, Feb. 3, 1910, May 14, 1911, May 16, 1912.

104. Ibid., May 14, 1911.

6. Ethical Socialists

1. *New Age*, Feb. 3, 1910.

2. Stanley James, "Arthur Penty: Architect and Sociologist," *American Review*, 9 (April 1937), 83-85.

3. A. J. Penty, *The Restoration of the Guild System* (London, 1906), p. 4.

4. Ibid., pp. 46, 57, 73.

5. Ibid., pp. 90, 42, 29.

6. Ibid., pp. 45, 43.

7. Ibid., p. 9.

8. Penty to H. G. Wells, July 23, 1906. H. G. Wells papers, University of Illinois Library, Urbana. A copy of the prospectus is included with the letter.

9. A. R. Orage, "Politics for Craftsmen," *Contemporary Review*, 5 (June 1907), 782-794.

10. Philip Mairet, *A. R. Orage: A Memoir*, rev. ed. (New York, 1966), p. 42.

11. *New Age*, Aug. 25, Oct. 20, 1910.

12. Ibid., Oct. 12, Aug. 31, 1911.

13. Ibid., March 7, Feb. 22, Jan. 18, 1912.

14. The fictional portrayals of Hobson include "Horace Meldrum" in H. R. Barbor, *Against the Red Sky* (London, 1922); "Ryan" in Paul Selver, *Private Life* (London, 1929); and "Gallacher" in C. E. Bechofer-Roberts, *Let's Begin Again* (London, 1940). Beatrice Webb refers to Hobson as one of her pet aversions in her unpublished diaries, 35, Feb. 18, 1920, Passfield papers, British Library of Political and Economic Science, London. See also C. B. Purdom, *Life over Again* (London, 1951), pp. 144, 279.

15. The talk was published in the *International Socialist Review*, 9 (September 1908), as "Confessions of a New Fabian," pp. 184-197. References are to pp. 186, 191.

16. Barbor, *Against the Red Sky*, pp. 237-238; *New Age*, Nov. 30, 1911, Feb. 15, 1912.

17. Notes refer to the published version of the articles, S. G. Hobson, *National Guilds*, ed. A. R. Orage (London, 1919), pp. 4, 44, 212, 106.

18. Ibid., pp. 273, 212.

19. G. D. H. Cole, *A History of Socialist Thought*, III, *The Second International, 1889-1914* (London, 1953-60), pt. 1, p. 243.

20. Hobson, *National Guilds*, pp. 64, 218, 133, 56, 258.

21. Ibid., pp. 10, 5, 20, 98.

22. *New Age*, Aug. 28, Sept. 11, 1913.

23. For Cole's intellectual development see L. P. Carpenter, *G. D. H. Cole* (Cambridge, 1973), and J. M. Winter, *Socialism and the Challenge of War* (London, 1974), chs. 4, 5.

24. Anthony Farley [S. G. Hobson], *Letters to My Nephew* (London, 1917), p. 306.

25. See Frank Mathews, "The Building Guilds," *Essays in Labour History*, ed. Asa Briggs and John Saville (London, 1971), pp. 284-331. Additional information can be found in S. T. Glass, *The Responsible Society* (London, 1966); Niles Carpenter, *Guild Socialism* (New York, 1922); Branko Pribicevic, *The Shop Stewards Movement and Workers' Control, 1910-1922* (Oxford, 1959). See also Hobson's articles in the *Guildsman*, March 1920, December 1921, and June 1923.

26. R. E. Dowse, *Left in the Centre* (London, 1966), pp. 65-69.

27. Hobson's funeral is described in Purdom, *Life over Again*, p. 279. The quotation is from Farley, *Letters to My Nephew*, p. 306.

28. *New Age*, July 11, 1912.

29. Ibid., March 17, Sept. 22, Aug. 25, 1910.

30. Ibid., Oct. 20, 1910, Jan. 9, 1913.

31. Ibid., June 2, Oct. 20, 1910.

32. Ibid., Nov. 24, 1910, Nov. 21, 1912, May 25, 1911, July 11, 1912, Dec. 14, 1911, May 22, 1911, July 18, 1912.

33. Ibid., Sept. 21, 1911, Sept. 22, 1910, May 22, 1913, Oct. 17, 24, 1912.

34. Ibid., July 13, 1911, Nov. 3, 1910.

35. Ibid., March 9, 1911, May 23, Sept. 12, 1912.

36. Ibid., Jan. 8, May 12, May 30, 1912, July 24, 1913.

37. Ibid., Sept. 7, June 8, 1911.

38. Ibid., Sept. 5, 1912.

39. Ibid., Dec. 18, 1913.

40. Ibid., Nov. 13, 1913.

41. Ibid., Nov. 21, 1912.

42. Ibid., March 9, 1911, Dec. 5, 1912.

43. Ibid., Feb. 8, 1912.

44. Ibid., May 2, 1912, Jan. 23, March 15, 1913.

45. Beatrice Hastings, *The Old "New Age": Orage and Others* (London, 1936), p. 10. Miss Hastings' harsh judgments about Orage reflected the bitterness of their parting. But her assessment is confirmed at critical points by C. E. Bechofer-Roberts in his fictional portrayal of Orage as "Whitworth" in *Life Begins Again.* See especially pp. 183-185, 198-203. For the other citations see *New Age*, Feb. 16, 1911; Edwin Muir, *An Autobiography* (London, 1954), pp. 170-175, 181; *New English Review* (Nov. 15, 1934).

46. Ibid., Aug. 14, 1913, May 30, 1912, July 31, 1913; G. D. H. Cole, *The World of Labour* (London, 1913).

47. Several recent studies have examined Orage's work as a literary critic. See Wallace Martin, *The New Age under Orage* (Manchester, 1967), ch. 2, and his Introduction to the volume *Orage as Critic*, ed. Wallace Martin (London, 1974). See also Tom Gibbons, *Rooms in the Darwin Hotel* (Nedlands, Western Australia, 1973, ch. 4. Three collections of Orage's articles were published: *Readers and Writers, 1917-1921* (New York, 1922), *The Art of Reading* (New York, 1930), and *Selected Essays and Critical Writings*, ed. Herbert Read and Dennis Seurat (London, 1935).

48. Orage to George Bernard Shaw, Jan. 30, 1911, Shaw papers, British Museum, London; *New Age*, July 20, 1911, Nov. 13, 1913.

49. *New Age*, June 12, 1913, Feb. 15, 1912.

50. Ibid., May 18, 1911.

51. Ibid., July 27, 1911, May 21, 1914, Sept. 25, 1913.

52. Ibid., Jan. 8, 1914. See also the discussion of Orage's work as a critic in Martin, *New Age under Orage*, ch. 13.

53. Phillip Mairet, *A. R. Orage: A Memoir*, rev. ed. (New York, 1966), p. 75. For an account of Douglas's scheme see John L. Finlay, *Social Credit: The English Origins* (London, 1972). Its relationship to Orage and the *New Age* is discussed in Chapter 4.

54. *New Age*, May 8, 1913.

55. Orage, *Readers and Writers*, p. 153.

56. The quotations are drawn from Roland Kenney, *Westering* (London, 1939), pp. 328 ff.; and C. S. Nott, *Teachings of Gurdjieff* (London, 1961), pp. 27, 65, 77, 151.

57. Orage to Herbert Read, Sept. 19, 1922, Herbert Read papers, University of Victoria Library, Victoria, British Columbia. Orage's life at Gurdjieff's institute is described in Nott, *Teachings of Gurdjieff*.

58. A. R. Orage, "An Editor's Progress," *Commonweal*, Feb. 10, 17, 24, March 3, 1926.

59. C. S. Nott, *Journey through This World* (London, 1969), pp. 16-18; Mairet, *Orage*, p. 99.

60. Orage's separation, at Gurdjieff's insistence, from his New York congregation is described in Nott, *Journey through This World*, pp. 15-16.

61. *Selected Letters of Edwin Muir*, ed. P. H. Butter (London, 1974), p. 80; Nott, *Journey through This World*, p. 37; Martin, *Orage as Critic*, p. 14.

62. Eric Gill, *Autobiography* (London, 1940), pp. 94-98.

63. Ibid., pp. 110-111, 113.

64. *New English Weekly*, Nov. 15, 1934; Eric Gill, "The Failure of the Arts and Crafts Movement," *Socialist Review*, 4 (December 1909), 290.

65. Gill, "Failure of the Arts and Crafts Movement," pp. 298-300.

66. Gill, "A Preface to an Unwritten Book," *The Highway*, 3.25 (October 1910), p. 5; Gill, *Autobiography*, p. 144.

67. Gill, "Church and State," *The Highway*, 27 (December 1910), 45-46.

68. Gill, "Masters and Servants," ibid., 26 (November 1910), 23-24.

69. Gill to E. R. Pease, Jan. 19, 1911. Shaw papers.

70. Gill to William Rothenstein, Dec. 12, 1910, *Letters of Eric Gill*, ed. Walter Shewing (London, 1947), pp. 34-36.

71. Gill, *Autobiography*, pp. 166, 271-272.

72. Ibid., p. 164. The affinities between Gill and D. H. Lawrence are discussed in Rayner Heppenstall, *Four Absentees* (London, 1960), p. 195. See also Robert Speaight, *The Life of Eric Gill* (New York, 1966), pp. 118, 166.

73. Shewing, *Letters*, pp. 43-44; Speaight, *Life of Gill*, pp. 61-62.

74. *The Game: An Occasional Magazine*, 1 (October 1916), 3-4; Gill to Henry Atkinson, June 20, 1917, *Letters*, pp. 90-91.

75. Shewing, *Letters*, pp. 97, 133.

76. The Ditchling community is discussed in Speaight, *Life of Eric Gill*, pp. 110 ff. See also the *Letters*, p. 133.

77. Speaight, *Life of Eric Gill*, pp. 109, 113, 146, 221.

78. According to Gill, Morris failed, for all his greatness, to perceive "the point at which humanity was corrupted" and hence rested his gospel on sentiment. See Speaight, *Life of Eric Gill*, p. 266.

79. Quoted by Speaight, *Life of Eric Gill*, p. 276.

80. Cushing Strout, "Ego Psychology and the Historian," *History and Theory*, 7 (1968), 289-290.

81. Ludwig Binswanger, "The Existential Analysis School of Thought," trans. Ernest Angel, *Existence*, ed. Rollo May, Ernest Angel, Henry F. Ellenberger (New York, 1958), pp. 206-207.

82. Muir, *Autobiography*, p. 104.

83. Ibid., p. 124.

84. Edwin Muir, *Poor Tom* (London, 1930), pp. 101-105; 121. The episode is also treated in the *Autobiography*, pp. 110ff. The relationship between Muir's novels and his life is discussed by Elgin Mellown, "Autobiographical Themes in the Novels of Edwin Muir," *Wisconsin Studies in Comparative Literature*, 6 (Summer 1965), 228-242.

85. Muir, *Autobiography*, p. 123.

86. Ibid., pp. 144-145.

87. *New Age*, Dec. 11, 1913.

88. Ibid., Dec. 18, 1913.

89. Muir, *Autobiography*, pp. 126-127.

90. Ibid., pp. 149-150. See also Willa Muir, *Belonging*, p. 24.

91. Many of Edward Moore's aphorisms were published as *We Moderns* (London, 1920), from which I have drawn the quotations.

92. Ibid., pp. 59, 92.

93. Ibid., p. 92.

94. Muir, *Autobiography*, p. 151.

95. Ibid., pp. 157-159, 128.

96. *Guildsman*, March 1918; *New Age*, Sept. 2, 1920.

97. Muir, *Poor Tom*, pp. 189-190.

98. Ibid., pp. 164-165, 191-192, 235-236.

99. Willa Muir, *Belonging*, p. 48.

100. Muir, *Poor Tom*, p. 254.

101. Michael Hamburger, "Edwin Muir," *Encounter* (December 1960), 46-53.

102. Muir's poetic development is traced in Elizabeth Huberman, *The Poetry of Edwin Muir* (New York, 1971). See also R. P. Blackburn, "Edwin Muir: Between the Tiger's Paws," *Kenyon Review*, 21 (1959), 419-436.

103. Muir to Stephen Spender, July-November 1936, *Selected Letters of Edwin Muir*, p. 83.

104. See the somewhat different assessments of Muir's final views on life in Huberman, *Poetry of Edwin Muir*, pp. 214 ff.; Hamburger, "Edwin Muir," pp. 51-53; and P. H. Butter, *Edwin Muir* (London, 1966), pp. 114-117.

105. Herbert Read, *The Cult of Sincerity* (New York, 1968), pp. 178-184.

106. Herbert Read, *The Contrary Experience* (London, 1963), pp. 49, 54.

107. Ibid., pp. 161-167.

108. Ibid., p. 201; *New Age*, June 17, 1915.

109. Part 2 in Read's autobiography, *The Contrary Experience*, covering the years 1915 to 1918, consists of letters written to a friend in Leeds. For the quotations in this section see pp. 70 ff.

110. *New Age*, June 8, 1916; Read, *Contrary Experience*, p. 93.

111. *The Guildsman*, April 1917.

112. Read, *Contrary Experience*, pp. 65, 77, 82.

113. Ibid., p. 124.

114. Ibid., p. 102. Correspondence between Orage and Read regarding the latter's role on the *New Age* can be found in the Read papers.

115. For Read's view of poetry and criticism see Worth Travis Harder, *A Certain Order: The Development of Herbert Read's Theory of Poetry* (The Hague, 1971). The quotations are on pp. 20, 58-59. See also Kathleen Raine, "Herbert Read as a Literary Critic," *Sewanee Review*, 77 (Summer 1969), 405-425.

116. Read, *Contrary Experience*, pp. 169 ff.; Harder, *A Certain Order*, pp. 95 ff.

117. Read, *Contrary Experience*, pp. 345, 193; Harder, *A Certain Order*, pp. 111-119, 134.

118. Herbert Read, *The Green Child* (New York, 1948), pp. 117-118, 137, 149, 173, 180, 176. In his biographical study, *Herbert Read: The Stream and the Source* (London, 1972), George Woodcock offers a very different interpretation from that suggested here. He argues that the novel is a study of the hatred of life and attributes the death of Olivero to his destruction of his vital other self. See pp. 71 ff. But see also Harder, *A Certain Order*, p. 139, and W.

R. Irwin, *The Game of the Impossible* (Urbana, 1966), pp. 134-138.

119. Read, *Green Child*, pp. 173, 180, 176, 193.

120. Read, *Contrary Experience*, pp. 28, 351.

121. Ibid., p. 69; Woodcock, *Herbert Read*, pp. 57, 15.

7. British Marxists

1. H. M. Hyndman to G. Wilshire, Jan. 20, 1906, Wilshire papers, microfilm copies in the British Library of Political and Economic Science, London; Hyndman to M. Hillquit, March 28, 1906, Hillquit papers, Wisconsin Historical Society, Madison.

2. Harry Quelch, *The SDF: Its Objectives, Its Principles, and Its Work* (London, 1907), p. 191; The Social Democratic initiative in the cause of the unemployed is discussed in Kenneth Brown, *Labour and Unemployment, 1900-1914* (London, 1971), pp. 97 ff.

3. *Social Democrat*, October 1907.

4. Ibid., August 1909; T. Rothstein to K. Kautsky, May 18, 1909, Dec. 13, 1909, Kautsky correspondence, International Institute for Social History, Amsterdam.

5. Hyndman's lectures are printed in *Justice* during November and December, 1907; Hyndman to Kautsky, May 15, 1911, Kautsky correspondence.

6. *Social Democrat*, May 1909; Hyndman to Kautsky, May 11, 1911. Kautsky correspondence. See also C. Tsuzuki, *H. M. Hyndmann and British Socialism* (Oxford, 1961), ch. 10; Walter Kendall, *The Revolutionary Movement in Britain, 1900-1921* (London, 1969), ch. 3; Norman Etherington, "Hyndman: The Social Democratic Federation, and Imperialism," *Historical Studies*, 16 (April 1974), 89-103.

7. *Justice*, July 27, 1907, Oct. 3, 1908.

8. *Justice*, Oct. 31, 1908; *Social Democrat*, November 1908; *Justice*, Sept. 18, 1909.

9. *Justice*, April 4, 1908.

10. Ibid., April 4, 11, 1908.

11. *Social Democrat*, March 1908.

12. *Justice*, Feb. 19, 1910; Social Democratic Party, *Report of the Annual Conference*, 1910, pp. 4-6; *Social Democrat*, March 1911; *Justice*, Jan. 29, 1910.

13. *Social Democrat*, March 1910; Social Democratic Party, *Report of the Annual Conference*, 1910, p. 11; *Justice*, June 25, 1910.

14. *Justice*, July 2, 1910.

15. *Social Democrat*, April 29, 1911; *Justice*, Jan. 21, Sept. 9, July 22, 1911. The resistance of various sections of the working classes to the Socialist appeal has been discussed in several recent studies. See Gareth Stedman Jones, *Outcast London* (Oxford, 1971), ch. 19, and especially his "Working-Class Culture and Working-Class Politics in London, 1870-1900: Notes on the Remaking of a Working Class," *Journal of Social History*, 7.4 (Summer 1974), 460-508. See also Paul Thompson, *The Edwardians* (London, 1975), chs. 15,

16; and Standish Meacham, *A Life Apart* (Cambridge, Mass., 1977), ch. 7.

16. *Justice*, January 21, April 8, 1911.

17. For accounts of the SLP's development in these years see Kendall, *The Revolutionary Movement in Britain*, ch. 4; D. W. Chewter, "The History of the Socialist Labour Party in Great Britain from 1902 to 1921," B. Litt. thesis, Oxford, 1966; Eugene Burdick, "Syndicalism and Industrial Unionism in England until 1918," D. Phil. thesis, Oxford, 1950. Further details are provided in Raymond Challinor, *The Origins of British Bolshevism* (London, 1977), pp. 177 ff.

18. *The Socialist Labour Party: Its Aims and Methods* (Edinburgh, 1908), pp. 9-10.

19. *Socialist*, March 1906.

20. T. Bell, *Pioneering Days* (London, 1941), pp. 27-28; Nan Milton, *John Maclean* (Bristol, 1973), pp. 19-20.

21. Bell, *Pioneering Days*, p. 42; *Socialist*, December 1907; Kendall, *Revolutionary Movement in Britain*, p. 72.

22. *Socialist*, November 1907, November 1909, March 1906.

23. *Socialist*, October 1905; *The Socialist Labour Party*, p. 23.

24. See Chewter, "History of the Socialist Labour Party," pp. 65 ff.; J. Carstairs Matheson to James Connolly, April 12, 1908, James Connolly papers, National Library of Ireland, Dublin.

25. *Socialist*, December 1908; Chewter, "History of the Socialist Labour Party," p. 90.

26. Connolly to Matheson, Dec. 20, April 8, 1908; June 10, 1909, Connolly papers.

27. *Socialist*, March, April, 1910, February 1911.

28. Kendall, *Revolutionary Movement in Britain*, pp. 72-74; see also James Hinton, *The First Shop Stewards' Movement* (London, 1973), p. 124; I. S. McLean, "The Labour Movement in Clydeside Politics, 1914-1922," D. Phil thesis, Oxford, 1971, pp. 152 ff.

29. *Socialist*, January 1910.

30. *Industrial Syndicalist*, July 1910. British syndicalism is examined in Burdick, "Syndicalism and Industrial Unionism." See also Chewter, "History of the Socialist Labour Party," pp. 95 ff.

31. *Industrial Syndicalist*, July, August 1910, January 1911; *Justice*, Sept. 10, 1910.

32. *Industrial Syndicalist*, July 1910; *Socialist*, February 1911.

33. Burdick, "Syndicalism and Industrial Unionism," p. 227; J. T. Murphy, *New Horizons* (London, 1941), p. 42; *Justice*, November 11, Oct. 7, 1911; *Anarchist*, May 3, 1912; *Syndicalist*, May 1912.

34. Hyndman to Wilshire, Oct. 13, 1911, Wilshire papers. *Justice*, July 18, 1911.

35. For accounts of the conference see H. W. Lee and E. Archbold, *Social Democracy in Britain* (London, 1935), pp. 176-180; Tsuzuki, *Hyndman and British Socialism*, pp. 174-176.

36. *Justice*, Oct. 28, 1911.

37. Ibid., Nov. 11, 25, 1911.

38. Ibid., Dec. 2, 9, 16, 23, 30, 1911.

39. Leonard Hall to Williams, October 1911; Leonard Hall, "The Strike and the Vote," "Industrial Unionism," and unidentified newspaper clippings. All are in the British Socialist Party papers.

40. Hyndman to Wilshire, Jan. 26, April 4, 1912, Wilshire papers. Mann's letter of resignation appears in the *Social Democrat*, September 1911.

41. *Justice*, Aug. 3, 17, March 9, 1912.

42. Irene San Carlos in *Social Democrat*, July 1912.

43. *Justice*, Nov. 2, 16, 1912; letter from F. B. Silvester to an unidentified newspaper; the clipping is in the British Socialist Party papers.

44. *Justice*, March 29, 1913.

45. *Justice*, Aug. 9, April 4, May 31, 1913. See also the reports on the BSP in the *Socialist Annual* in 1913 and 1914.

46. *Justice*, July 12, 19, 1913.

47. Ibid., July 26, 1913.

48. *Fabian News*, August 1914.

49. These tensions within the BSP are discussed in Kendall, *Revolutionary Movement in Britain*, ch. 3.

50. *Justice*, March 9, 1916.

51. Ibid., Oct. 1, 22, 1914; H. M. Hyndman and E. Belfort Bax, "Socialism, Materialism and the War," *English Review*, 29 (December 1914), 52-69.

52. Ibid., July 22, 1911, Sept. 10, 1914, Jan. 28, 1915.

53. *Socialist Record*, April 1913; *Justice*, Jan. 15, 1915. For discussions of the patriotic offshoot of Social Democracy see Roy Douglas, "The National Democratic Party and the British Workers' League," *Historical Journal*, 15 (1972), 533-552, and J. O. Stubbs, "Lord Milner and Patriotic Labour," *English Historical Review*, 87 (October 1972), 717-754.

54. Kendall, *Revolutionary Movement in Britain*, pp. 92-98. See also James Hulse, *The Formation of the Communist International* (Stanford, 1964), ch. 1.

55. *Call*, March 23, 1916; *Justice*, Jan. 20, 1916.

56. Contrasting perspectives on the conference can be found in the *Call*, May 4, 1916, and *Justice*, April 27, 1916. See also Tsuzuki, *Hyndman and British Socialism*, pp. 233-235, and Kendall, *Revolutionary Movement in Britain*, ch. 6.

57. *Justice*, June 8, 1916.

58. Ibid., Sept. 23, 1910. Quelch is quoted in Kendall, *Revolutionary Movement in Britain*, p. 176.

59. For Maclean's agitation against the war see Nan Milton, *John Maclean* (Bristol, 1973), pp. 79-117, and Kendall, *Revolutionary Movement in Britain*, pp. 88-120.

60. See especially Hinton, *First Shop Stewards' Movement*. See also Kendall, *Revolutionary Movement in Britain*, chs. 7, 8; Chewter, "History of the Socialist Labour Party"; McLean, "Labour Movement in Clydeside Politics."

61. Hinton, *First Shop Stewards' Movement*, p. 100.

62. Ibid., p. 68.

63. Ibid., pp. 96-99.

64. The formation of the committee is discussed in McLean, "Labour Movement in Clydeside Politics," pp. 16 ff.

65. Kendall, *Revolutionary Movement in Britain*, p. 133, McLean, "Labour Movement in Clydeside Politics," discounts the influence of Maclean.

66. See Milton, *Maclean*, for the fullest account of his career. See also Tom Bell, *John Maclean* (Glasgow, 1944).

67. *Justice*, Sept. 10, 1914.

68. Maclean's relationship with the Clyde Workers' Committee is described and judged differently by Hinton, *First Shop Stewards' Movement*, pp. 123-133, Kendall, *Revolutionary Movement in Britain*, pp. 118-122, and McLean, "Labour Movement in Clydeside Politics."

69. Rothstein is quoted in Hinton, *First Shop Stewards' Movement*, pp. 239-240.

70. British Socialist Party, *Report of the Seventh Annual Conference*, 1918, pp. 15, 30, 27.

71. Ibid., 34.

72. Quoted in Kendall, *Revolutionary Movement in Britain*, p. 134.

73. Hinton, *First Shop Stewards' Movement*, p. 306.

74. Kendall, *Revolutionary Movement in Britain*, p. 297. See Hinton's criticism of Kendall's interpretation in the *Society for the Study of Labour History Bulletin*, 19 (Autumn 1969), 42-49.

75. Hinton, *First Shop Stewards' Movement*, p. 324.

76. Guy Aldred quoted in Milton, *Maclean*, p. 13.

77. Ibid., p. 25.

78. Ibid., pp. 118-121, 204-205, 234-236, 295-296.

79. Ibid., pp. 149 ff.; British Socialist Party, *Report of the Seventh Annual Conference* (1918), p. 16.

80. Quoted in Milton, *Maclean*, pp. 248-250; Kendall, *Revolutionary Movement in Britain*, p. 202.

81. Milton, *Maclean*, p. 217.

82. *Vanguard*, December, May, 1920.

83. Ibid., November 1920.

84. Ibid., December 1920. The response of the SLP to these developments is discussed in Challinor, *Origins of British Bolshevism*, pp. 195 ff.

85. Ibid., December 1920.

86. Maclean to James Clunie, Nov. 24, 1922. This correspondence is included in an appendix in James Clunie, *The Voice of Labour* (Dumferline, 1958), pp. 81-101.

87. For Gallacher's views see his books, *Revolt on the Clyde* (London, 1936), pp. 124, 214-215, and *Last Memories* (London, 1966), p. 153. Support for Gallacher's view of Maclean is presented by McLean, "Labour Movement in Clydeside Politics," pp. 224-242. The other quotations are drawn from Maclean's letters to Clunie, *Voice of Labour*, pp. 81-101.

88. John Maclean to Agnes Maclean, Aug. 28, Oct. 14, 1923; Agnes Mac-

lean to John Maclean, Oct. 29, Nov. 7, 14, 1923, Maclean papers, National Library of Scotland, Glasgow. Most of these quotations also appear in Milton, *Maclean*, pp. 292-304.

89. Sylvia Pankhurst is quoted by Milton, *Maclean*, p. 297. See also p. 291.

90. Snowden is quoted by Milton, *Maclean*, p. 13. The contrasting views of Maclean are also presented in A. McArthur and H. Kingsley Long, *No Mean City* (Glasgow, 1935), p. 181. See also "John Maclean," *Collected Poems of Hugh MacDiarmid* (New York, 1962), pp. 242-243.

91. Tsuzuki, *Hyndman*, pp. 233 ff.

92. Ibid., p. 260; Hyndman to Charles E. Russell, Dec. 19, 1919, Charles E. Russell papers, Library of Congress, Washington, D.C.

93. Hyndman to A. M. Simons, April 1917, Algernon Simons papers, Wisconsin State Historical Society, Madison.

94. *Justice*, May 1, 1909.

95. Hyndman to George Bernard Shaw, Jan. 2, 1914, Shaw papers, British Museum, London; R. T. Hyndman, *The Last Years of H. M. Hyndman* (London, 1923), pp. 266 ff., 239 ff.; Hyndman to A. M. Simons, April 1917, Simons papers.

96. Hyndman, *Last Years of H. M. Hyndman*, pp. 122, 95 ff. His classical and functional approach to society, as contrasted with Romantic or medieval approaches, is apparent in his *Introduction to the Life to Come* (London, 1926). The essay was written in 1913.

97. Hyndman to Shaw, n.d. 1920, Shaw papers; Hyndman to Russell, Dec. 19, 1919, Russell papers.

98. Hyndman to Russell, June 1918, Jan. 5, 1920, July 26, 1920, Russell papers.

99. Hyndman to Shaw, n.d. 1920, Shaw papers; Hyndman to Russell, July 20, 1921, Russell papers.

100. Lee and Archbold, *Social Democracy in England*, pp. 242 ff; Tsuzuki, *Hyndman*, p. 262.

101. Lee and Archbold, *Social Democracy in England*, p. 271.

8. THE FABIAN CONVERSION TO PARTY POLITICS

1. H. T. Muggeridge to G. R. S. Taylor, Jan. 7, 1907. Fabian Society Archives, Nuffield College, Oxford.

2. Sidney Webb to H. G. Wells, June 15, 1907, Wells papers, University of Illinois Library, Urbana.

3. Henry Macrosty to L. Haden Guest, Dec. 17, 1906, Fabian Society Archives.

4. H. T. Muggeridge to G. R. S. Taylor, Jan. 7, 1907, Fabian Society Archives; Hubert Bland, *Socialism and the Labour Policy* (London, 1906).

5. See the unsigned "Reply to the Shaw Draft," probably written by Hobson or Taylor, Fabian Society Archives. Shaw's fears are expressed in a letter to Webb, Oct. 21, 1907. *Collected Letters of George Bernard Shaw*, II, *1898-1910*, ed. Dan Laurence (New York, 1972) p. 717.

6. Holbrook Jackson to Edward Pease, Dec. 11, 1906, Fabian Society Archives. See also *Fabian News*, February 1907.

7. The talk is printed as an appendix in Samuel Hynes, *The Edwardian Turn of Mind* (Princeton, 1968).

8. The lecture is summarized in the *Fabian News*, November 1906. The published version appears in *The Fortnightly Review*, 86 (November 1906), 785-798. The relationship of Wells to the Fabian Society is discussed most fully in Norman and Jeanne Mackenzie, *The Time Traveller* (London, 1973), chs. 12, 13. See also Hynes, *Edwardian Turn of Mind*, ch. 4; Margaret Cole, *The Story of the Fabian Society* (London, 1964), pp. 117-124; Edward Pease, *History of the Fabian Society*, 3rd ed. (London, 1963), ch. 9; and Anne Fremantle, *This Little Band of Prophets* (New York, 1960), ch. 12.

9. The "Report of the Special Committee" can be found in the Fabian Society Archives.

10. G. B. Shaw to H. G. Wells, Sept. 22, 1906. Shaw, *Collected Letters*, II, 654.

11. S. G. Hobson to H. G. Wells, Feb. 14, 1906, Wells papers; Beatrice Webb is quoted in Mackenzie, *Time Traveller*, p. 199; G. B. Shaw to H. G. Wells, Sept. 14, 1906, Shaw, *Collected Letters*, II, 652.

12. The meetings are reported in the *Fabian News*, January 1907. See also Mackenzie, *Time Traveller*, pp. 216 ff.

13. *New Age*, June 13, 1907; G. B. Shaw to H. G. Wells, May 5, 1907, Wells papers.

14. *New Age*, June 13, 1907; H. G. Wells to Miss Murphy, n.d., Fabian Society Archives.

15. S. Webb to G. B. Shaw, May 28, 1907, Passfield papers, British Library of Political and Economic Science, London; *New Age*, June 13, 1907; the essay, "First and Last Things," appears in vol. XI of *The Works of H. G. Wells* (New York, 1925).

16. G. D. H. Cole, *A History of Socialist Thought*, III, *The Second International* (London, 1953-60), pt. 1, pp. 204-205.

17. Wells, *New Worlds for Old* (New York, 1908), pp. 273-275.

18. Wells, "Socialism and the Middle Class," p. 703; Wells, *Experiment in Autobiography* (New York, 1934), pp. 389, 400-404; *New Age*, Oct. 17, 1907; *Works of H. G. Wells*, XII, *Tono Bungay* (New York, 1925), 216, and XIV, *New Machiavelli* (New York, 1925), 274; *Fabian News*, October 1908.

19. Wells, *New Machiavelli*, pp. 228-229, 352.

20. Ibid., pp. 352-353, 379.

21. Ingvald Rahnen, *H. G. Wells and His Critics* (Oslo, n.d.), pp. 114-115. Wells' relationship with his wife is discussed in Mackenzie, *Time Traveller*, pp. 261-263. Dorothy Richardson, with whom Wells had an affair in these years, concluded that he viewed people as "nothing . . . but the foolish hope of an impossible unanimity in the service of a plan" and maintained a "stoical disregard of the personal." See her autobiographical novel *Dawn's Left Hand* (London, 1931), p. 247, where Wells appears as Hypo Wilson. Writing in 1969, Gloria Glikin Fromm viewed Miss Richardson as "Wells's most author-

itative 'biographer' thus far" and maintained that her novels uncovered a self that Wells "tried to conceal." To accept the "little man deep within him," Miss Fromm concluded, was "to be divided" and "tantamount for Wells to failure and extinction." See her article, "Through the Novelist's Looking Glass," *H. G. Wells: A Collection of Critical Essays*, ed. Bernard Bergonzi (Englewood Cliffs, N.J., 1976), pp. 157-177.

22. Wells, *New Machiavelli*, p. 379. For the later thought of Wells see Warren Wagar, *H. G. Wells and the World State* (New Haven, 1961). Wells comments on the Fascists and Communists in *Experiment in Autobiography*, p. 563.

23. *Fabian News*, February 1907; Fabian Minute Books, March 31, Fabian Society Archives.

24. *Fabian News*, February 1908, January, February, April 1909.

25. Sidney Webb to H. G. Wells, June 15, 1907, Wells papers.

26. Webb to Graham Wallas, July 23, 1908, Wallas papers, British Library of Political and Economic Science, London.

27. *Nation*, March 30, 1907.

28. R. C. K. Ensor, "Permeation," *The Webbs and Their Work*, ed. Margaret Cole (London, 1949), p. 65; Sidney Webb to Beatrice Webb, Feb. 21, 1908, Passfield papers.

29. Beatrice Webb, *Our Partnership* (London, 1948), p. 387; Webb to Edward Pease, Aug. 12, 1908, Webb correspondence, Shaw papers, British Museum. The decision of the Webbs to write a minority report and undertake a campaign to convert the public to their views has been treated in a number of studies. For differing perspectives see Mary Hamilton, *Sidney and Beatrice Webb* (London, 1933), pp. 198 ff.; Joan S. Clarke, "The Breakup of the Poor Law," *The Webbs and Their Work*, ed. Margaret Cole (London, 1949), pp. 101-118; Kitty Muggeridge and Ruth Adam, *Beatrice Webb* (New York, 1968), ch. 12; G. R. Searle, *The Quest for National Efficiency* ((Berkeley, 1971), pp. 235-236; José Harris, *Unemployment and Politics* (Oxford, 1972), pp. 245-264.

30. Webb, *Our Partnership*, p. 424.

31. Ibid., pp. 427, 424.

32. Ibid., pp. 434, 443.

33. Ibid., p. 434.

34. Ibid., pp. 421, 435, 428, 423.

35. Sidney and Beatrice Webb, *The Public Organization of the Labour Market: Being Part Two of the Minority Report of the Poor Law Commission* (London, 1909), p. 304; Webb, *Our Partnership*, p. 417. See also Sidney and Beatrice Webb, *The Prevention of Destitution* (London, 1911), ch. 10, "The Moral Factor."

36. Webb, *Our Partnership*, pp. 385, 443.

37. George Bernard Shaw to Beatrice Webb, June 26, 1909, Shaw correspondence, Passfield papers; Masterman is quoted in Muggeridge and Adam, *Beatrice Webb*, p. 186; Burns is quoted in Harris, *Unemployment and Politics*, p. 267; for Churchill's views see Bentley B. Gilbert, *The Evolution*

of *National Insurance in Great Britain* (London, 1966), pp. 271-273.

38. Webb, *Our Partnership*, pp. 456, 447.

39. Ibid., pp. 476-477; Hamilton, *Webb*, p. 208.

40. Webb, *Our Partnership*, p. 453; Churchill is quoted in Harris, *Unemployment and Politics*, p. 265; A. M. McBriar, *Fabian Socialism and English Politics* (Cambridge, 1962), p. 277.

41. Webb, *Our Partnership*, pp. 467-472; Beatrice Webb to Sidney Webb, Nov. 18, Oct. 14, 18-19, 1910, Passfield papers.

42. Shaw to Sidney Webb, March 22, 1911, Passfield papers; Ensor's "Memorandum" is included in the Fabian Minute Books for 1910, Fabian Society Archives.

43. *Collected Letters of George Bernard Shaw*, II, 717; Shaw, *Collected Writings*, XXX (London, 1939), 300.

44. Shaw to Beatrice Webb, March 24, 1902, Shaw correspondence, Passfield papers; *Collected Letters of George Bernard Shaw*, II, 662; Shaw to Edward Pease, July 25, 1907, typed transcription in Shaw papers. (The original is in the Burgunder Collection at Cornell University.)

45. Shaw to Ramsay MacDonald, July 17, 1903, Labour Party Letter Files, Transport House, London; *Collected Letters of George Bernard Shaw* II, 661, 717; *New Age*, Aug. 29, 1907.

46. Sidney Webb to Beatrice Webb, June 20, 1907, Passfield papers.

47. Shaw to Clifford Allen, Jan. 13, 1912, Shaw to Edward Pease, Dec. 13, 1911, Shaw papers; *Fabian News*, February 1912.

48. *Fabian News*, January 1911; Shaw to Beatrice Webb, June 26, 1909, Passfield papers.

49. Bland discusses the Fabian mission in a lecture, "The Faith I Hold," presented to the Society during 1907. It is reprinted in *Essays by Hubert Bland*, ed. Edith Nesbit Bland (London, 1914). see also Hubert Bland to Shaw, Oct. 13, 1910, Shaw papers; Bland to Edward Pease, Dec. 5, 1911, Fabian Society Archives; *Fabian News*, August 1912.

50. The lecture is included in Bernard Shaw, *The Road to Equality: The Unpublished Lectures and Addresses*, ed. Louis Crompton (Boston, 1971), pp. 155-194. See also the report in the *Fabian News*, January 1911; Shaw to C. C. Fabb, Dec. 15, 1910, and Shaw to F. Catmur, March 23, 1911, Shaw papers.

51. *Fabian News*, April 1911; Bland to Shaw, March 7, 1911, Shaw papers.

52. Beatrice Webb, unpublished diaries, 28, April 21, 1911, 31, July 12, 1913; Beatrice Webb to Shaw, June 17, 1913, June 13, 1914, Shaw papers; Shaw to Beatrice Webb, March 22, 1911, Passfield papers.

53. Erich Strauss, *Bernard Shaw: Art and Socialism* (London, 1942), p. 64.

54. *Fabian News*, April 1906; *The Religious Speeches of Bernard Shaw*, ed. Warren Sylvester Smith (University Park, Pa., 1963), pp. 21, 38, 35.

55. After one of his lectures at the City Temple R. J. Campbell wrote Shaw: "Last night's meeting has made such a Shaw cult at City Temple that I

think I had better clear out and allow you to be elected minister herewith." R. J. Campbell to Shaw, Oct. 9, 1908, Shaw papers: *Religious Speeches of Bernard Shaw*, p. 19.

56. *Religious Speeches of Bernard Shaw*, p. 59; Shaw, *Collected Writings*, XV, 5-6.

57. *Fabian News*, March 1914; *Beatrice Webb's Diaries, 1912-1924*, ed. Margaret Cole (London, 1952), I, 21.

58. The development of the *New Statesman* and Shaw's relationship to it are discussed in Edward Hyams, *The New Statesman: The History of the First Forty Years* (London, 1963), pp. 1-70. See also Stanley Weintraub, *Journey to Heartbreak* (New York, 1971), for a narrative of Shaw's activities in these years. Shaw's role on the paper is also discussed in the letters of Clifford Sharp to Beatrice Webb, March 31-April 12, 1912, Oct. 26-8, 1916, Passfield papers.

59. *Beatrice Webb's Diaries, 1912-1914*, p. 31.

60. Recent analyses of the play include Louis Crompton, *Shaw the Dramatist* (Lincoln, Neb., 1969), chs. 10-12; Margery Morgan, *The Shavian Playground* (London, 1972), ch. 12; Charles Berst, *Bernard Shaw and the Art of Drama* (Urbana, Ill., 1973), ch. 9; Maurice Valency, *The Cart and the Trumpet* (New York, 1973), pp. 335-352; Alfred Turco, Jr., *Shaw's Moral Vision* (Ithaca, N.Y., 1976), ch. 8. For the quotation see Martin Meisel, "Shaw and Revolution: The Politics of the Plays"; *Shaw, Seven Critical Essays*, ed. Norman Rosenblood (Toronto, 1971), p. 131.

61. Crompton, *Shaw*, p. 153.

62. The lecture is included in Shaw, *Road to Equality*, pp. 279-333. For the circumstances of the talk see Weintraub, *Journey to Heartbreak*, p. 290.

63. Shaw, *Road to Equality*, pp. 317, 280, 311.

64. Ibid., pp. 280, 315, 290.

65. Ibid., pp. 284-285, 327, 322-323.

66. Weintraub, *Journey to Heartbreak*, p. 290; Crompton, *Shaw*, pp. 192-193; Morgan, *Shavian Playground*, p. 222.

67. For a summary of the play see Crompton, *Shaw*, pp. 169 ff. See also Turco, *Shaw's Moral Vision*, ch. 9, and James Hulse, *Revolutionaries in London* (Oxford, 1970), pp. 213-220.

68. For discussions of Shaw's later work see Morgan, *Shavian Playground*, chs. 16, 17, 18, and McBriar, *Fabian Socialism*, pp. 82-92. See also the later essays in Bernard Shaw, *Practical Politics*, ed. Lloyd Hubenka (London, 1976).

69. The Manifesto appears in the *New Age*, Jan. 18, 1912. See also the report in the *Fabian News*.

70. Henry Slesser, *Judgment Reserved* (London, 1941), p. 43.

71. Clifford Sharp to Beatrice Webb, Feb. 24, 1912, Passfield papers; *Fabian News*, August 1912.

72. *Beatrice Webb's Diaries, 1912-1924*, I, 70; Beatrice Webb, unpublished diaries, 34, Sept. 22, 1917; Clifford Sharp to Beatrice Webb, March 31-April 12, Feb. 24, March 22-29, 1912, Passfield papers.

73. *Beatrice Webb's Diaries, 1912-1924*, I, 6.

74. Cole's role in the Fabian Society is discussed in L. P. Carpenter, *G. D. H. Cole: An Intellectual Portrait* (Cambridge, 1973), ch. 1. See also Margaret Cole, *The Life of G. D. H. Cole* (London, 1971), and J. M. Winter, *Socialism and the Challenge of the War* (London, 1974), chs. 4, 5.

75. *Fabian News*, February 1911; August 1912; Webb to Edward Pease, Jan. 25, 1911, Passfield papers. The Webbs stated their objections to syndicalism in a supplement to the *Crusader*, August 1912. Their views are summarized in McBriar, *Fabian Socialism*, pp. 100-103. See also Winter, *Socialism and the Challenge of War*, pp. 37-40. Beatrice Webb's "Open Letter" to the Committee of Inquiry on the Control of Industry is included in the Passfield papers.

76. Sidney Webb to Beatrice Webb, Dec. 9, 1913, Passfield papers.

77. *Beatrice Webb's Diaries, 1912-1924*, I, 6, 9-10.

78. *New Statesman*, April 12, 1913. See also Hyams, *New Statesman*, pp. 13 ff.

79. *New Statesman*, July 12, May 24, April 26, April 19, 1913.

80. Ibid., June 21, April 12, 1913.

81. Ibid., June 7, 1913.

82. Ibid., May 31, April 12, 19, July 19, May 3, 1913.

83. *Beatrice Webb's Diaries, 1912-1924*, I, 16; *New Statesman*, July 19, 1913.

84. Clifford Sharp to Beatrice Webb, March 31-April 12, 1912, Passfield papers; Beatrice Webb, unpublished diaries, 32, March 8, 1914.

85. *Fabian News*, Aug. 12, 1914.

86. *Beatrice Webb's Diaries, 1912-1914*, p. 19.

87. Beatrice Webb, unpublished diaries, 32, May 19, 1915.

88. The work of the committee and Webb's role is discussed in Royden Harrison, "The War Emergency Workers' National Committee," *Essays in Labour History, 1886-1923*, ed. Asa Briggs and John Saville (Oxford, 1972), pp. 245-264.

89. *Beatrice Webb's Diaries, 1912-1924*, I, 46; Winter, *Socialism and the Challenge of the War*, p. 211.

90. See Ross McKibbin, *The Evolution of the Labour Party, 1910-1924* (Oxford, 1974); Harrison, "War Emergency Workers' National Committee"; Winter, *Socialism and the Challenge of the War*, chs. 7, 8.

91. McKibbin, *Evolution of the Labour Party*, pp. 96-97, 244. Harrison, "War Emergency Workers' National Committee," p. 259, concludes that Clause 4 "did not indicate" the "presence of a coherent ideology" but served as a "rallying point around which adherents of different ideologies and the representatives of different interests assembled." Much the same conclusion is reached by Rodney Barker, "Political Myth: Ramsay MacDonald and the Labour Party," *History*, 61 (February 1976), 45-56. For a different view see J. M. Winter, "Arthur Henderson, the Russian Revolution, and the Reconstruction of the Labour Party," *Historical Journal*, 15.4 (1972), 753-773.

92. See R. E. Dowse, *Left in the Centre* (London, 1966), pp. 32, 48; and

David Marquand, *Ramsay MacDonald* (London, 1977), pp. 227-233.

93. *Beatrice Webb's Diaries, 1912-1924*, I, 106, 141; Beatrice Webb, unpublished diaries, 34, April 1, 1918; McKibbin, *Evolution of the Labour Party*, ch. 9.

94. See Margaret Cole, *The Story of Fabian Socialism* (London, 1961), pp. 189-207.

95. *Beatrice Webb's Diaries, 1912-1924*, I, 162; *Beatrice Webb's Diaries, 1924-1932*, II, ed. Margaret Cole (London, 1956), pp. 73, 265-266.

96. *Beatrice Webb's Diaries, 1912-1924*, I, 227, 163, 225; *Beatrice Webb's Diaries, 1924-1932*, II, 23, 14, 79.

97. *Beatrice Webb's Diaries, 1924-1932*, II, 294-295, 307-309.

Conclusion

1. The larger historical context for this development is discussed in Anthony Giddens, *The Class Structure of Advanced Societies* (London, 1973), chs. 11, 14, 15, and especially pp. 284-287.

2. Joseph Clayton, *The Rise and Decline of Socialism in Great Britain, 1884-1924* (London, 1926), p. viii.

3. The continuing resistance of the working classes to the Socialist appeal is discussed in Stuart Macintyre, "British Labour, Marxism and Working Class Apathy in the Nineteen Twenties," *The Historical Journal*, 20.2 (1977), 479-496, and Ben Plimlott, *Labour and the Left in the 1930s* (Cambridge, 1977).

4. See David Coates, *The Labour Party and the Struggle for Socialism* (Cambridge, 1975), and Ralph Miliband's articles, "Moving On," *The Socialist Register* (London, 1976), and "The Future of Socialism in England," *Socialist Register* (London, 1977).

5. E. J. Hobsbawm, "The Left and the Crisis of Organisation," *New Society* (April 13, 1978), 63-66.

UNPUBLISHED SOURCES

ROBERT BLATCHFORD CORRESPONDENCE, Manchester Central Reference Library, Manchester.

BRITISH SOCIALIST PARTY PAPERS, British Library of Political and Economic Science, London.

EDWARD CARPENTER PAPERS, Sheffield City Library, Sheffield.

JAMES CONNOLLY PAPERS, National Library of Ireland, Dublin.

THOMAS DAVIDSON PAPERS, Yale University Library, New Haven, Conn.

R. C. K. ENSOR PAPERS, Corpus Christi College, Oxford.

FABIAN SOCIETY PAPERS, Nuffield College, Oxford.

JOHN BRUCE GLASIER CORRESPONDENCE, Archives of the Independent Labour Party, Bristol.

JOHN BRUCE GLASIER DIARY, in possession of Malcolm Glasier.

MORRIS HILLQUIT PAPERS, State Historical Society of Wisconsin, Madison.

KARL KAUTSKY CORRESPONDENCE, International Institute for Social History, Amsterdam.

LABOUR PARTY LETTER FILES, Transport House, London.

HENRY DEMAREST LLOYD PAPERS, State Historical Society of Wisconsin, Madison.

JAMES RAMSAY MACDONALD PAPERS, Public Record Office, London.

JOHN MACLEAN PAPERS, National Library of Scotland, Edinburgh.

ALFRED MATTISON PAPERS, Brotherton Library, Leeds.

PASSFIELD PAPERS, British Library of Political and Economic Science, London.

HERBERT READ CORRESPONDENCE, University of Victoria Library, Victoria, British Columbia.

CHARLES E. RUSSELL CORRESPONDENCE, Library of Congress, Washington, D.C.

GEORGE BERNARD SHAW PAPERS, British Museum, London.

ALGERNON SIMONS CORRESPONDENCE, State Historical Society of Wisconsin, Madison.

GRAHAM WALLAS PAPERS, British Library of Political and Economic Science, London.

H. G. WELLS PAPERS, University of Illinois Library, Urbana.

H. GAYLORD WILSHIRE PAPERS, microfilm copies in the British Library of Political and Economic Science, London.

INDEX